SYLVIA SIDNEY

~Paid by the Tear

Also by Scott O'Brien:

Kay Francis – *I Can't Wait to be Forgotten* (2006)
Classic Images Magazine – "Best Books of 2006" Laura Wagner – "O'Brien has a way with words as he beautifully examines Kay's films. He skillfully uses Kay's own diary to paint a picture of an independent woman ahead of her time."

Virginia Bruce – *Under My Skin* (2008)
Daeida Magazine – David Ybarra (editor) – *Under My Skin* is a well-researched, tactful, and skilled examination into the tragedy of a talented, beautiful and popular figure in film history, desperate to fall in love at any cost. Highly recommended."

Ann Harding – *Cinema's Gallant Lady* (2010)
San Francisco Gate – Mick LaSalle – "Scott O'Brien has managed to come up with a thick, fact-filled, smart and very readable biography of this enormous talent. Harding deserves to be known, and the public deserves to know her."

Ruth Chatterton – *Actress, Aviator, Author* (2013)
Huffington Post – Thomas Gladys – "Best Film Books of 2013"

George Brent—*Ireland's Gift to Hollywood and its Leading Ladies* (2014)
Huffington Post - Thomas Gladys - "Best Film Books of 2014"

SYLVIA SIDNEY

~Paid by the Tear

"They used to pay me by the teardrop"
~Sylvia Sidney (1972)

*"Whenever you need tears ...
just tell me when to cry"*
~Sylvia Sidney to director Richard Fleischer
while filming *Violent Saturday* (1955)

A biography by

Scott O'Brien

Sylvia Sidney
© 2016. Scott O'Brien. All rights reserved.

All illustrations are copyright of their respective owners, and are also reproduced here in the spirit of publicity. Whilst we have made every effort to acknowledge specific credits whenever possible, we apologize for any omissions, and will undertake every effort to make any appropriate changes in future editions of this book if necessary.

No part of this book may be reproduced in any form or by any means, electronic, mechanical, digital, photocopying or recording, except for the inclusion in a review, without permission in writing from the publisher.

Published in the USA by:
BearManor Media
P O Box 71426
Albany, Georgia 31708
www.bearmanormedia.com

Printed in the United States of America
ISBN   978-1-59393-942-7 (paperback)
          978-1-59393-943-4 (hardcover)

Book & cover design and layout by Dan and Darlene Swanson • www.van-garde.com

Sylvia Sidney publicity shot for *Merrily We Go to Hell* (1932) (Paramount)

Contents

	Foreword (by Richard Kramer) xi	
Chapter 1	From Cradle To Broadway	1
Chapter 2	Nice Women & Bad Girls	27
Chapter 3	"Mr. God" & the "Idiot"	51
Chapter 4	Merrily We Go To Hell	79
Chapter 5	Accent on Transition	107
Chapter 6	"One Should Never Legalize a 'Hot' Romance"	133
Chapter 7	Hollywood: Dead End	161
Chapter 8	Motherhood: "A Great Leveling Agent"	195
Chapter 9	Screen Comeback: 1944-1947	217
Chapter 10	Jeanne d'Arc & Judy Garland	239
Chapter 11	Stage, Screen and Television	259
Chapter 12	Auntie Sylvia	283
Chapter 13	Exit Laughing … All the Way to the Bank	309
Chapter 14	"I've Been Playing Those Rotten-Mother Type Roles"	335
Chapter 15	A Mother's Shrine to Her Son	365
Chapter 16	*Beetlejuice* & Beyond	389
	Acknowledgements	419
	Credits	425

Be a Good Girl (1989) (*ABC's thirtysomething*) Sylvia as Rose Waldman. Here with Melanie Mayron and Phyllis Newman (courtesy of Richard Kramer)

Sylvia Sidney ~

by Richard Kramer

What did I have for lunch yesterday? It could have been anything, although it probably wasn't, as I have the same thing for lunch every day (tunafish) which still doesn't help me remember. And yet – I remember the first time I saw the late great actress Sylvia Sidney, in the pretty much forgotten movie *Summer Wishes, Winter Dreams*. It was 1973, Google tells me. She played Joanne Woodward's mother, and the moment that electrified me, that dug right in, was when she had a heart attack in a movie theatre and croaked out the words "Cancel my appointments!" Who was this old beauty, with the gravelly voice and the slightly *far-bisseneh* face that somehow perfectly complemented that beauty?

So I did a little sleuth-

SummerWishes,WinterDreams
(1973) (Columbia)

Fury (1936) (MGM)

ing, which wasn't so easy, then.

I found out she had been a movie star, in films like William Wyler's *Dead End* and Fritz Lang's *Fury*. I learned that she had left Hollywood, at the height of her success. Yes, she had been someone. And she was still someone. And we wanted her to know we knew that, so we carved out a role for her on *thirtysomething*, never thinking we'd get her. We saw her as Rose Waldman, the grandmother of Melanie Mayron's Melissa, on an episode titled *Be a Good Girl* that I had written and was to direct. Rose was a big personality, a star, not of stage and screen but the *schmatta* business, specifically discount *schmattas* for ladies who wanted to be stylish on a budget and for whom bargain-hunting was a bloodsport. She was based on Jenny Loehmann, who famously sat on a throne in the main area of her store, insulting the terrified ladies who dared to try on the clothes. ("Buy that, save a few dollars, but the way that looks on you I promise you'll lose your husband.") Rose was a widow, and a diva, and a nightmare, but she adored (or seemed to) her grand-daughter Melissa, who adored her in return.

Rose was a lot of fun to write, as part of the trick of that was to be sure the audience remained seduced by her until the end, when her façade crumbles and she stands revealed as a pathetic, isolated old lady, whose grip on the family's story about itself Melissa must, in the end, challenge, conquer, and put to rest (which Ms. Mayron, magnificently, did; she won the Emmy for the performance).

But a step at a time, here. Not all my colleagues even knew who Sylvia Sidney was. Retired, the casting people told me. Not well. What about Helen Hayes? What about the Mildreds, Natwick or Dunnock? No to all; there was one Rose, and one Rose only. And through some chain of events we got her Connecticut address and sent her the script, prepared to never hear back from her and move on to some lesser old lady, still plugging along for the SAG insurance. But we did hear back. I got a call, at home, late one night.

"Who the hell is this?" a raspy voice demanded, as if I'd been the one who had called her. I told her who I was, and she told me (without bothering to mention that she was Sylvia Sidney) that she'd known many writers who were better than me, including Clifford Odets. "He was a very attractive man," she said. "We were all in love with him, although he could only talk about himself and his penis. I don't know what you look like. Frankly, I don't care." I heard my caller inhale a cigarette, which I could tell was unfiltered. "Anyway," she said. "I'm getting bored now. I don't like this old lady you've written. But I know her. *Vey iz mir*, as they say in the Klondike! So I'll play her for you. Good night." She wasn't done yet, though; she called back within a minute. "One more thing," she said, again not introducing herself. "You have a line where the little girl (the little girl being the thirty-something Melissa) refers to 'a Helen Hayes kind of grandma.'" We did have that line, meant to convey an apple-cheeked, potpourri-strewing Mrs. Santa Claus, the opposite of what Melissa's actual grandma was like. "Well," Miss Sidney said, "I'm not saying that. Nosirree. Helen Hayes is one of my oldest and dearest friends. And in her mind, she's Michelle Pfeiffer …" Inhale. Puff. "Who's a very talented girl."

And we were off. I was to learn the nicety-skipping was more method than madness, a trick that may have helped her survive a fifty-year-plus career. It certainly played right into who I thought Rose was. *Be a Good Girl* was about three generations of women and the damage that had trickled down and been passed on from the top. The great Phyllis Newman played Rose's disappointing daughter, Elaine, and a host of aging Jewish lovelies played the various cousins and aunts who gather miserably in Rose's mansion, kept to a comfortable fifty-eight degrees at all times. (A moment I'll never forget, from this very vivid six weeks … I noticed that one of these ladies, playing Aunt Cookie, I think, was wiping away tears after a rehearsal. I asked her what was wrong. "Look at her," she said, nodding in Sylvia's direction. "I always felt maybe, maybe I could look like her, if my face had worked out a little differently.")

A month before we were to shoot I was already talking to her about what we were going to do, which had never happened before with a guest player. She called me, with ideas, complaints (not many), expressions of excitement. She wanted to provide her own costumes. "I don't want to look like some Bella from the Bronx," she said. "Rose wears Chanel, and she's earned it. Like I did." (Note: These quotes are pretty much verbatim, as I kept good journals at the time.) As our start date approached I asked if she had any questions, only to be told *"You should have questions for me, Mr. Kramer. Remember: I'm the one who's Sylvia Sidney."* Imperious as a statement like that might seem, I came to see it as part of her charm. She was able to say something like that and play with the idea of her saying it at the same time; Sylvia was always, from what I could see, both herself and the idea of herself, which may be some sort of stumbling, awkward definition of what it means to be a star.

Then, suddenly, there she was—tiny, stunning, a few days early ("I gave myself some time to see old friends. Unfortunately, they're all dead"), in a Bond-girl leather pantsuit, with her two pugs and a bag of needlepoint. She spouted some unsolicited abuse about the actress Mae Questel, who had provided the voice of Betty Boop in the 30's; Ms. Questel had just played Woody Allen's nagging mother in the film *New York Stories*, and she had been on the flight with Sylvia. "It was Woody this, Woody that, Woody go-fuck-yourself," Sylvia said, rolling the enormous eyes which she was very good at. "I chose *not* to tell her that he came to me first, and that I told him in plain Yiddish I couldn't play a cartoon. He pleaded with me, for months, but I told him to jump in a lake." She nudged her dogs with her shoe. "Malcolm and Petey. The black one is Malcolm. For Malcom X. What a great man he was. Gone, of course. The good ones all are. Odets! Kennedy! Except Paul Newman. Classy. To the manor born, you know."

It was to go on like this for the coming weeks. She was sharp, with it; she could be impatient and a bit nasty, as if she sensed it was expected of her, this Lady of the Golden Age.

Sidney as *Auntie Mame* in a cross-country tour (1958-1959)

She didn't care for our cinematographer, for example, who kept moving her around like a bunch of grapes for the still life in his head. Once, I remember, she got up, put her hands on her hips, and said "Would you get this over with? I'm an actress. Not a roll of Tums!" But she sat down again, rolling those eyes; she was never an actual pain in the ass, she just played the part of one.

And the volunteered-from-nowhere stories kept on coming. She left Hollywood, she announced one day, when she realized that she had played ten roles in a row in which she found herself standing over an ironing board asking, "What will Poppa say?" She had a rumored but never substantiated romance with the much older B.P. Schulberg, father of Budd and the head of Paramount. "He never laid a finger on me," she told us. "The poor man just needed someone to talk to! And I could listen, and learn. I would go home and read Tolstoy and then discuss it with him! And his wife would bring us cashews, while we chatted about serious things. It was very innocent." One day, while submitting to before-shooting fluffs and touch-ups, she said "And as for *Auntie Mame*, I was wonderful. Roz played it for laughs. I found the heart!"

And here's my favorite. I noticed that during lighting set-ups she would click away at her needlepoint and murmur the nonsense word "Vinduz … Vinduz … Vinduz … ." I asked her what she was saying. "That was Fritz Lang," she told me, who had directed her in two famous roles. "He always used to say that. Finally I went to him and I said 'Fritz? Tell me, please. Why do you always sit there saying "Vinduz" to yourself?'" And he looked at me, and said – "Silly," which is what people called me. "I'm only saying vinduz we finish this fucking picture?"

I like to think we were fun for her. Melanie was, I know that. Sylvia loved her, and called me one night (late, of course) to tell me she was the finest actress she had ever worked with, but I shouldn't tell her till we were done and she and the pugs were back in Connecticut, so as not to jinx Melanie's game. I remember how little I had to tell her, how she became Rose, how she understood this dazzling old bat's grace and monstrousness. If there's one favorite moment I have in the completed show, it's one that Marshall Herskovitz, the executive producer, handed me with his usual generosity, one for which I wish I could claim credit. Rose/Sylvia had just made a comment that her daughter, Phyllis Newman, declared was "prejudiced". Momma turned on her. "Don't you talk to me about prejudice, Elaine," she warned. "I'll have you know I hired the first black saleswoman in Philadelphia." She snorted, triumphant as ever, "Black people love me!"

We did, too. We shot for eight days. At the end of the last one, she said to me "Well, Mr. Director, I hope you were satisfied. Did I stink?" "You were okay," I told her, still too scared of her to risk effusion. "Thank you." She curtsied. "I live for praise. And don't even think about hugging me." I did, though. She didn't stop me. She snorted, headed for the elevator with Malcolm and Petey. I stopped when I heard her call for me. "If Rose ever comes back," she said, "Promise me. You'll go first to Mae Questel."

Richard Kramer - November 2015

Writer/producer/director - (thirtysomething, Queer as Folk, Tales of the City)

Playwright - Theatre District **(Joseph Jefferson Award)**

Novelist - These Things Happen **(2012) (Lambda Literary Award)**

Flashback - 1934

Sylvia puffed on a cigarette in her Manhattan apartment, while writer Dena Reed for *Silver Screen* fired away questions. Sylvia looked out the window over the sea of rooftops. At age twenty-four, she knew what life was about—that is, *her* life. Sylvia brought the interview to an end, saying,

> *Work is the only satisfactory thing in life. I learned that early. I myself can't imagine a life without work. What will become of us, if we never have learned to depend on our own resources—our brains, and fingers and talents? No, work and laughter are the only things to cling to. I hope I'll act until I'm old.*

Sidney got her wish—joining the ranks for Helen Hayes and Lillian Gish, as having one of the longest theatrical/cinematic careers in history.

c1915 - Sophia Kosow with her father Victor (1886-1970)

Chapter 1
From Cradle To Broadway

May 1932, New York City. Childhood memories flooded Sylvia Sidney as she looked out onto the streets. East 137th Street, Longwood Avenue ... places she had lived, but it was all so long ago. Her father still lived in the Bronx on Morris Avenue. When was the last time she had seen him? Was she four, or five? Victor Kosow—the man who first abandoned her mother Beatrice when Sylvia was just nine months old. The couple reconciled, only after Kosow agreed to remain faithful. He broke his promise. Beatrice filed for divorce and was granted a decree on March 1, 1915. And now, seventeen years later, Sylvia was going to see Victor Kosow face-to-face. His surprise phone call had been unsettling. He made threats that if she wasn't nice to him, he would make things difficult for her and her mother, and ruin Sylvia's reputation.[1] What did he *really* want? Was it just money? Why meet at an attorney's office? She had always been known as the daughter of Dr. Sigmund Sidney, and now this.

Sylvia arrived at her destination with her head full of questions. She entered Brooklyn attorney Jacob Gelfand's office expecting to be greeted by her long-lost father. He was nowhere around. Instead, she sat in front of Gelfand, who began to solve the riddle of this father-daughter reunion. "I arrived there on time, but my father was late," she recalled. "In the meantime, the attorney said my father was very much in need of money." As she let the news sink in, Mr. Kosow eventually made his appearance. Sylvia noted, "We greeted each other ... rather coldly."

Four years after her divorce, Sylvia's mother remarried in 1919 to Dr. Sidney, a dentist. Sylvia was eight at the time. She and her new stepfather grew especially fond of each other, and Dr. Sidney adopted her when she was twelve. He was the only father she had ever known. She had no reason to reveal the identity of her real father. He had never made any effort to see her, or contribute to her welfare. Now, she was confronted by a complete stranger, and what he had to say, she found disheartening. Kosow told Sylvia that her adoption was invalid. He was going to have it annulled.

> He threatened to make public that I was not the true daughter of Dr. Sidney. I asked him what he had ever done for me or for mother to deserve any of the glory we were getting. But then I saw that all of this was getting us nowhere. I asked him to say exactly what he wanted. He asked me to buy him a house. He said I would have to buy it myself and later present it to him. He said good houses could be picked up in Brooklyn for $15,000.[2]

Sylvia was uncomfortable with Kosow's idea. She made a counter offer of substantial sums of money from time to time, but he refused, calling it charity. So, things turned even uglier.

> He then began to rant and rave about going to theaters where my pictures are shown. He said he had good connections with newspaper columnists. All this made me ill. So I got up to go. I promised to get in touch with him and give him my decision.

Summer 1932 - Sylvia with Beatrice and Sigmund Sidney

Sylvia Sidney, actress and film star, had managed to keep Kosow's existence a secret. The possibility of invasive publicity was imminent. She found consolation in the company of her mother and Dr. Sidney, now residing at the Century Apartments in Central Park West. They assured Sylvia that at the time of her adoption in 1922, Kosow had the necessary legal notice of the procedure by publication. It would be over a year before Sylvia's secret hit the newsstands. By that time, she and her stepfather had teamed with an attorney. Together, they had what appeared to be a foolproof defense: extortion.

Sylvia's mother released her own pent-up feelings to the press. "Kosow did not appear when he might have been of help to Sylvia. Never did he display any interest. He never paid a penny for his child's support. But when fame and fortune came to Sylvia, he came along with threats against her. He wanted a huge sum of money. I assure you that neither Sylvia or her parents will submit to extortion."[3] Kosow told the press that he didn't want money or publicity. "I am her father," he said. "I want Sylvia, and her mother, and Dr. Sidney and the law to know it." Reporters noted the similarities between Kosow and his daughter—the eyes, small full lips and nose. "She has her good looks from her papa," he wagged.⁴ Kosow argued that he didn't visit Sylvia as a child because he had trouble finding her. "It took plenty of money to keep in touch with her"—was another baffling excuse. He claimed not to have known about the adoption until 1932.

Following New York Supreme Court Justice Isador Wasservogel's decision, the case was withdrawn. No money was exchanged. Kosow agreed to recognize the adoption and never again question the legality. As for a statement, Kosow remarked, "I owe apologies to no one."⁵

It made sense to put Victor Kosow in Sylvia's past, permanently. His reappearance in 1932, in one respect, brought unexpected relief. "I let the case go to court because I thought it best to clear it up there and then," Sylvia said afterward. "It was all very painful and unpleasant publicity, but I am glad I went through with it."⁶

Victor Kosow (nee Avigdor Kossowski/Kosovsky) was born in the Jewish settlement of Grodno, Russia, December 10, 1886. Grodno consisted of two small villages. Victor grew up in Lunna, a hundred miles east of Warsaw. (After WWI Lunna became part of Poland). His father and mother, Moshe and Leah Kosovsky, operated a brick factory. The couple had three sons and four daughters. With his earnings, Moshe established a Hekdesh (hostel) that served as a rest stop for travelers, as well as refuge for the underprivileged. Victor's schooling focused on the study of Judaism.⁷ At age 15, Victor sailed on the *Rotterdam* to New York City. Passports issued in the 1920's describe Victor as 5' 8" with a medium build, dark brown hair and eyes, and ruddy complexion.⁸

Kosow learned the trade of a cutter and clothing salesman. He and Rebecca Saperstein, a dressmaker, married August 28, 1909. The couple resided on East 137th St. in the Bronx. Rebecca, was born April 12, 1887 in Bialystok, Poland (then part of Imperial Russia), a heavily populated and mostly Jewish city. She had been taught Hebrew at school and spoke Yiddish at home. Rebecca arrived in New York in 1906, following a year of persecution and martial law, known as the Bialystok Pogrom. Numerous Jewish citizens and officials were murdered by Russian troops. Violent outbreaks and looting of Jewish stores left a path of more bloodshed. On Sundays, priests fueled the fire of hate preaching that Jews were killing the Christian God. Rebecca's nephew Albert would recall in 1973,

> It was because of sermons like that ... a mob would develop, start fires ... and kill. And the police would stand by. Jews were not organized in groups to fight back. They were submissive. Soldiers would just join in the general fun of killing Jews. I grew up thinking of Russian soldiers as murderers. And the same way of many of the Christian neighbors. I had personal experience which I still carry to my present day.[9]

Albert told of an incident that occurred when he was five. He and a friend were walking home one Sunday when a bunch of boys, fresh out of church, began throwing rocks at them, screaming, "Jews, Jews Jews!" "One of those sharp stones hit me within 1/4 inch of my left eye. I would have been blinded for life, because I only have vision in my left eye. This is the kind of memory that stays with you for life."

As Rebecca witnessed the bloody horrors of Russian pogroms upon her people, her family was forced to separate. In 1931, veteran writer/editor Adele Whitely Fletcher interviewed Rebecca, now known as Beatrice Sidney.

Beatrice was fourteen the day the soldiers stood her brother-in-law up against a great stone wall and bayoneted him, not with one comparatively kind death-thrust but, viciously, six times. It was this that determined her to get away with as many members of the family as she could possibly take with her.[10]

Carefully, to avoid suspicion, Rebecca began selling family possessions. Each kopeck brought them closer

c1906 - Sylvia's mother, Beatrice (Rebecca Saperstein) (1887-1979)

to escape. Beatrice had knocked three years off her age in telling Fletcher her tragic story. In reality, Beatrice was eighteen by the time the family had funds to stand on the deck of a steamer, America-bound. Her mother, one brother and three sisters made the journey. Halfway across the Atlantic, her widowed sister gave birth to a baby girl. Beatrice left behind her brother Jacob, whose son Albert would play a significant role in the life of Sylvia Sidney.

Stories of the trials and tribulations that her family had endured in the old country left a lasting impression on Sylvia. In the 1930's, she was alarmed about the rise of Nazism and spoke on behalf of the Hollywood Anti-Nazi League. As Vice-Chairman of the Motion Picture Artists Committee, she raised funds on behalf of Republican Spain's fight against fascism. Before Europe entered WWII, Sylvia supported the Committee of 56—actors lobbying to boycott German trade. Sylvia honored her Jewish background, but explained in an interview, "I've no orthodox religion." With the exception of her grandmother, the Saperstein side of the family did not practice Orthodox Judaism.

A year after her marriage to Victor, Rebecca gave birth to their daughter, Sophia Kosow, on August 8, 1910. Rebecca's income as a dressmaker (she became a designer for merchant John Wanamaker) gave her and Sophia sustenance during Victor's "disappearances." After a separation in 1911, the couple reconciled and relocated to Longview Avenue, but promises were broken and it wasn't long before Victor abandoned his wife and daughter. After her divorce, Rebecca went by the name Beatrice Kosow. She and Sophia moved from Longwood Avenue to West 145th St. Beatrice signed an agreement that allowed Victor to see his daughter every other Sunday. After 1916, he failed to show. In the aftermath, little Sophia shared the weight of her mother's emotional burden. She became withdrawn and stayed that way far too long.

"When I was a little girl," Sylvia reflected in 1934, "I wasn't really a little girl at all. I did none of the things that other little girls did. I wanted none of the things that other little girls wanted. I was painfully shy. I am certain that all of this shyness was caused by all the trouble between my mother and father. It is not so much that I remember definitely unpleasant episodes between them; it is more that I lived with a saddening and permeating sense of my mother's tears."[11] Whenever little Sophia's heart-shaped face looked out onto the Bronx neighborhood street teaming with children, her grave blue-green eyes indicated that she wasn't interested in having playmates. Neither did she like the sound of her name when children stood beneath her window yelling, "Sophie!"[12] Beatrice Kosow realized she had a problem child.

In 1923, Victor Kosow would return home to Poland and marry his cousin's daughter, Rivka. They returned to the U.S., where Rivka changed her name (ironically) to Rebecca. The couple had two sons Albert and Edgar, Sylvia's half-siblings.

1923 - Victor and his second wife, Rivka

April 8, 1919. Manhattan. Beatrice Kosow stood at the altar next to the respected Dr. Sigmund Sidney. In the background the petite, shy, eight-year-old Sophia (soon to be called Sylvia, per her insistence) wondered what it would be like to have a father in her life, let alone a new father. Questions Sylvia had were silent ones. Despite her bull-headedness, words were always a struggle for her. But, the fates were listening. It would be her stuttering problem that bonded Sylvia with Sigmund. Before long, there were sessions with elocutionist Joseph G. Geiger, and dancing lessons (that she hated) to help overcome her handicap. A voracious reader, little Sylvia talked frankly about adult subjects with Dr. Sidney. In 1933, Sylvia would reflect, "Dad has always been so tender, so thoughtful, so *wise* for me that I am used to that sort of thing and that sort of man. I suppose that I have a 'father complex'—or Freud would say so."[13]

Sigmund Sidney (nee Solomon Haimowitz) was born in Romania in 1888. When he was nine, he and his family immigrated to New York City. In 1909, he graduated from the New York School of Dentistry.

c1917 - Dr. Sigmund Sidney (1888-1961)

In 1911, he took legal steps to change his name to Sigmund Sidney. His draft card (1917) indicated he was flat-footed and had a lame right arm. For many years, Dr. Sidney's small office was located on the second floor at 42nd St. and 8th Ave. The plaque on the door read: Dr. Sidney, Dentist. Plates Repaired While You Wait. Reasonable Prices.[14] People described him as a light-hearted, pleasure-loving man—a nice balance for young Sylvia, whose mother tended to more sedate and moody. Sylvia also had occasion to visit her Grandmother Saperstein. "My grandmother was orthodox," explained Sylvia, "but never in my life have I witnessed such tolerance and understanding. Always her attitude was 'That is not my way, but it may be a good way.'" It was obvious that Sylvia had deep affection for this woman, who, on special occasions would cook the meals. "She cooked us Russian food," said Sylvia. "Blinis. And a spicy stew called schaschlick." Most importantly, her grandmother taught Sylvia needlepoint beginning at age seven—a skill which would afford Sylvia much acclaim in her later years.

According to Sylvia, her early education was less than spectacular. She attended Public School No. 3 in Greenwich Village, and was a rebel from the start. Occasionally, she would calmly get up from her desk and walk home. "Sylvia," the teacher would say, "you can't go home. School isn't over yet." "But I'm going home just the same," Sylvia would announce. And home she went.[15] The playful pastimes of other youngsters continued to elude her. She was stubborn. After one childish offense her mother sent Sylvia to bed. At dinnertime Beatrice brought her dinner on a tray, reminding her, "You'll stay in bed until you apologize." Sylvia stayed in bed all the next day. When Beatrice asked if she was ready to apologize, Sylvia instructed, "No, Mother. Anyway, it's a rainy day so I don't want to go outside."[16] Her only run-in with Dr. Sidney occurred after some friends arrived at their home. "One of them asked where my mother was," recalled Sylvia. "'She's upstairs,' I said. My father was furious. 'Your mother,' he said, right in front of the guests, 'is never *she*.' But that's the only reprimand I remember from him. Little girls can always wheedle their way around grown men."[17]

An attempt by Dr. and Mrs. Sidney to place Sylvia in a girl's boarding school was another failure. She avoided classmates. She preferred the company of adults and ate her meals in the kitchen with the cook and gardener. Her only companion was the school dog, named Roger. Looking back, Sylvia reflected, "I don't really think I could have endured the months I spent at that school if it hadn't been for Roger. I really was frightfully unhappy." She knew that he was always waiting for her outside by the school steps. A harrowing episode in which the headmistress kept insisting that Sylvia eat bread and butter (which she detested), finally convinced her parents to bring Sylvia back home. Due to Beatrice's work schedule, Sylvia spent a great deal of time with an aunt in the Bronx. Grandmother Saperstein was right. It wasn't possible to transform Sylvia into a 'normal' child who enjoyed games and giggly companions.

In 1921, Beatrice's brother Jacob and his family arrived at Ellis Island. They too, had used their entire savings for passage to America. After a warm family welcome, they settled in Paterson, New Jersey. Upon completing high school in June 1923, Jacob's son Albert, who was four years older than Sylvia, was invited by Dr. Sidney to live in New York. With Sigmund's help and encouragement Albert could prepare to study dentistry. Initially, Sylvia saw Albert's presence as an intrusion. The two would sit and glare at each other. "I was moody.

And Albert was moody," she recalled. "For days we would glower at each other without speaking. Then suddenly, without any apparent reason, we would talk and laugh and be the best friends in the world." In the meantime, the Saperstein clan frequently had big family dinners. Plates were filled with plenty of good Russian food.

c1918 - Cousin Albert Sabin (Abraham Saperstein), who would develop the oral polio vaccine

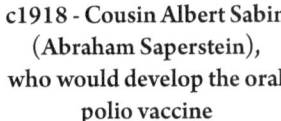

On November 8, 1922, Surrogate James A. Foley finalized the adoption of Sylvia Sidney—a name that would garner public attention and fame within a few years. Sylvia spent her allowance on theater and movies. She was particularly taken with Doris Keane in the stage revival of *Romance*. On stage, Keane opened a door into another world. "It meant escape to me," said Sylvia, "though I did not realize it then. I only knew that when I was in the theater, or watching a movie, I forgot myself. I wasn't Sylvia Sidney anymore. I was the character I watched before me."[18]

In March 1924, Sylvia got her first taste of "celebrity." Her name appeared in the *Brooklyn Daily Eagle* announcing her debut at the Little Theatre. Her impersonation of Jackie Coogan brought down the house. On another occasion she offered nine character impersonations with as many costume changes to ovations and cheering. Friends encouraged Beatrice to prepare Sylvia for the stage.

Sylvia's time at Washington Irving High School was short-lived. "I dropped out of high school," she would admit, with a trace of revolt in her voice. "I hated the regimentation of school. I hated math. So I got

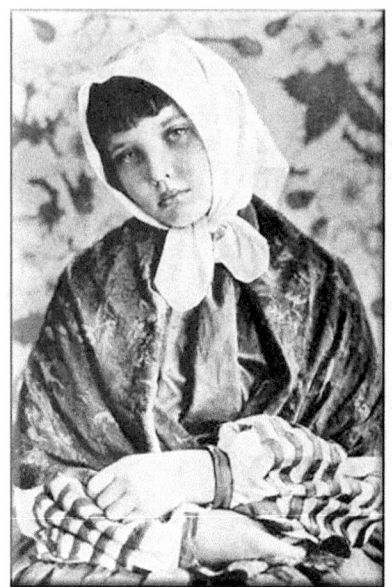 

c1922 - Playacting: A somber look, or a Jackie Coogan smile

this awful mental block. Besides, I didn't have a sense of responsibility."[19] Dr. Sidney, whose business was prospering, relocated his family to Lower Manhattan, 201 West 11th Street. Cousin Albert would recall, "We moved down closer to the Village … to a very, very nice apartment. He was making quite a bit of money as a dentist. My aunt was always dressed very gorgeously."[20]

In 1925, after Sylvia received a circular announcing classes at the Theatre Guild School, she was determined to enroll. Beatrice caught Sylvia in her bedroom dressed in an evening gown, fur and hat, starring into a mirror at an imaginary hero. She turned around, struck a pose, and launched into a speech on why she should attend dramatic school. One florid gesture knocked the mirror over, shattering the glass. Bewildered, Beatrice shook her head and walked back downstairs muttering to herself.[21] Sylvia's performance was not in vain. At age fifteen, she was accepted into the Theatre Guild School. Out of 700 applicants, 105 were awarded $500 scholarships. Of these, only 60 students would be retained. The Manhattan school was considered a stepping stone to professional acting. Winifred Lenihan, famous for her role in *St. Joan*, was the school's director. She told *The New York Times* that the primary goal was to train genuine and "highly competent" talent.

Sylvia passed the scrutiny of the school's board of directors. She was then judged and rated, along the with others, based on a recitation. Following this, she anxiously awaited the final verdict—handed to her by an office-boy. She slit open the envelope and read their decision—she was to stay. Included in this group was Peg Entwistle, remembered for her suicide leap from the Hollywoodland sign in 1932. Entwistle opted out of the school for an offer with the Jewett Players in Boston. Sylvia signed the Guild contract with the understanding that upon graduation, they could option her services at $50 a week. She pointed out, "The first thing they did was to make my voice over. I talked the way children so often do, way up high. They told me, 'You must learn to place your voice. You aren't using your own voice at all.' It wasn't easy to do the things they said. But gradually I began to get somewhere."

Vocal coach Dagmar Perkins, along with director Winthrop Ames, worked wonders for Sylvia. Her temper subsided. She had contentment. She matured. In acting, Sylvia appeared to find escape and release from her childhood torments. Sylvia was never happier. She began to enjoy intimate talk with other girls. She began to like boys. She was devoted to her studies. Cousin Albert noted, "I had to share a room with my cousin. I used to be kept awake at night because when I got through studying, she would have me read lines to her. So, I got to learn about Shakespeare, indirectly."[22]

At the end of the first term, May 1926, twenty-one students remained. All had the experience of playing many parts under the vigorous and exacting direction of talents like Laura Hope Crews and Guthrie McClintic. For the school's first public performance, Sylvia was selected to play the title role in *Prunella*. The 1906 play, directed by Winthrop Ames, was given a professional outing at the Garrick Theatre. Sylvia got to wear (and keep) the original costumes worn by Marguerite Clark in the 1913 Broadway production. The illusive nature of this charming fable details the cloistered beauty Prunella, reared by her watchful aunts. Her days are confined to lessons and needlepoint, until Pierrot serenades her, carries her into the moonlight and out into the real world. An audience of parents, doting relatives, critics and a few Broadway scouts witnessed Sylvia's exquisite interpretation. A critic for the *New York Evening Post* enthused, "Miss Sylvia Sidney's fragile charm and quiet grace, her vague and eloquent demureness, have been seized upon by those scouting among the nooks for new talent. Someone ought to beseech her to put her fingers in her ears against the siren song of quick success. She is better than that."[23]

The play proved so popular that extra matinees were added. Following *Prunella*, students anticipated spending the month of July in Scarborough, performing four weeks of summer stock. *Liliom* was scheduled first, and Sylvia assumed, as did many other students, that she would play Louise, the daughter. Instead she was assigned to paint scenery. Linda Watkins got the role. School director Lenihan adhered to the ensemble spirit and a strict set of rules and regulations—which, eventually, led to Sylvia's undoing. Prior to opening night curtain, Sylvia was paged back stage to curl Miss Watkin's hair. Sylvia was up to the task, which she performed to Linehan's satisfaction. "I'm going out," Sylvia told her afterward. A note of defiance underscored her exit. Outside, she was met by a young beau who took her for a drive. It

Prunella (May 1926) Sylvia displayed "quiet charm, and delicate grace"

had a calming effect. Sylvia began to realize there were other roles in the world besides Liliom's daughter. It was after midnight when they returned. Waiting up for her was Winifred Lenihan. There were words. Miss Lenihan fired Sylvia from the troupe. Dr. and Mrs. Sidney were faced once more with their problem child. A decade later Sylvia defended herself, saying, "Those days are past. Maybe I was a hellion but I did hate what I considered the snootiness of the place. Everybody was too grand to suit me so I just raised a little hell." [24]

Sylvia shrugged off her dismal, but gratefully acknowledged, "Mr. Winthrop Ames gave me one of the most precious things I have today—my voice. Mr. Ames told me I could never become an emotional actress with that voice and finally taught me how to place my voice correctly." For several weeks Sylvia's attempt to find another stage opportunity proved challenging. For encouragement, Beatrice bought something special at a Paris auction, no less, for her daughter's sixteenth birthday. It was the dressing table that had belonged to the famous French actress, Sarah Bernhardt. Sylvia would take it on her travels for years to come, considering it good luck.

Sylvia toyed with becoming a film extra. She played a bit in Lya de Putti's American film debut, *Sorrows of Satan* (1926) directed by D.W. Griffith.[25] Sidney is recognizable in an elaborate wedding scene, leading the bridal procession. For this, she was paid five dollars. *Prince of Tempters* (1926) provided more extra work. Sylvia also persisted in visiting the offices of stage managers. Describing herself as "a gawky kid with hair down her back and carrying a pile of books," she mentioned getting a round of rebuffs, such as, "Look what wants to be an actress—my God, throw it out, quick!"

While Sylvia attempted to find work, cousin Albert walked out of the Sidney home. He disappeared completely for six months. "Everyone said he was terribly ungrateful," Sylvia remembered, "And then he suddenly reappeared. He had taken a job at Luna Park [as a barker] to get enough money to study what he wanted to study. He knew he would not stick to dentistry."[26] Albert had become absorbed in the world of infectious disease. He recalled later, "I made some money ... so I wouldn't have to ask for everything. The first two years in dentistry was very similar to two years of medicine. I wanted to be able to *do* something. And I was very quickly introduced into a world that excited me." Albert was not aware that Dr. Sidney had taken out

Age 16. Sylvia leaves the Theatre Guild to face *The Challenge of Youth*

a life insurance policy on him—an investment, in case something untoward happened—or better yet, as Albert bluntly put it—a subterfuge. Upon hearing his nephew's decision, Sigmund told Albert that he would no longer support him.

Albert moved into a rooming house while attending Washington Square College. Sylvia missed her cousin terribly. He had cued her at home when she rehearsed. He had given her incentive and sympathized with her ambitions. The Saperstein family threw a dinner party to honor Albert's new endeavor. Cousins gathered around the table and talked about Albert's future. During this festive occasion, everyone became aware that Grandmother Sapertstein wasn't herself. As the evening wore on, it was obvious the family cornerstone of tolerance, patience and understanding, was failing. She was lost only in thoughts of her youth in old Russia. It was on this note that Sylvia was finally paged for her first professional stage appearance in the aptly titled, *The Challenge of Youth*.

Tryouts for *The Challenge of Youth* began in October 1926, prior to opening at Poli's Theater in Washington D.C. Sylvia signed on for the principal feminine role as Desire Adams, the epitome of flaming youth in a small New England town. Ads for the play teased, "A courageous and frank exhibition of why the average youth is called a member of the younger degeneration."

Sylvia packed her bags and stood on tip toe for good-bye kisses at the station from her mother, Dr. Sidney and cousin Albert. Before she knew it she was sitting at her dressing table opening night, telegrams stuck to the mirror and flowers filling the room. The evening of the second performance Sylvia put extra pep into her "degeneration" and fainted in the middle of the first act. There was a gasp from the audience as she fell, stage center, into a crumpled heap. The curtain came down and a physician in the house demanded Sylvia have an immediate appendectomy. She refused. "I wouldn't listen," Sylvia recalled. "I finished the show loving every minute of it."[27] The doctor had misdiagnosed. With the help of adhesive tape, she completed the week-long run, after X-Rays indicated a torn ligament from jumping over a banister in one scene.

D.C.'s *Evening Star* was highly critical of the play's subject matter—a girl who "polluted the family home with a wild party." "There have been other productions in which evil was viewed by proxy," said the critic, "but they have been subjects of comment only in hopelessly vulgar circles." *Variety*, to the contrary, found *The Challenge of Youth* rather "dull stuff," except when the father (Charles Waldron), a college professor, discovers his daughter (Sidney) with a boy ... in her bedroom. "But for a blur at times in her enunciation," said the review, "[Sidney] promises something worthwhile." Jewish real estate tycoon Morris Cafritz concurred with this assessment and feted Sylvia with an after theater supper party. The event was held in the Chanticleer Room at *Club Le Paradis*, one of D.C.'s ritziest, "hottest" rendezvous. In spite of Prohibition and frequent raids, many brought flasks of booze to classier supper clubs. Shortly after sixteen-year-old Sylvia's night of celebration, an undercover policewoman noted 44 intoxicated patrons at *Le Paradis*. By court order the popular night spot was padlocked for one year. *The Challenge of Youth* met a swift and permanent closure. It was reportedly being revamped for rewrites, but never opened on Broadway. Due to her torn ligament, Sylvia was finally confined to bed for two weeks.

"By sheer youthful gall," as Sylvia put it, she became the replacement for Grace Durkin, who had replaced Dorothy Stickney in *The Squall*. The play was one of the more successful exploiters for the fall of 1926. Press agent Richard Maney plastered enlarged photos of the play's most sinful episodes outside the 48th Street Theatre. Maney later described *The Squall* as "a three act horror." The location, contemporary Spain. The focus, a wanton gypsy girl, Nubi, who escapes from a traveling caravan. A farmer and his wife (Blanche Yurka) "rescue" Nubi, welcoming her into their God-fearing household. Nubi proceeds to seduce the farmer's son, the farmer, and the hired hand. Sylvia, in the minor role of Anita, the son's fiancée, had only to endure these antics for a few weeks. Still, it qualified as her official Broadway debut.

And, for this, she was late. She laughed about it years later. "It's true. I had snared the part by sheer youthful gall. When they told me they couldn't use me because they wanted a blonde I told them to get me a blonde wig. And, that furthermore, I was the girl who could play the part. They were so startled by this that they ... sent me out to get a blonde wig."

The evening of her first performance Sylvia sat in her dressing room. She hadn't the vaguest idea how to put on a wig. As she headed toward the stage, the play's star, Blanche Yurka, stopped her. "I want to check you my dear," she instructed. "This great lady had a fit," said Sylvia. "'That wig,' she announced. 'It looks ghastly.' I was due to make my entrance in three minutes." Sylvia's cue came and went. On stage, her co-stars were forced to ad-lib. The stage manager finally rescued her from Yurka's clutches. Sylvia's Broadway debut was a tad late, but she was completely humiliated. "I've never forgotten that awful experience," Sidney recalled in 1958. "The fear of being late still haunts me. To this day, I'm always the first one at the theater in the evening."[28]

The Squall afforded Sylvia a few weeks salary and paved the way for a more a promising opportunity. By the end of January 1927, she was rehearsing her first lead role in the Broadway hit, *Crime*. In 1998, she recalled standing in a lineup of young women applying for a part in the play. Producer Al Woods looked her over and said, "With that nose you gotta be Irish." Without missing a beat, she answered back, "With that nose I'm Jewish." "She can act!" cried Woods. "We'll start rehearsals on Wednesday." She was taken back when handed her heavy copy of the script. "I had a part *that* thick!" she laughed.[29]

Due to her age, Sidney had been advised not to accept any big parts. She asked director Winthrop Ames for his opinion. He asked how much they were paying her. "I told him $150 a week," she recalled. "He looked at me and said, 'You're ready.'"[30] Running for 186 performances, *Crime*, by Samuel Shipman and John B. Hymer, touted a cast of "unknowns" who would all make their mark in Hollywood: Chester Morris, Douglass Montgomery, Kay Johnson, Jack LaRue and the luminous Kay Francis.

During a two-week tryout in Philadelphia, *Crime Wave* (original title) left audiences intoxicated by the thrills and suspense they saw on stage. Critics predicted a prosperous run in New York. Producer Woods gave Sylvia a silver coin on opening night, February 22, at the Eltinge Theatre. The charm brought her luck. Organized crime was the topic and the play carried out the message with cold-blooded businesslike precision. James Rennie, played the high-brow gang leader Eugene Fenmore, who plots high class robberies. Sylvia was cast as Annabelle, a clerk at Macy's who, along with boyfriend Tommy (Douglass Montgomery) manages to save $130 for a honeymoon. While spooning on a Central Park bench, the young couple are robbed at gunpoint by two of Fenmore's bullies. Tommy turns bitter and decides to rob a poker game where gang members hang out. Annabelle tags along, and before they know what's happening they are given a choice: be turned over to the police, or be decoys in a major jewelry store heist. As suspense builds, audiences begin to wonder if Annabelle and Tommy will spend their "honeymoon" in prison.

Critic Arthur Pollock described *Crime* as an "appealing, human melodrama." "Probably the most popular member of the cast," cheered Pollock, "was a newcomer named Sylvia Sidney ... with gifts for the theater that make her always natural and effective."[31] *The New York Times* nodded, "Although all of the cast are well selected and drilled, the most ingratiating performances are by Miss Sidney and Mr. Montgomery." Sylvia admitted that audiences were dazzled by the brief distraction of Kay Francis in a gold dress. Biographer George Eells said, "Sidney maintained that Kay had stolen the play from her."[32] Sylvia gave credit for her own success to Al Woods, who instructed her on how to *listen*. "And once you learn to listen," said Sidney, "you begin to know how to act."

When drama critic Alexander Woollcott referred to Sidney as a "miniature Katharine Cornell," the reputable actress made an appearance backstage. "I shall never forget our first meeting," said Sylvia. "Cornell came to my dressing room. We stood in the doorway and eyed each other from head to foot before either of us spoke a word.

Sylvia's first Broadway "hit" *Crime* **(1927) with Douglass Montgomery**

My director stood there paralyzed, wondering if we were going to claw each other's eyes out!"³³ Sylvia became an ardent fan of Cornell after seeing her in *The Green Hat*. "Unconsciously I developed little mannerisms like hers," she admitted, "and they became so noticeable that I did not go to see her anymore." Following their dressing room encounter, Sidney mentioned having "great fun" with Cornell over luncheon, comparing notes.

After Broadway, *Crime* hit the Chicago Adelphi Theatre for a ten week run. There was talk of Sylvia co-starring with Claudette Colbert in *The Third Day*, John van Druten's adaptation of a Czech play. It was about a girl who is driven insane by her sister's indiscretions. John Colton's adaptation of the same play, titled *The Devil's Plum Tree*, preempted the Van Druten version when it opened at the San Francisco Curren Theatre starring Ruth Chatterton. Sylvia stayed on with *Crime* until it closed in Boston at the end of October. Remaining original cast members included Sidney, Kay Johnson and Chester Morris. In 1960, Morris recalled his association with *Crime* and producer/agent Al Woods. "Al was really responsible for my getting to Hollywood and for getting into that kind of money. I'd made a test with Sylvia Sidney when we were playing in *Crime*." Aside from the Sidney-Morris screen test, Sylvia also appeared in two films for First National during the Broadway run of *Crime*. These were shot at Cosmopolitan Studios on 125th Street.

Broadway Nights (1927) was a rags-to-riches tale starring Lois Wilson. Sylvia (unbilled) was among numerous guest stars playing themselves amidst the glamour of Manhattan nightlife. Also making their film debuts were Ann Sothern and Barbara Stanwyck. In April 1927, it was reported that Sylvia was in the Ben Lyon film *Dance Magic*— a saga about a girl (Pauline Starke) who leaves the confines of a strict New England religious community to dance on Broadway.³⁴

These minor celluloid appearances did not garner Sidney much mention. In the fall of 1927, she was seen lunching at the Tavern with German film producer Carl Laemmle. Whatever their discussion, Sylvia was more determined than ever to find another stage vehicle. Sidney indulged in what she referred to as "a procession of Broadway flops," before a disappointing and unexpected Hollywood misfire.

(Endnotes)

1. "Sylvia Sidney to Fight Suit," *New York Sun*, November 20, 1933
2. "Sylvia Airs Adoption Row," *Pittsburgh Post-Gazette*, November 20, 1933 (subsequent reports said the amount asked was $18,000)
3. "Sylvia Airs Adoption Row," *Pittsburgh Post-Gazette*, November 20, 1933
4. "Sylvia's Father Didn't Know of Adoption Till '32," *Brooklyn Daily Eagle*, November 22, 1933
5. "Sylvia Sidney Suit Dropped by Father," *New York Times*, December 3, 1933
6. "Behind the News with Sylvia Sidney," *The Daily News (Perth)*, June 10, 1937
7. Details on the family of Moshe Kossowski are taken from: JewishGen Shtetlinks: http://kehilalinks.jewishgen.org/lunna/Kosowski.html
8. Passport Application, dated February 28, 1920 (residing at 924 Tiffany St., Bronx) His WWI Draft card (June 5, 1917) lists his age as 30, and birth year as 1886. His father, Moshe Kosovsky was listed "Morris"
9. Saul Benison, "Interview with Dr. Albert Sabin," November 10, 1973 (DRC, University of Cincinnati)
10. Adele Fletcher Whitely, "The True Story of Sylvia Sidney," *Modern Screen*, December 1931
11. Gladys Hall, "Untold Secrets of the Stars," *Motion Picture*, April 1934
12. Laura Benham, "Sylvia Breaks All the Rules," *Screenland*, September 1934
13. Faith Service (pen name for Gladys Hall), "I Could Live Without Love," *Motion Picture*, March 1933
14. Mignon Rittenhouse, "One Step to Broadway," *Picture Play*, May 1932
15. Adele Fletcher Whitely, "The True Story of Sylvia Sidney," *Modern Screen*, December 1931
16. Dora Albert, "No More Impulses, says Sylvia Sidney," *Photoplay*, July 1937
17. Cleveland Amory, "Sylvia Sidney," *Observer Dispatch*, September 15, 1977
18. Gladys Hall, "Untold Secrets of the Stars," *Motion Picture*, April 1934

19 Marian Christy, "Lifestyle: Sylvia Sidney, Older, Wiser," *Oregonian*, November 28, 1978
20 Saul Benison, "Interview with Dr. Albert Sabin," November 10, 1973 (DRC, University of Cincinnati)
21 Jon Slott, "Sentimental Sylvia," *Screen and Radio Weekly*, 1935
22 Saul Benison, "Interview with Dr. Albert Sabin," November 10, 1973 (DRC, University of Cincinnati)
23 John Anderson, "Two on the Aisle," *New York Evening Post*, June 18, 1926
24 John J, Kelly, "Sylvia Is Back, Just As She Said," *Plain Dealer*, September 19, 1937
25 Adele Whitely Fletcher, "The True Story of Sylvia Sidney," January 1932 (principal photography for *Sorrows of Satan* was completed by July 1926 at Paramount's Long Island studio. Reshoots and new scenes added through September)
26 Katherine Albert, "Sylvia Sidney Plays Truth," *Modern Screen*, June 1936
27 Margaret Reid, "Who Is Sylvia?" *Screenland*, August 1931
28 "A Tardy Triumph For Sylvia Sidney," *Philadelphia Inquirer*, July 20, 1958
29 Sylvia Sidney during interview at the National Arts Club in New York City, June 2, 1998
30 William A. Raidy, "You'll Get No Book from Sylvia Sidney," *Times-Picayune*, March 7, 1976
31 Arthur Pollock, review of *Crime*, Brooklyn Daily Eagle, February 23, 1927
32 George Eells, *Ginger, Loretta and Irene Who?* Putnam, c. 1976, pg. 201
33 Elizabeth Yeaman, "An Actress Who Is Different," *Hollywood Daily Citizen*, January 14, 1931
34 *Motion Picture News*, April 29, 1927 (one week of filming had taken place); also mention of Sidney in *Dance Magic*: "Kane Begins Filming On Kelland's Novel," *Seattle Daily Times*, May 8, 1927

1929 photograph by Edward Steichen

Chapter 2
Nice Women & Bad Girls

Sylvia's success in *Crime* offered no career guarantees. As she put it, "After that, I reverted to routine and picked a couple more flops, *Mirrors* and *Don't Count Your Chickens*, both of which died on me almost immediately."[1] *Mirrors*, by Milton Gropper, had a tryout in Hartford, Connecticut, on Christmas Day 1927. *Variety* reported that with some "expert trimming" the play could have "possibilities." The theme was familiar—debauchery in the suburbs—traditional morals turning upside down—similar to turf explored in *The Challenge of Youth*. This time, however, Sylvia's character rebels against all the sexual shenanigans, boozing and depravity going on—and her parents are among the participants. *Variety's* review pointed out, "A particular bright spot is the playing of Sylvia Sidney. Miss Sidney plays with such simplicity and intelligent avoidance of overacting, that the conclusion is inescapable that of this young lady more will be heard anon."

Mirrors opened in January at Broadway's Forrest Theatre. *The New York Sun* huffed, "*Mirrors* is not only vulgar, it is also miserably snide." *The New York Times* concurred, adding that "one can hardly endure it all until the final curtain." *Mirrors* closed after thirteen performances. Cast as the callow youth, who Sylvia fancies, was blonde-headed

Raymond Guion—later known as Gene Raymond. In 1931, he and Sylvia would team for Paramount's *Ladies of the Big House.*

Don't Count Your Chickens, by Robert Riskin and Edith Fitzgerald, went through several name changes before a Cleveland tryout in March 1928. The rowdy comedy, starring Mary Boland as a scatter-headed divorcee, met with qualified approval by local critics. Sylvia played Boland's daughter, who confesses her "intimacy" with a free-spirited suitor who doesn't believe in marriage. The frantic Boland concocts a plan for her daughter to pretend to be pregnant in order to nudge her suitor into matrimony. One reviewer felt the subject matter "tickled a majority of the women in the audience," and said that Sidney "gave a first-rate performance, playing earnestly with quiet sincerity." The vitality of Boland and efforts of Sidney weren't enough. *Don't Count Your Chickens* collapsed on the road, after playing Detroit.

Sidney's next effort, *The Breaks,* also came to a screeching halt. Opening at Broadway's Klaw Theatre, the melodrama lasted eight performances. The action took place in Lovelady, Texas, replete with corn liquor, cotton fields, poor white trash, sheriffs, handcuffs, and a heavy dose of cursing. The *New York Evening Post* gave a brief nod to "Miss Sylvia Sidney ... quite nice when she wasn't fluttering and clasping her hands in fear." To be fair, Sylvia was a last minute replacement. She only had two days of rehearsal to perfect her hand-clasping and Southern drawl. Critic Gilbert Gabriel felt that Sidney "with her pert, triangular face and beseeching voice, is the one spoonful of sugar [in] this otherwise tasteless evening."[2] *The Breaks* was directed by Augustin Duncan, the elder brother of Isadora. He had been influential in establishing the Theater Guild. *The Breaks* was Augustin's comeback after losing his eyesight in the summer of 1927.

May 1928 came and went before Sylvia received an offer for a 14-week engagement at Elitch Gardens in Denver. She was assigned as the troupe's ingénue, and promised a variety of parts. Fredric March was the designated leading man. Others in the cast included leading lady Isobel Elsom, Florence Eldridge (March's actress-wife), and C. Henry Gordon. Blistering hot weather didn't stop patrons from enjoying the opening play, *Baby Cyclone. Behold the Groom* and the crowd-pleaser *Nightstick* followed. *The K Guy* offered a rather lame spoof of movie-makers. More impressive were the controversial *The Command to Love* by Fritz Gottwald and a revival of the 1893 hit *The Second Mrs. Tanqueray*. On August 8, the cast celebrated Sylvia's 18th birthday with a big party. Sylvia returned to Elitch decades later, celebrating her 66th birthday while starring in *Sabrina Fair*.

Sidney returned to New York with twelve more plays on her résumé. Prior to her engagement at Elitch, she signed with producer Jed Harris for a new play, *Rasputin*, to be produced that fall. *Rasputin*, she learned, had been set back indefinitely. Sidney filed a claim against Harris, through Equity, and received two weeks salary ($600) in settlement. Luckily, by October, Sylvia found a play which virtually "tore the house down," *Gods of the Lightning*. Reviews paid tribute to Sidney's "genius." Walter Winchell cheered, "Sylvia Sidney, one of the finest of the younger actresses, comes into her own with great emotional acting that gripped the heart strings and opened the tear ducts of those who occupied the front pews. She is a mighty fine actress, this Sidney lass, not given to overplaying nor fraudulent impersonating." Winchell underscored what had been true all along—Sylvia Sidney was a natural born actress.

The controversial *Gods of the Lightning*, also brought Department of Justice officials to the October 24 opening at Broadway's Little Theatre. They took notes. The subject matter was still a "hot" topic as far as the law was concerned. *Gods and the Lightning*, written by Maxwell Anderson and Harold Hickerson, was inspired by the sensational trial of two Italian anarchists Nicola Sacco (a shoemaker) and Bartolomeo Vanzetti (a fish peddler). In 1927, after seven years of incarceration, the men were finally executed. In the play, Charles Bickford portrayed a red-headed, belligerent strike leader, James Macready. Macready hates wealthy men, big business, religion and the military—accusing the former pair of manipulating the latter. Macready and his partner, Dante Capraro, are involved with a raucous group of eastern seaboard teamsters who are on strike.

Much of what follows parallels the incidents surrounding Sacco-Vanzetti. Macready and Capraro are arrested for robbery, and murder. Evidence is thin, but political expediency demands that someone be charged for the crime. In court, the biased judge pronounces their death sentence. Sylvia's big moment, as Rosalie, Macready's fiancée, occurs the evening of the execution. As the clock strikes midnight, a hush falls over a grimy lunchroom where the play began. Rosalie emits a blood-curling scream, crying, "Don't whisper it! That's what they'll want you to do—keep quiet about it—say it never happened—two innocent men killed. They're *killing* them!—Shout it! Cry out! Run and cry! Only—it won't do any good ... now." Curtain. The point being—murder was at work, not justice.

Critics found the heroes in *Gods and the Lightning* far from heroic, but as the *Evening Post* admitted, "It leaves one miserable, angry, ashamed and deeply disturbed." *The New York Times* pointed to Sidney in the final act: "She acts this searing episode with an unadorned poignancy that recapitulates and compresses all the emotions of *Gods of the Lightning* into one living moment."[3] Critic Pierre de Rohan joined the chorus for Sidney, saying, "Few artists of her youth have ever plumbed the emotional depths of a role so exacting and few of any ages could do as well." The public, however, too familiar with the *real* case, had had their fill of Sacco-Vanzetti. The play closed after twenty-nine performances.

Nonetheless, Sylvia's blood-curdling scream reached Hollywood. Years later, she explained, "The Fox films representative came to hear me scream, and he was so impressed he signed me up to scream in the movie *Thru Different Eyes*. Producers have thought of me ever since when they needed an outraged banshee."[4] On December 5, *Film Daily* reported Sylvia was headed for Hollywood (accom-

Gods of the Lightning (1928)

panied by her mother). *Thru Different Eyes* was an inventive piece of work, and seen today, the silent version (the talkie version is apparently lost) impresses. Film historians such as William K. Everson and scenarist DeWitt Bodeen consider *Thru Different Eyes* a forerunner of the Japanese *Rashomon* (1950)—a murder trial in which various

Thru Different Eyes (Fox) with Florence Lake

witnesses tell conflicting versions of the same crime. *Thru Different Eyes* was based on a play by Milton Gropper, who had written Sidney's short-lived, *Mirrors*.

The fluid camerawork of Ernest Palmer in *Thru Different Eyes*, captures chaos in the court pressroom prior to a sensational murder trial. Sidney shows up in a cloche hat and white fox fur accompanied by her friend (Florence Lake) who connives a way for them *both* to see the overcrowded proceedings. On trial is Harvey Manning (Edmund Lowe), who has been accused of murdering his best friend, an artist named Jack Winfield (Warner Baxter). Two versions of the alleged crime precede Sidney's "outraged banshee" and a climactic finish. First, the defense attorney represents Manning and his wife as a devoted couple. Baxter is a seducer, who tries to cajole the wife into running away with him to Italy. The camera then dissolves back to the defense attorney in court. Sidney's friend wisecracks, "Say, he's going to be my lawyer next time I kill a guy!" Sylvia stares straight into the camera looking hopeless and forlorn. The prosecution steps up. He portrays Manning and his crowd as a raucous bunch of boozers and wife swappers. Back in court, following deliberation, Lowe faces the jury.

The verdict, "Guilty!" is followed by Sidney's ear-piercing scream. Heads turn in her direction as she rushes forward to tell her sad story. "All his life this man Winfield has destroyed things," she sobs. "But I loved him! I still love him! Every time I look at my baby I see him." In flashback, Sidney describes how she tailed Baxter on the evening in question. There is a rousing scene where Sidney confronts Baxter inside the Manning home. She wants marriage and respectability. "Why pick on me?" he snarls. "There were others!" With gusto she offers Baxter a well-deserved slap across the face. He grabs her. They struggle. She sees a gun on the desk. The wife is upstairs when she hears a shot ring out. Lowe pulls in the driveway. They find Baxter's body, while Sidney quietly slips away. Not knowing what else to do, the couple claim it was a suicide.

It's a powerful scene that Sidney gives us at the climax. It is difficult to understand her dislike for the film. New York critic Arthur Pollock thought of all the cast members, "Miss Sidney, with the benefit of her stage training, appears to have somewhat the best of it in a major-minor speaking role."[5] *The New York Times* praised *Thru Different Eyes* as being "ingeniously conceived," noting that director Blystone's "sagacious guidance" had allowed the major players to give "capital performances."

Contract or no contract, Sylvia had had enough of Hollywood. The lights burned her eyes and she loathed the disconnected manner in which scenes were shot. While she thought director Jack Blystone "a lovely man," she found the experience bewildering. "I had never been so miserable in my life," she said afterward. "They said I was hard to handle and I guess I *was* pretty disagreeable."[6] In 1936, she elaborated, "It was those topsy-turvy days when Hollywood suddenly found its voice and began signing up speaking stage talent. The change from stage to screen was too sudden. I felt when I was making the picture that the world wouldn't declare a half holiday to see it when it was released—or me, either. To be frank, I didn't expect to ever return to Hollywood. I had always been happy on the stage, it was a medium I understood, and my family and friends were in the east."[7]

Sidney also ran into problems with one of the Fox studio leading men. She never specified who, but revealed to writer/editor Adele Whitely Fletcher that during production he knocked on her dressing room door and before she knew it his hands were all over her. He suggested they could have lunch in *his* dressing room, or ... his beach house. Sylvia freed herself after rebuffing him, but he persisted, telling her there was no need for her to be lonely. "I'm not yet sufficiently lonely to be interested in you," she replied, holding the door wide open. She counted it as the only unpleasant experience in her career up to that point.[8] The Fox roster in the leading man category included: co-stars Warner Baxter and Edmund Lowe, Charles Farrell, and George O'Brien. They all had beach houses in the Malibu film colony. Whoever her lothario was, his libido was put to rest by mid-March when *Film Daily* reported that Sidney had "bag and baggaged to Manhattan."

Sylvia cancelled her two-year Fox contract, called her mother from the studio, and told her to meet her at the train station. "I was bound and determined to get out of Hollywood," she recalled. "I was also determined that I was going to make it back to New York in time for the Mayfair Dance ... at the Ritz Carlton Hotel. The food was great, everyone brought a bottle. Eddie Duchin played, and nobody gave a

Fox starlet, Sylvia Sidney

damn about Prohibition. ... I guess the Mayfair Dance was symbolic about all I had missed in being away from New York. If you were invited there it meant you had arrived in the theater."⁹

Sylvia wasted no time getting back on stage. She signed with a stock company in Rochester, run by George Cukor and George Kondolf. When asked about it years later, she was dismissive. "Oh *that*," she said. "I was only with them for a week."¹⁰ In truth, she appeared in three different productions at the city's Temple Theatre. First, was the satirical comedy *The Royal Family* (parodying the Barrymore clan). Sidney was praised for revealing "both comedy and emotional ability." This was followed by a curiosity titled *The Silent House*. Through hypnosis, Sylvia falls under the spell of an unscrupulous Chinese, Ho Fang, who intends to pilfer the inheritance of a young heir (Alexander Kirkland). Rochester's *Democrat Chronicle* complained, "If thirteen or fourteen of the killings were omitted there would be no weakening of the general effect of butchery." Kirkland and Sidney, the review claimed, "played the hero and the heroine in pleasant juvenile fashion."

The real lure for Sidney was the title role in the Ann Harding success, *The Trial of Mary Dugan*. As a "Follies" girl and mistress of an older man, Dugan is accused of murdering her wealthy benefactor.

While circumstantial evidence piles up against her, Dugan's brother (Kirkland), a young attorney, comes to her rescue. Things move swiftly toward a sensational climax, proving that Mary Dugan was being framed. Opening April 29, Rochester critic George L. David found the play "uncommonly excellent. Miss Sidney played Mary Dugan with fine judgment and graceful restraint." David was impressed how easily Sidney could rouse audience sympathy, as she took the witness stand.

Bette Davis and Miriam Hopkins had worked the previous fall with Cukor-Kondolf, and Davis was fired. "George Cukor—that's 'Cu' as in cucumber," she would grumble, "played a very important part in my life. He was the first person to fire me."[11] Cukor found Davis disruptive during rehearsals and disinclined to take direction. "It was useless to argue with her," he said.[12] As for Sidney's departure, she had another offer. She signed on with producer L. Lawrence Weber for the Broadway-bound comedy *Nice Women*.

First-nighters at Broadway's Longacre Theatre were impressed with how Sidney nailed comedy in *Nice Women*. For Sylvia, wise-cracking her way into the arms of an older, wealthy bachelor was new turf. One critic called the play "futile" and "guileless," but complimented Sidney's tough on-stage virgin, saying, "Miss Sidney managed with sly petulance … to edge a not very scintillating role with humor." Percy Hammond agreed, "With flaming lips, eyes like deep mysterious Broadway caverns … Miss Sidney leaps rather gracefully over the boundaries, making remarks and doing things that shock those of us who belong to an elder and subtler generation of sinners."[13] After two months of spouting an abundance of slang and brash theories about sex, Sylvia decided to make an about turn and play the title role in *An Old Fashioned Girl*. Shortly before the play opened, Sidney and thirty-year stage veteran Elsie Ferguson were guests of honor at the Actor's Matinee Club held at

Nice Women (1929) with Robert Warwick

the Lyceum Theatre. The invitation was yet another feather in Sidney's thespian cap—this time from fellow colleagues.

An Old Fashioned Girl, a satire by Maureen Watkins, debuted at the Flatbush Theatre in Brooklyn in October 1929. The opening night audience voiced disapproval during intermission. At midnight their ordeal was over. It required three lengthy acts for Watkins' lowdown on temperamental actresses. On stage, Helen MacKellar played a volatile blonde star, who throws tantrums at her producer (Edward Arnold) while a stage-struck lass (Sidney) keeps stealing the spotlight. Audiences were left wondering *who* the old-fashioned girl was. Bright spots in the play were few, but they all belonged to Sylvia. "The audience delighted in the work of little Sylvia Sidney, who carried off whatever honors there were to carry off last night," noted one savvy critic.[14] Following opening night, the most remarkable thing about the play was Sidney herself, carrying a cane, her foot encased in a plastic cast. She blamed Edward Arnold for that. "I wore a costume that had a long train," she explained years later. "He was standing on my train and when I started to walk, my ankle gave way. He was just as big and heavy then as he is now. I didn't find out until the next day it was broken."[15]

Sidney's mishap took place in the middle of the third act. When she came to, she insisted on going on with the performance. "Next day they put a cast on," she recalled, "and I went through the rest of the run leaning picturesquely on a cane. And adoring it. I'd park myself in the center of the stage and take every scene for myself. The ankle didn't hurt me a bit. Someone really should have killed me."[16] When the play closed for revisions, Sylvia, instead of being killed off, signed on for another play, *Cross Roads*.

The legendary Guthrie McClintic was at the helm of *Cross Roads* when it opened at the Morosco in November. Playwright Martin Flavin had two other successes running at the same time: *The Criminal Code*, which ran five months, and *Broken Dishes* with Bette Davis, running close to six. *Cross Roads*, his only failure of the season, lasted twenty-eight performances. Despite McClintic's intelligent direction, the play collapsed under the weight of melodramatic plotting. Sidney played a pretty co-ed at a Mid-Western college. Her romance with a medical student (Eric Dressler) is upset following a quarrel. He wants to leave school and marry. She insists he stick to his studies. After Dressler gets drunk in a speakeasy and is arrested, Sidney, to get even, accepts a ride with an intoxicated campus roué (Franchot Tone) in his new Packard. The car crashes into telephone pole and Tone dies. "The result," said critic

Lamar Trotti, "is a rather horrible example of what a good playwright can do ... when he had two other plays to worry about."[17] Another review barbed, "*Cross Roads* does not equal its two competitors from the same pen." Trotti did mention that the only good thing about the play was Sylvia Sidney. Critics agreed that she offered a fully realized character—as Brooks Atkinson's review put it, "a coherent image of sensitive, earnest young womanhood, by all odds the finest work she has done." *Cross Roads* closed just in time for the Christmas holiday. Sylvia took time out to see a few plays and celebrate a New Year and decade.

In early 1930, playwright Robert Riskin decided to revamp his play *Don't Count Your Chickens*. Retitled, *Many a Slip*, Riskin gathered some of the original cast. It turned out to be a career boost for both Riskin and Sylvia. The Greenwich Village tale of a mother who concocts a phantom pregnancy for her daughter (Sidney) to pressure her boyfriend (Douglass Montgomery) to propose marriage, fared better with Riskin in the director's seat. The play opened at New York's Little Theatre on February 3, and ran for fifty-six performances. The witty banter and slapstick made an impression on some. The *New York Evening Post* commented that *Many a Slip* provided plenty of laughs, while playing off Sidney's propensity for tears. "Miss Sidney has her usual quota of sobbing to do," said the critic, "and is made to appear thoroughly miserable throughout the play." Critic Lamar Trotti protested, "Miss Sidney is one of the few really young actresses who can act ... but one can easily tire of three hours of tears by any woman." The *New York Times* countered, "Miss Sidney presents the role of the girl with delicacy and understanding." After Broadway, *Many a Slip* toured for two months before ringing down the final curtain in Chicago. Robert Riskin would become a towering figure among Hollywood screenwriters. He teamed frequently with director Frank Capra for such classics as *It Happened One Night* (1934).

Sylvia's young co-star in *Many a Slip*, seventeen-year-old Tom Brown, who played her brother, developed a huge crush on her. "Gosh, I was walking around in the clouds," Brown recalled two years after the fact. "Sylvia always came to my dressing room before the opening curtain, we'd be together between acts, and we'd go out to supper after the show—Sylvia, my mother and myself." By the end of the run, Tom's mother, musical comedy actress Marie Francis, had other engagements. Tom, who had been saving his money to buy an engagement ring, was worried when Sylvia didn't bother to come around. After a couple of days he inquired if he had said something to offend her. "No Tommy," Sylvia replied, "but I've missed your mother terribly. I just adore her." He then asked what that had to do with her coming to see him. "Heavens Tommy," Sidney shot back. "Where'd you ever get the idea that I was interested in *you*?"[18] This embarrassment soured Brown on romance, temporarily.

Tom Brown wasn't the only one dazzled by Sylvia. In July, syndicated columnist Walter Winchell revealed, "That was some fight between Horace Liveright and Milton Raison over Sylvia Sidney, the actress, in a nightclub." The twenty year age difference between publisher/producer Liveright (age forty-seven) and Raison, a press agent, didn't discourage them from sparring. Both men were hotheads. Liveright, a self-professed socialist and Wall Street gambler with a profile like John Barrymore, was a devoted philanderer. Sylvia's future husband Bennett Cerf had bought his way into Liveright's publishing house in 1923. Cerf said of Liveright, "He was quite vain. He had flair. He sure charmed the hell out of me."[19] Cerf added that it was not unusual for Liveright to be

Many a Slip (1930) with Dorothy Sands

reasonably drunk. Although Sylvia's preference was for older men, it is unlikely that Sylvia succumbed to the charms of Liveright or Raison. Their altercation took place shortly after she filmed a Vitaphone short for Warner Brothers titled, *Five Minutes from the Station.*

After her bitter disappointment with *Thru Different Eyes*, it's surprising that Sidney took another try at celluloid. Vitaphone studio, located in Brooklyn, gave vaudeville stars an opportunity to make a quick buck filming musical comedy shtick. The fact that *Five Minutes from the Station* lasted less than 14 minutes and was shot in continuity may have influenced Sidney's decision. She played a discontented housewife on a tight budget whose husband (Lynn Overman) invites the boss (Burton Churchill) home for dinner. When they show up she is polite, but anxious, as she tries to butter up the boss and champion her husband's potential. Dinner begins to burn after the boss reveals he has someone else in mind for promotion. In tears, Sidney gives Churchill a good chewing out, while Overman looks on aghast. The boss likes her gumption and offers Overman a job as his assistant. Sidney throws her arms around Churchill and beams, "I'm going to kiss you, if they *shoot* me for it!" She does and everybody is happy.

Audiences (and critics) were used to Vitaphone shorts taking their minds off the Depression. *Film Daily* called *Five Minutes from the Station* "A flat number," another critic called it "so-so," but these were unfair assessments. The short succeeded as an entertaining slice of life. When asked by her publicist John Springer in the 1960's about her experience at Vitaphone, Sidney replied, "I've heard that I appeared in a short, but I've absolutely no recollection of it." More importantly, Sidney soon grabbed hold of a stage role that put Hollywood mogul B. P. Schulberg and publisher Bennett Cerf in her pocket. It was titled, appropriately, *Bad Girl.*

In August 1930, Sylvia was directed for the first time by Marion Gering, who would soon transfer his talent to the movies. Gering had guided Bette Davis in her Broadway debut *Broken Dishes* (1929). In 1953, he recalled, "I had a play called 'Bad Girl' and was looking around for an actress who could play the role without looking like the 'bad girl' the title implied. Then I remembered that in the previous season Sylvia Sidney had a role in a play called 'Nice Women.' So, casting against type, I sent for Miss Sidney."[20]

Bad Girl was based on the sensational, best-selling novel by Vina Delmar. Beatrice Sidney was not pleased at the prospect of her daughter participating in the project. Sylvia admitted, "When my mother read the script she hit the ceiling. She felt it was a 'dirty' play and if I did it my career would be ruined. I thought it was a good play and a terrific role, and I signed the contracts. I guess my mother still saw me as a child because we ended up not speaking ... . I moved out on my own into the Beaux Arts Hotel on East 44th Street."[21]

Bad Girl's debut at the Bronx Windsor Theatre was disrupted by a police raid before the final curtain. Charges were made that producer Robert Newman, Sylvia, and leading man Paul Kelly, were "staging an indecent performance."[22] The problem: a scene in a maternity hospital wherein 'bad girl' Sylvia is writhing in agony during childbirth. Forewarned, the District Attorney and several police officers were in attendance opening night. For co-star Paul Kelly a ride in the paddy wagon was no big deal. He was still on parole. An ex-con, Kelly had spent 1927-29 in San Quentin for manslaughter after bashing his best friend's head against the wall. For Sylvia, the experience was new territory.

Sidney received a summons to appear in court. Her photo made the front page of *Brooklyn Daily Eagle* with the headline, "'Bad Girl' in Bad." In 1972, someone showed Sylvia one of these sensational clippings. She was delighted. "I gave birth to a baby on stage," she enthused. "All done in shadows. I remember they had the paddy wagon parked outside the theater. What happened is that we eventually had to clean up the show."[23] Indeed, some of the objectionable lines and situations were deleted before the play opened at Broadway's Hudson Theatre, October 2. (The charges were finally dismissed on November

7.) A San Francisco columnist blamed all the controversy on a moral revival being waged by the Catholic Drama League. The smarter critics agreed that the play had a refreshing element of truth and underlying tenderness. Following all the brouhaha, headlines helped *Bad Girl* gross a whopping $12,000 a week. Critic Arthur Pollock admitted that the maternity scene "was played in a manner that left little to the imagination." "The old idea ... that babies arrive in cabbages," said Pollock, "was knocked higher than a cocked hat."[24]

The "bad girl" in *Bad Girl* was from the Bronx. Her name was Dot. Her live-in boyfriend, Eddie (Kelly) made $40 a week at a radio store. When Dot tells Eddie she is pregnant, they agree to marry. Neither believes the other wants a child. The controversial second-act hospital scene was done in silhouette, using a gauze curtain. The lighting outlined cast members—grotesquely enlarged for effect. Nurses scurried about while the doctor reassured the pain-wracked Dot in the throes of childbirth. In the final act, Dot's affection for the baby is obvious. Act III, Scene II, titled "Between Traffic Lights"—finds the couple headed home in a taxi. The driver speeds over a bump in the road, provoking Eddie to scold, "You ain't driving no hook-and-ladder!" Dot and Eddie realize they *both* love the baby. New York critic Gilbert Gabriel praised Kelly's "brilliantly disciplined" performance coupled with the "volatile, more softly shadowed playing of Miss Sidney" as the finest performances of the year.[25]

A review in the *Standard Union* cheered, "Sylvia Sidney is a complete revelation. At last she emerges as a top-ranking performer. Playing with a sensitive charm and finished virtuosity, she makes the simple-minded heroine a living, poignant being. She handles the dialogue, full of tough expressions and Bronx slang, with unaffected ease." International News reporter David Sentner observed the first-night audience stand up and cheer Paul Kelly whose ex-con status was a indeed

Bad Girl (1930) with Paul Kelly

a main attraction. "They cheered," said Sentner, "because they were with him and because he showed he was a gosh darned good actor."

By the time *Bad Girl* closed, Kelly's parole term had expired. He married actress Dorothy Mackaye, the widow of the dead chum he had "unintentionally" killed. The new Mrs. Kelly affectionately called her new husband '"Bratface." Sylvia, in a surprise turn, was headed to Hollywood, where over the next few years she would be teamed with her director Marion Gering for no less than six Paramount films.

B.P. "Ben" Schulberg, managing director of Paramount Studio on the West Coast, was in the audience of *Bad Girl* one evening with his wife Adeline "Ad" Jaffe Schulberg. Their son, Budd Schulberg described in his 1981 memoir,

Mother prided herself on her ability to spot upcoming actors … who were still 'unknowns.' And so that evening, it was Ad who raved about young Sidney's promise and urged that they go back to her dressing room to introduce themselves. It could have been a scene from one of my father's movies: the stylish matron … and the elegant, prematurely grey, tycoon at the height of his power and confidence going back stage to introduce themselves to the fetching ingénue.[26]

The next morning, Adeline suggested that Schulberg telegram Sidney for an interview at Paramount Pictures Building on Broadway. Sylvia retained vivid memories of their meeting that same afternoon. It was pouring rain.

> I went up to his receptionist and said that I wanted to see Mr. Schulberg. She was a little snotty. 'And who may I say is calling?' says she, and I say, 'Tell him it's Sylvia Sidney.' Well, all at once the whole attitude changes. 'Oh, yes, Miss Sidney. I'll let him know that you are here.' Couldn't be nicer.

> I go into his office. He gets up from his desk. Tall, white hair, beautiful hands, cigar. The first thing he says to me? 'I hear you're a hellion, a hell cat.' I looked him right in the eye and said, 'Well?' Schulberg laughs. 'They were right,' he says, and then, 'Look here, I've a got a contract for you. Five hundred a week.' 'Forget it,' I tell him. 'I'm making seven fifty a week on Broadway now.' I was about to leave when he says, 'Well, I'm really sorry you won't take it, because your first film on the contract will be *An American Tragedy*. Well, my young

heart was saying, 'I'll die, I'll die, I'll die,' and then I went totally bananas and said 'Okay ... I'll sign ... what time shall I be there?' So that's how Schulberg got me; by dangling Theodore Dreiser under my nose.[27]

Sidney had loathed Hollywood, determined never to go back, but Schulberg's persuasive attitude compelled her to do just the opposite. He emphasized how talkies had been perfected since her previous experience. The very mention of *An American Tragedy* and she was suddenly ambitious to be involved. "I've never changed my mind so completely in all my life," she admitted.[28] There was also the thirty-nine-year-old married Schulberg himself. Sidney felt an instant attraction to the man.

A few days prior to Sylvia's departure for the west coast, Dr. Sidney telephoned insisting that it was improper for her to travel across country alone. "Mother *had* to accompany me," recalled Sylvia. "But you'll remember that mother and I were not speaking, so dad devised some story that I had called him and had asked him to ask her to accompany me to Hollywood. Of course she couldn't say 'no,' but I can still see us sitting on opposite sides of the compartment just glaring at each other all the way to California."[29]

Much to Sylvia's surprise, a few days after arriving in Hollywood (January 1931), she ended up being a last minute replacement for Clara Bow. Sidney wasn't enthused, at first. "I couldn't see myself in a Clara Bow part," she said. "When I read the story I found that it might have been written for me." The film was *City Streets*, directed by Rouben Mamoulian.

I got a call one night from Paramount. I was to be at the studio tomorrow! There had been a meeting at Schulberg's house;

the picture with Clara Bow was to be cancelled. Mamoulian said, 'There's a gal who can play the hell out of this part, and she's here!' They asked, 'Who?' He said, 'Sylvia Sidney. She can run away with the part!' If it hadn't been for him, I would have never stayed with films.[30]

Once cameras began to roll, Sidney was impressed with the expertise and guiding hand of director Mamoulian. Her *real* comfort and support, however, was unquestionably the presence of B. P. Schulberg—a man she would soon learn to walk ten or twelve feet in front of, as rumors began to circulate about their relationship. Avoiding being caught together by news cameras kept people guessing. Sixteen-year-old Budd Schulberg visited Paramount during production of *City Streets*. He later recalled,

> I watched mother's new rival on the set of *City Streets*, sitting close to my father while one of his new favorite directors, the brooding Rouben Mamoulian, put her through her paces. I sat with Father, Sylvia and Mamoulian in the intimacy of the projection room, never sensing that the drama going on around me was more intense than the acting on the screen.[31]

(Endnotes)
1 Margaret Reid, "Who Is Sylvia," *Screenland,* August 1931
2 Gilbert Gabriel, review of *The Breaks, New York Sun,* April 17, 1928
3 J. Brooks Atkinson, review of *Gods and the Lightning, New York Times,* October 25, 1928
4 "Sylvia Sidney in Good Voice for Screaming in New Film," *Richmond Times Dispatch,* March 7, 1946

5   Arthur Pollock, review of *Thru Different Eyes, Brooklyn Daily Eagle*, April 15, 1929
6   Margaret Reid, "Who Is Sylvia?" *Screenland*, August 1931
7   Sylvia Sidney, "Studio Storms Too Realistic for Sylvia," *Lodi News-Sentinel*, December 31, 1936
8   Adele Whitely Fletcher, "The True Story of Sylvia Sidney," *Modern Screen*, December 1931
9   Jeff Laffel, "Sylvia Sidney," *Films in Review*, September/October, 1994
10 Jeff Laffel, "Sylvia Sidney," *Films In Review*, September/October, 1994
11 Charlotte Chandler, "*The Girl Who Walked Home Alone: Bette Davis a Personal Biography*, Simon & Schuster, c. 2006
12 Victoria Wilson, *A Life of Barbara Stanwyck: Steel-True 1907-1940*, Simon and Schuster, c. 2013, pg. 287
13 Percy Hammond, review of *Nice Women, Trenton Evening Times*, June 16, 1929
14 Review of *An Old-Fashioned Girl, Brooklyn Daily Eagle*, October 8, 1929
15 Louis Sheaffer, "Miss Sidney a Quick-Change Artist in *The Fourposter*," *Brooklyn Eagle*, March 19, 1953
16 Margaret Reid, "Who Is Sylvia?" *Screenland*, August 1931
17 Lamar Trotti, review of *Cross Roads, Macon Telegraph*, December 8, 1929
18 E.R. Moak, "Nix on Dames," *Picture Play*, December 1932
19 Bennett Cerf, "Notable New Yorkers," Columbia University Library Oral Research, undated, 1967
20 Mark Barron, "Doings on Broadway," *Leader-Republican*, March 19, 1953
21 Jeff Laffel, "Sylvia Sidney," *Films in Review*, September/October 1994
22 "*Bad Girl* Hearing Delayed," *New York Times*, September 21, 1930
23 Arthur Bell, "Sylvia's Souvenirs," *New York Times*, December 17, 1972
24 Arthur Pollock, review of *Bad Girl, Brooklyn Daily Eagle*, September 23, 1930
25 Gilbert W. Gabriel, "Critic 'Finds' Two New Stars in *Bad Girl*," *Plain Dealer*, December 14, 1930
26 Budd Schulberg, *Moving Pictures: Memories of a Hollywood Prince*, Stein & Day, c. 1981, pg. 353
27 Jeff Laffel, "Sylvia Sidney," *Films in Review*, September/October, 1994
28 James Robert Parish, *Paramount Pretties*, Castle Books, c. 1972, pg. 265
29 Jeff Laffel, "Sylvia Sidney," *Films in Review*, September/October 1994
30 Gregory J.M. Catsos, "Sylvia Sidney," *Filmfax*, November 1990
31 Budd Schulberg, *Moving Pictures: Memories of a Hollywood Prince*, Stein & Day, c. 1981, pg. 353

City Streets with Gary Cooper (Paramount)

Chapter 3
"Mr. God" & the "Idiot"

Paramount prepared *City Streets* for their biggest star Clara Bow. Since the arrival of talkies, Bow's career was in trouble. She worked with director Rouben Mamoulian to overcome her fear of the microphone, but had a nervous collapse before cameras began to roll. Her problems were compounded by unsavory publicity from a sensational trial involving her personal secretary. Ben Schulberg reassured AP reporters, "Sylvia Sidney, who was brought to Hollywood from the New York stage and whom we regard as a sensational screen discovery will take Miss Bow's place." It was Mamoulian, however, who campaigned for Sidney as Bow's replacement, and he was an ideal match for the young actress. "If it hadn't been for Mamoulian," Sidney recalled, "I would never have been a movie star. I refer to him as Mr. God."[1] In 1994, Sylvia underscored Mamoulian's influence, during an interview with Jeff Laffel.

> Anything you write about me in the movies must start with Rouben Mamoulian. He and I worked together at the Theatre Guild and he was hired to direct *City Streets*. Mamoulian worked with me, gave me tips ... he carried me through that picture. He was a great teacher and a great director, and I will

always be indebted to him for his genius and for his confidence in me. I was just a kid, but he had faith.[2]

City Streets, an underworld romantic-melodrama, was based on a story by Dashiell Hammett titled *The Kiss-Off*. In the hands of director Mamoulian, the film was brutally atmospheric with multiple murders, yet it avoided explicit violence. The expressionistic camerawork of Lee Garmes was an added plus. Gary Cooper starred as The Kid, a carefree youth and circus sideshow sharpshooter. Sidney's poignant appeal and unaffected ease registered on screen as Nan, the stepdaughter of bootleg racketeer, Pop Cooley (Guy Kibbee). Nan's tough Bronx attitude provides grit for the Cooper-Sidney romance. The Kid tires of Nan's nagging him to join the beer racket and make some *real* dough. He finally tells her, "Why don't you get yourself a racketeer." In a matter of hours Nan is implicated in a murder her stepfather committed. Pop reassures her, "The mob won't let you down." She soon realizes he is only saving his own skin. While Nan serves time, Pop convinces The Kid to join the racket.

Upon her release from jail, the embittered Nan distances herself from the mob. She tells her stepdad, "Can the 'Pop' stuff. Sell it to somebody who wants it." When the racket leader (Paul Lukas) forces his attentions on Nan, he decides to snuff out The Kid. In a surprise twist, both Cooper and Sidney end up being taken "for a buggy ride." The edge-of-the-seat climax wherein The Kid uses his fancy car as a weapon, provides him and Nan a breathless escape from the world of crime. The finish is an inventive piece of work with an unexpected dash of humor. Author James Robert Parish observed, "Mamoulian's technical originality did much to showcase Sylvia's performance." When Cooper visits Sidney in jail, they are separated by mesh grillwork. "Boy, you're good to see," she smiles, "I wish ... I wish I could just

City Streets - "I wish ... I wish I could just touch you" (Paramount)

touch you." The camera closes in to show her fingers pushing through the mesh that divides them. There is a brief kiss as they brush lips together. Back in her cell, Sidney is in a reflective mood. Cooper's voice and her thoughts echo in tandem on the soundtrack. This voiceover, as Parish points out, was "a startling new cinematic technique."[3] Mamoulian's ability to underscore the palpable on-screen simpatico between Cooper and Sidney was a highlight of *City Streets*. *Variety* echoed the critical reaction to Sidney's performance. "Picture is lifted from mediocrity through the intelligent acting and appeal of Sylvia Sidney. From a histrionic standpoint she's the whole works. She won't be unknown long." New York's *Standard Union* raved, "A throbbing picture, surcharged with action. *City Streets* unlike *Little Caesar* has no particular moral to deliver. It wisely contents itself in showing a vivid and graphic canvas of fiend-like thugs." *Screenland* cheered, "Sylvia is a smash hit in her screen debut, by far the finest actress of the new ingénue crop." *Film Daily* agreed, "Miss Sidney carries the burden of the piece and handles her lines and situations with ease and conviction."

Prior to filming *City Streets*, *Variety* reported that Sylvia's co-star from the stage success *Crime*, Kay Francis, was assigned to bolster the marquee. Her role as the gangster's moll went to Wynne Gibson. Gibson's frantic display lacked the silky edge of Francis, who had lost favor with Paramount after negotiating a new contract with Warner Bros.[4] As far as playing opposite the 6' 3" Gary Cooper, Sylvia mused, "It's a pain in the neck if you ask me. Even if you don't, it is. I should be used to the face-lifting, because I played opposite Charles Bickford on the stage and he's no midget."[5] Sidney, who stood at 5' 4", relayed that Cooper warned her, as a newcomer to Hollywood, about employing servants who "told phony pity stories meant to get you to cough up a lot of money."[6] Cooper had problems, alright. He was underweight, exhausted from overwork, anemia, jaundice, and depression. *City Streets* was a tough shoot. In 1998, Sylvia recalled dancing around the cameras, in the wee hours of the morning, trying to stay awake. While doing this, she would sing, "Fight on for Paramount!" It managed to do the trick, until Schulberg caught her in the act. "Whoa!" Sylvia remembered. "It was *not* nice." Mamoulian confirmed that the average working day on *City Streets* was 16 hours. "I remember doing a scene at midnight with Cooper and Sidney," he recalled, "and they fell asleep during the take."[7] Soon after the film's release, Cooper sailed to the Mediterranean for a six-week cure.

City Streets hit theaters after the release of *Little Caesar* (Edward G. Robinson) and just prior to Cagney's *The Public Enemy*—both enormous gangster hits for Warner Bros. *City Streets* is considered the most sophisticated of the trio, and most overlooked. In 1936, the film was banned from re-release by Joseph Breen of the Production

Code Administration (PCA). Aside from its casual amorality, Breen felt the film indicated that the law couldn't cope with illegal activities. Mobster Al Capone took it as a compliment. Years later, Mamoulian visited a Chicago nightclub and was given a surprise embrace by Capone's brother. He told Mamoulian how much Big Al had loved *City Streets*—it had "class." Capone (who died in 1947) had seen it eight times. "I was puzzled by his enthusiasm for a time," Mamoulian reflected in 1975. "Then I realized it was because I hadn't shown the dirty work."⁸ The lack of on-screen killings, or a tragic finish, place *City Streets* outside the typical gangster genre. In 2008, *City Streets*, after decades of obscurity, was among the films nominated for The American Film Institute's "Top 10 Gangster Films."

Dashiell Hammett had mixed feelings about *City Streets*, but he was enamored with Sidney. In an April 1931 letter to his lover Lillian Hellman, Hammett wrote, "Last night I went to see *City Streets* and found it pretty lousy, though Sylvia Sidney makes the whole thing seem fairly good in spots. She's good, that ugly little baby, and currently my favorite screen actress."⁹ Hammett's "ugly little baby" avoided seeing the rushes during production. "It actually gives me indigestion to see myself on the screen," Sylvia explained to columnist Robbin Coons. "I just see how terrible I am and want to go away and hide. It's the same way seeing myself in a completed picture, but I'd rather take it all in one dose than suffer the agony day by day—like having my leg cut off by inches." Her attitude wasn't helped any by cameraman Lee Garmes. "Garmes couldn't stand the sight of me," Sidney admitted. "He thought I was the ugliest thing that ever happened. He told me, 'You're un-photographable!' That tends to make an actress insecure."¹⁰

Numerous comments were made about Sylvia's looks. "I'm not pretty," she agreed in one of her first interviews. "Now don't be politely hypocritical. I have a mirror."[11] A Cleveland critic described, "Miss Sidney ... isn't pretty in the conventional sense. There is no dazzle about her. Her charm is great, but it is not the obvious charm of a Hollywood eyeful. She is an actress ... rather than a beauty exhibit."[12] Sidney thought her face was her bane and her fortune. "My face is against me," she sighed. "I have that funny crushed-by-life look and I'm doomed to weep and wait."[13] In one of her last interviews (1999) Sidney recalled Paramount producer Jesse Lasky asking, "What are we going to do with the ugly kid? The ugly kid who can act."[14] While weeping and waiting, Sylvia was assigned one of Paramount's "star suites" adjacent to Ruth Chatterton.

In December 1930, Paramount had announced that Sidney would co-star with Phillips Holmes in *Confessions of a Co-Ed* . The film was touted as a build-up prior to their teaming for *An American Tragedy*. Fortunately, production was delayed in order to make *City Streets*, which showcased Sidney to better advantage. In early March, *Confessions of a Co-Ed* was postponed again to film *An American Tragedy*, originally set to be directed by Sergei Eisenstein. Eisenstein's replacement, Josef von Sternberg, arrived fresh from filming his protégée Marlene Dietrich in *Dishonored*. Sidney's relationship with von Sternberg was not a happy one. "He was an idiot," she snorted years later. "He didn't give a damn about actors at all. He had scripts typed with no punctuation marks. *He* wanted to be all the punctuation. Watch the film today [1994], and listen to how everyone in it is 'sing song.'"[15] Along with von Sternberg's volatile temper, she found him to be dictatorial and arrogant.

An American Tragedy was adapted from Theodore Dreiser's 1925 novel based on an actual 1906 murder case. Dreiser tackled subjects

An American Tragedy with
Phillips Holmes (Paramount)

such as birth control, capital punishment, and the American obsession with wealth and physical beauty. Filming began in March 1931. Sylvia played Roberta Alden, a factory worker whose pregnancy stands in the way of her boyfriend Clyde Griffiths' (Phillips Holmes) pursuit of a wealthy socialite (Frances Dee). After failed attempts to terminate her pregnancy, the lovelorn Roberta drowns in a lake while Clyde flees the scene. He is faced with the inevitable capture, trial and execution. In his novel, Dreiser claimed society was the villain, not Griffiths. On screen, the viewer has no sympathy for either.

Location shooting for the drowning scene was at Lake Arrowhead. Von Sternberg was not pleased when Sidney told him she couldn't swim. "I had been cautioned by the assistant director to say I couldn't swim," recalled Sidney, "because von Sternberg was going to dump me in the middle of that lake, and the water was freezing! My head was dumped in a barrel of water instead."[16] Sidney was deeply disturbed by von Sternberg's treatment of her co-star. "Phillips Holmes ... a lovely young man," recalled Sylvia. "We all knew he was having trouble with his homosexuality and we were warm to him. Von Sternberg terrified him. He didn't have to be so rough on Holmes, who eventually ended up killing himself. Well, I can't blame *that* on von Sternberg, but he was a dreadful person. Oh God, I hated him."[17]

Holmes, three years older than Sylvia, was discovered at Princeton University during his sophomore year (1927-28). He played the female lead in the school's all-male Triangle Club production of *Napoleon Passes*. Paramount director Frank Tuttle spotted Holmes on campus and cast him the film *Varsity* (1928). By 1931, Holmes' career was building momentum despite his reputation for avoiding publicity. A 1932 news item from *The Brooklyn Times* noted, "He has never been engaged or rumored romantically." Sylvia mentioned Holmes' struggle with depression and alcohol. He made headlines in 1933 when he crashed into a parked car. His passenger was co-star Mae Clarke, who broke her jaw. Months later, she sued Holmes, claiming that he was intoxicated at the time.[18] Years later, Clarke euphemized, "He was too beautiful to be in love with."[19]

As his screen career faded, Holmes moved in with torch singer Libby Holman, who had a weakness for fragile younger men (among them, Montgomery Clift). Holman was known for her intimate affairs with both men and women. Sylvia was mistaken in her remark about Phillips' suicide, but understandably so. In 1941, Holmes joined the Royal Canadian Air Force. On August 12, 1942, his aircraft collided with another plane. There were no survivors. It was his younger brother, actor Ralph Holmes, who committed suicide in 1945, following a break-up with his wife ... Libby Holman.

Phillips Holmes received mixed reviews for his moody, introspective performance in *An American Tragedy*. *Variety* felt he was "physically perfect," but "colorless." *The New York Times* said Holmes "walks dolefully through his part." Cleveland critic W. Ward Marsh found Holmes to be "touching." Of Sidney, Marsh said, "Here is a genuinely great screen actress." Star reporter for *Variety* Cecelia Ager (an early champion of Orson Welles) praised Sidney's acting as a big step forward for her career.

> It is she who gives the picture its most genuine moments. Her realness, her rare naturalness, overcoming direction that mistakes clumsy restraint for profundity, makes her share of the film alive ... there's no one else like her. She gives to Roberta Alden more intelligence, more force, than Dreiser's own conception of his character.

An American Tragedy was banned in Italy and England. Censor boards in New York also protested allusions to abortion and had them deleted. Theodore Dreiser was definitely not pleased with what he saw on screen. He sued Paramount, claiming that the indictment on society's role in creating social-climbers like Clyde Griffiths had been ignored. A Supreme Court Justice ruled in favor of Paramount, saying Dreiser was paid handsomely ($150,000) and had avoided story conferences prior to production. Following the Los Angeles premier, Louella Parsons railed, "Mr. Dreiser ought to send a sincere congratulations to Paramount and Josef von Sternbeg for building up an intense, gripping drama, beautifully directed and excellently produced." Parsons' assessment of the film was, perhaps, too generous. As Jerry Vermilye points out in his analysis of the film, "The lawyers who virtually take over the dramatic action during the film's final scenes, Irving Pichel and Charles B. Middleton, are encouraged to allow their sonorous voices and melodramatic tendencies go a bit overboard."[20] In her *5001 Nights at the Movies*, the reputable Pauline Kael deemed Sidney responsible for the film's best scenes. "Sylvia Sidney is so appealing," wrote Kael, "that the pathos of Roberta's situation is intensified." Dreiser also approved of Sidney's thoughtful performance. He was delighted, two years later, when Sylvia was cast in a film adaptation of his novel *Jennie Gerhardt*.

After completing two more films, Sylvia flew home to New York for a vacation and attended her first premier—the August 5 opening of *An American Tragedy* at the Criterion. It was memorable for all the wrong reasons. On stage, Sidney was greeted with thunderous applause and literally stopped the show. Once outside, the crowd clamored around her demanding autographs. In a panic, she was swept to the door of her limo. The car pulled away before Sylvia realized that her mother had been left behind. She reportedly beat on the chauffer-window, crying, "I want my mama—I want my mama." The laughing crowd made way so "mama" could tend to the sobs of her daughter.[21] Years later, Sidney reflected on her evening from hell.

> I was not prepared for what the fans did. They were all screaming and yelling behind the line. I was arriving at the theater in the limo with my mother and I looked out at the fans and thought, 'What the hell is this all about?' I was

confused and frightened. Then I had to sit myself down and watch this movie—which I had already seen at the studio.

I had bought a special yellow chiffon evening gown for that night. Well, the fans started grabbing and pulling at me, and they tore it! I got absolutely hysterical and started crying. It was a horrible experience. What did I know? I didn't realize that because of the success of *City Streets*... that I was considered a star.[22]

Understandably, Sidney avoided the Los Angeles premier. Columnist Mollie Merrick was impressed how the audience burst into long applause when "Sidney gave them a close-up which wrenched at their hearts." "This girl," wrote Merrick, "creates the same emotional sympathy for which the stars of silent days were famous."

In 1978, Sidney's only comment on *An American Tragedy* was, "I was the girl who got murdered. Frances Dee was the rich bitch. I didn't think it was very good."[23] By that time, Dreiser's story had been "immortalized" on screen by director George Stevens in *A Place in the Sun* (1951). Montgomery Clift essayed the role played by Holmes, Elizabeth Taylor played the "rich bitch" and Shelley Winters offered a less sympathetic version of Sidney's "girl who got murdered."

Confessions of a Co-Ed was filmed after, but released a month prior to *An American Tragedy*. In this campus soap opera Sylvia jumps from the freshman class to motherhood in one semester. She falls for a smooth talking college senior (Phillips Holmes) who is only after one thing. Much against her better judgment, Sylvia gives in. An ensuing

Confessions of a Co-Ed with Phillips Holmes and Norman Foster

escapade with another co-ed gets Holmes expelled. He sails away on a steamer to South America. His best friend (Norman Foster), clueless about baby-to-be, comes to Sylvia's rescue with a proposal of marriage. *Co-Ed* was touted as being based on jottings of an anonymous college girl—an obvious publicity fib. Mordaunt Hall for *The New York Times* barbed, "It's no wonder that the author should prefer to remain anonymous, for it is a most trivial and implausible story." Hall was even less enthused by co-directors Dudley Murphy and David Burton.

Confessions of a Co-Ed was a routine tale kept interesting by Lee Garmes camerawork, dialogue with occasional snap, and good chemistry between Sidney and Holmes. Holmes plays another opportunist who is "almost in love." He appears more comfortable in his role than he was in *An American Tragedy*, but Sidney received most of the praise. A Los Angeles critic said, "It is her work alone that lifts the picture from a class of mediocrity." A *Boston Herald* critic agreed, "Miss Sidney ... has brought to the screen a technique all her own, and one which we rise to ap-

Bing Crosby serenades Sidney and Holmes in *Confessions of a Co-ed* (Paramount)

plaud." The film's "high spot" for an Ohio critic was Bing Crosby and the Rhythm Boys crooning "Out of Nowhere" at a frat house party. *Motion Picture* magazine nodded, "The real hit of the picture is Bing Crosby, the baritone with sex appeal." After the film's release, Crosby made his first solo national radio broadcast. The rest, as they say, is history.

Sylvia would refer to *Confessions of a Co-Ed* as a "real bomb"—"one of the most horrible pictures ever made." During production, she failed to impress co-star Dickie Moore. "I was a little taken back," said Sylvia, "when I was introduced to Dickie Moore, the infant whose mama I was supposed to be. I said to him, 'Do you think you'd like me to be your mama in this picture?' He responded. 'Did you see me in *Seed*?' I had to say that I had not. 'Or, in *Aloha*?' Again I had to say that I hadn't. He turned to the director and shrugged, as if to say, 'What sort of mother is this woman going to make?'"[24] Five-year-old Moore was a veteran of fifteen films. Another co-star commented that Sylvia never upstaged. "Being a trouper, she doesn't resent or envy anyone else his success," enthused Norman Foster. "There is room for all good actors is her credo."[25]

Co-director Dudley Murphy was aware that Sidney and B.P. Schulberg were an item. He recalled, "Had I been a better politician, I would have played up to her." Instead, the studio cancelled Murphy's contract. Years later, Schulberg asked him if he knew the reason why— then informed him that Sidney said Murphy was "on the make for her" during the shoot of *Confession of a Co-Ed*. Murphy was not shy about responding to attractive women. By summer, he was in the arms of Miriam Hopkins, and a few months later, Ann Harding (both married). In between these flings, Murphy married the eighteen-year-old daughter of a Fox executive. As Murphy himself put it, "I had very little respect for the politics of the movie business."[26] If anything positive came out of the production it was Sylvia's close friendship with her sorority sister co-player Dorothy Libaire, wife of director Marion Gering. Gering, who had directed Sidney in Broadway's *Bad Girl* had also signed a Paramount contract. He would direct Sylvia in her final release for 1931, *Ladies of the Big House*.

Sylvia now resided in Clara Bow's plush dressing room—considered number one on the Paramount lot. Former occupants included Gloria Swanson and Pola Negri. "The only thing I want in it that it hasn't already is a couch," said Sylvia, "a place to lie and rest" (and do elaborate needlework between "takes"—something for which she had gained a reputation). Sylvia's car and chauffeur were allowed to drive on the lot, whereas Claudette Colbert, Carole Lombard and Miriam Hopkins were made to park outside the studio gate. Sylvia Sidney had indeed "arrived."

Louella Parsons complained that she and Sidney might become "great friends" if not for the persistent chaperoning by Paramount's publicity department. "I don't know if it was her idea," said Parsons, "or Paramount's to have someone listen in on our conversation." Sidney had every reason to avoid Parsons. After declaring, "There is no better actress than Miss Sidney in Hollywood," it wasn't long before the columnist spared no opportunity to take jibes at Sidney's expense. Sidney admitted being petrified of such women. Regarding her first interviews, she said, "I was asked some of the most extraordinary questions. I don't see why, just because one is in pictures she should be asked questions that are not only personal but insultingly so. I turned around and asked the interviewer the same questions. That didn't set so well."

When Hale Horton, for *Screenland* magazine, informed Sylvia he wanted to do a rags-to-riches story about her, she protested, "You can't write that sort of thing! I've never dressed in rags! And never to my knowledge have I missed a meal. My father always made a decent income from his dentistry work. We had a comfortable apartment down in Greenwich Village." After she calmed down, Sylvia was more reflective and told Horton, "I don't suppose I'll ever be perfectly happy. Perhaps my moodiness forbids—or maybe it's just because I'm never quite satisfied." Horton, who was visiting her at home in Beverly Hills, noted her "highly emotional nature," and that Sylvia seemed most content to "mooch around" the house (as she put it). Interviewers blamed Sidney's Russian background and Slavic melancholy. When Horton peeked into her large bedroom suite and balcony, Sylvia snipped, "It's fun being sick up here. I almost wish I were sick right now." She abhorred snoopy fan magazine writers, and being gossiped about. Rumors about her and Schulberg had begun to surface.

Among Sidney's biggest fans was MGM's Joan Crawford. Director

Mervyn Le Roy introduced the two at a special luncheon and preview of Samuel Goldwyn's *Street Scene*. A select group including Norma Shearer and producer-husband Irving Thalberg, had been invited into Goldwyn's private screening room. Sylvia was accompanied by her mother. Following the screening, Crawford and husband Doug Fairbanks Jr. approached Sylvia. "I think that you're just simply grand," Crawford told her. "You're really my favorite actress, and I've been wanting to meet you ever since the first time Douglas and I saw one of your pictures. Now, I go to see everything you do three or four times."[27] Observing all this was reporter Barry Spencer, who noted, "Sylvia just beamed. She was so pleased." The fact was, she was petrified. A few years later Sidney commented, "I met Miss Crawford once and was scared stiff. I knew all about Joan Crawford, about her stacks of fan mail. I couldn't think of a thing to say. I was so nervous I couldn't eat my lunch."[28]

For *Street Scene*, Sylvia was borrowed by the prestigious producer Sam Goldwyn. The brooding, Depression-themed story, was a Pulitzer Prize-winning play by Elmer Rice. Sylvia landed the lead role of a budding young girl whose life is hampered by her sordid, stagnant tenement surroundings. As Rose Maurrant, Sidney provided, as critic Richard Watts, Jr. put it, "one of the most satisfying characterizations of the year." The location was familiar territory. Most of Sylvia's life had been mere subway fare from the crusty West Side tenements that served as background for the story. Other critics offered an array of superlatives for Sidney, the film, and director King Vidor.

Street Scene was much more than a photographed stage play. Some noted the "visual freedom" director Vidor and veteran cameraman

Street Scene with William Collier Jr. (United Artists)

George Barnes (assisted by Greg Toland) created on screen. They had literally liberated the camera from its tripod, mounting it on wheel devices that created a restless momentum as the drama unfolded. Viewers felt like bystanders rather than an audience in a movie theater. Another plus for *Street Scene* was Alfred Newman's musical score. The film was interspersed with musical motifs—themes that Newman attributed to his idol George Gershwin. Lone clarinets and fragments of jazz tones greeted a montage of Manhattan skylines. Beulah Bondi, in her screen debut, along with seven other players from the original New York production populated the film.

Two days in the life of Rose Maurrant (Sidney) offered seduction, eviction, a new birth, and a double murder—entwined together between casual sunrises. A typical mix of tenement characters swelter in the heat, finding relief in ice-cream and gossip. Rose's embittered mother (Estelle Taylor) has turned to adultery—with the milk collector, no less, to work out her frustrations. Head gossipmonger (Beulah Bondi) thrives on this bit of scandal. "A woman her age!" she rails. "You get married for better or worse!" Worse, is Rose's equally frustrated, domineering father (David Landau), who ends up killing the illicit lovers not so much out of jealousy, but resistance to change. The cast does justice to these characters, but Sidney appears to be fresh and more *real*—whether she's rebuffing the advances of a married co-worker or encouraging the hopes of Sam, her law school boyfriend (William Collier Jr.). She empathizes with her mother, but still loves her dad—pleading with him to be "nice and gentle." Following tragedy, life in the big city continues to move nowhere in particular. A glimmer of hope in *Street Scene* suggests that Rose and Sam have been propelled toward a new life away from what they believe to be the real culprit: their surroundings. Curiously, Vidor had penciled in on his copy of the script that "It's not our surroundings that defeat us."[29]

The filming of *Street Scene* on the back lot of United Artists took longer than expected. Production was prolonged after Sylvia broke her vulnerable ankle. The injury occurred in an automobile accident. As Sylvia braced herself to meet the shock, the impact on her ankle broke the bone. Doctors insisted that for proper healing she shouldn't walk for a month. After two weeks she was back on the lot (in a wheelchair) for rehearsals. Tightly bandaged, she forced herself to complete the picture. As a "reward," she was invited to the New York red-carpet premier at the Rivoli.

Sylvia's second New York premier was less traumatic. After dining with Dr. Sidney, the two stepped into a limo outside the restaurant. A motorcycle escort with siren heralded her arrival at the theatre. "I've never been so impressive in all my life," she joked. She still wasn't prepared for the reception and hysterical ovation following the film. One eyewitness wrote that after several bows "[Sidney] was so nervous that she could not talk. She kissed her hands as the sign of her appreciation."[30] Her trepidation was understandable. Staring back at her from the audience were: Tallulah Bankhead, Gary Cooper, Al Jolson, Claudette Colbert, Irving Berlin, Judith Anderson, Groucho and Harpo Marx, and veteran director D.W. Griffith.

Motion Picture Daily praised, "Sylvia Sidney gives the tragedy-ridden girl an understanding that again evidences her pronounced competence as a dramatic actress of real force." A Dallas critic admired her "dramatic genius—the supreme art of artlessness." Columnist Mollie Merrick lauded Beulah Bondi. "She is like some priestess of shabby places—some clairvoyant of the sordid—some augur of implacable tragedy. The acting honors go to Beulah Bondi." Bondi so impressed Goldwyn that he offered her a seven year contract. "I knew that those things meant seven years of slavery," recalled Bondi, "so I didn't take it."[31] In *The Film Daily* nation-wide poll of leading critics, *Street Scene* placed second in the coveted "Ten Best Films of 1931."

In 1999, American artist Mel Odom interviewed Sylvia at her New York apartment. Odom commented that he had recently acquired a print of *Street Scene*. Plain-spoken and vinegary until the very end, Sidney groaned, "What would anybody want with a copy of *Street Scene*?" Odom explained that he found the film to be a revelation, and her performance "extraordinarily fresh." After profusely praising Sam Goldwyn, Sidney stated that there was no adlibbing, and confirmed, "Elmer Rice was on the set all the time." It was Rice who had recommended Sidney to Goldwyn. When studio executive Joseph Schenck heard that she had been cast, he sent a less than enthusiastic wire from New York warning Goldwyn, "SYLVIA SIDNEY FINE ACTRESS BUT QUITE HOMELY ... YOU SHOULD HAVE GOODLOOKING

PEOPLE."[32] When Odom praised how drop-dead gorgeous she was, Sidney chuckled, "Honey, they always called me the ugly kid."[33]

Sidney emphasized to Odom that Vidor's success was as a *movie* director and seemed hesitant to pay him a compliment. "All I knew was that I was doing *Street Scene* and I did as I was told," she said. "I don't remember any particular relationship with him."[34] Sidney referred to directors like Vidor and Hitchcock as "cinema men." She also shared with Odom that producer William Brady and playwright Rice had asked her to perform in the original play. She refused. Brady told her, "You'll regret it." Erin O'Brien-Moore got the role. By the time *Street Scene* opened on Broadway, Sidney was on the west coast filming *Through Different Eyes* for Fox. When she returned to New York, she went to see *Street Scene*—a huge hit, which would rack up 601 performances. Sidney admitted that there may have been a flash of "it could have been *me* on stage," but she didn't give it any further thought.

While in New York for the premiers of *An American Tragedy* and *Street Scene,* Sylvia spent time with her family and celebrating her twenty-first birthday. Her cousins were in awe. This displeased her. "I couldn't bear them acting as if I were a celebrity," she said afterward. "Talking to me with constraint. I wanted it to be as it had always been. I wanted our talk to be of family things ... of new babies ... of new apartments ... of the way Albert promised to make a great name for himself."[35] Cousin Albert's first research project had been published in the *American Journal of the Chemical Society.* He was in the 1931 graduating class of New York University Medical School.

When George Jean Nathan recommended Sylvia for the role of

Lavinia in Eugene O'Neill's *Mourning Becomes Electra*, O'Neill approved. Sylvia, still in New York, called Schulberg to tell him the good news. Schulberg told her that such a part would do nothing the enhance her screen career. She needed to follow up with another screen success. The role went to Alice Brady.

Sylvia retreated to her home in the Hollywood Hills, not too far from Ronald Colman and Ann Harding. She spent time in her den, flanked by books (her pet extravagance—mostly contemporary authors), a caricature of her by New York's Ralph Barton, and a life-mask of her heart-shaped face by fellow actor Richard Cromwell. Sylvia described herself as a "hermit." She told Radie Harris, the columnist with a wooden leg, "I came out this time with the determination to work, not as a sightseer or tourist. In fact, I've become quite a hermit. I live sort of high up on a hill with a glorious view and once I'm up there, I don't ever want to come down!"[36] "I don't blame you," wagged Harris. "You're sitting on top of the world."

"On top of the world," in Sylvia's case, meant being sent to prison again. A third teaming for Sidney and Holmes, *Break-Up*, to be directed by Dorothy Arzner, was abandoned. In its place, *Ladies of the Big House* co-starring Gene Raymond began filming in September. The story's author was Ernest Booth, a "lifer" in Folsom prison. For the screen, he created a gripping, inside look at life behind bars. Sidney played a flower shop girl who rebuffs a tough mobster with "connections" in high places. She and Raymond, newlyweds, suffer the consequences. Both end up in prison—Raymond on death row—Sidney, facing a life sentence. Forget justice. They've been framed for a crime neither committed. In the climactic scene, Sidney risks her life breaking jail, in order to reveal new evidence that is being suppressed.

Despite an impacted wisdom tooth, Sylvia completed filming in

Ladies of the Big House - **Acting with an impacted wisdom tooth. With Gene Raymond and Robert Emmett O'Connor (Paramount)**

mid-November. Upon release, *Ladies of the Big House* was applauded. *The New York Times* mentioned the "cold and rather terrible fascination" on display during the prison scenes. "Both Miss Sidney and Mr. Raymond," said the review, "give good, honest performances." Critic Harold W. Cohen deemed the film "an authentic document of prison life." He qualified, "This is due principally to the excellent acting of Sylvia Sidney, who has the uncanny knack of making the most trumped-up situation seem like the most natural thing in the world." Under the helm of director Marion Gering, the film wasn't bogged down with trial scenes that had consumed the last half of *An American Tragedy*. The cheerless atmosphere and genuinely convincing performances in *Ladies of the Big House* kept audiences on edge.

Publicity shot, *Ladies of the Big House* (Paramount)

As 1931 came to a close, Sidney had established herself as the embodiment of the Depression heroine. In 1978, she admitted to film historian Karen Kay, "Since I was a good crier, and one of the youngest of the good criers, that was the mold I was put into. It never occurred to me that it was in the nature of an image."[37] The triumvirate of *City Streets*, *An American Tragedy* and *Street Scene* secured Sidney's film career, showed her best assets as an actress and guaranteed her star status. It seems remarkable that she wasn't considered for an Academy Award. When nominations were announced, columnist Mollie Merrick slammed all of the female contenders in the Best Actress category except Irene Dunne in *Cimarron*. "All told the acting prize should go to Miss Dunne," Merrick wrote, "unless you want to give it to Sylvia Sidney for practically everything she has done on the screen."[38] In December, Merrick came close to linking the names of Sylvia and Ben Schulberg—both in Palm Springs attending the winter sports. Merrick lumped together: Sylvia, Phillips Holmes, their respective mothers, Schulberg and Adolph Zukor. In his 1972 tome *Paramount Pretties* James Robert Parish pointed out that B.P. Schulberg was (by the summer of 1931) considered a "definite part of Sylvia's life"— along with a Spanish-styled home and Malibu Beach house.

In May 1931, Sidney declared, "I'm rather a flat sort of personality so far as the public is concerned. I have no past. I suppose I'm the sort that just won't get a past. Some people never do." Sylvia was lying through her teeth. She openly admitted that she preferred the company of men and that women distrusted her. The idea of women lunching together? "Gosh! I don't get that at all," said Sylvia. "What fun can that be?"[39] As rumors circulated around Sylvia's relationship with Schulberg, his seventeen-year-old son Budd was, to put it mildly, *not* a fan of Miss Sidney. Years later, he admitted to thoroughly savoring every second of the drowning scene in *An American Tragedy*.

How good it felt to watch that drowning scene, and to see Sylvia being pitched into the lake, floundering and going under. What an ideal solution. If only I could take Sylvia rowing ... tip the boat over, watch the little homewrecker go down for the third time, and swim ashore insisting it was an accident. The perfect crime. The family saved.[40]

The embodiment of the Depression heroine,
smiling near Malibu Beach

(Endnotes)

1. Gregory J.M. Catsos, "Sylvia Sidney," *Filmfax*, November 1990
2. Jeff Laffel, "Sylvia Sidney," *Films in Review*, September/October 1994
3. James Robert Parish, *Paramount Pretties*, Castle Books, c. 1972, pg. 267
4. "Par Says Kay Francis Goes to Warners as Iz," *Variety*, February 4, 1931
5. Hubbard Keavy, "Screen Life in Hollywood," *Macon Telegraph*, February 8, 1931
6. Marian Christy, "Lifestyle: Sylvia Sidney Older, Wiser," *Oregonian*, November 28, 1978
7. David Luhrssen, *Mamoulian: Life on Stage and Screen*, University of Kentucky, c. 2013, pg. 53
8. "Rouben Mamoulian Revisited," *California Courier*, August 7, 1975
9. Dashiell Hammett, *Selected Letters of Dashiell Hammett, 1921-1960*, Counterpoint, c. 2001, pg. 74 (*City Streets* was initially titled *After School*, then *The Kiss-off*)
10. Gregory J.M. Catsos, "Sylvia Sidney," *Filmfax*, November 1990
11. Leo Rabbette, "Clara Bow's Rival is a Scream," *Omaha World Herald*, March 8, 1931
12. William F. McDermott, "Hollywood and Beauty - Film Comment," *Plain Dealer*, May 9, 1931
13. Elizabeth Borton, "Hollywood From the Inside," *Boston Herald*, July 13, 1931
14. Mel Odum interview with Sylvia Sidney, YouTube
15. Jeff Laffel, "Sylvia Sidney," *Films in Review*, September/October 1994
16. Gregory J.M. Catsos, "Sylvia Sidney," *Filmfax*, November 1990
17. Jeff Laffel, "Sylvia Sidney," *Films in Review*, September/October 1994
18. "Charges Holmes Intoxicated," *Tonawanda Evening News*, October 6, 1933 (Details an amended complaint filed two months after Clarke's original suit against Holmes)
19. Mae Clarke, *Featured Player: An Oral Autobiography of Mae Clark*, Scarecrow, c. 1996, pg. 52 (In March 1934, Clarke dropped her suit against Holmes in which she charged "grossly negligent" driving)
20. Jerry Vermilye, *More Films of the 1930's*, Citadel, c. 1989, pg. 50
21. Mollie Merrick, "Movieland," *Richmond Times Dispatch*, September 22, 1931
22. Gregory J.M. Catsos, "Sylvia Sidney," *Filmfax*, November 1990
23. Joseph G. Boyd, "Sylvia Sidney is Still a Presence to Reckon With," *Milwaukee Sentinel*, October 11, 1978
24. Elizabeth Borton, "Hollywood From the Inside," *Boston Herald*, July 13, 1931
25. Radie Harris, "Sylvia Sidney - The Little Girl with the Big Emotions," *Silver Screen*, September 1931

26 Susan Delson, *Dudley Murphy: Hollywood Wild Card*, University of Minnesota Press, c. 2006, pg. 107
27 Barry Spencer, "Joan Crawford Pays Tribute to Sylvia Sidney," *Seattle Daily Times*, August 23, 1931
28 Frances Fink, "Catlike Smile," *Picture Play*, March 1935
29 Raymond Durgnat, Scott Simmon, *King Vidor, American*, University of California Pr., c. 1988, pg. 119
30 Mordaunt Hall, review of *Street Scene*, *New York Times*, August 27, 1931
31 A. Scott Berg, *Goldwyn: A Biography*, Simon & Schuster, c. 1989
32 A. Scott Berg, *Goldwyn: A Biography*, Simon & Schuster, c. 1989
33 *Actress Sylvia Sidney Talks With Designer Mel Odom 1999*, https://www.youtube.com/watch?v=aVL-ozea5qo
34 *Actress Sylvia Sidney Talks With Designer Mel Odom 1999*, https://www.youtube.com/watch?v=aVL-ozea5qo
35 Adele Whitely Fletcher, "The True Story of Sylvia Sidney," *Modern Screen*, February 1932
36 Radie Harris, "Sylvia Sidney – the Little Girl with the Big Emotions," *Silver Screen*, September 1931
37 Karyn Kay (interviewer) *Close-Ups-The Movie Star Book*, Galahad Books, c. 1978, pg. 446
38 Mollie Merrick, ""Notes on the Passing Show," *Dallas Morning News*, October 6, 1931
39 Charles Grayson, "That Big Little Girl Who Came From Broadway," *Motion Picture*, September 1931
40 Budd Schulberg, *Moving Pictures: Memories of a Hollywood Prince*, Stein & Day, c. 1981

An alluring Sylvia in *Merrily We Go to Hell* (Paramount)

Chapter 4
Merrily We Go To Hell ...

*"I know what the papers
have said ... I'm not blind"*

Sylvia Sidney (1933)

After signing a new Paramount contract (December 1931), Sidney was scheduled to reteam with Gary Cooper in a remake of *The Miracle Man* (1919)—a career hit for silent star Betty Compson. Producer Adolph Zukor convinced Sylvia that she was destined to do the talkie version. Before cameras rolled in mid-December, Chester Morris replaced Cooper, who was still on an extended leave. The production came to an abrupt halt on December 30, when Tyrone Power Sr., in the title role, collapsed on the set. He succumbed to a heart attack. His son, Tyrone Jr., who was promised a bit part in the film, was at his bedside. "No one suspected he was ill," Power Jr. later recalled, "he died in my arms. The small part I was to play in *The Miracle Man* did not materialize."[1] Hobart Bosworth, a close friend of Power Sr., took over the role of the patriarch-healer. Sylvia received top-billing, but the action was strictly ensemble. It did not showcase her talent.

Miracle Man with Chester Morris and Boris Karloff (Paramount)

Sidney played a con-artist who turns copious tears into bundles of cash. She and her boyfriend (Chester Morris) team with a pickpocket (Ned Sparks) and a fake cripple (John Wray) to fleece wealthy folks out of what tough guy Morris calls "sucker's dough." Sidney plays tough, and it's no surprise when she gives tavern owner Boris Karloff a slap across the face for getting fresh. Thanks to Morris, Karloff ends up unconscious at the bottom of a stairwell. To avoid a run-in with police, the con-artists escape to a small town which has no booze or doctors. The local "Patriarch" (Bosworth) heals all ills free of charge and citizens get high on God instead of illegal hooch. The hotel clerk reassures them that nonbelievers "are headed straight for eternal damnation." Morris sees dollar signs and comes up with a master plan to profit from "miracles." He campaigns for funds to build the Patriarch a church.

Bosworth's saintly old man is fully aware of the vice that motivates these intruders. He allows a greater power to work things out. Sidney, sans makeup, pretends to be his long-lost niece. Morris smirks approvingly, "You look as if you've never seen a gin bottle." However, Sidney has a change of heart. She provides the film's best moment as a witness to the Patriarch's miracle cures. Amazed and frightened, her eyes register the impact of what she has seen. "Something's *got* me!" she tells Morris, who is more determined than ever not to be fooled by "bunk." "Money will buy the miracles I want!" he persists.

The predictable finish isn't helped any by the lethargic tempo that leads up to it. Sylvia was becoming increasingly discouraged with the quality of her film assignments. Columnist Mollie Merrick complained, "the pathos of *The Miracle Man* is laid on with a heavy hand."[2] In Los Angeles, Jimmy Starr found the film "far from satisfying." "Sylvia Sidney," said Starr, "seems to be wasted. Chester Morris battles hard … but in vain. Hobart Bosworth tries desperately, but … hasn't the proper timing." Virginia Bruce and Robert Coogan effectively register as cripples who are cured, but *The Miracle Man* died at the box office. According to Sylvia, Zukor was the only one who wanted to see it. Years later she declared, "It was a lulu." Sidney may have "cried superbly" according to one Milwaukee critic, but she would fare better in her next release, *Merrily We Go to Hell*.[3]

Sidney and Fredric March teamed for director Dorothy Arzner's final film at Paramount. The studio teetered on the edge of bankruptcy, and Arzner would rather freelance than take a mandatory pay cut. In *Merrily We Go to Hell*, March, fresh from his success in *Dr. Jekyll and Mr. Hyde*, is hooked on a more conventional (albeit illegal) formula—cognac. He's stewed when he meets heiress Sidney at a swank penthouse party. They marry. March becomes a successful playwright, and, bottle in hand, has an open affair with his selfish leading lady. March is still tipsy when Sidney ups and leaves him. "Well … merrily we go to hell!" he toasts repeatedly in a scenario that floats on booze, grim realities, and a garnish of light humor. The team of Sidney and Fredric March make a heady concoction—they have chemistry.

Sidney's girlish enthusiasm upon meeting March is infectious. She's aware he has a problem—a nice guy whose thirst masks a great deal of pain. She wants to see him conquer his demons. Despite some choppy transitional scenes, the look in Sidney's eyes bolsters the film's continuity. While March carries on his affair, Sidney cautions him, "Being a modern wife gives me privileges." She hits the speakeasies with Cary Grant (the leading man in March's play), but not for long. Sidney leaves March, then finds herself critically ill in a maternity ward. Before they reunite, she loses her baby. March, by this juncture, realizes that he's been drinking to a phantom love. He finally has the capacity to say the three little words she has longed to hear. The talent of the stars turns a predictable conclusion into a touching, effective finish.

Merrily We Go to Hell was among the most financially successful films of 1932. Not surprisingly, the Hays office objected to the title. The film received mixed reviews, but no one complained about the acting. "The acting is way above the story," wrote Larry Reid for *Movie Classic*. Columnist Jimmy Starr deemed the film "a smart little bit of celluloid that eases into heavy drama [and] grasps the heartstrings." Starr found the Sidney-March combo "natural and completely minus the usual actor-ish affectations." In 2009, film editor/critic Glenn Erickson reassessed, "Dorothy Arzner's fine direction brings out the humor in the witty, fresh script. March is easy to forgive, and Sylvia Sidney is as heartbreaking as ever."[4]

Cary Grant and Fredric March join Sylvia
in *Merrily We Go to Hell* (Paramount)

Sidney bobbed her long hair for *Merrily We Go to Hell*. She was pleased with the results, and liked the film. In 1978, Columbia University professor Karen Kay interviewed Sidney, complimenting her "striking performance," saying that by the end of the film, her character ... "has balls!" Sylvia interrupted. "Excuse me. It was kind of an avant-garde picture ... a very protected gal who always lived in great luxury and didn't know what it was to be hurt. Finally, she ends up a *woman* —for the thirties, anyway."[5]

Sidney inadvertently aided population control in Asia following the release of *Merrily We Go to Hell*. A still shot from the film, featuring Sylvia in a black lace dress ended up on the cover of a popular Japanese condom package. New York journalist Liz Smith recalled in 2013, "We used to scream with laughter when Sylvia told us how she had starred unwittingly on prophylactic boxes all over Asia."[6] Sylvia admitted to being furious upon first hearing about the condoms, she wanted producer Walter Wanger to sue. Later on, she found it amusing and wished she had collected royalties. In 1992, Sylvia offered more details to writer Eve Golden,

> It was '35 or '36, I'd just come back from doing a Hitchcock picture in London, *Sabotage*, and I walked into Walter Wanger's office. There on his desk was this big package, and when I opened it, out fell condoms from the Orient. Mr. Wanger told me, 'You can go into any drugstore in the Far East and ask for a "Sylvia Sidney" and you get a condom with your picture on it!' It was a heavily retouched photo from *Merrily We Go to Hell*. I screamed at him, 'We've got to put a stop to this, we've got to sue,' but he said to me, 'Don't be ridiculous—there isn't a man in the Far East who doesn't think of you when he goes to bed with a woman!'[7]

Sylvia was pleased with co-star March. He made her laugh. But, the feeling wasn't always mutual. "I was shooting *Merrily We Go to Hell* and I had an early call," said Sidney. "Well, I had been a naughty girl the night before and fell asleep where I was not supposed to be sleeping and forgot all about it. I got there dreadfully late and I apologized, but Freddy March … was so furious that he didn't talk to me for days."[8] Sidney and March also showed up for a few seconds in Paramount's *Make Me A Star* (1932) based on the novel *Merton of the Movies*. Playing themselves, they are seen signing autographs while attending a premier.

After … *Hell*, Sylvia tested to play a Christian slave girl in Cecil B. DeMille's *Sign of the Cross*. She was his original choice. It was generally conceded that Sidney would get the role, which would have reunited her with Fredric March.⁹ DeMille finally decided on Elissa Landi. Doug Fairbanks Jr. pushed for Sylvia to co-star with him in Warners' *Scarlet Dawn*—filled with romance and revolution in modern Russia. Paramount could not be persuaded to loan her out. Fairbanks, who had co-written the role with Sidney in mind, offered it to Nancy Carroll. Sylvia also got a call from George Cukor asking if she wanted the lead opposite John Barrymore in *A Bill of Divorcement* for RKO. "No, George," she told him, "I'm simply too tired." After completing seven films, she wanted a break. She reflected years later, "So he used another girl who nobody had ever heard of ... and it made Hepburn a star." Sidney laughed, "Just too tired. Isn't that awful? But I *was* tired. No regrets. I would have liked to have done it in retrospect."¹⁰

Before DeMille, Fairbanks, or Cukor began filming, Sidney hadn't worked in two months. Her refusal to Cukor was likely due to the storyline of *A Bill of Divorcement* hitting too close to home. Cukor's offer coincided with Sylvia being contacted by her long, lost father Victor Kosow (May 1932). *A Bill of Divorcement* detailed a bittersweet reunion between father and daughter. Kosow's phone calls and threats left Sylvia feeling only animosity. She was faced with revealing the ruse of her "happy" infanthood with Dr. and Mrs. Sidney. Kosow was already in cahoots with the son of publisher William Fawcett, who displayed a Sphinx-like image of Sylvia's face in his syndicated post (April 1932) "Screen Oddities." The caption read, "Sylvia Sidney is Hollywood's mystery girl. She has never revealed her true name."¹¹ It would be over a year before the real "scandal" made headlines. So, instead of Barrymore, Fairbanks, or being fed to the lions, Sylvia opted for hara-kiri, *Madame Butterfly*, and the arms of Cary Grant.

To complicate matters, Schulberg was going through his own "hell" with Paramount. After years of success, forty-year-old B.P

Schulberg was in trouble. His compulsive gambling, drinking, womanizing—his affair with Sylvia Sidney, were blamed for Paramount's decision to "demote" him. The studio was feeling the weight of the Depression. Financial losses were up to $20 million. It was time to cut costs. In June 1932, Paramount's co-founder Jesse Lasky, along with Schulberg, were forced out. In 1985, B.P.'s brother-in-law, actor Sam Jaffe, put it bluntly. "Ben couldn't take that kind of success. He went crazy. He gambled, he screwed and he drank. He was screwing every girl that came along. He was fired. He ruined himself."[12]

Ironically, it was B.P. who brought Mae West to the screen while he was still production head. West would be credited with pulling Paramount out of its financial hole. In a 1934 news article, Schulberg revealed that he had telegraphed Mae offering her a part (and not much money) in the George Raft film *Night After Night* (1932). "I was sure she would turn it down," said B.P. "To my amazement she accepted. That's how Mae West got into the movies."[13] Sidney, out of sheer loyalty, stuck by Schulberg. His first film as an independent producer, *Madame Butterfly*, began shooting in October.

"With a face like mine, of slightly Oriental cast," Sylvia remarked, "I always dreamed of playing an Oriental character."[14] Nevertheless, playing Cho-Cho-San, a Japanese geisha girl, entailed hours of make-up artistry. *Variety* reported that facial blisters from heavy make-up kept Sidney out of close-ups for over a week. Co-star Cary Grant, who was replacing Gary Cooper in the film, called Sylvia a "grand little trouper" for what she endured. He never forgot it. "She had to have the corners of her eyes taped back as far as they would go," he said in a 1936 interview. "I hap-

Cary Grant woos Cho-Cho San in *Madame Butterfly* (Paramount)

pened to pass by her dressing room when the makeup men were removing that tape and I almost keeled over. Beneath the tape and the makeup, were huge, inflamed blisters. And she hadn't whimpered."[15] Instead, Sylvia sat in a dentist's chair contemplating her blisters. The headrest supported her heavy wig and its elaborate ornamentation. Grant indicated that Sidney still managed to pull pranks between takes, making the set ring with "her wonderful laughter."

The tragic romance of *Madame Butterfly*, based on David Belasco's 1900 play, follows the trials of Cho-Cho-San after she marries a dashing American naval lieutenant, B.F. Pinkerton (Grant). Pinkerton leaves Cho-Cho-San with empty promises when his fleet sails away. Her consolation: false hopes and ... a child. When Pinkerton reappears three years later, he is accompanied by his new wife. The film underscores familiar strains from Puccini's opera, as the devastated Cho-Cho-San sends her son away and proceeds to (honorably) take her own life. The plot was antiquated, but *The New York Times* felt it was buoyed by "the persuasive acting of Sylvia Sidney."

Lionel Collier, for England's *Picturegoer*, also singled out Sidney: "It was not a great picture but her performance undoubtedly was. I could never hope to see a more perfect characterization of the pathetic little figure of Puccini's opera." A Portland drama editor praised, "Of all the American film players who lately essayed oriental roles, including Richard Barthelmess, Edward G. Robinson, Ramon Novarro, Helen Hayes ... Miss Sidney is by far the most credible."[16] Sidney was up to the challenge of her assignment, genuinely tragic, especially during her visit to the U.S. Consulate where she inquires after Lt. Pinkerton, who had promised to return to her in the Spring. Three Springs had passed. "And he not come back yet," she pleads. She reaches into the heart of the Consulate (and the viewer), inquiring if robins in the United States nest as frequently as those in Japan. The film had some fine moments, but failed to soar toward the climactic conclusion. Decades later, New York critic Pauline Kael reassessed *Madame Butterfly*, slamming that it was "every bit as bad as you might expect."

Sidney's own opinion on *Madame Butterfly*? "It's as corny now as it was then," she snipped in a 1972 interview. She complained that, for years afterward, musicians at Hollywood nightspots would strike up the tune "Poor Butterfly" the moment she walked through the door. At a later revival in Rochester, however, Sidney paid tribute to Grant. "I got the surprise of my life," she admitted. "At the end of the film, I saw a close-up of Cary Grant and it was one of the most extraordinary pieces of acting I had seen. He was more talented than we thought he was."[17] Paramount's new sensation, Mae West, had enough savvy to offer Grant leads in her box-office hits *She Done Him Wrong* and *I'm No Angel*. Playing a Mae West sex object boosted Grant's popularity.

Sidney felt that Cho-Cho-San was obsessed with "one overwhelming idea." "When she met frustration," said Sylvia, "death was the only

Geisha girls (and off-camera friends) Dorothy Libaire and Sylvia in *Madame Butterfly*. Louise Carter (center) (Paramount)

door by which she could leave the emptied room of life." As for herself, Sylvia acknowledged, "I would always have something left. I might be deeply in love with a man tonight. I won't say that I am and I won't deny it. Only time will tell this story." She, rather candidly, referred to her relationship with Ben Schulberg. Sylvia shared these intimate feelings with Gladys Hall, a trusted, professional writer and founding member of the Hollywood Women's Press Club.

> I know what the papers have said. I'm not blind and neither is the rest of the reading public. But he is not free—and I am not speaking—yet. Tomorrow night I might be told that the man has gone out of my life forever. I would, undoubtedly, at once think of killing myself. For a moment. For an hour. I would probably jot down a few heart-rendering fare-

well notes. Then—then I would stop suddenly and say, 'But I can't do this! I forgot—I am working. There is that big scene to shoot. If I fail to appear, the rest of the cast will suffer. There are those among them who may lose their jobs.'[18]

Sidney concluded her sage observations about suicide by saying, "The love of a man would not, today, be sufficient motive. Not for a normally well-balanced girl or woman. So many doors are open ... that to close one door is no longer fatal."

"Opening the door" regarding her relationship with Schulberg, took the edge off of being seen together in public. Schulberg and his wife were legally separated. Schulberg judiciously had blamed his "bad disposition" for the split. Prior to this, columnists had kept mum. "Everybody knew it, but nobody dared to print it," said fan writer Elisabeth Goldbeck. Much had been written about Beatrice Sidney living with Sylvia at Malibu Beach. In truth, Mrs. Sidney would pop in only occasionally, then sail back to New York via the Panama Canal. Sylvia's only companion, aside from Schulberg, was her Doberman Pinscher, Zim. The time had come for Sylvia to put all nonsense to rest. She explained, "It's so perfectly silly. I've always lived alone, ever since I've been on the stage. I do in Hollywood. My mother went out there and stayed with me while I was getting settled, but as soon as my house was finished she came back to join my father. When I come to New York, they don't expect me to do anything else but live by myself. We've always let each other alone."[19]

Gossips suddenly felt free to predict romance and marriage. Dorothy Manners disclosed, "It is believed by their intimate friends that the dramatic ingénue from Paramount will be the next Mrs. Schulberg." However, Sylvia still enjoyed her independence. Reporter Helen Louise Walker, who often took actors to task, egged Sylvia about marriage. "I should hate to lose my freedom," Sylvia replied. "I hate roots or ties. I am even afraid of possessions. That is probably the real reason why I have never married." She also stated, "I can't stand people feeling responsible for me. That makes me feel so tied down, so *captured*. I must live my own life in my own way. I've *got* to!"[20] The real question for Sylvia was determining if Ben Schulberg was husband material. She got her answers in spades.

Publisher Bennett Cerf, who would marry Sylvia in 1935, assessed the Sidney-Schulberg romance thusly,

> Sylvia broke up the Schulberg household. She thought she was just vamping Mr. Schulberg, and it ended up being one of the great love affairs of Hollywood. He fell in love with her; she fell in love with him. He was old enough to be her father, but a fascinating man—a fascinating man.[21]

Benjamin Percival Schulberg

Percival Schulberg was born, January 19, 1892, in Bridgeport, Connecticut. His parents, Simon and Maria, came to the U.S. from Russia in 1887. Simon was a self-employed junk dealer, then shoemaker. The family moved to New York in 1895. As a boy, young Percival registered at school as Benjamin "Bennie" Schulberg to avoid being teased about his first name. By 1912, he was an editor for *Film Reports*, a small trade paper. He met pioneer director Edwin S. Porter, who hired him as a scenario editor and publicity manager. In due time, B.P., a man of intellect and skill, was publicist for Famous Players Film Co. under Adolph Zukor. Schulberg came up with the idea of dubbing Mary Pickford as "America's Sweetheart" (1914), and by 1917, was ap-

B.P. Schulberg

pointed general manager. In 1919, he founded his own company, Preferred Pictures. As his bank account grew, so did Schulberg's capacity for drinking, poker and philandering.

B.P.'s wife, Adeline "Ad" Jaffe Schulberg (whom he married in 1913), had grown up in New York's poverty-stricken Lower East Side—filled with Jewish immigrants. Ad's surroundings influenced her political views. She was an active socialist. In 1922, the Schulbergs, along with their eight-year-old son Seymour "Budd" (born 1914), and daughter Gladys "Sonja" (born 1918), relocated to Hollywood. Ad became active in child welfare and education, and helped organize birth control clinics along the West coast. She also produced a second son, Stuart, born in 1922. The Schulbergs befriended Louis B. Mayer and his wife Margaret. The families alternated Sunday brunches at their homes. The two men operated their respective independent companies at the Mayer-Schulberg studio until 1924, when Mayer merged with Metro-Goldwyn-Mayer. There was some bitterness between the two men during the transition, but Ad Schulberg remained close to the Mayer family.

The Plastic Age (1925), an immense box-office hit for Schulberg, skyrocketed his "discovery" Clara Bow, to fame. She became the "It" Girl, as well as one of his extra-marital flings. Preferred Pictures, however, was unable to compete with major studios and filed for bankruptcy. Adolph Zukor again hired Schulberg to head West Coast Productions for Paramount. B.P. became a powerful man in Hollywood. His salary grew to $10,000 a week. The family, despite Ad's socialist leanings, resided in a mansion in the swank Hancock Park section of Los Angeles.

B.P. displayed his ingenuity as a publicist when he coined the phrase, "If it's a Paramount Picture, it's the best show in town!" As he twirled the gold chain of his diamond-studded watch, Schulberg became the studio's top producer. He oversaw the first film to win an Academy Award for Best Picture, *Wings* (1927). Schulberg developed the careers of Gary Cooper, Fredric March and Cary Grant. He brought Marlene Dietrich and Emil Jannings from Germany.

1932 proved to be a year of weighty transitions for the Schulbergs. On February 2, B.P. announced to the press that he had separated from his wife. "My fault," he said. "A nervous temperament made me let off steam at home."[22] The couple had already signed a property agreement dated September 30, 1931, while Sylvia was filming *Ladies of the Big House*.[23] Their son Budd would recall the midnight battles in his parents' bedroom. In his 1981 autobiography, Budd admitted to his "callow but bone-deep hatred" of Sylvia Sidney.

> I would give Miss Sidney no quarter. In my eyes there was nothing she could do to redeem herself, nothing to modify my preconception that Sylvia Sidney was simply the latest (and in Father's case the most destructive) of the pretty little vampires who sucked his blood to fatten their studio careers. ... I knew that discretion on Mother's part would not protect us from the country club gossip. I could not have been more "mortified" by the public scandal that I knew was spreading ... .[24]

Budd found Sylvia "painfully appealing," but that didn't stop him from envisioning her face on his punching bag. "I went to my punching bag and hit it hard," he recalled, "seeing the provocative little face of Sylvia Sidney bobbing in front of me. Or I would belt her Mama for good luck. For I had heard—rightly or wrongly ... that her mother [was] encouraging the affair ... both on the make for big studio success." According to Budd, gambler/producer Felix Young was a frequent "beard" for the B.P. and Sidney rendezvous. While attending a December 1931 Christmas party at Young's home, Budd spied Sylvia among the revelers. "Flushed with champagne and studio success," sniffed Budd, "young Sylvia was looking particularly piquant and sexy that day. Again, a primitive desire for revenge and murder crept into my mind. I left the party."[25]

Budd's rash assessment of Sylvia's talent was delusory. Her achievements on screen were based on talent and ability, *not* Schulberg or Paramount. She had no reason to climb the Hollywood ladder to success on her back. Sylvia had proven that with her first release, *City Streets*—a picture that Mamoulian campaigned for her to do. Playwright Elmer Rice had championed Sidney for the role in *Street Scene*, a Samuel Goldwyn Production. And Budd's own mother, Adeline, was the one who told B.P. to sign Sidney to a contract before Louis B. Mayer or Jack Warner. The only role of consequence that Schulberg offered Sylvia was *An American Tragedy*. If anything, it was Sylvia who stuck by *Schulberg*.

Budd and his father still attended the Friday night fights together, but their camaraderie was now underscored with tension. According to Budd's autobiography, B.P. "was hardly a devoted father."[26] Since 1924, Ben Schulberg had been more devoted to wild parties and gambling than hearth and home. By mid-1931, it became an open secret that B.P. spent most evenings at Sylvia's Malibu beach house. When Budd could stand it no more, he determined to rescue his father from the clutches of his "luscious little plum-blossom," Sylvia Sidney. Budd hopped into his Duesenberg (a gift from his father) and drove to her house. Once out of the car, Budd followed the wooden walk to the front door and let himself in, unannounced. Sylvia and her mother were sitting on an oversized couch while B.P. paced back and forth, scotch high-ball in one hand, and puffing on his cigar. Budd stood there in a rage, trembling. B.P. was in midsentence when he saw his son.

> The eyes of my father bulged in disbelief. Sylvia and her mother stared, waiting to see what I would do. When I finally spoke, it was with a new voice—and words I had never used before, certainly not to my father. 'You son of a bitch! You're coming home with me right now!'

The eighteen-year-old grabbed his father by the arm, forcing him outside and into the Duesenberg. Such dramatics were pointless. Apparently, venting against Sylvia gave Budd satisfaction. He wanted to blame someone—why not Sylvia Sidney?

Budd's praises were reserved for his mother (who he admitted was "undemonstrative")—her patience, loyalty and "discretion." She could do no wrong. In a matter of months Ad Schulberg was indulging in a love tryst with the head of MGM. She was Louis B. Mayer's first serious extramarital affair. Obviously, Ad's twelve-year friendship with Mayer's wife Margaret and his children was no reason to rule out infidelity. And then there was Mayer himself, adamant about upholding strong family values in MGM films. As biographer Matthew Kennedy pointed out, "Never mind that Mayer's crusade was to ferret out all adultery and fornication among his staff; or that he was married … or that Ad's and Mayer's politics could not have been more discordant."[27]

Following her separation from B.P., Ad Schulberg was actually thriving. She used her new independence and connections in the Hollywood community to form her own talent agency representing writers, and such big names as Dietrich, Fredric March, Herbert Marshall and director Edmund Goulding. A lavish tea-party inaugurating the Schulberg-Feldman Agency was held on July 18, 1932. Budd would defend his mother's love affair, saying that for her to refuse the advances of such a "despot" as Louis B. Mayer might quash her newfound career. "What was she to do?" Budd pleaded. "She was a free woman now, or almost, still extremely attractive, and challenged through no fault of her own to establish her identity."[28] Mayer's biographer, Scott Eyman, assessed the situation differently.

> Mayer had liked and respected Ad ... a summer 1932 meeting with her in his office ...evolved into an admission that he and Margaret too had moved apart ... . They had stopped sleeping together. ... For both partners, it seems to have been a matter of sexual relief and mutual comfort, both of them revenging themselves on their spouses.[29]

From the plethora of issues that surrounded the Schulberg marriage since 1922, one could surmise that there wasn't much of a marriage to break up.

Before Budd left for Dartmouth in late summer 1932, he overheard the last big quarrel between his parents in their Malibu home. Budd's diary noted, "Dad was over tonight. Awful row. Poor Mom has her hands full." B.P.'s recent demotion at Paramount included a substantial cut in pay. Ad Schulberg, the "responsible" mother (and socialist) who held the family together, wanted to send daughter Sonja to an exclusive girls' school in Paris, and Stuart to a boarding school in Santa Barbara. Although she had a promising new business, Ad was outraged when her husband suggested a reasonable cut in financial support. "You know the trouble with you Ad," said B.P., "you love money. Well, there are other things in life." Ad interrupted, "You think that Sidney woman loves you! She and her mother would drop you in a minute if you weren't still so important." B.P. countered,

> That Sidney woman, as you insist on calling her, could go out tomorrow morning and double her salary at Warners or MGM. After all, you were the first one to sing her praises when you saw her on the stage. You were the one urging me to sign her. What makes you think she's not in greater demand now than she was when she was still a minor New York actress? If she were as selfish and greedy as you say she is, wouldn't she have jumped to one of the other studios long before this? Be fair, Ad. ... goddamn it, be fair![30]

B.P. argued that whenever he was feeling low, Sylvia gave him confidence and restored his faith in himself. He felt that Ad was always tearing him down. "God-damn-it Ad!—if you don't stop lecturing me I'm walking out of here." Indeed, he stormed out of the house. In a matter of days he and Sylvia headed south to Mexico for a brief respite in Agua Caliente.

Sidney, on a very personal level, was also put on the defensive. She told journalist Ben Maddox, "I know of no actress who has married primarily to advance herself. They are not designing. Norma Shearer is the one star who has married an influential man. But Norma married for love. Remember, she was a big star before her marriage and I'm sure she would have been just as big even though she had not married Irving Thalberg. Marriage has nothing to do with a girl's career. Gossips are the main cause for unsuccessful marriages in Hollywood.[31]

On the surface, B.P. remained optimistic about being an independent producer. His salary was lower, but he retained a percentage of the profits. At the end of August 1932, he was set to make eight films for Paramount release, the first being *Madame Butterfly*. However, the string of mediocre assignments that followed took its toll on Sylvia, emotionally and professionally. One could say she was being used. Maybe she was. Her contract ($2,000 weekly) was with Paramount, not Schulberg. As far as choosing her own film roles, Sidney frankly stated in 1978, "I had no say." But, Sylvia had fallen in love. She didn't want to let Schulberg down as he struggled to succeed. In 1989, Sidney revealed to director Richard Kramer that Schulberg was a lonely man. "They often faced each other over dinner at a long, long table," said Kramer, "similar to the scene in *Citizen Kane*—and Schulberg would just chat with her. She said he was lonely—a father figure."[32]

In an interview with Cecelia Ager, *Variety's* first female reporter, Sylvia remarked, "I'm not satisfied with my work in pictures so far. There's so much I have to learn. Maybe I have no career, no future in pictures. I'm always surprised that anyone stays through my pictures. I can't." Sylvia shared her concerns about succumbing to tendencies she had noticed in other film stars—their obsession with how they look on screen, their make-up and coiffures. Sylvia told Ager that she wanted to retain the innate individuality that had made her in the first place. She wanted both light and shade in her work, and to avoid being typecast. The real question was whether or not she could trust Paramount. Ager said that Sylvia

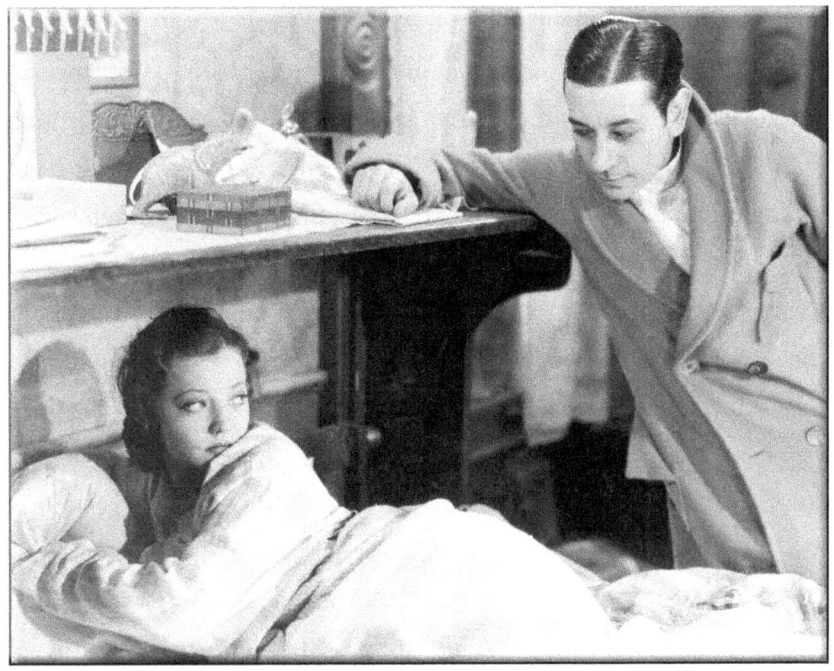

Pick Up with George Raft (Paramount)

had confidence that the studio would protect her. It was clear to Ager that Sidney suffered from "wishful thinking," and headlined her column "Pollyanna Tete-a-Tete with Li'l Syl Sidney Who Trusts Her Studio."[33]

Pick-Up, which began filming in January 1933, was to reunite Sidney with Gary Cooper. Just as he had with *Miracle Man* and *Madame Butterfly*, Cooper opted out. He headed to the prestigious MGM lot to co-star with Joan Crawford in *Today We Live*. Crawford was still a big fan of Sylvia's at this juncture, but not for long. Joan telephoned Sylvia inviting her to a cocktail party for Leopold Stokowski. Sylvia hung up on her. She thought it was a gag and returned to her knitting. She was distressed to read in the paper that Crawford indeed hosted a party for the famous conductor. "How was I to know," she moaned. "I have never heard Joan's voice over the phone before. I thought she'd be the last person in Hollywood to invite me to a party."[34] The truth of the matter was, Sylvia Sidney maintained a reputation of not mixing socially with Hollywood elite. Not to worry, Bing Crosby had stepped in line to declare Sylvia as his favorite screen actress, as had Salt Lake welterweight Red Millet, who was famous for knocking out referees.[35]

In *Pick-Up*, George Raft falls for Sidney, and, according to Paramount publicity: "She makes a man of him." Male characters in *Pick-Up* are prone to swagger, including Mussolini who pops up in a newsreel. Raft brags to Sidney, "I've got a mind of my own." "Sure you have," she smirks reassuringly, tightening her apron strings. The story, by Vina Delmar, who wrote the play *Bad Girl*, has a good mix of action and humor. Sidney, with trademark intensity and emotional punch, creates a definite person out of Mary, a sketchily written role. After serving a two-year prison sentence, Mary falls for a taxi driver named Harry (George Raft). The two move in together. He wants to marry her, but Mary already has a husband (William Harrigan)—and he's behind bars. By the time the marriage is annulled, Harry walks out on Mary for a society playgirl (Lillian Bond). At this juncture, the ex-husband breaks out of prison with murder on his mind.

"The censors seem to have been amazingly lenient," reported *Hollywood Citizen News*. "The hero and heroine live together without benefit of clergy, and nobody has said tut, tut!" Drama editor for the *Oregonian* thought *Pick-Up* "one of the best" of Sidney's career. *Boston Herald* noted, "Miss Sidney scores her points quietly, efficiently. She is always in character. Mr. Raft is in and out of his ... one cannot dodge the impression she is patiently and ever so subtly teaching him how to act." To be fair, Raft made no pretense of being a great actor. Sylvia had nothing but respect for the man, and considered Raft a real gentleman. "What he lacked in talent," she said, "he made up for in charm."[36]

Pick-Up was surefire hokum, but as the *Hollywood Reporter* indicated, "it was far above average" and did well at the box-office. One interesting tidbit concerns the opening line—just as Mary is released from prison: "Here are your clothes. The ones you wore when you came in." It was spoken by Jane Darwell, who wasn't in the film. Director Gering wasn't pleased with the woman cast as the matron (Eleanor Lawson), and asked Darwell to dub over her voice.

Unexpectedly, Sidney returned to the stage in early 1933. She signed for a two week engagement in the Franz Molnar fantasy, *Liliom*, playing Julie, a servant girl, instead of the daughter role she had been denied back in 1926. Sylvia told reporters that she wanted to "keep in practice." The Pasadena Community Playhouse production opened February 28. Opening night was sold out. The title role of a bull-headed carousel barker was played by Arthur Lubin, long before he became a director of hit comedies starring Abbott and Costello. Los Angeles critic W. E. Oliver thought the revival was a "well-staged, worthwhile effort," adding, "Miss Sidney's Julie is a unique creation ... and is responsible most for giving conviction to the play." Following the premier, Ben Schulberg hosted a party at his home

Expectations were high for Sylvia's fourth outing with director Marion Gering, *Jennie Gerhardt*. Based on Theodore Dreiser's 1911 novel, Jennie was a naive girl who is seduced by a U.S. Senator (Edward Arnold). The senator dies before she gives birth to his illegitimate

child (Cora Sue Collins). Eventually, Jennie sacrifices her true love, Lester Kane (Donald Cook), a wealthy manufacturer. Their illicit romance could lose Lester his career and substantial inheritance. Jennie learns this bad news from a socialite (Mary Astor), who is out to nab Lester for herself. Astor brought bite and intelligence to her role. She would quip, years later, that viewers should have had sympathy for the *men* who fell for Jennie. "Sylvia's chest measurement was formidable," said Astor, "she had bedroom eyes and a lovely moist mouth, but she suffered and suffered, because she was pure."[37]

Jennie Gerhardt does a good job showing disparity in the American class system. At the start, we witness Jennie's poverty-stricken family. She and her mother scrub floors and do laundry for rich folks. Jennie displays childish wonder at her employers' luxuries, while her siblings steal coal from the train yard in order to cook meals and keep warm. On the other hand, we hear Donald Cook (in a standout performance) jest, "Father seems upset because we only made about 6 million last year!" Entitlement amongst the wealthy is underscored when Cook's sister (Dorothy Libaire) snaps at Jennie, "Speak when you are spoken to!" Libaire is outraged when her brother's flirtation turns serious, "A cheap woman like that ... a *servant*!" The tearjerker scenario was similar to the hugely popular *Back Street* (1932) starring Irene Dunne.

Leon Shamroy offered his fluid, mobile camerawork to *Jennie Gerhardt*, and make-up artist Wally Westmore convincingly transformed Sylvia from a girl of twenty to a matron in her fifties. Mordaunt Hall for *The New York Times* praised, "Miss Sidney makes her actions very natural. There is true pathos in the grief she encounters." Hall acknowledged director Gering's "laudable sincerity," but felt the film lacked "the necessary suspense ... a story told in monotone." The sequence leading up to the death of Jennie's daughter, in particular, felt

Sylvia and Donald Cook in Theodore Dreiser's *Jennie Gerhardt* (Paramount)

strained and deliberate. It was Sidney's emotional driving power that moved the film forward. Toward the finish, her rueful helplessness feels appropriate—her face skillfully registering the repression described in Dreiser's novel.

Jennie Gerhardt was a definite step above the average programmer and notches above many of Sidney's previous films. Sylvia had wanted to play the part ever since she first read Dreiser's novel at the impressionable age of fifteen. She received a congratulatory telegram from Dreiser himself: "Yours is a beautiful interpretation of Jennie Gerhardt. My compliments and thanks."³⁸ Two years after the film's release, Sylvia reflected, "*An American Tragedy* was a grand part to play, but *Jennie Gerhardt*— there was the picture and the role! The whole company enjoyed making that film. We all worked as we had never worked before. We previewed it in San Diego—and the fleet was in. You can imagine what the houseful of gobs ashore, in a Mae West mood, did to our tragedy. When we came out of the theater we said let's put the picture on the shelf and forget we ever made it."³⁹

After the San Diego preview, scenarist Vincent Lawrence inserted a scene in the park, with Jennie and Lester, that gave a dash of humor and lifted what Sidney called "a low spot."

Sylvia had been hopeful while doing *Jennie Gerhardt*, but had qualms about director Marion Gering. In 1966, Sidney's publicist, John Springer, remarked that most of Sylvia's Paramount films were made quickly and inexpensively by "such scarcely-inspired directors as Marion Gering." Sidney added, "They thought Gering who had directed the *Bad Girl* play, could 'handle' me. I was supposed to need 'handling' then because I was inclined to be impatient with some of the trimmings surrounding stardom. I was discontented with the shoddiness of many of my movies."[40]

Amid much controversy, it would be another nine months before a Sidney feature film was released. She put Paramount in an uproar and made a lot of people angry. Several columnists snickered that Sylvia was so accustomed to being nicknamed "The Brat" that she had begun to like it.

(Endnotes)

1. Allan Donn, "In His Father's Footsteps," *Picture Play*, May 1937
2. Mollie Merrick, "Hollywood – In Person, *Cleveland Plain Dealer*, April 1, 1932
3. Dawn O'Dea, review of *The Miracle Man*, *Milwaukee Sentinel*, April 30, 1932
4. Glenn Erickson, review of *Merrily We Go to Hell*, DVD Savant, March 29, 2009
5. Karyn Kay (interviewer), *Close-Ups: The Movie Star Book*, Galahad Books, c. 1978, pg. 446
6. Liz Smith, "Broadway Lights Up," *Chicago Tribune*, June 28, 2013
7. Eve Golden, "Grand Dame," *Movieline*, December 1992
8. Jeff Laffel, "Sylvia Sidney," *Films in Review*, September/October 1994
9. Mollie Merrick, "Cecil de Mille is Coy," *Dallas Morning News*, July 1, 1932
10. Jeff Laffel, "Sylvia Sidney," *Films in Review*, September/October 1994
11. Capt. Roscoe Fawcett, "Hollywood Oddities," *Evening Star*, April 20, 1932
12. Sylvia Shorris and Marion Abbott Bundy, *Talking Pictures: With the People Who Made Them*, New Press, c. 1994, pgs 32-40
13. John C. Moffitt, "Mae West: Who, What and When," *Dallas Morning News*, June 15, 1934
14. James Robert Parish, *The Paramount Pretties*, Arlington House, c. 1972, pg. 269
15. Gordon Crowley, "Cary Grant Wins With Four Queens," *Motion Picture*, January 1936
16. Fred M. White, review of *Madame Butterfly*, March 4, 1933
17. Hillel Italie, "Sidney Wastes No Time on Nostalgia," *Daily Gazette*, December 7, 1990
18. Gladys Hall (using pen-name Faith Service), "I Could Live Without Love, Says

Sylvia Sidney," *Motion Picture*, March 1933
19 Elisabeth Goldbeck, "Sylvia Sidney's Tired of All Those Rumors," *Motion Picture*, October 1932
20 Charles Grayson, "That Big Little Girl Who Came from Broadway," *Motion Picture*, October 1931
21 Bennett Cerf, *Notable New Yorkers*, Columbia University Libraries - Oral History Research, October 19, 1967
22 (AP) report, *Evening Tribune* (San Diego), February 3, 1932
23 "Wife Sues B.P. Schulberg," *Variety*, March 25, 1938 (mentions 1931 property agreement)
24 Budd Schulberg, *Moving Pictures: Memories of a Hollywood Prince*, Stein and Day, c. 1981, pgs. 354-355
25 Budd Schulberg, *Moving Pictures: Memories of a Hollywood Prince*, Stein and Day, c. 1981, pg. 431
26 Budd Schulberg, *Moving Pictures: Memories of a Hollywood Prince*, Stein and Day, c. 1981, pg. 135
27 Matthew Kennedy, *Edmund Goulding's Dark Victory: Hollywood's Genius Bad Boy*, University of Wisconsin, c. 2004, pg. 140
28 Budd Schulberg, *Moving Pictures: Memories of a Hollywood Prince*, Stein and Day, c. 1981, pg. 485
29 Scott Eyman, *Lion of Hollywood: The Life and Legend of Louis B. Mayer*, Simon & Schuster, c. 2008, pg. 194
30 Budd Schulberg, *Moving Pictures: Memories of a Hollywood Prince*, Stein and Day, c. 1981, pgs. 489-490
31 Ben Maddox, "Why Girls Say 'Yes,'" *Silver Screen*, October 1932
32 Conversation with Richard Kramer, May 12, 2015
33 Cecilia Ager, "Pollyanna Tete-a-Tete With Li'l Syl Sidney, Who Trusts Her Studio," *Variety*, June 2, 1932
34 Margaret Angus, "Stormy Sidney," *Screenland*, May 1936
35 T.D. Kemp, Jr., "The Human Side," *Charlotte Observer*, September 25, 1933 (Millet's declaration for Sidney appeared in an interview with Virginia Moody, *Idaho Statesman*, April 22, 1932)
36 "Sylvia Sidney at New York's Town Hall," *Films in Review*, 1973, v. 24, pg. 324
37 Mary Astor, *A Life on Film*, Dell Pub., c. 1971, pg. 106
38 James Robert Parish, *The Paramount Pretties*, Arlington House, c. 1972, pg. 270
39 Leonard Hall, "Sylvia's Two-Way Personality," *Screenland*, November 1935
40 John Springer, "Sylvia Sidney," *Films in Review*, January 1966

Chapter 5
Accent on Transition

In early summer 1933, Sylvia and B.P. were seen at Rouben Mamoulian's dinner-dance at the Ambassador Hotel. Filmland society, surrounded by the Latin rhythms of Xavier Cugat, also included: Marlene Dietrich, Joseph von Sternberg, Myrna Loy, Gary Cooper, Jean Harlow, Cecil B. DeMille, and Claudette Colbert. Schulberg and Sylvia persisted in the habit of not being photographed together. Dorothy Manners observed, "In spite of the fact that there is no particular reason for it, Sylvia always walks ten or twelve feet in front of Mr. Schulberg when they are entering a theater or leaving a cafe. It's all very amusing to everyone—except the news cameramen."[1]

Her contract renewed (May 1933), Sidney was assigned to play a gypsy—a carnival prop for a knife-thrower who beats her. Maurice Chevalier comes to her rescue. The film was titled *The Way to Love*. Sylvia wasn't exactly enthused about portraying another sad-faced waif, or being called upon to sing, "It's Oh, It's Ah, It's Wonderful," with the relentlessly cheerful Chevalier. After a month behind the lens, production halted while Sylvia underwent an operation to have a stone removed from a salivary gland. Her throat kept swelling up, making it difficult for her to speak. Following a brief recoup, she

Sylvia bowed out of *The Way to Love* (Paramount)

walked out on *The Way to Love*, after $100,000 had been spent on the production. On July 31, Sylvia boarded a plane to New York accompanied by her mother and Schulberg. In turn, Paramount filed charges against Sidney, calling her behavior "professional anarchy."[2]

Prior to Sidney's walkout, Schulberg had announced his plans for a sojourn to Europe. Sylvia decided to tag along, claiming "complications" following surgery. "If it doesn't take," she said, "I'll have to have another operation for the complete removal of a gland, which will leave a scar on the outside of my face."[3] Emmanuel Cohen, vice-president in charge of production at Paramount, told reporters that no less than three Los Angeles physicians had given the go-ahead for Sidney to return to work on a film that was two-thirds finished. An executive committee for The Academy of Motion Picture Arts and Sciences sent a telegram to Sidney, asking her to reconsider. It read: "No leading player has ever been known in the history of the stage and screen ever to violate the ethics of the profession."4 This pompous epistle was signed by: Adolphe Menjou, Chester Morris, Warner Baxter and Hedda Hopper. Some predicted a "finis" to Sylvia Sidney's film career.

Paramount knew that Sidney was having physical problems before filming began. They had persuaded her to do *The Way to Love* by promising to concentrate on her role and get her through "as soon as possible." Instead, they focused on co-star Edward Everett Horton so he could fulfill his role in *Design for Living*.5 After a month of filming, Sylvia had only worked ten days. It also became obvious to her that the film was being thrown to Chevalier—her own role reduced in importance. Naturally, she was upset. When her neck pain became unbearable, Sylvia contacted her cousin Albert Sabin and followed his advice—surgery.

On August 10, came a report that the "equally rebellious" Ann Dvorak would replace Sidney in *The Way to Love*. Dvorak had walked out on Warner Bros. eight months prior. She felt that her studio was "selling her down the river," and took a European honeymoon. On August 19, Sylvia boarded the *Il de France* for Europe (Schulberg had left two weeks prior). Before sailing, she snapped at reporters," No, I'm not going to marry B.P. Schulberg, film magnate. I don't care if he is supposed to have been divorced."6 Schulberg, who was still married, had told reporters, "What Sylvia needs is rest and relaxation."7

After arriving in Paris, Sidney headed to Cannes where she received a great deal of attention from the French press. From there she headed to London. During her sabbatical, Sidney made a surprise return to acting by way of a BBC variety broadcast. She joined Ion Swinley to

August 19, 1933 - Aboard *Il de France*, headed for Paris, and the arms of Ben Schulberg

perform the balcony scene from Shakespeare's *Romeo and Juliet*. Swinley, known for his magnificent voice, had been leading man at the Old Vic Company. Sidney cabled Paramount on September 14, to okay the five-minute broadcast. Permission was granted.

Sylvia and Schulberg arrived back in New York on the *S.S. Paris*, September 26. Also on board were Marlene Dietrich (boarding as Marie Magdalene Sieber), her daughter Maria, and the playwright Robert Sherwood. Sidney's five weeks abroad hadn't completely solved her problem. She went under the surgical knife a few days later at the office of Dr. Leo Winter [oral surgeon]. Sidney later revealed the details of her physical dilemma and subsequent surgeries.

> I was doing a costume test one day when I felt a severe pain in my neck. I was in absolute agony, and I called my cousin Albert Sabin. He recommended a doctor at Cedars of Lebanon who insisted that I be operated on immediately. It wasn't a goiter, but there were stones in the gland. It got to a point where I couldn't speak. Paramount was furious. Finally, when I had the [second] operation, they realized that I wasn't faking it; that I really was terribly sick. But by

that time I guess the damage had been done. I was known as 'difficult.' Well, maybe that was true. I wasn't going to be pushed around.⁸

Sidney returned to her home on North Roxbury Drive in Beverly Hills before beginning her next Paramount assignment. She and Schulberg spent late October in Palm Springs going over a script for *Reunion*, a saga of WWI espionage, that would team her with Herbert Marshall. This project was put on hold, permanently. As Sylvia predicted, when *The Way to Love* premiered in October, the *Los Angeles Examiner* declared the film, "practically all Chevalier."

Sidney faced more headlines when Victor Kosow filed a lawsuit against his long lost daughter. In the aftermath, Sylvia no longer had to relay poppycock about Dr. Sidney being at her cradle side. *Modern Screen* had run "The True Story of Sylvia Sidney" (December 1931) which detailed,

> Across the crib the eyes of the young mother and father met. Then, gently, Beatrice Sidney stooped to kiss her baby's tiny hand. 'She will be free, Sigmund,' Beatrice said softly. 'Our little Sylvia ... .' The man came around to his wife's side. He understood. 'Free,' he said. 'That is a beautiful word.'

This little fantasy was concocted by Adele Whitely Fletcher. Fletcher had been editor for several fan magazines, and should have known better. Never mind that Sylvia was eight years old before Sigmund Sidney ever laid eyes on her.

Camera-ready after a controversial five month sabbatical

After Kosow's charges were dropped (December 2), Sylvia was set to join Fredric March and director Marion Gering on the Paramount lot. *Good Dame* began filming in December, and the end result was less than satisfying. In *The Films of Fredric March* (1971), author Lawrence J. Quirk called *Good Dame*, "possibly the worst film of his career ... a confused and meandering trifle." Wisecracks and tough-talk didn't slide easily off March's lips. (Doug Fairbanks Jr. was the studio's original choice for the role). Sidney fared better, but her sobs and smiles were wasted. Storyline: After being fired from a carnival, a card shark (March) and stranded chorus girl (Sidney)—both outsiders who don't fit in with respectable society, quarrel their way into matrimony.

Carnival scenes added flavor to *Good Dame*, as did some snappy dialogue. Not long after they meet, March suspects chorus girl Sidney is only

Good Dame with Fredric March (Paramount)

playing "innocent." "C'mon, baby, take 'em off," he scoffs. "Take *what* off?" she asks. "The wings," he replies. Sidney sees through March from the get-go: "Guys like you think just because a girl's in the chorus all you gotta do is buy her a dish of chow mein." Midway into the film, the wisecracks lose their punch. Bits of business fall flat. The mismatched lovebirds continue to bicker until they melt into a fade-out kiss. With four screenwriters on board, *Good Dame* lacked charm and imagination. What the film needed was Frank Capra. Gering's direction felt indifferent.

Hollywood critic Arthur Forde, found *Good Dame* entertaining, but pin-pointed the film's major problem: "Fredric March cannot play a hard character which he is called upon to do. Jack La Rue ... could have played March's part to perfection." La Rue, as the carnival owner, filled his usual role as the "heavy." Snippets from New York reviews: "A couple of good actors wasting their talents" (*World Telegram*), "Story and dialogue are pretty uninspired" (*American*), "Not one of March's better pictures" (*Sun*). *Variety* noted, "Sidney delivers a more even performance. She holds straight to the character." Harrison Carroll praised Sidney's "flair for comedy." "Given a chance to wipe her tears at last," said Carroll, "Sylvia Sidney proves an apt comedienne."

Sidney's only comment on the film made reference to her "walk-out" earlier that year, and the fact that March was leaving Paramount for good. "Freddy March and I did penance in a thing called *Good Dame*," she told Milwaukee journalist Joseph Boyd in 1978. "The reason it was called that was because I had an Airedale whose registered name was 'Good Dame.'" "Was the *picture* a dog?" Boyd inquired. "It was a monster," said Sylvia.[9] The only compensation for Sylvia was having her favorite cinematographer Leon Shamroy on board. He was behind the lens for six Sidney features (1933-1937).

Thirty Day Princess, Sylvia's third and final film with Cary Grant, was a frothy tale of subterfuge. The clever scenario was from the pen of legendary writer-director Preston Sturges (among others). Marion Gering directed Sylvia for the sixth and final time. In a dual role, Sylvia faced the camera as both the Princess of the mythical kingdom of Taronia and a struggling young actress who doubles for her highness when she is diagnosed with "galoosh" (Taronian for "mumps") prior to a goodwill tour of America.

Sidney charms her audience as the phony princess, while mangling the English language. "You may kiss ... our hand," she coyly coos to Grant—the fall guy she has agreed to seduce for a total of ten grand. This sum is promised by a wealthy investor (Edward Arnold) who has his capitalist eyes on Taronia's rich natural resources. Grant, a publisher, refers to Arnold as one of "the thieves of Wall Street" and wants to expose his Taronia bond scheme. Predictably, Grant discovers he likes the scent of royalty and is completely smitten. Before long, Sidney is inviting him to "kiss ... our lips." The love-match is jeopardized when the princess's fiancé shows up.

The film loses steam when reporters connive to expose the royal impersonator, but things pick up again when the King of Taronia (Henry Stephenson) arrives to investigate rumors. Just in time, the two Sidneys resume their true identities and everybody is happy. Afterward, the King learns the truth. His curiosity is piqued as he gazes at the remarkable resemblance between his daughter and her imposter. "Have you royal blood in your veins?" he asks. "I don't think so, your majesty," she replies. The king nods reflectively, "Well my dear, you never can tell!" Obviously, he had sown some wild oats. Such tomfoolery would never have got past the censors a month after the film's release. The Production Code Administration (PCA) (July 1934), fueled by the Catholic Church, ruled out such risqué innuendo.

A Dallas critic felt that the film succeeded "under the bewitching power of Miss Sidney who is gracefully comic and tellingly romantic"—then added, "Sidney introduces her seldom-used smile for excellent results."[10] In her 1982 tome, *5001 Nights at the Movies*, the highly opinionated Pauline Kael commented that Sidney in *Thirty Day Princess* "is such a skillful technician that you can't distinguish between her technique and her personal charm. She operates in that

Thirty Day Princess with Cary Grant (Paramount)

area where acting and witchcraft come together."[11]

Grant was said not to have enjoyed making the film. His personal life had been turned upside down. Filming began immediately after he returned from England with a new bride, actress Virginia Cherrill. She balked when Grant carried her over the threshold of a house he shared with Randolph Scott near Griffith Park. Scott seemed in no hurry to move out. After the completion of *Thirty Day Princess* the newlyweds relocated. According to Cherrill, domestic troubles (drinking and violence) surmounted. Cherrill was quite candid about their relationship in later years. By fall, the couple separated—Grant was found unconscious and ended up at the Hollywood Receiving Hospital having his stomach pumped after telling physicians he had taken poison.[12] Cherrill fled home to mother, and Grant went back to Scott—a more harmonious match. Grant's next Paramount feature was titled, ironically, *Kiss and Make-Up*.

Like Sidney and producer Schulberg, Grant and Scott faced the wagging tongues of gossipmongers. Columnist Jimmy Fidler reported that the two men were "carrying the buddy business a bit too far" and referred to them as "The Inseparables."[13] Schulberg and Adolph Zukor didn't approve of their handsome, athletic male stars sharing domesticity under the same roof. By the end of December 1934, Virginia Cherrill filed for divorce and was paid $25,000 to keep her mouth shut (along with $1,000 a month alimony).[14] As British biographer Geoffrey Wansell put it, eventually "Grant managed to conceal the contradictions in his personality with the same steely professionalism that he brought to his screen performances."[15]

Despite his marital woes, Grant offered *Thirty Day Princess* his trademark style. Critic Walter Ramsey noted, "Grant does just about his best work to date."[16] However, it is Sidney's natural emotional range that brings the nonsensical story "to life" whenever she lights up the screen. When asked about co-star Grant, Sylvia observed, "A man who keeps his own counsel … there's little getting to know him."[17]

Sidney headed for New York. She wrote to Los Angeles columnist Reine Davies that she loved the rush of the city. "I'm pleasantly lost in the crowds," she cheered. "After seeing shows, going places and buying clothes for a couple more weeks, I'll be eager to work." Sylvia also spent time with her five-year-old godson, her aunt's child on the Saperstein side. "I adore him, " said Sylvia. "We have the grandest times together. We go shopping and play long hours, but I never buy him toys that are meaningless. I buy him things to build with, that will show him the result of his own ingenuity. Things that stimulate his imagination and inventiveness."

Sidney was slated to film *Limehouse Blues*, reuniting her with George Raft. In July 1934, it was reported that she was having more glandular trouble. Jean Parker took the feminine lead. For her twenty-fourth birthday, Sylvia celebrated with an informal dining party. Guests included Dorothy Libaire and husband Marion Gering, Rouben Mamoulian, Elissa Landi, B.P. Schulberg and others.

Fans would wait another seven months for a Sylvia Sidney feature. By that time, Sylvia was no longer anchored to Schulberg, romantically, or professionally. Hints of a rift in their relationship began in February 1934, when Louella Parsons blabbed, "There was rejoicing in Hollywood today. The Schulbergs ... dined with the Sam Jaffes at the Colony Club. Two nights before that, Ben Schulberg, who is always seen in a ringside seat at the fights with petite Sylvia Sidney at his side, sat alone. Is the Sidney-Schulberg romance cooling?"[18] Three days later, the "rejoicing" ended. Parsons' spies reported that Schulberg had "whisked" Sidney off to the desert resort of La Quinta. Parsons apologized for misinforming her readers. She invited Sylvia and Cary Grant to guest on her CBS radio show on April 18. Sylvia advised women in the audience about the importance of "charm," before doing a sketch with Grant. By August, Parsons was back on her soapbox reporting that Sidney and Schulberg had come up against a "serious misunderstanding." The columnist was finally on to something.

In July, Budd Schulberg had returned home from Dartmouth, prior to a two-month visit to Russia. Adelaide threw a big party at her Malibu Beach home the eve of his departure. Who should show up (unannounced) but B.P. Schulberg—as columnist Alma Whitaker

Fall of 1934 - Romance with B.P. Schulberg was "definitely at an end"

put it, "to the astonishment of the movie colony." Whitaker indicated that the "ripple" from this event instigated "storms hovering over the so-called Sidney-Schulberg romance." Intermittent lulls in these summer storms found Sylvia and B.P. "shopping for a house" (according to Walter Winchell), or dancing at the Trocadero, inviting friends to their table for drinks and toasts.

On October 25, 1934, Schulberg told the Associated Press that his romance with Sidney was "definitely at an end." He also mentioned a possible reconciliation with his wife, Adelaide. In November, a United Press release reported that Ben and Ad (whose tête-à-têtes with Mayer had petered out) were on a "second honeymoon" in Colorado Springs. The "Daily Picture" section in numerous newspapers featured a photo of the happily reunited couple, describing them as "a picture of domestic happiness." Perhaps this newfound happiness came from commiserating about the tax liens filed against both of them by the federal government (Schulberg: owing $19,910 on his 1933 wages, and Adelaide owing $24,240).

Behold My Wife, originally titled *Red Woman*, was the last B.P. Schulberg production for Sidney. Filming began following the Schulberg reconciliation. In early 1934, Warners released *Massacre*, a progressive look into the ongoing plight of Native Americans and how government agencies and corporate interests exploit native peoples. The role of a crusading, college-educated Sioux went into the able hands of Richard Barthelmess. *Behold My Wife* introduced Sylvia as a college-educated Apache, who takes pity on a white man (Gene Raymond) after he is shot in a Phoenix saloon. The melodrama was based on an improbable tale from 1894, *The Translation of a Savage*, by Canadian author Gilbert Parker. It had been filmed twice as a silent film, detailing the life of a Hudson Bay "savage girl" named Lali who had a "bird-like laugh" and "ran like a deer." By the finish, Lali has become "civilized"—regenerated into a "woman of today." Parker hints that Lali's transformation was abetted by the dash of "good white blood—Scotch blood" running through her veins.[19] It comes as no surprise that Parker was a staunch imperialist—a reputation that landed him a job as propagandist for England during WWI. Parker convinced numerous influential Americans to favor the British cause.

On screen, Sylvia's character was rechristened Tonita Storm Cloud. She becomes the bride of a wealthy, booze-loving, New York scion (Gene Raymond), who proposes marriage only to spite and disgrace his status-seeking family. His parents had snubbed the young woman (Ann Sheridan), a mere stenographer, who he really loved. Under the direction of Mitchell Leisen, the first twenty minutes build momentum and suspense, but once Raymond heads west and into a saloon on an Apache reservation, the plot unravels into the implausible. It is at this juncture that Sylvia, fetchingly dressed in native costume, appears. She falls in love while saving Raymond's life, but she can't save the film.

Behold My Wife - with Gene Raymond. "I smelled up the screen, " said Sidney. (Paramount)

Near the climactic finish, Tonita is allowed to sum up the idiocy of the elitist white class. "You're no good. No good at all. Any of you."

The New York Times thought *Behold My Wife* "abnormally improbable," and advised Sidney to "read her scenarios before she agrees to appear in them." Los Angeles critic Eleanor Barnes expected a tribal committee from a reservation to take revenge on Paramount "with Indian clubs and protests."[20] Ads for the film howled, "*Behold My Wife* - I Married a Savage!" Jerry Hoffman, for *Los Angeles Examiner* rated it as "heap good drama." His review was peppered with the usual politically incorrect asides, but he found the film "at all times deeply engrossing." Hoffman found Sidney to be "lovely and sincere," and added that Ann Sheridan "registers with an emotional sequence." Gene Raymond was often singled out for handling his role with "finesse." In the long run, however, Sheridan was the only one who came out ahead in this opus. Her standout turn spared her the drudgery of doing more work as an extra.

Gene Raymond paid compliments to co-star Sidney. "We don't take each other very seriously," he grinned. "We had played together on Broadway. We did *Ladies of the Big House* together, always kidding. The interesting thing about Sylvia is that when she's not working she's just the opposite of the sad, wistful girl you see in pictures. She's always bubbling, carrying on a running fire of conversation with everybody."[21] Sylvia admitted to being frank during conversations. "I am completely without tact," she explained in an interview. "I'm compelled to say what I think and I can't help showing people how I feel about them. If I like a person, he knows it. If I don't—well, he knows that, too. I can't turn charm on and off. People must understand that about me and accept my complete tactlessness."[22] Sylvia kept her temper at bay, by shutting her mouth and walking out of the room. "I stopped having rages. It seemed silly to play big emotional scenes that I didn't get paid for. I save the fireworks for the camera now." Her own opinion of *Behold, My Wife*? "I smelled up the screen," she grumbled.

Following the release of *Behold My Wife* (December 1934) Schulberg severed his relationship with Paramount. By April, he joined the producing forces at Columbia Pictures. Once again, Sylvia was off-screen for several months. During her sabbatical she enjoyed a lengthy vacation in New York and Florida. Happily, she found herself in the throes of a "hot" romance, which would eventually turn quite serious.

It had been reported that Sylvia and Doug Fairbanks Jr. would co-star in Vina Delmar's story, *End of the World* for Paramount. By the time cameras rolled, instead of Fairbanks, Sidney faced Herbert Marshall in *Accent on Youth*. Along with director Wesley Ruggles (brother of actor Charlie Ruggles) they created one of the box-office champions for 1935.[23] The film, based on a successful play by Sam Raphaelson, was about a middle-aged playwright (Marshall) who tackles the problems of a May-December romance in his latest play. He then quite unexpectedly finds himself in a similar situation with his young secretary (Sidney). Life imitates art. The cultivated, mellifluous voice of Marshall, coupled with engaging chemistry between costars, combined for diverting screen fare. What *Accent on Youth* lacked was the necessary brisk tempo for complete success. A Brooklyn critic thought the film "unenterprising." Sidney was unimpressed with director Ruggles. She had her reasons and offered them.

> Wesley Ruggles ... was another son-of-a-bitch! Marshall had lost a leg in World War I, but he used to cover this handicap. On stage, you never noticed it. When he was in films, you didn't notice it. It was only apparent in *Accent on Youth*, because Ruggles' set was too difficult for Marshall to walk around on. The other directors had accommodated Marshall.[24]

Sylvia also butted heads with scenarist Claude Binyon. Binyon remarked, "When Sylvia appeared in *Accent on Youth* ... she took exception to a remark I made about her performance and stated quite frankly that she needed no advice from a writer. I decided immediately, that Miss Sidney was on her way out."[25] After the crash of 1929, Binyon had created the *Variety* headline: "Wall Street Lays an Egg." Sidney wouldn't have to suffer the wit or suggestions of Binyon again, nor director Ruggles, nor costume designer Travis Banton whose "dreadful" fashions, as one critic put it, gave Sidney "more weight than a big fudge sundae." However, Sylvia liked her role in *Accent on Youth* enough to repeat it on stage in 1938 and 1941. In fact, playwright Raphaelson had originally written the play with Sidney in mind, but Paramount wouldn't release her for a return to Broadway.

Herbert Marshall joined Sylvia for *Accent on Youth* (Paramount)

Sidney owed Paramount one more picture, and was demanding $4,000 weekly against her $2,500. While on vacation in New York—hobnobbing with her new boyfriend, and enjoying the baths at Elberon, her negotiations reached an impasse. Independent producer Walter Wanger came to her rescue. She decided to sign with Wanger, on loan-out. By mid-September—it was good-bye to Paramount. Sidney was negotiating with Wanger, exclusively. She was back at the Malibu Beach home she rented from Richard Barthelmess, and ready to begin what turned out to be one of her favorite films, *Mary Burns, Fugitive*. "It was so obvious that Paramount didn't know what to do with me," said Sylvia. "There was something about Mr. Wanger's quiet, intelligent handling of a situation that inspired faith in everyone in the cast."[26] As the picture took shape, the story began to mean something to Sylvia. She sang nothing but praises for her director, William K. Howard. "I learned more about picture making, about how a film was put together, from Howard than from almost anyone. He was one of my gods. He was one of the only directors in America at the time that 'cut' in the camera. Fritz Lang did it and so did Hitchcock, but I think Bill Howard was brilliant."[27]

Howard recalled that, at first, Sidney wasn't that keen about *Mary Burns, Fugitive*. He explained, "She was going to be married; her old contract was just ending; she just wasn't much interested. The first day on the set I decided to be very efficient, entirely business-like—I'd show this young woman that I knew my job." On the second day, Sylvia arrived on the set at 7:30 a.m. Filming didn't wrap until 11 p.m. Howard apologized, and was surprised when she smiled and told him it was alright. She was enjoying it. She was excited about her part and Howard got excited about her acting. "She has a quality rare on the screen," said Howard. "You feel it in that courtroom scene where she is sentenced to fifteen years. Remember how she repeated it, 'fifteen years, fifteen years.' Well, you can't tell a person how to do a scene like that. Either they can do it or they can't. She was such a grand person to work with. She was marvelous every minute."[28]

In the hands of William K. Howard, *Mary Burns, Fugitive* is both personal and expressionistic, offering a skeptical view of American justice. It is a disturbing piece of work. Mary (Sidney) runs a popular roadside café. There's a new man in her life named "Babe" Wilson (Alan Baxter), who claims to be in the oil business. She appears infatuated with him. Wilson drops by to propose marriage, but their rendezvous is interrupted by gunfire and a police raid. Wilson escapes, while Mary is left begging for an explanation. The law nabs Mary, suspecting that she is Wilson's gun-moll. "Babe," it turns out, is a notorious racketeer. Blazing headlines feed the public what they want to hear—anything but the truth. In other words, people think that Mary Burns deserves what's coming to her.

After being mercilessly badgered by the state prosecutor, Mary "confesses" under duress, and ends up in prison where she is grilled by an FBI agent named Harper (Wallace Ford). This "protector of the law" is willing to set up a "jail break" and put Mary's life at risk as "bait" to track down "Babe" Wilson. No matter that Harper is placing the life of an innocent, young woman in jeopardy. After Mary's "escape," the desperate eyes of gang members as well as the long arm of the law follow her every move. This cinematic twist countered the films, sanctioned by J. Edgar Hoover, that glorified the FBI.

Mary's "happy interlude" finds her employed in a hospital, bringing trays of coffee to snow-blinded patient (Melvyn Douglas). Before long, he's proposing marriage without having laid eyes on her. The FBI uses this turn of events to let "Babe" know that his gal is two-timing him. At a critical moment, it's Mary, gun in hand, who solves the problem of public enemy "Babe" Wilson. As author Bob Herzberg surmised in his *The FBI and the Movies*: "If films like *G-Men* and *Let 'Em Have It!* were love letters to an all-knowing, always perfect FBI, *Mary Burns, Fugitive* was a refreshing bit of hate mail."[29]

Film Daily reported that *Mary Burns, Fugitive* was "ingenious ... just the type of picture that fits Sylvia Sidney perfectly, and she scores handsomely." One critic marveled, "she plays it with a realism that makes viewers almost forget they are in a theater." The *San Francisco Chronicle* concluded, "Melodrama it may be, but the tale is so capably told that it becomes extraordinarily exciting ... thanks to superb direction by William K. Howard." Sidney received nothing but praise for a performance that increased her box-office stature. In 2009, writer Moira Finney joined the chorus.

> Sidney won my heart playing a plucky, almost fatally naive hash slinger. The movie, which is a hybrid of the 'woman's picture' and the socially aware *I Am a Fugitive From a Chain Gang* [1932], limns the downfall and rise of a person whose unexamined life is turned on its head by chance and by the coldness of the justice system. The gradual assertion of this over-

Mary Burns, Fugitive - with Pert Kelton. (Paramount)

whelmed young woman's will to survive was more riveting for me because of the petite Sylvia Sidney's ability to convey such a highly feminine blend of fear, outrage, and her growing understanding of the thinness of civilization's veneer ... a perfect embodiment of the Depression era victim and survivor."[30]

Occasionally, Sidney referred to *Mary Burns, Fugitive* as her personal favorite. She would point out that director Howard's reputation for drink did not interfere with his professional responsibilities. "Bill was an alcoholic," said Sylvia. "He was always calling for Coca Cola, which we all knew was spiked with gin." She noticed that he wrote scene numbers scheduled for the day on his shirt cuff, so he wouldn't lose track.

> I remember one day Leon Shamroy, the director of photography, said to Bill that he needed a master shot of me entering a building, and Bill told him that you didn't always need a master shot ... that once you establish that particular place, you don't have to say over again, 'Look how big that place is.' I tell you, I have more respect for him than for almost any other director I ever worked for. And isn't it a shame that so few people remember him today?[31]

Sylvia mentioned Howard's successes: *The Power and the Glory* (1933) with Spencer Tracy, and *Fire Over England* (1937) with Olivier. Howard directed over fifty films and is credited with developing an innovative "flashback" narrative that predates *Citizen Kane* (1941). In a 1970 interview, Academy Award-winning photographer James Wong Howe answered without hesitation that William K. Howard was the best director with whom he had ever worked.

Sidney's association with Wanger under a four-year contract was exactly what she needed, career-wise. Her "liberation" from Paramount would translate into some of her finest screen work. She had more money than she knew what to do with. "Naturally, I couldn't handle it," she commented to *The New York Times* in 1945. "Who could?" Still, she held on for three more years, becoming more successful, more wealthy ... and more unhappy. And, it didn't take long for Sylvia to discover that she couldn't handle a honeymoon either, let alone marriage.

(Endnotes)

1. Dorothy Manners, "Looking Them Over," *Movie Classic*, July 1933
2. "Walks Out on Chevalier," *Omaha World Herald*, August 1, 1933
3. "Scarring Feared by Sylvia Sidney," *Trenton Evening News*, August 2, 1933
4. "Actors Plead Miss Sidney's Return to Job," *Hollywood Citizen News*, August 1, 1933
5. "Sylvia Sidney Consults Doctors," *Variety*, August 8, 1933
6. "Sylvia Sidney, Sailings, Denies Wedding Plans," *Omaha World Herald*, August 20, 1933
7. Art Arthur, "Reverting to Type," *Brooklyn Daily Eagle*, August 7, 1933
8. Jeff Laffel, "Sylvia Sidney," *Films in Review*, September/October 1994
9. Joseph G. Boyd, "Sylvia Sidney Still Is Presence to Reckon With," *Milwaukee Sentinel*, October 11, 1978
10. John Rosenfield Jr., *Thirty Day Princess*, *Dallas Morning News*, June 3, 1934
11. Pauline Kael, *5001 Nights at the Movies*, MacMillan (edition), c. 2011 pg. 760
12. George H. Beale, "Hospital Treats Cary Grant, Star of Films, Who Denies Death Try," *Berkeley Daily Gazette*, October 5, 1934
13. Jimmy Fidler, "Jimmy Fidler in Hollywood," *State Times Advocate*, June 17, 1936 (First quote from William Mann's *Behind the Screen*, Viking, c. 2001, pg. 154)
14. Miranda Seymour, *Chaplin's Girl: the Life and Loves of Virginia Cherrill*, Simon and Schuster, c. 2009 ($25,000 was a division of community property)
15. Geoffrey Wansell, *Cary Grant – Dark Angel*, Arcade Pub., c. 2011
16. Walter Ramsey, review of *Thirty Day Princess*, *Modern Screen*, August 1934
17. Marian Christy, "Lifestyle: Sylvia Sidney, Older, Wiser," *Oregonian*, November 28, 1978
18. Louella Parsons column, *Syracuse Journal*, February 7, 1934
19. Gilbert Parker, *The Works of Gilbert Parker*, Scribner, c. 1913, pg. 7
20. Eleanor Barnes, review of *Behold My Wife*, *Illustrated Daily News*, December 6, 1934
21. Dorothy Ann Blank, "What I Know About the Women I Have Loved," *Screen Book*, March 1935
22. Katherine Albert, "Sylvia Sidney Plays Truth," *Modern Screen*, June 1936
23. *International Motion Picture Almanac, 1936-37*, Quigley, c. 1936

24 Gregory J.M. Catsos, "Sylvia Sidney," *Filmfax*, November 1990
25 "In Hollywood," *Advocate*, October 24, 1937
26 Dora Albert, "No More Impulses," *Photoplay*, July 1937
27 Jeff Laffel, "Sylvia Sidney," *Films in Review*, September/October 1994
28 "Picture Plays and Players - William K. Howard, Director of *Mary Burns, Fugitive*, in New York," *New York Sun*, November 21, 1935
29 Bob Herzberg, *The FBI and the Movies: A History of the Bureau on Screen and Behind the Scenes in Hollywood*, McFarland, c. 2006, pg. 41
30 Moira Finney, "Sylvia Sidney: 'Paid By the Tear,'" Movie Morlocks (on-line), February 4, 2009
31 Jeff Laffel, "Sylvia Sidney," *Films in Review*, September/October 1994

October, 1935. Cerf and Sidney prior to the honeymoon that never happened

Chapter 6
"One Should Never Legalize a 'Hot' Romance"
- Bennett Cerf

"One should never legalize a 'hot' romance," remarked Random House publisher Bennett Cerf after his brief marriage to Sylvia Sidney. At 37, the tall, brown-eyed and bespectacled Cerf held a crush on Sylvia ever since seeing her in *Bad Girl* on Broadway. The moment Sylvia walked on stage, Cerf told his date, "That's the most beautiful girl I ever saw, and I'm going to meet her if it's the last thing I do on earth."[1] It took him a few years. When Sylvia relocated to Hollywood, Cerf religiously followed her career in the papers. He told *everyone* about his crush. "I considered her my personal property," he admitted. When Cerf learned of the Schulberg-Sidney affair, he resented it. His hopes soared, however, when director Ernst Lubitsch and his wife asked Cerf to join them *and* Sylvia for an evening out on the town. Sadly, Sylvia came down with pneumonia. Cerf's big opportunity finally arrived on New Year's Eve 1934, in New York. He attended a big party at the home of Goldwyn publicity chief Lynn Farnol. Sylvia attended the event with story editor Richard Halliday. Halliday, well aware of Cerf's big crush, made the introductions, "Mr. Cerf, this is Mrs. Cerf." Cerf was completely tongue-tied.

For the next hour, Cerf could not muster the courage to engage Sylvia in conversation. He finally told his date that they ought to leave. When he went up to Sidney to say goodbye, she said, "You're the strangest young man I have ever met in my life. I've been hearing about this publisher who was determined to meet me. Then finally I meet you and you never say one word to me."[2] Cerf, feeling some semblance of normalcy, replied, "Well, Miss Sidney, we've been here about an hour, and I've just been so dazzled by you. If you'd like me to tell you every move you have made in that hour, I can because I've never taken my eyes off you." Sidney acknowledged, "Don't you think I know that?" After a brief pause, she added, "Are you game?" Cerf gave her a puzzled look—which quickly transformed into unbridled joy when she suggested that they both leave the party. He wasted no time in leaving word for Halliday to take care of his date. Welcome, 1935.

A cross-country courtship ensued. Their appeal to each other was understandable. Cerf was an author, lecturer, raconteur, and partygiver. His guest list for one typical party Sylvia attended included: Gertrude Stein and Alice B. Toklas, George Gershwin, novelists Edna Ferber and William Saroyan, and Cerf's former girlfriend Miriam Hopkins. Cerf's relaxed, cheerful style had appeal. More importantly, he helped shape the country's literary and cultural life. His influence at Random House broke the Federal censorship ban on the James Joyce masterpiece *Ulysses*. Cerf published Marcel Proust and underwrote the career of William Faulkner. And, he was generous. It was his theory, "If you're going to have two people for dinner you might as well have forty." Although she was less inclined than Cerf to enjoy large social gatherings, it would appear that Sylvia was in good hands. However, her heart belonged to her career.

Rumors of the Sidney-Cerf romance surfaced, but Sylvia remained silent. It was mentioned that she was often seen at the Trocadero and the Clover Club with writer Norman Krasna. Other intellectuals in the arts also enjoyed her company—Sidney Kingsley, and George Jean Nathan. Her escorts were confined to a select few, and for good reason. Sylvia harbored an unnerving impulse to do harm to any man who didn't measure up. "If a man ever says a dumb thing to me," she stated, "I feel like kicking him. Even if a man says something that makes me know that I am cleverer than he ... I feel repulsed."[3] It was Walter Wanger who finally disclosed Sylvia's plans to marry Cerf, during the shoot of *Mary Burns, Fugitive*. Cerf's father, Gustave, adored Miriam Hopkins, who would curl up in the elder gentleman's lap. Gustave was displeased with his son's intention to marry Sidney. He thought she was "a fresh, spoiled brat."

An Associated Press release scoffed that the movie colony knew more about the nuptials than either of the principals involved. Sylvia's trousseau had been described by stylist Rene Taylor (a two piece woolen suit in shades of dubonnet accented with a sable scarf and close-fitting velvet hat); Cerf's purchase of a large square-cut diamond was old news by the time the two wed, October 1, 1935. The ceremony took place in a Phoenix, Arizona hotel suite. When Cerf went to the courthouse to find someone to officiate he was told that the judge was in the middle of a murder trial. Cerf replied, "My name is Bennett Cerf and I'm marrying a girl named Sylvia Sidney." Within five minutes the murder case was adjourned. Judge Marlin T. Phelps accompanied Cerf to the hotel. "We couldn't get rid of him," said Cerf, afterward. "We kept reminding him he had a murder case."[4] In attendance were

Sylvia's mother, actress/chum Dorothy Libaire, screenwriter George Oppenheimer, and Cerf's father, the disgruntled Gustave. "Am I really married?" the nervous bride exclaimed afterward.

Following a luncheon, Mr. and Mrs. Cerf chartered a plane bound for Hollywood. Pilot Paul Mantz, technical advisor to Amelia Earhart, had to make a forced landing in Banning. The couple motored the last 75 miles of the trip. It was a precursor of things to come. Sylvia was baffled by the brevity of her wedding. "I can't realize I'm married," she told reporters. "I expected the ceremony to last a half hour." Marital bliss didn't last much longer. "The time we decided to marry," said Cerf long afterward, "was the time we should have been saying goodbye to each other."[5]

While Bennett and Sylvia were saying their "I do's" the Hollywood trade papers announced Sidney's role in the upcoming feature *Trail of the Lonesome Pine*. Cerf understood that Sylvia had only a few days left to complete *Mary Burns, Fugitive*, before an extended honeymoon. Apparently, Sylvia was ready for the marriage to be over with *before* the honeymoon. In 1994, she admitted to the folly of becoming Mrs. Cerf. "He wanted to go on some kind of honeymoon around the Panama Canal," she laughed. "Or, the Suez. All that I know is that I didn't want to go; that I didn't want to be married to him anymore." She mentioned being drunk as a skunk and asking a friend, "How do I get out of going on this honeymoon?" She had jumped into marriage too quickly. "What saved me was … *Lonesome Pine*," she insisted.[6] Cerf felt that decisions had been made behind his back. He was accurate on this score.

After three days in Hollywood and numerous parties for the newlyweds, Cerf was invited by Walter Wanger for a man-to-man talk. Over lunch, Wanger chastised Cerf for forcing Sylvia to give up her opportunity of appearing in *Trail of the Lonesome Pine*, the first outdoor Technicolor film. Wanger told him that Sylvia would love to do it, but decided to go along with Cerf's plans instead—a honeymoon cruise, followed by an extended stay in New York. Unruffled, Cerf countered, "She's already a big star. She'll find some other picture." Wanger offered to show Cerf the Technicolor tests that Sylvia had made up at Lake Arrowhead. Cerf, who obviously hadn't read the trade papers, was becoming suspicious. Sylvia was being counted upon for the lead. "She looked glorious," admitted Cerf after seeing the Technicolor footage. He immediately confronted her. "This has all been cooked up behind my back, hasn't it?" Sylvia confessed that she was dying to make the picture. "Well," he argued, "what the hell can I say?"[7]

Cerf ended up spending one day with Sylvia on location at Big Bear, before returning home to New York, alone. He began to ask himself if he was cut out to be the husband of a movie star. The following month he flew back to Hollywood for a brief Thanksgiving reunion. Sylvia was soon sporting around in a new canary-yellow coupe Cerf purchased for her. Regardless, there were "troubles" in the marriage. When asked, Sylvia brushed them aside, saying that she was planning on visiting New York and spending Christmas with Cerf. After they brought in the New Year, the couple decided to separate.

In January 1936, Sidney announced, "We decided to call it quits." Officially, their marriage lasted three months. "It was more like a week," Sidney admitted years later. "We fought constantly, and he went home to his father."[8] Cerf reluctantly let go of his dream bride. "I was mad for her," he recalled in 1967. "As she later said, 'You know, you were never really in love with me. You were in love with a dream,' which was true. And she said, 'For about six months I was so crazy about you that I lived up to your dream, then I got damn tired of it.'"[9]

It was a shrewd assessment of their relationship. The separation wasn't easy. Cerf would dredge up memories from the past and then get angry at his propensity for self pity. "You can't forget it very quickly," observed Cerf. "My pride was hurt. Everybody talked about this great wonderful romance between the young publisher and the ravishing young star. And to have to end it so quickly was embarrassing for both of us. We've often agreed since what fools the two of us were."[10] One interesting side-note is Cerf's remark that B.P. Schulberg had threatened to kill him over Sylvia.[11] Cerf provided no further details. The rapid bust-up of Cerf's marriage could well have been a life-saver.

Louella Parsons announced that the end of Sylvia's marriage came as a surprise to no one. Sylvia's close friend and wedding attendant, Dorothy Libaire, also filed for divorce from director Marion Gering, the day after Sidney filed (March 26). In court, Sidney told Superior Judge Harry P. Archbald that Cerf quarreled with her over the time she gave to her career. "We just found that things did not click," she explained. The decree was granted on April 9. Libaire won her decree on April 16. "Show people should never marry," said Dorothy. "They should just see each other whenever they feel like it." This sage advice was given to her by ex-husband Gering.

In his autobiography, Cerf detailed, "I'd read an item about myself—for three years after the marriage it was always 'Bennett Cerf, ex-husband of Sylvia Sidney,' which used to drive me absolutely crazy. Gradually the tag disappeared and my memories of her disappeared too—the poignant ones, the ones that hurt." In August 1936, Cerf's name would pop up in the scandalous Mary Astor custody trial. He was one of the "ten men" mentioned in her infamous "purple" diaries. According to Astor's testimony, they saw each other several times. Cerf came close to being subpoenaed in what was essentially a month-long media circus. Cerf had escorted Astor to the Princeton-Dartmouth football game the previous November, prior to his return to Hollywood to "save" his troubled marriage. Cerf admitted that his and Astor's "weekend together ... didn't work." "We were too busy moaning about our own misfortunes to console anybody else," he explained.[12] At the time, Astor was on the rebound from an affair with playwright George S. Kaufman who was prominently featured in her diary. Cerf would wait another four years before his happier, enduring marriage to Phyllis Fraser, who became an editor of children's books at Random House.

Columnist Mollie Merrick had made mention of *Trail of the Lonesome Pine* in August 1935. She said that Marsha Hunt was being groomed at Paramount to replace Sylvia in case she didn't "fall into line." At that time, the picture was titled *Feud*. Director Henry Hathaway revealed years later that Joan Bennett had also been considered for the role, but he felt she wasn't right. She never let him forget it, always telling him, "You son of a bitch! You knew that when you were making the test that I wouldn't get it even if I was good."[13] Hathaway insisted on Sidney, and he got her.

Initially, Sylvia didn't jibe with Hathaway, but once filming got underway she was enthusiastic. Filming at Big Bear in the San Bernardino Mountains and Moon Ridge (8,000 feet above sea level) was no picnic. *Trail of the Lonesome Pine* was the first extensive (month long) location shoot for Sidney. "It was murder!" she said. Freezing cold induced Sylvia to wear layers of long underwear under her wardrobe. While watching the dailies producer Wanger complained to her, "Dammit, you're get-

Happily knitting on the set of *Trail of the Lonesome Pine*.
As June Tolliver (inset) (Paramount)

ting fat."[14] Sylvia responded by imbibing what she called "lethal but quite wonderful wine toddies," prepared by her chauffeur, that gave her face and feet a pink glow. "I'd get bombed out of my mind by five o'clock in the afternoon," laughed Sidney, "but I really looked good in the film!"[15] Lucky for Sidney, color photographer Robert Bruce had to get all close-ups completed by 3 p.m., otherwise the setting sun would cast a yellowish tinge on her face. Sylvia was pleased with Technicolor. "The picture is not just a glorified travelogue," she stressed. She felt the actors looked "simple and real." Greasepaint, heavy powder, eyeshadow, and lip rouge were avoided. Sylvia appreciated the subdued colors of her simple clothing. "Rather than make *them* important," she stressed, "we wanted the story to stand out."

Sylvia also pacified herself with an electric heating pad and her collection of Ray Noble phonograph records. When co-star Fred MacMurray was asked about the film he responded, "I don't think Miss Sidney was very happy during that picture. We were on location most of the time. I don't think she enjoyed the mountains like Hank Fonda and I did."[16] MacMurray biographer, Charles Tranberg, noted that the two actors "were essentially shy men who didn't say much but enjoyed each other's company just for the pleasure of having somebody to fish with."[17] Between scenes would find the duo casting their rods into Big Bear Lake.

James Fox Jr.'s 1908 novel *Trail of the Lonesome Pine* had previously been released in three silent film versions. Director Hathaway held to the original narrative and provided a sympathetic look at feudin' mountain folk along the Kentucky-Virginia border. For decades, the Tolliver and Falin clans were at each other's throats. Undying hate had become a religion. Into this mix a big city engineer (MacMurray) arrives on the scene. In the process of acquiring land for a coal mine and

Trail of the Lonesome Pine with Fred MacMurray, Henry Fonda, Fred Stone (Paramount)

railroad, MacMurray unexpectedly falls for June Tolliver (Sidney). He soon discovers he has competition—her mountain boy cousin Dave (Fonda). While MacMurray wrangles with clan hostilities, he encourages Sidney to get an education and sends her to Louisville to stay with his sister. She goes along with the idea. She's clever and she's smitten. Her schooling, newly acquired manners and fashion sense, however, rapidly lose their meaning when she returns home to learn that her little brother (Spanky McFarland) has lost his life due to more Falin chicanery. She wants revenge, mountain-style.

Sidney, sans script, conveys volumes of feeling by simply using her eyes. She subtly mirrors the instinctive anguish and distrust her people have toward the encroachment of "civilization." Still, she's puzzled

Betrothed Cousins: Sidney and
Henry Fonda (Paramount)

by her betrothal to her cousin. "I don't ... *feel* nothin'," she tells her mother (Beulah Bondi). As Sidney's brooding fiancé, Fonda leans on the only education he knows, his rifle. The poignancy of Beulah Bondi, the crusty determination of Fred Stone as Judd Tolliver, and Robert Barret as Buck Falin, make the mix of anguish, feuds and undying hatred seem plausible. In one scene, Sidney telephones MacMurray from Louisville. She tells him that she's been reading about the American Revolution. "It was just like a feud," she chuckles. Indeed, the feuds of mountain folk were merely a reflection of a larger world where men employ even bigger guns in relentless games of war.

Despite a contrived prologue, and blaring soundtrack during gunfire and fistfights, *Trail of the Lonesome Pine* impressed. *The New York*

Times noted that outdoor Technicolor gave cinema "fuller expression." The review complimented the "cast of unusual merit," singling out director Hathaway and the art direction of Alexander Toluboff. *Variety* praised Sidney's performance of the hillbilly girl who reverts to type, as being "uncompromising in every detail." Another critic raved, "The portrayal by Sylvia Sidney reaches and sustains an emotional crisis that is breath-taking."[18] *Film Daily* predicted a sure-fire hit, and it was, breaking box-office records in all the major cities. Paramount was happy.

Henry Fonda, in a 1966 interview, stated, "It was my first experience with Hathaway. I'm still one of his fans. I liked working with Sylvia and Fred MacMurray. It was a good experience and a successful picture."[19] Sidney liked working with Fonda and the two would successfully team again.

After two months off, Sylvia headed for her first (and last) time to the prestigious MGM studio to work with director Fritz Lang in his first American film, *Fury*. To do so, she had turned down the opportunity (and twice the money) to play opposite Ronald Colman (whom she adored) in *Under Two Flags*. That role went to Claudette Colbert. Lang was a refugee from Vienna. He had arrived in the United States in 1934 to escape the Nazis, after refusing Hitler's request that he run the film industry for the Third Reich. "That made it even more important for me to back him up, to work for him," said Sidney. "My parents also were refugees." [20]

Fury was adapted from the short story *Mob Rule*, by Norman Krasna. It was based on an actual lynching that took place in San Jose, California in 1933. Two men accused of kidnapping, were presumed guilty by local folk, who took the law and a long rope into their own hands. In the aftermath, a mob of 6,000—women, children and men—were seen "spitting and striking the corpses as they were taken away."[21] Just as appalling was California Governor James Rolph's reaction. He approved the deeds of an "aroused people" and said the lynching was a "fine lesson for the whole nation."[22] Lynching and mob violence had escalated during the 1930's, frequently making news. It was under these circumstances that Krasna wrote his indictment against blind injustice. Fritz Lang and scenarist Bartlett Cormack turned Krasna's outline into a screenplay.

Lang was a tyrant on the set, but Sidney found the experience rewarding. Lang stipulated (nudged by Krasna, Sylvia's frequent escort) that Sidney be in the film before signing his contract.[23] Lang often kept her on the set fifteen and twenty hours at a stretch. She later mused, "I had stamina, I guess." Co-star Spencer Tracy agreed, "When Sylvia Sidney and I put in 21 hours a day on *Fury*, we did it because we knew Lang had something worthwhile."[24] When author Jeff Laffel interviewed her in the 1990's, he assumed that Sidney didn't get along with Lang. She was stunned. "Honey," she said, "you are *wrong* about that! I adored the man. What the hell… I made three pictures with him."[25] Not that Lang didn't make her miserable. "Fritz Lang was an egomaniac!" she insisted. "But I knew he'd get a good performance out of me!"

In *Fury*, we see Spencer Tracy, a mechanic with a bright future, en route to visit his schoolteacher sweetheart (Sidney). Taking a by-road, Tracy is picked up by a small town deputy, who suspects Tracy of being an accused kidnapper. On a shred of evidence (salted peanuts and a $5 bill), Tracy ends up in jail. Rumors spread and by the time Sidney rushes to the scene, an aroused lynch mob has set the building in which Tracy is incarcerated on fire. It is assumed that he was killed. In truth, he had escaped ... and wants revenge. After the real kidnappers are arrested, twenty-two members of the mob go on trial for murder. In a powerful scene Sylvia walks into a hotel room to discover her "dead" fiancé. She barely recognizes him. Anger has distorted his looks and character. Sidney pleads with him to appear in court and stop the madness. His "fury" is unrelenting. "I'm hanging twenty-two rats!" he snarls, then asks, "Why don't you think about *me*?" She backs off. "I *am* thinking about you," she says thoughtfully. "About what a swell guy you were ... when you were alive. I couldn't marry a dead man." Tracy storms out, but her words gradually sink in.

Fury, along with *San Francisco* (filmed simultaneously), were the films that made Tracy a star. "Spencer Tracy was very special," admitted Sylvia. "He was not only a great actor, but he listened as well. Tracy would say, 'Acting to me is always reacting!' Tracy and Fonda could be in long scenes where they didn't say anything. But you knew they were listening and *hearing* the dialogue." Sidney had known Tracy from Broadway. Even though Tracy knew that Lang was onto something, the two fought frequently. They grew to hate each other. Cinematographer Joe Ruttenberg said of Lang and Tracy, "They were always fighting, always fighting."[26]

Fury was uncompromising and unusual screen fare. Critics stood up and took notice. They appreciated the lack of comic relief. *The New York Times* called it the "finest original drama the screen has provided this year. A mature, sober and penetrating investigation of a national blight." *Photoplay* placed the film and performances of Tracy and Sidney in its "Best of the Month" category. British novelist, Graham Greene rated *Fury* as "astonishingly, the only film I know to which I have wanted to attach the epithet of 'great.'" Greene singled

Fury (1936) Sidney said of Spencer Tracy, "I'd give my eyeteeth to play opposite him again." (MGM)

out Sidney's performance: "She has never more deeply conveyed the pain and inarticulacy of tenderness."[27] On the 2005 DVD release of *Fury*, director Peter Bogdanovich praised Sidney, saying she was "an extremely good actress. She reminds me a little of Bette Davis without quite the posturing. She never really lets herself go over the top. She's very contained."

MGM didn't think they had a hit on their hands. Social commentary on the bloodlust of humankind didn't mix with Metro's glossy appetite. Joseph Breen, head of the PCA, had warned Louis B. Mayer that *Fury* avoid any hint of racial prejudice. Mayer deleted footage showing African-Americans. "I had a scene showing a group of Negroes," said Lang, "an old man, a very beautiful buxom girl, and a young Negro with two children—sitting in a dilapidated Ford car in the South listening on the radio." The broadcast was of a lynching trial which mentioned the high incidence of lynching in the U.S. "I had the old Negro just nod his head silently without a word," said Lang. "Mayer had this scene and others like it removed."[28] Initially, the studio thought so little of *Fury*, they planned to distribute it as part of a double-bill. Lang stated in an interview that prior to release, someone at Metro told a reporter, "Oh, a lousy picture. Don't watch it; it is by that German son-of-a-bitch, Lang."[29] Afterward, Lang was banned from MGM for twenty years.

Lang was adamantly against having the usual Tracy-Sidney fadeout kiss, but Metro insisted. In the 1960's Lang told Peter Bogdanovich, "I hated the [fade-out] kiss, because I think it wasn't necessary. ... You could have shown a close-up of Sylvia Sidney—she's very happy—he could look at her; period. It's such a coy ending now." When asked who was the ablest actor on screen Sidney didn't hesitate, "Spencer Tracy. I'd give my eyeteeth to play opposite him again."[30] This never happened, but she did co-star with Frank Albertson (who played Tracy's brother in *Fury*) on tour in the comedy *The Fourposter* in 1954.

Sylvia had had her fill of snooping columnists, Hollywood, and all the brouhaha that went with it. Writer/editor for *Silver Screen*, Elizabeth Wilson, said of Sidney, "An interview with her is always a duel of insults." Sidney chastised Wilson, arguing, "Why do you bother with me? You know you've written this story before seeing me. But I suppose I'll have to give you lunch anyway. Why don't you take me to lunch sometime?" Wilson summed Sidney up—"A nasty person, but I like her."[31] Sidney's attitude was understandable. Wilson's active imagination erroneously reported that Sylvia was "chipper as a meadowlark" on location during the *Trail of the Lonesome Pine* shoot where she "spent her honeymoon" with Bennett Cerf (who in fact, was nowhere around). Not to worry. Sidney would "escape" Hollywood and sail to London for a new picture.

England & Hitchcock

In May 1936, Sylvia left the United States for four months. According to one gossipmonger, B.P. Schulberg saw her off and "waved a mess of bye-de-bye-byes" to her at the Los Angeles depot."[32] His marriage to Adeline would finally dissolve in 1938. Not long afterward, he eloped with a socialite-turned-actress from Chicago named Helen McHale Keebler.

In New York, Sylvia boarded the ocean liner *Berengaria*. She told a swarm of reporters that after completing her next film, the British production *Sabotage*, she planned to venture to Lake Como with her mother. She was excited about working with leading man Robert Donat and director Alfred Hitchcock. It was Michael Balcon, executive-producer for Gaumont-British Films, who had signed Sidney the previous December. "I should have been a fool if I had let slip the opportunity of signing up such a brilliant actress," he enthused.[33] In the long run, Sidney's "escape" offered her something she hadn't bargained for—locking horns with Hitchcock.

After docking in Southampton, Sylvia boarded a train for London. Upon arrival, she offered a rather unexpected performance at the railroad terminus. British journalist Stiles Dickenson observed, "The greatest sensation of the London season so far, and the most surprising star so far is Sylvia Sidney. We all went to greet Sylvia. Even so, we were hardly prepared for Sylvia herself. She alighted from her carriage and as her welcoming admirers clustered around, she suddenly burst into tears and hid her face in her hands. Police came to the rescue and carried her bodily off the platform into the waiting car, anxiously followed by the reception committee of studio officials, speech and presentation flowers forgotten now."

Several hours later, after checking into her suite at Claridges, Sidney met her public. With averted eyes, she explained, "I'm just a worker. I've made seventeen pictures these last five years, because I love work so much. I think I should die if I had to give it up. Work is all I live for. Work—and being alone." Reporter Dickenson pondered, "Surely she's the shyest and most individual of all the lovely ladies who have come to grace London for us this summer season!"[34]

When Sylvia reported to the Shepherd's Bush studio to discuss the script with Hitchcock, she learned that leading man Donat was confined to a nursing home battling asthma, barely able to breathe. The actor only found relief by sucking medicated lozenges—his throat specially treated with cocaine.[35] Production was postponed. Donat was soon replaced by the less charismatic John Loder, a big disappointment for Sidney. When the cameras finally rolled, Sidney insisted on privacy. The producer set up a tent on the studio floor so she could rest between scenes, hidden from prying eyes. Regardless, she had difficulty with director Hitchcock's technique.

Prior to her arrival, Hitchcock was contemplating an original story for Sylvia, but decided instead to cast her in his adaptation of the Joseph Conrad 1907 novel *Secret Agent*. Hitchcock had called her sev-

Sabotage (1936). On the set with Alfred Hitchcock and John Loder (Gaumont-British)

eral times over radiotelephone while she was aboard the *Berengaria*, welcoming her profusely. When they met face-to-face, according to scenarist Charles Bennett, "It was a different matter. Sylvia just wasn't Hitch's type—although she gave a beautiful performance. She was continually resenting his treatment of her. Some years later, over lunch at Cock and Bull in Hollywood, Sylvia told me how much she had hated Hitch and never wanted to see him again."[36] Bennett admitted that although Hitchcock was brilliant, he was "tough to love and easy to hate."[37]

In *Sabotage*, Sidney was in a loveless marriage to Oscar Homolka, the manager of a small London cinema. The cinema is used as a front for foreign spies. She is unaware that her husband is involved with sabotage, a commissioned terrorist. From the outset the audience knows about him, but Sidney and her young brother Stevie (Desmond Tester), who lives with them, are clueless. Sidney's suspicions are aroused when an undercover agent from Scotland Yard (John Loder) begins asking her some disturbing questions. The suspense builds after Homolka gives Stevie a package with a time bomb inside. He instructs the boy to deliver the parcel to a Piccadilly Circus cloakroom by a specific time. Things go amiss. The boy dawdles. The bomb explodes in a crowded bus—the innocent brother, one of the victims.

Sidney had difficulty adjusting to Hitchcock's fiendish methods, especially when he instructed her how to play her big dramatic scene. She balked at the idea of having only a few frames of her face to indicate the battle going on inside her, juxtaposed with frames of her hands closing in on the knife as she prepares dinner, only to plunge it into her husband's abdomen. Sidney complained that the rest of her anatomy was being neglected. Hitchcock dismissed Sylvia's concerns, explaining that he had the camera all set up to move according to plan. There was no point in arguing the matter. She felt irrelevant and threatened to quit. Associate producer Ivor Montague was forthright when he recalled the crisis. "For this film we probably got the most accomplished actress we ever had: Sylvia Sidney. She had always acted a scene right through, and she badly needed words … to start a mood off for her. We were happy with her work. Many were the times I was called up from my office to find her weeping. She was not to be consoled. She wanted to go home." Montague resolved the issue thusly,

> I persuaded her to stay at least for the big scene [where] she learns that her husband has been the cause of the death of her small brother. 'Try this one,' I coaxed. Afterwards we

Preparing to kill husband Oscar Homolka in *Sabotage* (Gaumont-British)

would see. The scene, alas, contained barely a word. A real Hitch scene, made up of close-ups and inserts, eyes, expressions, forks, potatoes, cabbages. After playing it as directed, in total unhappiness, she broke down.[38]

Montague begged that she wait to see the rough cut. A few hours later, Hitchcock, the cutter Charles Frend, Sylvia and Montague watched the projected images. "Our star was dazed," confirmed Montague. "As she came out of the projection room she looked at Hitch. 'Hollywood must hear of this,' she said." She wasn't entirely convinced, however. "What did he teach me?" Sidney asked herself years later. "To be a puppet and not try to be creative … I really took exception to that."[39] In the 1960's, Hitchcock, true to form, told Peter Bogdanovich, "What terrible trouble it was to get any expression on

Sylvia Sidney's face. She had a kind of mask-like quality. Actually, I think that's what drove me to get around it through other means."[40]

"Mr. Hitchcock's technique is its own excuse," commented *The New York Times* critic Frank S. Nugent in his review of *Sabotage*. He thought Hitchcock had created a "masterly exercise in suspense." Nugent explained, "He builds ruthlessly to his climaxes and makes their impact hard and sudden. His players ... are held rigidly to the line of story advancement but, within the narrow limits Hitchcock permits them, contribute sound characterizations."

Nugent's succinct review hit the critique nail on the proverbial head. On the other hand, prominent London critic, C.A. Lejeune, was not happy. She was furious. In her review for London's *Sunday Observer* she railed that Hitchcock had "gone outside the code" with his "free-handed slaughter." At a cocktail press showing, she approached scenarist Bennett protesting that he and Hitchcock had manipulated the audience with suspense only to disappoint. "Charles, you should be ashamed of yourself for killing that child!" she fumed. Bennett was stunned. "What the hell are you talking about?" he shot back. "Read Conrad's *Secret Agent* and see for yourself. Blame Conrad for it!"[41] One can only image Lejeune's displeasure if Hitchcock had stuck to the finish in the novel where Sidney's desperately unhappy character commits suicide.

Interestingly, Hitchcock acquiesced to the vitriol of the powerful critic, saying he regretted his decision to have the boy killed. His prime rule from there out was that heroes and heroines be rescued at the last minute. He told Dick Cavett in a 1972 TV interview, "I made the mistake of not relieving (the audience) at the end of the suspense. If you put an audience through the mill like that, you must relieve it. The bomb must be found—and quickly thrown out of the window."

Cavett asked, "And if you had it to do over again?" "I'd never let the bomb go off," he replied. While the finish in *Sabotage* left Sidney's character (and audiences) holding a heavy emotional weight—the death of her young brother gave innocent victims of terrorism a "face."

Sidney would insist that while Hitchcock was a genius moviemaker, he was *not* great with actors. Case in point: Desmond Tester, the young actor who played her brother. "Hitchcock insisted on calling him 'testicle,'" said Sidney. "'Where's the testicle?' Hitchcock would cry ... to the amusement of the cast and crew and the total mortification of the kid."⁴² Sidney had to admit, "It never seemed to affect the boy's performance, which was very good."⁴³

While in England, Sidney engaged a private secretary, her first. "I didn't know what to do with her," she admitted long afterward. "So, I said, 'Take a letter ... Dear Mom ... ,' Who dictates a letter to your mother? So I sent her out to buy me some sweaters."⁴⁴ Sylvia spent her spare time preparing for her upcoming film, *Wuthering Heights*. Producer Wanger promised her the lead in the Emily Bronte classic. She reread the book for the fourth time after visiting the Bronte home, absorbing the country atmosphere and Yorkshire dialect around Haworth. Wanger, in the meantime, was conferring with Mussolini. Plans were underway to set up a studio in Rome. It was announced that Sidney and Henry Fonda would star in the first Walter Wanger Company of Italy feature, *Three Times a Loser*, to begin no later than June 1937.

After *Sabotage*, Sidney took a sojourn to Paris, where she lingered a few days, before heading to Cannes for sun and swimming. It was there that her mother joined her. By August, Beatrice and Sylvia were vacationing in Italy. Producer Wanger requested that Sylvia visit his Italian associates and pose for a photo with Mussolini. Wisely, she refused.[45] Sylvia was tightlipped when meeting with columnists during her stay in Europe. In Paris, Stiles Dickenson had joined Sylvia and Richard Barthelmess over cocktails at the Crillon Bar. When Barthelmess asked how she liked working in British studios, Sylvia glanced over at Dickenson, gave a quick smile and said, "Perfectly chawming, old chap, perfectly chawming." The most that Dickenson could drag out of Sylvia was that she found the experience, "interesting."

In September 1936, Sylvia and Beatrice boarded the *Conte Di Sevoia* in France, arriving home in New York on the 17th. On September 30, *Three Times a Loser* (retitled *You Only Live Once*) began filming—not in Italy, but Hollywood. After filming wrapped in November, Sylvia mentioned the prospect of her and Henry Fonda doing another Technicolor feature. "We understand our 'boss' Walter Wanger is going to reunite us in *Arabian Nights*," she enthused, "which probably will be filmed in Italy."[46] Wanger's dream of producing in Rome eventually came to a standstill. By the time Mussolini's son visited Hollywood in the fall of 1937, Il Duce was consulting with Hitler. Hollywood's relationship with Nazi Germany had already crumbled and the Anti-Nazi League made sure that the younger Mussolini got their message. He left town posthaste.[47]

(Endnotes)

1   Bennett Cerf, "Notable New Yorkers," Columbia University Libraries Oral History, October 1967

2   Bennett Cerf, "Notable New Yorkers," Columbia University Libraries Oral History, October 1967

3   Faith Service (aka Gladys Hall), "I Could Live Without Love, Says Sylvia

Sidney," *Motion Picture*, March 1933
4   Bennett Cerf, "Notable New Yorkers," Columbia University Libraries Oral History, October 1967
5   Bennett Cerf, "Notable New Yorkers," Columbia University Libraries Oral History, October 1967
6   Jeff Laffel, "Sylvia Sidney," *Films in Review*, September/October, 1994
7   Bennett Cerf, "Notable New Yorkers," Columbia University Libraries Oral History, October 1967
8   Arthur Bell, "Sylvia's Souvenirs," *New York Times*, December 17, 1972
9   Bennett Cerf, "Notable New Yorkers," Columbia University Libraries Oral History, October 1967
10 Bennett Cerf, "Notable New Yorkers," Columbia University Libraries Oral History, October 1967
11 Bennett Cerf, "Notable New Yorkers," Columbia University Libraries Oral History, January 1968
12 Bennett Cerf, "Notable New Yorkers," Columbia University Libraries Oral History, January 1968
13 Rudy Behlmer, *Henry Hathaway*, Scarecrow, c.2001, p. 138
14 Jeff Laffel, "Sylvia Sidney," *Films in Review*, September/October 1994
15 Gregory J.M. Catsos, "Sylvia Sidney," *Filmfax*, November 1990
16 Bee Bangs, "Solving the MacMurray Mystery," *Screenland*, February 1945
17 Charles Tranberg, *Fred MacMurray-A Biography*, BearManor, c. 2007, pg. 44
18 D. Mark Key, review of *Trail of the Lonesome Pine*, January 2, 1938
19 Charles Dennis, interview with Henry Fonda, *Toronto Telegram*, April 1966
20 Gregory J.M. Catsos, "Sylvia Sidney," *Filmfax*, November 1990
21 Gregory D. Black, *Hollywood Censored*, Cambridge University Pr., c. 1996, pg. 265 (In one interview, Sidney erroneously reported that *Fury* was based on the lynching of an innocent black man)
22 "Comments Laud Rolph," *San Diego Union*, November 28, 1933
23 Sidney Skolsky, "Hollywood," *Augusta Chroncle*, June 12, 1936
24 James Curtis, *Spencer Tracy: A Biography*, Knopf Doubleday, c. 2011, pg. 283
25 Jeff Laffel, "Sylvia Sidney," *Films in Review*, September/October 1994
26 James Curtis, *Spencer Tracy: A Biography*, Knopf Doubleday, c. 2011, pg. 284
27 Graham Greene, review of *Fury*, *World Film News*, August 1936
28 Barry Keith Grant, *Fritz Lang: Interviews*, University Press of Mississippi, c. 2003, pg. 103
29 Barry Keith Grant, *Fritz Lang: Interviews*, University Press of Mississippi, c.

2003, pg. 104

30 John J. Kelly, "Sylvia Is Back, Just As She Said," *Plain Dealer*, September 19, 1937
31 Elizabeth Wilson, "Interviewing Stars," *Silver Screen*, July 1936
32 "Talkie Town Tattler," *Motion Picture*, August 1936
33 Donald Spoto, *The Dark Side of Genius: The Life of Alfred Hitchcock*, Da Capo Pr., c. 1999, pg. 156
34 Stiles Dickenson, "Paris – London," *Screenland*, August 1936
35 Hettie Grimstead, "Why Dietrich Waited for Donat," *Screenland*, February 1937
36 Charles Bennett, *Hitchcock's Partner in Suspense: The Life of Screenwriter Charles Bennett*, University Press of Kentucky, c. 2014, pg. 71
37 Charlotte Chandler, *It's Only a Movie: Alfred Hitchcock A Personal Biography*, Simon & Schuster, c. 2008
38 Ivor Montague, "Working with Hitchcock," *Sight and Sound*, Vol. 49, Issue 3, 1980
39 Donald Spoto, *Spellbound by Beauty: Alfred Hitchcock and His Leading Ladies*, Random House, c. 2008, pg. 72 (Conversation October 23, 1984)
40 Peter Bogdanovich, *Who the Devil Made It: Conversations with Legendary Film Directors*, Knopf, c. 1997 (Interviews with Hitchcock took place January 1961, February 1963, August 1966, May 1972)
41 Patrick McGilligan, *Backstory: Interviews with Screenwriters of Hollywood's Golden Age*, University of California Press, c. 1986, pgs. 28-29
42 Jeff Laffel, "Sylvia Sidney," *Film in Review*, September-October 1994
43 Charlotte Chandler, *It's Only a Movie: Alfred Hitchcock A Personal Biography*, Simon & Schuster, c. 2008
44 Marylynn Uricchio, "Sylvia Sidney: a real pro for the Public Theater," *Pittsburgh Post-Gazette*, September 28, 1984
45 Matthew Bernstein, *Walter Wanger: Hollywood Independent*, Univ. of California Pr., c. 1994, pg. 127
46 Sylvia Sidney, "Studio Storms Too Realistic for Sylvia," *Lodi News-Sentinel*, December 31, 1936
47 David Welky, *The Moguls and the Dictators: Hollywood and the Coming of World War II*, JHU Press, c. 2008, pg. 52

Dead End - Sylvia thought Joel McCrea "an absolutely beautiful man" (below) with kid brother Billy Halop. "I was always ironing somebody's shirt," Sylvia would complain. (Samuel Goldwyn)

Chapter 7
Hollywood: Dead End

The exploits of Bonnie Parker and Clyde Barrow made headlines before they were gunned down by the law in May 1934. For their numerous robberies and killings, the duo gained a celebrity status. Public Enemy Number One, John Dillinger, was unimpressed. Learning of their demise, he snapped, "They were kill-crazy punks and clod-hoppers, bad news to decent bank robbers. They gave us a bad name."[1] *You Only Live Once*, the first Hollywood treatment for Bonnie and Clyde, starred Sylvia Sidney and Henry Fonda. Prior to Sylvia's voyage to England, Walter Wanger suggested that she tackle the role of Bonnie Parker. "I had visions of myself as a really wonderful character actress doing that kind of role," Sidney recalled. "I imagined me with a cigar in my mouth and standing against a car with a machine gun like in that popular photo of Bonnie."[2]

When filming began, director Fritz Lang called the cast together so he could act out each part himself. Sylvia warned Fonda, "You haven't seen anything, yet." Lang used Fonda's anger to create tension on the set. Sidney elaborated,

> Fritz would take me across the set from where Fonda was sitting and whisper in my ear. He had a thermos with home-

made soup in it and he would pour some for me. Fonda assumed that Fritz was giving me preferential treatment; giving me extra coaching. Well, Fonda would fume and mutter, 'That son of a bitch,' while all Fritz was doing was telling me how he had made the soup. And Fonda ... gave one hell of a performance.³

Years afterward, Sidney expressed disappointment in the film, stating, "I must say that by the time Wanger was finished with the story, he had taken a great deal of the life out of it."⁴ She complained that the parts had been romanticized. "We were two people in love on the run," she said, "*victims* of circumstances rather than creators."⁵ Henry Fonda's only gripe was about the autocratic Fritz Lang. In 1966, Fonda stated, "*You Only Live Once* was a successful picture and was a good picture. But it was absolute torture to make because Fritz Lang is and was a director who has absolutely no feeling for actors. He was a prick. He doesn't think of treating actors like human beings. They're puppets to him and he's the master puppeteer."⁶

"Master puppeteer" Lang chose to present Clyde Barrow (rechristened Eddie Taylor) as an ex-con with the odds against him, instead of a publicity-seeking thug and murderer. Lang's intent for *You Only Live Once* was to arouse audience sympathy. Eddie tries to go straight, but is railroaded back to prison for a murder he didn't commit. Sidney's role as Eddie's wife (Joan) was another reinvention. Joan, employed as a secretary for the Public Defender, is a complete innocent about life. After Eddie spends five months in a death cell, Joan, having lost faith in the system, supplies him with a gun, which is intercepted by the prison Chaplain (William Gargan). Eddie still managers to break out of prison—but with blood on his hands. The young couple flee to Canada

Cinema's original Bonnie and Clyde: Sidney and Fonda in *You Only Live Once* (United Artists)

only to have their car riddled with bullets (the fate of the *real* Bonnie & Clyde). During their escape, the media blames them for every crime in the country. Joan's heartfelt pledge to Eddie, "We're going on together. We have a right to live!"—isn't easily forgotten. (Following the film's premier, Sidney stated that she was against capital punishment.)[7]

In Lang's view, Eddie and Joan are escaping a callous "civilization" designed to protect a privileged few. In the Depression Era it was either the "system" or the narrow-minded "mob"—a world with no real heroes. At the finish, Eddie and Joan are liberated from earthly justice. "I think every serious picture [that] depicts people today should be a kind of documentary of its time," said Lang. "Only then … can you get the quality of truth into a picture."[8] This was the clue to Lang's unvarnished realism on screen.

Sidney's portrayal of Joan received nothing but plaudits from the critics. In New York, Howard Barnes was full of praise: "Miss Sidney plays with splendid understanding and emotional depth. The portrait is stamped with tragedy almost from the first, but it is human and always in character." *Photoplay* awarded "Best Performances of the Month" to Sidney and Fonda, placing the film in the "Best Picture" category, calling Lang's direction "even finer than in the much vaunted *Fury*." David O. Selznick telegrammed Lang to say, "I think it one of the greatest directorial jobs ever seen."

You Only Live Once did not fare well at the box-office. The grim subject matter wasn't for everyone. The *San Francisco Chronicle* nodded to the "superbly and tautly directed film" but described it as "relentless and almost painfully realistic" before arriving at its "cheerless conclusion." Wanger wrote to Lang admitting, "I'm afraid the general reaction is that our picture is a little heavy for what they call 'entertainment' in this country."[9] Like fine wine, *You Only Live Once* aged well. James Robert Parish noted in 1972, "In subsequent years, *You Only Live Once* gained considerable repute as an unheralded little masterpiece."

Sidney reflected later, "I enjoyed working with Henry Fonda. He was a wonderful actor, very natural. He'd say, 'Don't let the audience recognize that you're acting. Conceal your acting so they totally accept you as your character, and forget that they're watching a movie!'"[10] On a side note, Lang wanted to include the ironic touch of Sidney purchasing Lucky Strike cigarettes (Bonnie Parker's favorite) to give Fonda prior to being ambushed. Since that constituted advertising, it wasn't allowed. In 1945, Sidney and Fonda reprised their roles for radio's *Screen Guild Theatre*. In 1968, Sidney was her usual blunt self when asked about Arthur Penn's *Bonnie and Clyde* (1967) starring Warren Beatty and Faye Dunaway. "*That's* even worse," she railed. "I went to see it because I was interested—I don't see many movies—and there's that opening shot of a dame [Dunaway] with the most colossal teeth-capping job I've ever seen. And I don't think that I'm a prude ... but I've just never had any desire to peek into other people's bedrooms."[11] Penn's landmark film broke many cinematic taboos, and took the liberty of implying that Clyde Barrow was impotent.

In December 1936, Sylvia headed to New York for a month-long stay. She returned to Hollywood briefly to make an appearance at the Shrine Auditorium along with guest lecturer Ernst Toller, a German exile and playwright. Toller revealed to a crowd of 5,000, the rising threat of Nazism and the danger of Hitler's "vast machine of war." Sylvia spoke on behalf of the Hollywood Anti-Nazi League. She returned to New York and spent time attending plays with good friends like critic George Jean Nathan. Her travel routine was repeated in February. Volleying back and forth reflected her state of mind. Sidney was ready to leave Hollywood for good. Time out in Cuba gave her neutral territory in which to reflect. In the interim she witnessed the success of a new play, *Having Wonderful Time*. The previous summer, playwright Arthur Kober and producer Marc Connelly had offered Sidney the lead opposite John Garfield, but film commitments interfered. She suggested they hire her friend Katherine Locke, who would garner positive reviews and a real career boost thanks to Sylvia.

In March, Sidney signed (at $75,000) to play opposite Joel McCrea in a film version of the Broadway success, *Dead End*. Adapted for the screen by Lillian Hellman, the film became a classic of Depression realism. Producer Samuel Goldwyn insisted from the start that Sidney was to play Drina. The role was similar to her Rose Maurrant in Goldwyn's *Street Scene*—a soulful-eyed tenement girl determined to leave the slums. Sylvia's only reluctance was in working with director William Wyler.

In May 1937, *Variety* reported that Sylvia had injured her face at the Elizabeth Arden salon. She had fallen upon a glass table and was found lying on the floor. She was rushed to Cedars of Lebanon Hospital. According to Sylvia, she was exhausted from working so late on the set of *Dead End*. "I became faint, slipped and fell smack on my nose," she recalled. "Both my eyes turned black and blue. Within an hour, I was lying terrified in a hospital bed. Through the entire night, Walter Wanger paced the floor. After all, I was a Hollywood investment."[12] Sylvia returned to the set sporting an eye-patch. The cast of teenage boys called "Dead End Kids," stood around and gaped at her. "I looked more like a Dead End Kid than they did," she mused. Her forehead was sutured (18 stitches) and heavily bandaged. "That's a movie star?" Wyler shouted as she walked on stage. As soon as Goldwyn got word of what was going on, he flew down to the set to announce that he was driving her home. Goldwyn assured Sylvia that he would keep her on salary until she fully recovered.[13]

When filming commenced, Wyler kept Sylvia on the verge of tears. "He needled me and needled me," she recalled, "and he knew I had a concussion and my nose hurt. But that didn't stop him. He'd do thirty or forty takes of the same scene." She had trouble remembering her lines and Wyler's "technique" was undermining her confidence. She grew to despise him. Sidney would moan to Goldwyn, "I hate this goddamned picture!"[14] To make matters worse, after one strenuous day's shoot, Wyler was in hot pursuit of his leading lady. When Wyler biographer Jan Herman interviewed Sidney in 1990, she recounted,

Wyler was ... a sadistic son-of-a-bitch. He had a habit of treating you badly and then trying to make love to you. At least that was my experience with him. He was not nice to me on the set. But he tried very hard to get into bed with me. I had a wonderful little hideaway in Palos Verdes, and he showed up there one night. It was after we had a fight and I left the set. I just tore down to the beach. I guess he thought I was alone. Fortunately, Luther Adler was there with me. Nobody knew I was having an affair with Luther. If it hadn't been for him, I might have ended up in the crazy house. Wyler almost put me there.[15]

One day Adler was on the set. Wyler informed Sidney, "I can get an actress for $150 a week to do a better job than you're doing!" Adler, fuming, walked over to Wyler, grabbed a hold of him, and ordered, "Don't you *dare* talk to a talented person that way!" "Wyler left me alone after that," said Sylvia. The spurned Wyler had to wait a few months to satisfy his sexual desire in the arms of leading lady Bette Davis. While filming *Jezebel*, she was most compliant. "I adored Willie," cooed Davis. "He was the only male strong enough to control me. The sexual sparks were there from the beginning."[16]

As Sidney indicated, her affair with thirty-four-year-old Luther Adler was a godsend. Luther, also under contract with Walter Wanger, was in Hollywood for his film debut in the drama *Lancer Spy*. Adler came from a Yiddish theatrical dynasty, and was one of the founding members of the Group Theatre (1931), a primarily left-wing troupe of players producing plays dealing with social issues. The Group revolutionized American Theater by infusing it with "realism." *Dead End* fit in perfectly with the Group Theatre dynamic.

Kingsley's 1935 play *Dead End*, minus a few choice obscenities, spitting, prostitution, and syphilis, translated into relevant social commentary on screen. Along a dead end street on New York's East River, poverty thrives—only a block away from the shadow of luxury, wealth and power. The story (which takes place in 24 hours) focuses on Drina (Sidney), a shopgirl, footsore from walking the picket line for higher wages. "It's money that's coming to me for hard work!" she tells her younger brother (Billy Halop) who she is trying to raise and keep out of trouble. Drina's romantic attachment to Dave (Joel McCrea), an unemployed architect, is threatened by his infatuation with the courtesan (Wendy Barrie) of a wealthy racketeer. Real trouble begins when Dave recognizes the notorious gangster Baby Face Martin (Humphrey Bogart)—a local boy who made it big by being bad. Slum kids see Baby Face as a hero, whereas Dave, as Baby Face puts it, is "a sap working for peanuts." Lillian Hellman's scenario was keyed to enhance the dramatic contrast between helpless squalor and excessive riches. (Kingsley and Hellman —both liberals—were advocates of slum reform.)

The "Dead End Kids" (from the original Broadway cast) were a sensation upon the film's release. Their faces told unprintable things—they were the "real stuff." Wyler saw himself as their mentor and gave them preferential treatment—taking them for rides on his motorcycle. Wyler was also chummy with Bogart. Their only altercation was during the scene between Baby Face Martin and his mother (Marjorie Main). Following her line "You dirty rotten bum," she slaps him. There were numerous takes, and Main never held back. As Bogart's face began to swell, he turned to Wyler and fumed, "If she slaps me one more time, I'm going to wipe up the floor with her."[17] Joel McCrea, at odds with Wyler's tactics, recalled that the director "tended to look out for one or two actors in a picture, and ... shit on the rest."[18]

Sidney's opinion of Bogart was less than enthusiastic. "I'd known

Bogart from way before, when he was a very bad 'juvenile' in the theater. He was a *mean* young man, and ended up a rather mean *old* man. But that was his nature."[19]

Dead End received four Academy Award nominations, including Best Picture. *Variety* found Wyler's direction "faultless" and praised the leading lady. "Miss Sidney is excellent. Her sister-and-brother scenes are tender, moving and tragic." Dallas critic John Rosenfeld thought the film "one of the superior releases of the year. Miss Sidney again plays tragic womanhood with just the right blend of romance and realism. She is not to be excelled in such an assignment."

That fall, Sidney finally sat through *Dead End* at New York's Rivoli Theatre. "I have a phobia about seeing myself on the screen," she said afterward, "it makes me sick. I was sitting there loathing myself when the woman back of me said to her companion, 'Look at her. What a deadpan! That's what Hollywood does to a person. No expression.' From then on whenever I came on the screen she sniffed, 'Deadpan.' Finally when the lights came on ... I turned around and stared. When she recognizes me, I said to myself, I will slap her down." The woman (apparently) didn't bat an eye. Sylvia mused, "When your public doesn't even recognize you, you can't get grand with them!"[20] When asked about *Dead End* decades later, she replied, "I ironed shirts and made goo-goo eyes at Joel McCrea, who was an absolutely beautiful man."[21]

While filming *Dead End,* Sidney took a break (May 28) to appear once more at the Shrine Auditorium. Several organizations banded together to fight the potential boycott of film stars whose political biases leaned left. "They were tired of being called Communists, Reds and other names," reported *Variety*. A resolution drawn by scenarist Herbert Biberman received support from actors contributing to various anti-Nazi causes, such as raising funds for medical aid in Republican Spain's battle against fascism. Both Sylvia (as vice-chairman of the Motion Picture Artists Committee) and playwright Clifford Odets had already donated ambulances. Speakers at the Shrine included Spanish Ambassador Fernando de los Rio, Father Michael O'Flannagan of Dublin, and Sylvia Sidney. Some of Sylvia's Hollywood friends objected when she participated in such affairs. The political climate in New York, particularly among the Group Theatre, was more in tune with Sidney's—another motivation for her to leave Hollywood behind.

Sidney's long-time admirer (and ladies man) George Jean Nathan, had nudged her toward returning to the stage. Nathan, among the nation's most feared drama critics, declared, "When it comes to substantial dramatic equipment in general, there is perhaps no young woman on the screen so competent as Sylvia Sidney. Her dramatic talents, save for her beautiful performance in United Artists' *Street Scene*, are continually wasted."[22] In Nathan, Sidney had a champion and she finally heeded his advice. When the Theatre Guild offered her a lead in the message drama *To Quito and Back* (by Ben Hecht) she grabbed at the opportunity. Hecht had recently renounced Hollywood, along with his fabulous salary. *To Quito and Back* was his first solo effort since collaborating with Charles MacArthur for such uproarious hits as *The Front Page*. In August 1937, Sylvia arrived in New York for rehearsals. She enthused to reporters, "After an absence of seven years from the stage, I'm returning to my first love. Seven years is a long time—long enough to forget the differences between motion picture and stage technique. But I am excited about my part, because it's unlike anything I've ever done in pictures."

Sidney's three-room apartment on East 73rd was refurbished

To Quito and Back (1937) - with Leslie Banks.
Critics targeted "movie star" Sidney

while she filmed *Dead End*. She and her dachshund, Strudel, felt right at home. Dr. and Mrs. Sidney lived close by, as did other family members. "I don't mind supporting my relatives," volunteered Sylvia. "You have no idea how many new ones discover you when you become a picture star." Sylvia finally resigned to wearing large, silver-rimmed spectacles. "I can't see without them," she admitted, "that's all there is to it. I decided that the not-so-glamorous Sidney woman would have to come down to earth."

At a Boston tryout (September 1937), *Variety* reported that *To*

Quito and Back "glibly but artfully spread a Communistic gospel. Only those hungry for an evening of weighty words will come out raving." The three-hour plot consisted of a New York novelist (English actor Leslie Banks) who abandons his wife and runs off with his much younger secretary (Sidney) to revolution-ridden Ecuador. Uncertain of his purpose there, he deserts his secretary, only to be killed in an uprising against fascist rule. On Broadway, the play died after 46 performances. Critics took an uncalled for opportunity to aim fire at "movie star" Sylvia Sidney. *Variety* admitted that her role "came out of the rewrites as a wooden toothpick ... small, inconclusive and phoney."

Leslie Banks' line to Sidney proved prophetic, "I think we're unreal. We're here for no good reason. And we talk too much." The *New York Post* gloated, "Mr. Hecht, in writing those lines, has reviewed his own play. Miss Sidney seemed to be parroting lines whose meaning, if any, escaped her." Others felt that Sidney suffered from "movie technique." Critic George Ross summed up the overall critical reaction: "*To Quito and Back* was greeted in such vicious contempt by the reviewers that they might as well have expressed their opinions with machine guns instead of typewriters—singling out Miss Sidney for their direct hits."

Sidney shrugged off the bad notices. "Yes, some of the critics got pretty rough with me. Didn't I hate them for their reviews? No—because in most instances they were perfectly right."[23] Sidney was not the only film star to meet defeat that season. Henry Fonda's return to the stage in *Blow Ye Winds*, which critics found listless, folded after 36 performances. It was his last play for eleven years. If anything, Sylvia was more determined than ever to align herself with the Group Theatre. Now romantically linked with Luther Adler, she was eager to gain firsthand experience of the famous "method." Adler was currently offering a dazzling performance in the Group's hit *Golden Boy*.

Capping her decision to permanently relocate to the east coast, Sylvia purchased a 114-acre farm in Flemington, New Jersey. "I've bought a real farm with cows and chickens and things that grow," she enthused. "It's the only thing I've ever done to please myself—and I've worked since I was sixteen. I bought the farm because I long for harmony, peace and rest." A well-preserved brick and frame dwelling (built in 1780) with a seven-foot open fireplace was refurbished with modern improvements by the time Sylvia returned from making her Hollywood heyday swansong.

When news came that Walter Wanger had sold *Wuthering Heights* and that Merle Oberon had the lead, Sylvia was devastated. For the last year she was reading everything about the Brontes she could get her hands on. "I was dying to do it," she recalled. "The script was bought for me and Charles Boyer, but I had a terrible fight with Wanger, because I refused to do *Algiers*." *Algiers* would have also paired Sidney with Boyer, but newcomer Hedy Lamarr would have the romantic lead. "My character was just another slum girl," complained Sidney. "Even though the slums this time were the Casbah!"[24] When it came to being in the same film as Lamarr, Sidney balked, "You've gotta be kidding! I'm not putting my face up against that!"[25] In retaliation, Wanger sold *Wuthering Heights* to Goldwyn. This upset motivated Sylvia to abandon Hollywood after completing her third film for Fritz Lang.

Director Lang teamed with composer Kurt Weill (best known for *Mack the Knife*) to underscore the message in *You and Me* (1938)—a crime-does-not-pay fairytale. Photographer Charles Lang Jr. experimented with montage and camera angles. The first half of the film has an inviting, rhythmic charm that pulls you right in. Dashes of humor and an occasional dose of social commentary underscore the plight of ex-cons trying to make a go of it in a civilization that revolves around the almighty dollar.

The fantastic premise of a department store manager, Mr. Morris (Harry Carey), employing some twenty-five ex-cons as salespeople, is intriguing. We find ex-con Sylvia selling lingerie, and former gangster George Raft handling sporting goods. Their romantic feelings are obvious, but Sidney is still on parole and forbidden to sign legal contracts—such as a marriage license. They marry (illegally) anyway, though Raft is ignorant of Sylvia's criminal past. The film drags down into a weighty mix of misunderstandings. Raft's anger toward Sidney's deception is overdrawn. When Sidney lectures the ex-cons, things pick up again. She instructs them (with the help of a chalkboard) that running a department store is more profitable than robbing one (Lang's subtle comment on the joys of capitalism). The risqué ending in which Raft finds Sidney (no longer on parole) in a maternity ward after she gives birth to their son, was clever. "Joe, I've been thinking," she says. "Don't you think we ought to get married?" It brings a smile (and somehow passed the objections of the PCA), but it couldn't save *You and Me*. Lang's attempt to break the Hollywood formula felt "disjointed." "It was—I think deservedly—my first real flop," admitted Lang.[26] *The New Yorker* declared the film "the weirdest cinematic hash" ever seen.

Kurt Weill's stylistic numbers failed to gel with the rest of the film. Sidney revealed that she had specified in her contract that Weill do the score. She had a recording of Weill's *The Threepenny Opera*, knew that he was trying to establish a career after fleeing Germany, and wanted to help. Weill wrote a vocal number for Sylvia, "We're the Kind of People Who Sing Lullabies." She was delighted at the prospect and

You and Me (1938) - with George Raft and director Fritz Lang (Paramount)

began rehearsing with vocal coach Al Siegal ("discoverer" and mentor of Ethel Merman). The song was eliminated to tighten the plot. "So I suppose I'll never be a singing star," mused Sylvia. Lang later told Peter Bogdanovich, "*You and Me* was an unfortunate affair from the beginning. In the middle of the picture, Weill left. I wanted to make a picture that teaches something ... [that] life has a very peculiar way of making you pay for whatever you get."[27] Prophetically, when Lang tried to create dissension between Sidney and Raft, his "technique" backfired. Raft gave Lang an ultimatum to treat Sylvia with respect. "George almost killed him," recalled Sidney. "He was a tough pussycat, very much like his screen image."[28] As for Weill, in a letter to his wife, Lotte Lenya, he complained that the egocentric Lang, "makes you want to puke. I completely understand why he is so hated everywhere."[29]

The more Sylvia complained about Hollywood the more caustic remarks she received from vipers like Louella Parsons. In Parsons' review of *Fury* she grumbled, "You might have had almost any leading lady in place of Sylvia Sidney ... so little does she take advantage of what opportunities are offered her." Parsons summed up Sylvia's performance in *Dead End* as "incidental." Sylvia told the *Hollywood Citizen News*,

> I don't like Hollywood. I'm in a gold fish bowl every minute I'm out here, and it's no fun. In New York it's different. I can walk along the streets and nobody knows me. Even if they do recognize me, they don't pay any attention. I can live normally there, just like any other girl. Here I have to be on parade.

Shortly after Sylvia's statement, Parsons advised producer Walter Wanger to let Sidney go. "Our advice to him," she barked, "is to let her have the freedom she is asking for. No actress who ever expressed herself as being opposed to Hollywood ever helped the picture industry or herself."[30] In 1979, Sylvia took the opportunity to vent her feelings about professional snoops like Parsons and Hedda Hopper. She portrayed an aging Hollywood gossip herself in the primetime TV movie *The Gossip Columnist.*

"I shouldn't even be in Hollywood," Sidney admitted. "There is so much compromising. The man I admire more than anyone in the world is my Cousin Albert. He lives his life with complete integrity. Now he works for the Rockefeller Foundation and is completely happy. He is married to a lovely girl. They have very little money but their lives are ideal, for he is doing real work and living simply. In spite of the money, we picture people haven't a chance for real happiness. Our lives are too cluttered with nonessentials. We are living in too false a world."[31]

Upon completing *You and Me*, Sylvia reiterated her struggle with

c1935 - Albert Sabin, doing "real work" for the Rockefeller Foundation.

Hollywood to writer Nanette Kutner (former secretary to George Gershwin). Some had accused her of being a money grabber. "Listen," she said, "in my contract I'm supposed to be paid between pictures, even when I'm not working. I didn't think that was fair to my employers, so I refused sixteen weeks salary." It was a tough decision. Sidney was inundated with distant relatives demanding money. She had trouble turning them down. She had also invested in the farm. Her desire to live permanently in New York was stimulated by Luther Adler. Adler contributed greatly to her social consciousness and offered her diversified interests. He also lent a sympathetic ear. Kutner observed Sidney fighting within herself. "She tries hard, very hard," Kutner wrote, "but as long as she wages these inner battles ... ." By fall, Sidney bought out her contract with Wanger for the sum of $40,000, and moved on with her life ... and a new husband.

Luther Adler

Luther Adler was born May 4, 1903, in New York City. By the time he was five, he joined his parents on stage. Jacob and Sara Adler were major figures in Yiddish Theater. Like Sidney's parents, both were Jewish refugees. Luther and his older siblings, Jay and Stella, were raised to be devoted to the theatrical arts. For the Adlers, acting wasn't about money.

It was a sacred calling. Stella Adler put it like this: "In my family, in four generations, nobody was ever in business. I don't care who he is, Rockefeller—he's in a money game. Some of my cousins decided to be the Lerner Brothers and became multibillionaires. We always said, 'Well, there are the rich Adlers and the talented Adlers.' They never mixed." [32]

Stella pithily summed up her and Luther's relationship to their father: "He didn't have any children. He had actors." Jacob Adler was a task master, imperious, a force to be reckoned with. Luther recalled that his childhood was "miserable"—an endless round of performances in his father's repertory. Nonetheless it provided the boy with a versatile foundation for the stage. Luther's debut was in a 1908 production of the Yiddish play, *Schemdrick*. At age nine, he signed his first contract at $15 a week. He played a variety of roles, among them an aged man speaking in a cracked, faint voice—and occasionally, much to his resentment, the part of a girl. At seventeen he was in full charge of a traveling company, as manager, press agent and leading man.

Luther's Broadway debut was in *The Hand of the Potter* (1921). Often billed as "Lutha J. Adler," he impressed audiences as the young violinist in the Laurette Taylor hit, *Humoresque* (1923). *The New York Times* praised "the finely heroic vein" of Adler's performance. By 1929, he joined the cast of *Street Scene* (as the law student), and repeated his role during the Chicago run. After the ensemble Group Theatre was formed Luther and Stella co-starred in their production of *Success Story* (1932). Playing a volcanic Jewish youth, Luther's first real lead on Broadway was considered a triumph.

Stella augmented her stage skill studying the Stanislavsky "method" with Maria Ouspenskaya, and later in Paris, with Stanislavsky himself. From this profound experience, she evolved into an actress of unique power and was considered to be the best drama teacher in New York.

Luther and Stella Adler (publicity shot for *Awake and Sing*)

It was Stella who would discover the "quivering mass of sensitivities" in young Marlon Brando, who always gave her credit for providing him with a base to build his art, or as he put it, "how to be real." Luther and Stella carried the Adler theatrical legacy into new venues that reflected the times, and both made substantial impact on an art they had inherited.

Sidney first saw Luther on stage. "I saw him in a play—and once wasn't enough," she recalled in a 1941 interview. "I kept going back to see him. I thought he was the greatest young actor I had ever looked upon. But my repeated visits started talk backstage. People kept telling him 'Sylvia Sidney's out front again.' I was having lunch in Sardi's, when he came over and introduced himself, with the intention of finding out whether or not I was a case for a psychiatrist." The duo spent a great deal of time talking about acting and plays. In so doing, Sylvia experienced a wakeup call to the world around her.

It wasn't long before Adler proposed marriage. "What would you do if I said yes?" Sylvia asked. "I'd faint," he replied. "Someday," she smiled, "you're going to faint." In the interim, Adler received acclaim for what was perhaps his most famous role for the Group Theatre—*Golden Boy* (1937), co-starring Frances Farmer, who had recently abandoned Hollywood for the stage. As Joe Bonaparte, Adler played a young man torn between big money in boxing, or pursuing his dream as a violinist. Luther understood the author Clifford Odets' intention and offered a dazzling portrayal. Besides working out at the gym for his role, Adler also had his nose reshaped.

Prior to the London premier of *Golden Boy* (June 1938), Luther and Sylvia agreed to marry in England, on her birthday. On board the *Queen Mary*, Sylvia realized that she had forgotten her divorce papers from Bennett Cerf. She cabled to get the proper documents for the Caxton Hall Registry. The Sidney-Adler nuptials were delayed until August 13, 1938, at 8 a.m. sharp. Adler had (indelicately) inquired as to the earliest possible time that they could "get it over with." Bill O'Bryen (producer of *Golden Boy*) stood in as witness. Sylvia was dressed in brown with a large blue hat. Adler wore a grey business suit. Records from Dade County, Florida indicate that while Sylvia was beginning a new marriage, her mother Beatrice was in the process of ending hers with Dr. Sidney.[33] Sylvia made no official comment on the dissolution of their marriage. Beatrice leased an apartment at Central Park West, and Dr. Sidney moved in with his brother's family. He would remarry and settle in Queens, before his death in 1961.

"After the ceremony," said Sylvia, "Luther wouldn't talk to me for

**September 1, 1938 - Mr. & Mrs. Adler
arrive in New York on the SS *Champlain***

a half-hour. Said I sounded like a movie actress, giving my responses." Luther's attitude was a precursor to the kind of nonsense Sidney would have to put up with from others involved with Group Theatre. "My husband," Sylvia admitted, "has the world's most perverted sense of humor. He has given me some of the worst half-hours of my life. Life is never dull with Luther. He's a man of mad, mad impulses."

When the successful London run of *Golden Boy* closed, Luther and Sylvia crossed the Channel to Paris. After a brief honeymoon, they boarded the *Champlain*, arriving in New York on September 1. Two weeks later, Luther joined the touring company, and it wasn't long before the new Mrs. Adler was making a feature film, *One Third of a Nation*. For this, she did not return to Hollywood. From September

27 through early November, Sylvia joined cast members Leif Erickson, Sidney Lumet, Myron McCormick and director Dudley Murphy at the old Astoria studio on Long Island.

One Third of a Nation was the first play written for the Works Progress Association (WPA)—President Roosevelt's New Deal agency. The WPA provided jobs for millions of unemployed workers. Besides constructing roads and bridges, the WPA employed those involved in the arts. The film's title was taken from Roosevelt's second inaugural address: "I see one-third of a nation ill-housed, ill-clad, ill-nourished ... ." With a modest budget of $200,000, the crudely made, politically radical film had its pluses.

On screen, Sidney found herself (once more) as a shopgirl living in a substandard, dead end tenement with her unemployed father, mother and teenaged brother Joey (Sidney Lumet). A fire breaks out. Joey is seriously injured falling from a faulty fire escape. The wealthy tenement owner, Peter Cortlant (Leif Erickson), happens to be on the scene. Unaware that he *owns* the building, Erickson pays for Joey's hospital treatment which leaves the boy on crutches ... for life. A hearing at the D.A.'s office declares that no one is responsible for the fire, or resulting deaths, in spite of evidence that the tenement is a firetrap. The landlord is exempt from prosecution. After the verdict, Sidney's friend Sam, who doesn't like rich people, smirks "Capitalist Democracy!" Sidney, with her customary force, offers Erickson her own prosecution, "Your lousy tenements breed criminals and sick people and you don't know what kind of women. That's where some of your rent comes, Mr. Cortlant!"

In due time, Erickson develops a social conscience—he becomes de-

One Third of a Nation (1939) with Myron McCormick (Paramount)

termined to build new housing, which will be up to code. The crippled brother however, wants revenge. He burns down his enemy, the tenement, losing his own life in the process. The film offered grim images of charred bodies, a burning man leaping to his death, and earnest commentary underscoring how out of touch rich people are with the poor. Except for director Murphy's unfortunate use of flashback to detail a cholera epidemic, the film holds its own—a cinematic editorial of the Depression era.

The *New York World-Telegram* reported that when a rough-cut version was screened for the film's backers (a group of prominent bankers), one gentleman was outraged upon seeing a newsreel clip from Roosevelt's speech "I see one-third of the nation ... ." "This is New Deal propaganda," he yelled. "Strike that scene out!" It was cut. Impassioned dialogue such as: "Balance the budget? What with? Human lives? Misery? Disease? What was the appropriation for the army and navy for the last four years?"—all omitted from the screenplay. With numerous reshoots to avoid censorship, *One Third of a Nation* still ended up on the lower half of theater marquees.

The *New York Times* felt *One Third of a Nation* was "sensibly and vividly told by a diligent cast," adding that it contained "no appeal to government to correct the slum situation—except the mute appeal embodied in a grim picture." The critique nodded to "Sylvia Sidney for her vibrant and glowing performance." Although the end result was less than perfect, the film's vision of capital and labor working together still carries a palpable sense of grievance. In 2012, Kyle Westphal, Vice President of the Northwest Chicago Film Society, referred to *One Third of a Nation* as "a curious version of an extraordinarily important piece of American theatrical history." Sylvia herself commented, "[it] looked better on paper than it did on celluloid."

Sidney Lumet, who played Sidney's young brother would go on to direct such Academy Award-winning films as *The Pawnbroker*. In a *Rolling Stone* interview with Lumet, one of film industry's "warmest humanitarians" according to critic Roger Ebert, the director peppered his responses with numerous f-bombs. He commented on director Dudley Murphy, and offered ungracious remarks about his twenty-eight-year-old co-star, Sylvia Sidney.

> The director was maddening. And he knew nothing about actors or working with them. The star was Sylvia Sidney, who, you'll pardon my speaking badly of the dead, was a nasty old cunt. When it was time for my close-up, the director said, "Please give him the lines, instead of the script girl." She was so resentful that, she sat there clicking her knitting needles. Not one look at me. Just mumbling. The whole experience was lousy.[34]

Sylvia had admitted to being temperamental. When things didn't go smoothly, she was annoyed. "I got myself greatly disliked," she said. "But now—well, now I keep my mouth shut, and my hands busy

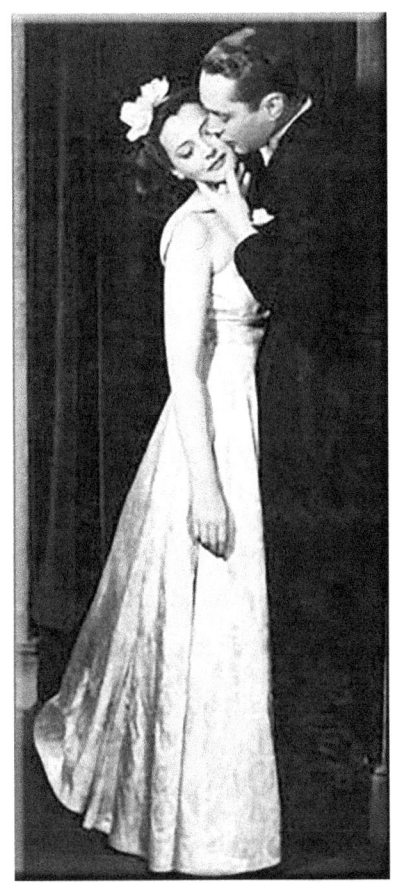

The Gentle People (1939) with Franchot Tone

with knitting needles."35 And, as Lumet pointed out, an abundance of mumbling. Perhaps Sidney still hadn't forgiven director Murphy for coming on to her during *Confessions of a Co-Ed.* As far as her young co-star, Sylvia would comment, "Sidney Lumet was destined to grow up to be a fine director."36

Shortly before her marriage to Adler, Sidney had performed as Eliza Doolittle in Shaw's *Pygmalion* on Cape Cod. Associate producer Richard Aldrich was impressed with Sidney's ability to play comedy. Eliza was a role Sylvia would perform numerous times during the 1940's. Soon after her marriage, Group Theatre founder/director, Harold Clurman, urged Sylvia to join them for their production, *The Gentle People.* She accepted Clurman's offer (at $150 per week), seeing it as an opportunity to enrich her skill for serious stage work. She would soon learn otherwise.

Much of the action in Irwin Shaw's *The Gentle People,* took place on a fishing boat moored at Coney Island. Sidney played Stella, the daughter of a Jewish lens grinder (Sam Jaffe) who owns the boat along with his crony, a Greek chef. When a racketeer named Goff (Franchot Tone) threatens the two harmless fishermen to pay "protection money" for the boat, they have no choice. To make matters worse, Goff seduces the gullible, unhappy Stella, who is growing tired of her boyfriend (Elia Kazan). Stella informs Goff that her father is saving up money for a new boat. Goff demands he hand it over. As a last resort, the two fishermen take Goff "for a ride." They bash him over the head, toss him overboard, in what *The New York Sun* called, "one of the most ludicrous murder scenes of recent stage history." The critic complained, "glaring improbability is the result. But the flaws are not the fault of the actors."

As for the "glaring improbability"—playwright Shaw subtitled his play "A Brooklyn Fable"—a fantasy. *The New York Times* praised, "Sylvia Sidney gives a beautiful, shining performance. Franchot Tone ... lacks something of the menacing hardness that would pull the whole play together and give it bite." In spite of being knocked around by the critics, word-of-mouth kept *The Gentle People* going for 141 performances, before closing at the Belasco in May, 1939.

Sidney was not pleased with her role, or her treatment by director Clurman. During private rehearsals, he excluded Sylvia from attending. She confronted him. "Look, I'm not doing anything with this part. I've been playing this kind of part in films, for which I get an awful lot of money. What the hell am I doing here?"[37] Clurman told her to relax. "All we want," he snipped, "is the Sylvia Sidney personality projected in the movies." Sylvia got the gist of his message—she was a box-office draw, and she resented it. So did Group Theatre actresses, who were bitter that outsiders like Sidney got the lead roles. Franchot Tone, who had left the Group Theatre in 1933, was looking forward to the camaraderie he had missed in Hollywood—but, only found hostility towards a production aimed at commercial success with "movie stars" in the leads.

Sylvia called her character, Stella, "a chippie from Brooklyn, with silver nail polish. All I did was rush back and forth putting on those silver fingernails, then hiding in the wings, wiping it off for the next act." Elia Kazan fell victim to Sidney's displeasure with the play. "I had a love scene with Sylvia Sidney," he recalled years later, "one I didn't enjoy playing, because the lady didn't interest me that way. She wasn't taken with me either; when we had to kiss, she'd leap up at me and bite me on the lips."[38] In the aftermath, the two were never on speaking terms. In 1941, Warner Bros. released a film version, *Out of the Fog*, starring John Garfield and Ida Lupino in the Tone and Sidney roles.

In a 1933 interview with Gladys Hall, Franchot Tone confessed to having been "seriously in love" with a Broadway co-star. "We didn't marry, because I felt it would be unfair to the girl," he explained. "She was very talented. She had a big career ahead of her. We broke it off and she has gone on, as I knew she would. She is a very successful star right now." Hall wagered, "I had a sneaking suspicion that this girl ... was none other than our own Sylvia Sidney."[39] Tone and Sidney's teaming in 1929's *Crossroads* was the clue. Now, ten years later, the simpatico remained intact. During the run of *The Gentle People* Sylvia and Franchot, both active in the battle to protect the WPA, flew together to Washington D.C. They presented President Roosevelt with 200,000 signatures (many from Group members) protesting budget cuts which affected the Federal Theatre Project. The two co-stars also hosted a cocktail fund-raiser for Committee of 56—actors lobbying for a total boycott of German trade—a push for government to take a stand against Nazism. This was in the aftermath of the deadly *Kristallnacht* riots. Throughout Nazi Germany, Jewish shops, homes

Lovers reunited? Sylvia and Franchot team to promote The Federal Theatre Project, and co-host a fundraiser to boycott German trade

and synagogues were burned and looted. Over 30,000 Jews were incarcerated in concentration camps.

On a lighter note, Sylvia participated in a testimonial for Luther's mother, Sara, celebrating her 50 years on stage. The eighty-year-old distinguished tragedienne performed the third act of Tolstoy's *Resurrection* for guests in attendance at the National Theatre.

During the summer of 1939, the Group Theatre troupe went to the country to study and prepare for the upcoming season. They could do this because of the financial gain from *The Gentle People*. During the hiatus, there evolved a complex tangle of personal and professional discontents. Sylvia was horrified by the way group members treated each other. Any admiration she felt for the ensemble spirit quickly vanished. As things unraveled, Franchot Tone became as disillusioned as Sylvia. In disgust, Sidney left for her farm in Flemington. Group members told Adler "that his wife was selfish."[40]

The stress of Group life wore on Sylvia. She was treated badly and doubted that Luther's association with them was good for his career. Theater historian Helen Krich Chinoy, author of *Group Theatre: Passion, Politics, and Performance in the Depression Era*, noted, "although Sylvia admired the acting of leading players, she became bitter about the Group's leaders and found the men destructive to talented, intelligent artists like Frances Farmer." Many Group members felt that Farmer's downward spiral into alcohol and mental illness was a result of playwright Clifford Odets' cruelty following their extramarital fling.[41] "Of course we were used," Sidney acknowledged, later. "They took lives and just broke them up."

In hindsight, it was the right decision for Sidney to leave the jealousy, contention and "brilliance," of the Group behind. During the run of *The Gentle People*, she missed several performances. *Variety* reported that she missed the final performance due to a "slight illness." Aside from being unhappy with the play, and her relationship with the Group, Sylvia felt miserable. Was it morning sickness? Indeed, she and Luther were expecting their first child.

Sylvia began a campaign. She would tell people, "The baby is on its way. I have to save." When Stella Adler learned of her sister-in-law's pregnancy she advised, "If you're going to start saving, you'd better save for a new nose for the baby!"—an obvious pan at brother Luther's prominent proboscis prior to his operation. Stella had her own nose bobbed before her movie debut in 1937. She was asked by Paramount to have her name altered to "Stella Ardler." The *Jewish Chronicle* reported, "Name changing is in style again among Jewish screen actors ... Stella Adler will henceforth be called Stella Ardler, to keep pace with her change in nose." Marlon Brando observed in Stella, "a marvelous actress who unfortunately never got a chance to become a great star, and I think this embittered her."[42]

While awaiting her "new arrival," Sylvia kept busy at the farmhouse by making hooked rugs and petit point covers for chairs. She was surprised by the exorbitant cost and poor selection of hooked rugs, and became determined to make her own. After searching through museums and art galleries for ideas, she met a curator at the Metropolitan Museum of Art who selected and repaired rugs for their collection. From this woman, Sylvia received valuable insight and technique. Sylvia's intrepid pursuit for achieving the "authentic look" of colonial rug hooking spoke volumes about her attitude toward things that really *meant* something to her—such as her technique as an actress—and, before long, her devotion as a mother.

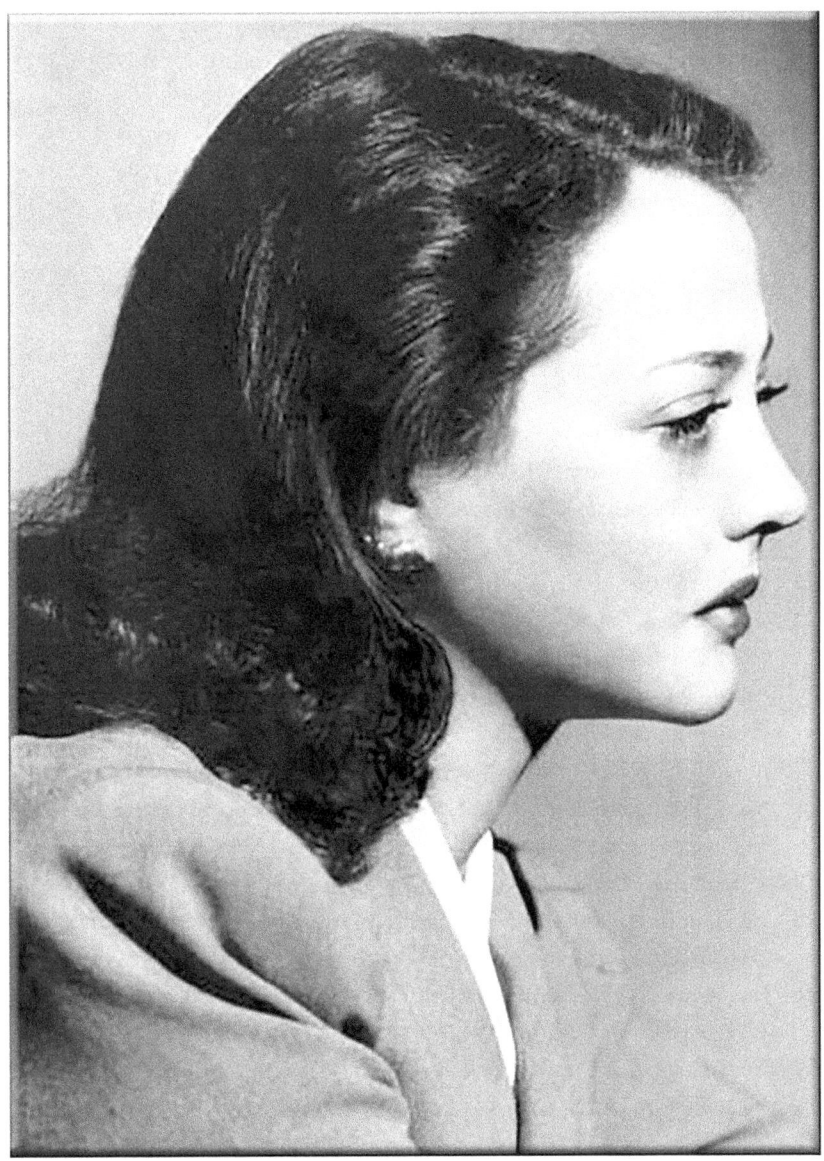

1939 - Facing a return to the stage, and .... motherhood

(Endnotes)

1. Kerry Seagrave, *Women Serial and Mass Murderers*, McFarland, c. 1992, pg. 231
2. Gregory J.M. Catsos, "Sylvia Sidney," *Filmfax*, November 1990
3. Jeff Laffel, "Sylvia Sidney," *Film in Review*, September-October 1994
4. Jeff Laffel, "Sylvia Sidney," *Films in Review*, September/October 1994
5. Arthur Bell, "Sylvia's Souvenirs," *New York Times*, December 17, 1972
6. Charles Dennis, article on Henry Fonda, *Toronto Telegram*, 1966
7. Jay Carmody, "Sylvia Sidney Cast Again In Hunted Woman Role, *Evening Star*, January 26, 1937
8. Gene D. Phillips, *Gangsters and GMen on Screen*, Rowman & Littlefield, c. 2014, pg. 86
9. Walter Wanger letter to Fritz Lang, dated March 8, 1937 (www.afi.com)
10. Gregory J.M. Catsos, "Sylvia Sidney," *Filmfax*, November 1990
11. Emerson Beauchamp, "Memory Lane Is Not Her Street," *Evening Star*, March 28, 1968
12. Nanette Kutner, "Hollywood is not for Me!" *Modern Screen*, July 1938
13. A. Scott Berg, *Goldwyn: A Biography*, Simon and Schuster, c. 2013, pg 291 (Berg's biography, and others repeat the story that filming was to begin in February 1937, but put on hold due to Sidney's accident. Sidney did not sign on for the film until mid-March 1937. Her accident at the salon took place at the end of April. *Dead End* began shooting in May) (Louella Parsons, in her May 1st column, incorrectly reported that the fall took place at the studio and required only 6 stitches)
14. A. Scott Berg, *Goldwyn: A Biography*, Simon and Schuster, c. 2013, pg. 291
15. Jan Herman, *A Talent for Trouble: The Life of Hollywood's Most Acclaimed Director, William Wyler*, Da Capo Press, c. 1997, pgs 169-170
16. Jan Herman, *A Talent for Trouble: The Life of Hollywood's Most Acclaimed Director, William Wyler*, Da Capo Press, c. 1997, pgs 177
17. Jan Herman, *A Talent for Trouble: The Life of Hollywood's Most Acclaimed Director, William Wyler*, Da Capo Press, c. 1997, pgs 171
18. A. Scott Berg, *Goldwyn: A Biography*, Knopf, c. 1989, pg. 270
19. Gregory J.M. Catsos, "Sylvia Sidney," *Filmfax*, November 1990
20. Daniel Tharnton, "Bloody But Unbowed," *Screenland*, May 1938
21. Jeff Laffel, "Sylvia Sidney," *Films in Review*, September/October 1994
22. Douglas Gilbert, "George Jean Nelson's Movie Favorites," *New Movie Magazine*, February 1935
23. Daniel Tharnton, "Bloody But Unbowed," *Screenland*, May 1938

24 Gregory J.M. Catsos, "Sylvia Sidney," *Filmfax*, November 1990
25 Anna Quindlen, "That Nice Girl Sylvia Sidney Is Back At Work," *Lakeland Ledger*, June 26, 1977
26 Barry Keith Grant, *Fritz Lang: Interviews*, University of Mississippi Press, c. 2003, pg. 103
27 Peter Bogdanovich, *Who the Devil Made It*, Knopf, c. 1997
28 Gregory J.M. Catsos, "Sylvia Sidney," *Filmfax*, November 1990
29 Foster Hirsch, *Kurt Weill on Stage: From Berlin to Broadway*, Hal Leonard Corp., c. 2004, pg. 160
30 Louella Parsons column, *Los Angeles Times*, May 16, 1938
31 Katherine Albert, "Sylvia Sidney Plays Truth," *Modern Screen*, June 1936
32 Stella Adler, *Stella Adler on Ibsen, Strindberg and Chekov*, Vintage, c. 2000
33 Florida, Divorce Index, Dade Co., (Beatrice vs. Sigmund Sidney) 1938. Certificate No. 770
34 Peter Travers, "The King of New York," *Rolling Stone*, January 25, 2008
35 James Robert Parish, *Paramount Pretties*, Arlington House, c. 1972, pg. 273 (original quote from 1936)
36 Jeff Laffel, "Sylvia Sidney," *Films in Review*, September/October 1994
37 Helen Crich Chinoy, *The Group Theatre: Passion, Politics, and Performance in the Depression Era*, Palgrave Macmillan, c. 2013, pg. 215
38 Eliz Kazan, *Elia Kazan: A Life*, Knopf, c. 1988
39 Gladys Hall, "Now Gable Does Have a Worry - Franchot Tone," *Motion Picture*, June 1933
40 Wendy Smith, *Real Life Drama: The Group Theatre in America*, Knopf Doubleday, c. 2013, pg. 376
41 Christopher J. Herr, *Clifford Odets and American Political Theatre*, Greenwood, c. 2003, pg. 59
42 Marlon Brando, *Brando: Songs My Mother Taught Me*, Random House, c. 1994, pg. 78

1946 - Sylvia and son Jacob "Jody" Adler

Chapter 8
Motherhood: "A Great Leveling Agent"

Sylvia and Luther welcomed a five-pound, eight-ounce addition to their busy lives. Jacob Luther Adler was born October 22, 1939, at Woman's Hospital in Manhattan. Luther was rehearsing a lead role in the Group Theatre's anti-fascist themed *Thunder Rock* when the hospital summoned him to see his newborn son. There were difficulties and for three days the couple had reason to worry. The baby's high temperature would not subside. The Group offered to cancel the play's premier in Baltimore. Luther's fears were underscored by the play's focal point revolving around the death-struggle of a sick child. Fortunately, the off-stage drama had a happy ending. At three weeks old, baby Jacob, with blue-eyes and curly blonde hair, weighed in at six-pounds, one-ounce, and Luther was being singled out with "raves" in Baltimore.

Jacob was named after his paternal grandfather. He was nicknamed "Jody"—which stuck. The summer prior to Jody's birth, Sylvia got a copy of John Steinbeck's *The Red Pony*. She read it aloud to Luther each night. "We fell in love with the little boy in it," said Sylvia. "We made up our minds that if we had a little boy we were going to call him

Jody." Sylvia confessed that on occasion she affectionately called him "Stinky." She also had to admit, "the only thing that is more fun [than acting] is seeing a baby's first smile." The Adler trio continued to use their apartment on East 56th Street, but weekends were spent at the 114-acre farm in the agricultural community of Flemington—a two-hour drive from New York City.

As Jody approached three-months of age, Sylvia took on the undemanding radio assignment of playing herself on the popular CBS serial *Pretty Kitty Kelly*. Sylvia acted as confidante to Kitty when the plot traveled to Hollywood. The story of Kitty (Arline Blackburn), an Irish émigrée and a victim of amnesia, revolved around her unexpected adventures (some involving murder). Following Sylvia's soap opera stint, she and Luther offered a dramatic skit for the *Kate Smith Hour* on ABC. Sylvia also played opposite Charles Boyer for radio's *Hollywood Playhouse* production of *Shadow Light*, which centered on a sightless millionaire and his beautiful wife.

When Jody was six-months old, it was announced that Sylvia would return to the screen. The press referred to it as a "comeback." Initially, she was considered for the female lead in Cagney's *City for Conquest*, but she opted to recharge her thespian skills on stage. In June 1940, she appeared for six evening performances of S. N. Behrman's *No Time for Comedy* at the Amherst Drama Festival. For this, Sylvia faced her husband for their first joint stage appearance. In charge of the festival was twenty-five-year-old actor/producer Harold J. Kennedy. Upon arriving at the swank summer theater, Sylvia and Luther made a point of visiting the Shrine Hospital children's ward, armed with an abundance of gifts.

Sylvia was visibly moved by the experience, giving her autograph freely. Except for a few of the older children, none had ever seen her on screen.

As far as who got top-billing in the Adler family, it was definitely Jody. During rehearsals at Kirby Memorial Theatre, eight-month-old Jody joined his mother on stage. He sported a light blue sweater she had made. Sylvia knitted all Jody's suits and sweaters. The infant Adler also made an unexpected "appearance" on radio during a promotion for *No Time for Comedy*. Sylvia and Luther were doing an interview sketch. Luther had the line, "I repeat the question. Who are you?" Before Sylvia could answer, a tiny voice in the audience squealed, "Ma!" It was Jody. The timing was perfect. The audience and Sylvia burst out laughing.

Years later, producer Kennedy described Sylvia at the time as a "shy, reticent, almost apologetic movie star who came to Amherst." He elaborated,

> I say apologetic because she was then very much in awe of and under the thumb of Luther, and his whole coterie of Group Theatre actors, all of whom looked down their noses at Hollywood and anyone connected with it. She had been in a number of films which even today [1978] rank as motion picture classics. But she always played the tearful heroine ... and she hated that type casting. She told me at that time she went to the movies one night ... and they showed a preview of a film she was starring in. As soon as her face came on the screen the man behind her said, 'Oh, God, there she is, crying again.' 'That did it,' said Sylvia.[1]

Producer Kennedy surmised that dyed-in-the-wool Group Theatre members refused to recognize what a great asset Sylvia was in keeping them afloat. Kennedy mentioned the highly profitable run of *The Gentle People*. Sylvia's name sold plenty of tickets. When the Group was considering the Billy Rose project *Clash By Night*, one member cavalierly indicated that Sylvia should be dropped from the project. "Sylvia," said Rose firmly, "is the money ball." Kennedy felt that Luther also failed to realize Sylvia's importance. "They made a number of cross-country tours," Kennedy noted, "in which [Luther] was co-starred and Sylvia was indeed 'the money ball.'"[2] Theron Bamberger, who ran summer stock's Bucks County Playhouse in Pennsylvania, offered Sylvia and Luther five hundred dollars to do a play. Luther protested, "But that's only two hundred and fifty dollars apiece." Theron didn't have the heart to tell Luther that four hundred of the sum was for Sylvia.[3] Kennedy observed that Sylvia was a good wife and mother and loyal Group member. "She went along with all of it," he said. But, not for long. Sylvia was about to make an abrupt about-turn.

The final parting of the ways for the Adlers and the Group involved Clifford Odets' *Clash By Night* and the fragile Frances Farmer. In 1973, Sylvia offered the details.

> I'm taking care of Fanny Farmer, who has just left her bridegroom Leif Erickson to move in with Cliffie Odets, in the same house and same company, mind you, and she's beginning to crack. I have the baby, and Luther and I are waiting around for a year—while our dear friend Cliffie writes Clash by Night for us— that's when Billy Rose, who produced it, called me the money ball. A week after that I read in the papers that Tallulah Bankhead's been signed for it. I lost my faith in people in the bargain.[4]

England had declared war on Germany in September 1939, a month prior to Jody's birth. Warner Brothers responded by releasing their top money-maker for the year, *The Fighting 69th*—recruiting James Cagney and George Brent for patriotic duty. A year later, Sylvia arrived on the lot. Her Hollywood agent, Mike Levee, signed her to play a fortune teller opposite Humphrey Bogart in the Warner film *Carnival*. It was a rehash of Warners' *Kid Galahad* (1937), and far removed from the trend of war-themed dramas. The plot was switched from the boxing ring to the big-top. In the original, Bette Davis played the right-hand-gal of hot-headed boxing promoter Edward G. Robinson. Bogart, also on hand, was as a rival promoter—a bad guy, who bribes Robinson to throw the big fight. For the remake, the bad guy was replaced by a killer lion.

Sylvia appeared on the *Carnival* set wearing a bright, red gypsy dress and carrying eleven-month-old Jody. Bogart was in the middle of a take in which his line is interrupted by a lion. Instead of a roar, Jody let out a big squeal. "What's that—a mouse?" grumbled Bogart. When Jody wasn't on the set, Sylvia eagerly displayed photos of him to cast members. Bogart politely begged off whenever she reached for her purse.[5]

Columnist Sheilah Graham reported on Sylvia's motive for returning to Hollywood: money. "I won't stay away too long from my farm in New Jersey," Sylvia explained. She enjoyed the cows and chickens and growing the food they ate. Getting up at dawn and retiring at dusk suited her just fine. Sylvia was contemplating doing two pictures a year—if Jody could tolerate the traveling. "I wouldn't travel without him," she emphasized. During their stay at the Chateau Elysee, Jody's playpen was prominently displayed in the center of the apartment.

Carnival (retitled *The Wagons Roll at Night*) placed Bogart in the original Robinson role. Fresh from his breakthrough performance in *High Sierra*, Bogart easily filled the shoes of the tough, cynical owner

The Wagons Roll at Night (1941) with Humphrey Bogart (Warners)

of a traveling circus. Sylvia, as his love interest, appears more rooted in reality. She sees through Bogart's schemes, and is ready to move on. She's tired of weaseling money out of anxious customers who want to know the "future." Sidney mentioned, "I like one thing about the character. She's a girl who can handle herself. She has maturity. She has intestinal fortitude, which we call guts—she doesn't let people push her around."[6] The script, however, afforded Sylvia Sidney no real opportunities. The meat in the Bette Davis performance was apparently tossed to the lions during the rewrite. Warner archivist Clive Hirschhorn felt the retread of *Kid Galahad* was "in every respect inferior" to the original, partially due to the "unexciting screenplay."[7]

The Wagons Roll at Night held as many thrills as a bag of popcorn. It came as no surprise when the vengeful Bogart ended up being cat food. As one New York critic put it, "The suspense … has a habit of lapsing into a coma every so often due to the injection of too much run-of-the-mill romance." At best, the romantic interludes between Bogart's kid sister (fifteen-year-old Joan Leslie), fresh from the convent, and his amateur lion tamer (thirty-six-year-old Eddie Albert) seem contrived. The same critic aptly summed up Sidney's return: "It's good to see Sylvia Sidney back on the screen, even in the thankless role of a fortune teller."[8] The *Syracuse Herald* echoed, "Sylvia Sidney invests a routine part of a gold-hearted moll with more warmth and charm than it deserves." The film might have worked had it reached into the darker clutches of film noir. Sidney compared director Ray Enright to Wyler. "He was a cutter, not a director. He'd do numerous takes. Then he'd say, 'Print it! Next shot!' with no enthusiasm."[9]

Warners, pleased with Sylvia's rushes, negotiated for a five picture deal. She tested for the second feminine lead in *The Great Lie*.[10] After filming wrapped on *The Wagons Roll at Night* (mid-November) Sylvia packed her bags and left for New Jersey. She was furious about losing the lead opposite John Garfield in *Fiesta in Manhattan*. Garfield had done a little casting of his own and requested Margo instead.[11] *Fiesta in Manhattan* revolved around a young couple transplanted from their native Mexico into the Harlem slums—a treatise on the struggle of immigrants. The film project eventually met a snarl with the Mexican government and was never made. Before Sylvia fled town, Louella Parsons revealed that Sylvia would probably join Bette Davis and George Brent for *The Great Lie*. The coveted part ended up in the hands of Mary Astor. Astor stole every scene she was in from Bette Davis and ended up winning Best Supporting Actress for 1941. She called her character, "a real bitch. I was delighted to test for it."[12] Instead of an Oscar plaque, Sylvia and Jody returned home with a 42-foot long hooked rug Sylvia had made for the hallway of their farmhouse.

Following her Hollywood misfire, Sidney headed back to the stage. It would be four years before she returned to the screen, enticed by the idea of playing opposite James Cagney. The difference between Bogart and Cagney, according to Sylvia, was that for Cagney playing a tough guy was just a role. "Bogart," she emphasized, "thought he was the character he played. There were many times when Bogart was *not* a very nice person." To illustrate her point, Sylvia told writer Jeff Laffel about a scandalous incident that occurred at the home of Bogie and Lauren Bacall. "I probably shouldn't tell this story," she said, "but what the hell. It was a hundred years ago." The incident took place shortly after Sylvia's divorce from Luther Adler in 1946. She was dating radio/film producer Carleton Alsop. Bogart saw them dining at Romanoff's and asked them to join him, Bacall and a few others at his home that same evening. They arrived to a house filled with a celebrity-studded crowd. The booze flowed freely. "At any rate," said Sylvia, "we were milling about having a nice time when Bogie came up to us."

> It was pretty obvious that he had had a number of large drinks and he was in a rather belligerent mood. Everyone knew that Bogart could be a bully when he got like that; he would select a person and keep at them and at them until he got to them. Tonight, for some reason, it appeared to be my turn. 'When are you gonna stop marrying Jew-boys, Sylvia' he said, and I could feel the nerves at the end of each hair on my neck begin to itch. And he said it again. 'You gotta stop marrying Jew-boys, Sylvia.' And trying to hold back my tem-

per, I said to him, 'Look, Bogie, we're all just trying to find our way. Till you married Betty (Lauren Bacall), you were in big trouble ... big trouble. So let's just leave this alone.'[13]

Bogart would not stop. "Jew boys. You gotta marry a gentile once in a while." Sylvia, having had a few belts of her own, threw her drink *and* glass in his face, then ran off. By the time Carleton found her she was angry at herself for letting Bogie get to her. Carleton persuaded her to come back inside ... and see the damage. Bogie was sitting on the toilet—blood flowing everywhere, as Bacall poured iodine on his wound—a gash that went from his temple to behind his ear. While Bogart grimaced and yelped, Bacall fired back, "Shut up. You deserved it." While they waited for a doctor to arrive, Bogie looked up at Sylvia and said, "You're a great kid, Sylvia. Didn't know you had that kinda fire."[14]

"You have to kill Bogart first," surmised Sylvia, "and then he respects you." The next day Sylvia's phone rang off the hook: Hedda Hopper, Louella Parsons, Sheilah Graham—gossip mongers had heard about the ruckus—they wanted facts. Before Sylvia had left Bogart's home the previous evening, both agreed to inform the press they hadn't seen each other in months. They stuck to the story and no one was the wiser. In truth, Sidney had first revealed the Bogie incident in 1979 to veteran reporter Vernon Scott. Prior to that, her comments on Bogart were variations of "I'd rather not talk about him."

In the spring of 1941, the Adlers decided to co-star in an extensive tour of Samson Raphaelson's sophisticated comedy *Accent on Youth*, which Sylvia had successfully essayed on screen. The play opened in Syracuse.

Accent on Youth- **on tour with husband Luther Adler**

Raphaelson was on hand for rehearsals and the premier performance, before the play headed to Detroit and Toronto—baby Jody tagging along with his nurse. Sylvia's close friend from her Paramount days, Dorothy Libaire, was in a supporting role, as was Kevin McCarthy.

Trouper that she was, Sylvia accompanied Luther to Kansas City to co-star in a previous commitment: a revival of *Two On An Island*. The week-long run of the Elmer Rice (who had penned *Street Scene*) comedy was well-received. Back on tour, the scheduled two-weeks at Chicago's Selwyn Theatre for *Accent on Youth* was held over for a month. From there, the Adlers headed to the Bronx and Brooklyn. Critic Arthur Pollock joined a standing-room-only crowd, and praised, "This can easily be called the best performance the borough has seen this summer. Sylvia Sidney was good before she went into the movies and Hollywood has not dulled her luster. Luther Adler is equal to anything. The two play beautifully together. The Adlers know what to do when they are doing nothing … [holding] the audience at every turn."

Sylvia and Luther took a second break on tour, to team in what many consider Adler's greatest characterization for the Group Theatre, *Golden Boy*. The week-long engagement was at the Maplewood Theatre in New Jersey. *Accent on Youth* closed the following week on Long Island. From there, Sylvia, Luther and Jody returned to their New Jersey farm that was fast becoming a mecca for actors, playwrights and artists.

In the fall, Sylvia signed on for two radio broadcasts for *Philip Morris Playhouse*: *Angels With Dirty Faces*, and her coveted role as Cathy in *Wuthering Heights*, co-starring Raymond Massey as Heathcliff. During a brief respite for the holidays, the United States entered WWII. From then on, Sidney made a point to combine her stage appearances with war bond drives. She joined Victor Jory for a touring company of the Broadway success *Angel Street* (known as *Gaslight* in England). It opened in Baltimore in February 1942. While at the National Theatre in D.C., First Lady Eleanor Roosevelt invited Sylvia and Jory for luncheon at the White House. The play eventually reached Chicago for an extended stay. Critic Berny Gavzer waxed ecstatic about Sidney. "If ever a role has existed to fit her personality, her ability to express emotion, certainly the character of Mrs. Manningham is it. Her interpretation of the over-lorded, belittled, piteously unhappy, befuddled, frightened target of an ingenious scoundrel is highly commendable. Her "Et tu brute?" expression has found its little niche."[15]

Another critic thought Sidney to be "masterful." Mrs. Manningham's tormentor in *Angel Street* was her cold, calculating husband (Victor Jory), who is determined to drive her stark raving mad. Sylvia and co-star Jory relieved tension during the Chicago run by playing gin rummy at the nearby Rhumba Casino. The duo also attended a fundraiser on behalf of tuberculosis patients. Jory spoke to the crowds and Sidney took a bow. The Chicago engagement closed after eight weeks. Before leaving town, Sylvia campaigned for a Stage Door Canteen in the Windy City. Hedda Hopper crowed that Sylvia in *Angel Street* had been an "enormous success." The Sidney-Jory combination wasn't easily forgotten. They would repeat their roles for *Broadway Television Theatre* in 1953.

In the summer of '42, Sylvia returned to Cambridge, Massachusetts, to star in Louisa May Alcott's *Little Women* at Brattle Hall. The charm and sentiment of Alcott's gentle, old-fashioned story, was a surprise turn for Sylvia, who played Jo. One Boston critic found her portrait "vivacious and sympathetic." "Miss Sidney ... endows Jo with fire or tenderness as the moment demands."[16] Audiences were enthusiastic in spite of the summer heat. One afternoon, Sylvia visited Harvard to assist with the school's War Bond Drive. The college band lured traffic toward the booth where she assisted students. Sylvia also joined Mayor Dennis Roberts of Providence, Rhode Island, for a patriotic fundraiser where they stood side-by-side singing "The Star-Spangled Banner."

Next up, Sylvia offered a revival of her Eliza Doolittle in *Pygmalion*. For this, she re-teamed with Philip Huston as Professor Higgins. The tour of Shaw's comedy hit the Atlantic Coast circuit, followed by the Subway Circuit. One performance was touted as a benefit for the Central Manhattan Branch of the Socialist Party. Proceeds went to the election campaign of 1942.[17] By the end of September, Huston left the cast to join the ac-

Angel Street tour (1942)

claimed Paul Robeson production of *Othello*. He was replaced by Staats Cotsworth, who was noted for his resonant, booming voice. *Pygmalion* enjoyed successful runs in Newark, Cincinnati, and Philadelphia, before closing at the Copley Theatre in Boston in early March 1943. A *Boston Herald* critic raved, "The best play that Sylvia Sidney has had since her return from Hollywood. She's not afraid to be common nor is the emergence of the fine lady overstressed and artificial."[18]

At the close of *Pygmalion*, Sylvia and Luther joined Paul Muni, Edward G. Robinson and a cast of several hundred for the Ben Hecht drama *We Shall Never Die*. Luther's sister Stella was on the production committee. Staged by Moss Hart, Madison Square Garden was transformed into a massive temple of mourning for the two million Jews killed by Nazis in Europe. The moving spectacle dramatized the contributions of the Jewish people to civilization, underscoring the theme: "Remember Us." It was a call for action—"the human spirit against massacre"—a push for America to support a State of Israel. Drama critic Lawrence Perry praised, "Luther Adler, Sylvia Sidney ... heightened their art as actors by a deep sincerity rising out of their own Jewish heritage."[19] *We Shall Never Die* was repeated at Constitution Hall on April 12, for Supreme Court justices, diplomats, legislators, and Mrs. Roosevelt. In response, President Roosevelt formed the War Refugee Board, which was reported to have saved 200,000 Jewish refugees during the last eighteen months of WWII.

After eight months of Eliza Doolittle and making audiences laugh, Sylvia opted for another eight-month tour in something darker, heavier and equally successful: *Jane Eyre*. For this, she re-teamed with her husband. Luther, as one journalist put it, "had more irons in the fire that you could shake a script at." While starring in *The Russian People* on Broadway, he did broadcasts for the Office of War Information, directed an army camp production of *You Can't Take it With You*, and served on the Board of Directors of the U.S.O. Army Camp Shows. Broadway snoop Walter Winchell reported that Sylvia and her sister-in-law Stella Adler were "Hatfield-McCoying"—possibly over Luther's schedule. Winchell rubbed it in further by saying, "The Luther Adlers are invariably seen together but have separate teepees."[20] "Winchell was a bad guy," Sylvia said years later. "His Monday morning columns set me trembling to see if he'd picked up on what I might have done the previous Saturday night."[21] It was shortly after Winchell's barb that the Adlers began their extensive cross-country tour in *Jane Eyre*.

Thanks to the acting Adlers, playwright Helen Jerome's 1936 stage adaptation of the Charlotte Bronte novel received its first Metropolitan New York offering. When *Jane Eyre* was first published in 1847, many women read it in secret. Ranked as one of the first feminist turns in literature, it was met with outrage and disapproval. The play version begins with Jane's employment with the brooding, tormented Mr. Rochester (Adler). She is governess to his illegitimate daughter. The presence of a female mental patient, in the west wing of the mansion, is quickly established. The oddly impersonal and passionate affair between Jane and her employer culminates on their wedding day with the revelation that Rochester was planning bigamy.

As staged by Luther Adler, Jerome's play maintained the tension, suspense and the novel's central theme: the gradual unfolding of the young heroine's independent and spiritual sensibilities. "Sylvia," said New York critic Robert Francis, "was the brighter spot of the evening. Luther, in spite of the fact that physically he doesn't measure up to our conception of Miss Bronte's hero, builds a thoroughly satisfactory portrait." A critic for the *Philadelphia Inquirer* nodded to the Adlers "illuminating and eloquent performances," and stated, "Miss Sidney accomplishes the formidable task of satisfying the mind and the imagination as well as the eye with her characterization." The handsomely staged production survived an occasional mishap, as when a 19-year-old socialite, dubbing piano for Sidney off-stage, began a Bach choral while Sylvia's hands were still raised in mid-air.

Sidney continued to push for the War Bond campaign. A Chicago

The Adlers tour in *Jane Eyre* (1943-44)

event raised two million dollars from ballyhoo provided by Sylvia Sidney and the Ringling Circus. Sidney's purchase of a $1,000 bond worth 40 Ringling tickets, she gave to forty youngsters in The Boy's Club who were involved in various phases of war work. Her appearance at the Apex Electrical bond rally was credited for selling $40,000 Series E bonds in the first half hour. In Cleveland, Sylvia was the first celebrity to appear at the WAVES recruiting lounge. The Adlers also joined Vice-President Wallace at Chicago's Victory Garden Festival. The Agricultural Department reported that victory gardens produced over eight million tons of food in 1943.

Upon reaching Los Angeles, *Jane Eyre* had a month's stay at the Biltmore. Critic Don Short praised the production's passionate love-making. "Sylvia Sidney's enactment of a love-starved soul," said Short, "won the admiration of all ... at the climax of each love scene she was acclaimed with outbursts of enthusiastic appreciation." Sylvia admitted that their version of *Jane Eyre* stressed romance. During a month-long stay at San Francisco's Geary Theatre, critics applauded the Adlers as "authentic" and "convincing." Heading north, by train, to Portland, Sylvia, wearing a mink coat and "saucy little hat" submitted to an interview. She said that *Jane Eyre* was "a very tough piece to handle." Her initial attraction to the role was the "terrific challenge." Asked if she liked playing opposite her husband, she curtly replied, "I wouldn't have done it for the past eight months if I hadn't." There were no more questions.

The popularity of *Jane Eyre* resulted in sold out houses and extended runs. Producer Jules Leventhal stated that, had Sylvia been willing, the tour could have played Canada. A film version of the Bronte novel, starring Joan Fontaine and Orson Welles, had recently been completed (with due respect to the Production Code). The 20th Century-Fox feature was released in the US following Sylvia and Luther's final performance at The Playhouse in Wilmington (January 1944). Sidney thought the play was a "natural" for the screen. "It should make one of the year's great films," she predicted.

So, what was Jody up to during his parents' transcontinental tour? He tagged along with a new friend, a silky black cocker pup. When *Jane Eyre* reached Los Angeles, Jody celebrated his fourth birthday. Sylvia made sure that the prop department created a doggie-house with Jody's name prominently displayed in bright colors. Jody knew just how much dehydrated dog food to prepare for his little pal. Sylvia ran

Publicity shot, 1943

errands around town accompanied by the pup on a red-leather leash. "Her dog and her dark glasses," noted one war bond saleswoman, "were the specially dramatic touches she indulged in. Her hair was brushed high with a pompadour. When she came over to buy a bond (a fat one, too) I noticed that she barely came up to my shoulder."[22]

Mention of a "rumored rift" in the Adler marriage continued to make news columns. Prior to *Jane Eyre* closing, columnist Dorothy Kilgallen blabbed that John Garfield was "trying to reconcile the Luther Adlers." Jimmy Fidler's column said that pals predicted divorce. The tour closed primarily because Luther had committed to a new play. In late summer 1944, Louella Parsons put it simply. "Sylvia and Luther Adler are separated and have been for nearly two years."[23] Walter Winchell's assessment was correct. Sylvia finally relented to the press, dryly explaining her decision to part ways with Luther Adler. "He was always missing," she said.[24]

Sylvia felt that being a mother was a boon to her career as an actress. "Having a child was a great leveling agent," she said. "Those babies couldn't care less that their parents were famous."[25] At the close of *Jane Eyre*, Sylvia took Jody into a New York hospital for a tonsillectomy. "There I stood," she recalled, "ready to sign Jody in one morning when the nurse asked, 'Who is the father?'" Sylvia politely explained that Luther Adler was in Chicago. The nurse insisted on Adler's written permission prior to the operation. "But I've *signed*," said Sylvia, "his father is in Chicago in a play." Wasting no time, Sylvia suggested that they phone him. They finally reached Adler, who was asleep. After some hysterics—learning his son was in the hospital, he calmed down to say, "Get him lots of ice-cream."[26] "*Finally*," said Sylvia, "the nurse took down his statement: 'I, Luther Adler, give permission to have my son Jody's tonsils removed.'" Motherhood—the great leveling agent—did not circumvent the right of male privilege.

(Endnotes)

1. Harold J. Kennedy, *No Pickle, No Performance*, Doubleday, N.Y., c. 1978, pgs. 202-203
2. Harold J. Kennedy, *No Pickle, No Performance*, Doubleday, N.Y., c. 1978, pg. 203
3. Harold J. Kennedy, *No Pickle, No Performance*, Doubleday, N.Y., c. 1978, pg. 204
4. Bernard Drew, "Sylvia Sidney - The Return of a Star," *The Herald Statesman*, c. 1973

5   "Sylvia Sidney Back From Farm," *Oregonian*, October 27, 1940
6   Carol Craig, "I Didn't Run Away," *Motion Picture*, March 1941
7   Clive Hirschhorn, *The Warner Bros. Story*, Crown Pub., c. 1979, pg. 221
8   C.R.R. review of *The Wagons Roll At Night*, *Knickerbocker News*, May 23, 1941
9   Gregory J.M. Catsos, "Sylvia Sidney," *Filmfax*, November 1990
10 "WB Tests Sylvia Sidney," *Film Daily*, October 4, 1940 (On November 7, 1940, *Film Daily* announced that Mary Astor had the role in *Far Horizon*—later retitled *The Great Lie*)
11 Richard E. Hays, "Amusements," *Seattle Daily Times*, November 28, 1940
12 Mary Astor, *A Life on Film*, Dell, c. 1967, pg. 152
13 Jeff Laffel, "Sylvia Sidney," *Films in Review*, September/October 1994
14 Vernon Scott, "Actress Glad Gossips Gone," *Spokane Daily Chronicle*, November 26, 1979
15 Berny Gavzer, review of *Angel Street*, *Daily Northwestern*, March 27, 1942
16 Helen Eager, "Sylvia Sidney Starred in *Little Women*," *Boston Traveler*, July 21, 1942
17 Harry Fleischman, "Life of the Party," *Socialist Call*, September 4, 1942
18 Elinor Hughes, review of *Pygmalion*, *Boston Herald*, February 24, 1943
19 Lawrence Perry, review of *We Shall Never Die*, *Evening Star*, March 14, 1943
20 Walter Winchell, "Man About Town," *Richmond Times Dispatch*, February 9, 1943
21 Vernon Scott, "Actress Glad Gossips Gone," *Spokane Daily Chronicle*, November 26, 1979
22 Mary Hampton, "Mary Hampton's Column," *Riverside Daily Press*, November 20, 1943
23 Louella Parsons column, *Philadelphia Inquirer*, September 15, 1944
24 Sheilah Graham, "Flashes From Hollywood," *Plain Dealer*, October 22, 1944
25 James Robert Parish, *The Paramount Pretties*, Castle Books, c. 1972, pg. 276
26 "In Hollywood," *Trenton Evening Times*, August 14, 1944

1944 - Sidney called it a "Drop-dead gorgeous" photo

Chapter 9
Screen Comeback: 1944-1947

After Jody's tonsil operation, Sylvia consulted doctors regarding his delicate health and sinus condition. It was decided that California's climate would prove beneficial. Sylvia wasted no time. She took a break from acting and would not return to the stage for three years. Upon arriving in California, she explained, "I came back this time, because of Jody's health. The doctors wanted him away from the eastern winter." By March 1944, Sylvia, Jody, a live-in nurse, and a housekeeper were residing at the Beverly Hills Hotel. "We had an extended and very happy family," recalled Sylvia in 1994.

> Though he was quite ill with pneumonia, Jody really enjoyed the train trip to Hollywood, and though he and I had always been close, I don't think there was ever a time in our lives that we were closer than on that train heading away from New York. It was one of the nicest times of my life having that little boy eat with me, sleep with me, read with me... it was ... wonderful.[1]

Before long, their "extended family" moved to a neighborhood on Ogden Drive so Jody could have playmates. Sylvia filled the back yard with swings, slides and sandboxes—making sure he got plenty of fresh air. When neighbor kids got rough and pushed Jody spinning into his sandbox, he was caught off guard. "Jody didn't want to fight," said Sylvia indignantly. "He doesn't know anything about fighting. He doesn't think that way."[2] She intervened, telling the bullies to behave themselves or leave. Their tune changed and Jody was soon having what he called a "tremense" time with his playmates. AP reporter Rosalind Shaffer observed, "Motherhood apparently has deepened and broadened Sylvia's personal life."

Although Sylvia envisioned filing for divorce proceedings in California, when asked about Luther, she would just shrug her shoulders. When Luther was asked why he didn't join his estranged wife and son in Hollywood he would answer, "That wouldn't be progress for me. People would say that I was compromising my art. Yes, that's what people would say." Who, exactly, would say such a thing? After a long pause, Luther replied, "My sister Stella."[3] Stella had already "compromised her art" by playing a ninth-billed bit in MGM's *Shadow of the Thin Man* (1941). Luther eventually followed suit, receiving seventh-billing as a villain in Dick Powell's *Cornered* (1945).

Stella had married Harold Clurman, a consummate man of the theater, in 1942. On a sojourn to Hollywood in 1944, Clurman, who was "compromising his art" at RKO, ran into Sylvia. He wrote Stella offering his impressions of their "estranged" sister-in-law on June 3, 1944.

> I see Sylvia occasionally. She has some money apparently but I believe she is a kind of wreck tho she looks pretty. It is almost sad: not her home life (divorce and separation), not her career (tho she hasn't found anything yet), not her sex life (tho

she appears to have one). But her being. A kind of ... powerless meanness and bitterness holds her fighting in its grasp. There is consequently no beauty of soul, no nobility, no richness of texture in her gaiety. Sylvia's troubles make her small. She seems not to be in touch with anything beyond her little world.[4]

Clurman then paid compliments to Stella, saying that her "stature" and "greatness" were never dimmed by her own "descents into the murky." Clurman was blinded by love. It was after a ten-year courtship that Stella finally relented and married him. His letter was designed to boost Stella's own self-esteem. Nonetheless, Clurman had zeroed in on an aspect of Sidney's persona that had some validity. Her disappointment with Hollywood, the turmoil that infested Group Theatre, her dissolving second marriage—left a bitter edge. Sidney lost her faith in people. Over the next few decades she gained a reputation of being cranky and difficult. Oddly enough, many of her co-workers and fans grew to love her for it! In mid-October, 1944, after months of no acting assignments, Sylvia, once again, faced Hollywood cameras.

Sidney had been tempted twice with film offers. In the summer of '42, producer Bill Pine paged her for *Tornado* (1943) to play a scheming showgirl who wreaks havoc in a coal-mining town. The cast included her old co-star from Broadway's *Crime*, Chester Morris. Nancy Kelly took on this assignment at Paramount's B-unit. *Tornado* was strictly low-budget, double-bill fare and soon forgotten. It was then announced that Sidney would film *Girls in Chains* (1943) for the prolific director Edgar Ulmer. Made in five days, this prison riot opus conflicted with Sylvia's *Pygmalion* tour. One wonders what Sidney was thinking. Poverty row films like *Girls in Chains* spelled a death warrant for washed up actors. Fortunately, the Cagney brothers came to Sidney's rescue.

Sylvia's agent offered her services to producer William Cagney, and his brother James. Glamour and intrigue promised new screen territory for Sidney, and that seemed to please her. She also needed the work. She had a son to support. At first, the Cagney brothers didn't deem her glamorous enough. They wanted Merle Oberon, but Merle didn't relish playing a half-caste (a reflection of her own "secret" past). Sidney put up a fight. She hired the flamboyant publicist Russell Birdwell, who had done wonders promoting the Howard Hughes' exploiter *The Outlaw*. "Here are two good reasons to see *The Outlaw*," screamed ads with Jane Russell's breasts prominently displayed. Birdwell hired one of Hollywood's top photographers. "That guy took some drop-dead gorgeous shots of me," recalled Sidney. She elaborated that Birdwell entered her photos in some "cockamamie contest" that named the 10 most beautiful women in the world. The first was Lana Turner. The second was Sylvia. Eventually, the photos reached *The Los Angeles Times*. "The next thing you know," said Sidney, "I was signing a contract."[5]

In *Blood on the Sun*, Sidney played an exquisite-looking Eurasian, a double-agent who lurks in the shadows while Tokyo news editor James Cagney investigates a plot by Japanese imperialists. Japan wants to overtake resource-rich Manchuria and eventually the United States. This all takes place in the late 1920's during the reign of Prime Minister Tanaka. The film is a highly fictional account of what was really going on, but it allowed a cocksure Cagney to make several narrow escapes and demonstrate his newly acquired skill with Judo. "Love your enemies? But first, get even!" snarls Cagney at the film's fadeout. In *Blood on the Sun*, Sidney's character kept audiences wondering whose side she was on.

Entering film noir as a double agent in *Blood on the Sun* (1945) (United Artists)

On screen, Sidney is much more than she appears—a professional spy and advocate for women's rights in Asia. "I was always taking a rap or getting pushed around in my pictures," Sylvia complained at the time, "but those days are over now."[6] As enticing as Sidney was, the script failed to provide her with a standout moment. Scenarist Lester Cole was more focused on action and political conspiracy. (A hardcore Communist, Cole became one of the Hollywood Ten in 1947.)

The romance that develops between Sidney and Cagney was bold for its time. Granted, Sidney (half-Chinese) appears to be more European, but, as professor of American studies Thomas Patrick Doherty points out, "*Blood on the Sun* approves of interminglings that were once unthinkable."[7] Miscegenation laws in California were still in effect three years *after* the film was released. Even so, the sting of racism fueled the casting of roles. A column in *Variety* declared "Orientals don't make good actors, [therefore] Caucasian actors will portray Japs in the William Cagney production."[8] This was a typical ploy in wartime Hollywood. Watching the film today, the cardboard caricatures of white actors (particularly Robert Armstrong and Marvin Miller) playing Japanese officials is uncomfortable to watch. In what should have been a boon-time for actors of Asian descent, Central Casting avoided hiring them. The Japanese had been cast elsewhere ... into internment camps by the War Relocation Authority.

Sidney joined the Cagney brothers in San Francisco for the premier of *Blood on the Sun*, where it was held over for eleven weeks. *Variety* enthused that Cagney was "the same rough and tumble character he's always been." Apparently, that's what mattered most, and the film grossed $3.4 million. *The New York Times* thought Sidney succeeded in being "bewitchingly mysterious." Another review thought she had "grown more beautiful during her absence from the screen." "Her dark beauty and dramatic finesse have been missed," agreed columnist Bob Thomas. Many critics thought it a "vivid" and "grand comeback" for Sidney. Louella Parsons asked Sylvia what it felt like to be a glamour girl. "You know," said Sidney, "I have spent more time in prison than any other actress. You don't know how wonderful it is to get out of jail!"[9] *Blood on the Sun* had a visual edge over its competitors in 1945, and received the Academy Award for Best Black-and White Art Direction.

Cagney liked working with Sidney, enjoyed her piquant humor and skill with Yiddish. He later recalled:

> One day Sylvia was making a costume test before the camera, and I watched her as she turned around, looking as elegant as any Shinto princess and twice as lovely. Now, Sylvia is Jewish, and I with my affection for Yiddish can't resist the opportunity to use it when I can. To tease her, from behind the camera I said, 'Zee gigt aus vi a Chinkeh!' ('She looks like a Chinese lady!') Without stopping her pirouette before the camera, she said, 'Fa vus nit?' ('Why not?') It is some accomplishment to be talented, beautiful and funny.[10]

Cagney and Sidney in *Blood on the Sun* (United Artists)

Sidney returned the compliment when Cagney was given a Career Achievement Award by the National Board of Review in 1981. The actor had recently completed *Ragtime* his first film in twenty years. Sidney approached the podium and after chiding Warren Beatty for changing the microphone position, the feisty actress purred, "I was happy to have appeared with [Cagney] in one picture. I wish it could have been more. Of course, now that he's working again, hope springs eternal." Cagney roared with delight. Sidney confirmed that Cagney was "one of the sweetest, kindest, gentlest men" she had ever known. "Mr. Mush," she smiled, "that was Cagney."[11]

During her return to the screen, Sylvia was seen about town with, as one columnist put it, "an array of interesting escorts." Winchell reported in the spring of 1944, that Sylvia and artist Fletcher Martin were "thicker than tapioca." Later that summer she and director John Brahm (*Hangover Square*) were considered "an item." As *Blood on the Sun* wrapped in the New Year of 1945, Sheilah Graham confirmed that Sylvia was "in love with artist Fletcher Martin." It came as no surprise when Martin, a handsome war correspondent/painter for *Life*, spent three weeks perfecting a portrait of Sidney for the popular magazine. The six-foot-two, mustachioed artist selected a sultry midnight-blue gown for his model. It would set off, as he put it, Sylvia's "restrained tempestuousness." By the summer of '45 Sidney was "table for two-ing" at the Beverly Hills Hotel wearing her leopard-skin cape, with Capt. Bill Atkinson, a New York banker. And, was the diamond she received from Ben Bogeaus (who would produce Sylvia's film *Mr. Ace*) merely a token of friendship?

Sylvia was amused when Jody began interrogating her dates. He insisted that each escort arrive before his bedtime (8pm). After Jody looked the man over, he would ask, "What do *you* do?" If Jody found the profession dull, he would take over the conversation with a few stories of his own, like the one he told about a dog whose father was a lion—punctuated with his favorite new word "tre-normous." Regardless of her rumored romances, Sylvia was adamant that her life was centered, in a healthy way, on Jody. She maintained, "When you are busy, you have a program for your child and it's a treat for him to see you and you are more of a novelty than if you are with him every hour of the day. I want my child to think for himself."[12]

Jody began piano lessons when he was four. He was precocious and inquisitive. He wondered why his mother was so tired when she tucked him into bed. "Mother, why do you go so early in the morning?" he asked. She explained that she had to work. "For money dear, so that you and Birdie [the nurse] and Socrates [his new bulldog] and I can have a house to live in and clothes to wear and something to eat." Jody offered to work himself so she could stay home. "But I'm not growing *up* fast enough!" he complained. Sylvia refrained from punishment, saying, "He's never done anything to be punished for." She once bargained to take Jody to a movie if he agreed to do a particular thing that he disliked. He didn't do it. So she told him they wouldn't go. "Oh, that's alright Mother," he said. "I can go on waiting some more."[13] Jody had the ability to perplex Sylvia with questions like, "Mother. What's distance?" Perhaps one influence that "explained" Jody was the progressive school in which Sylvia enrolled him.

Bill Cagney announced new projects to star Sidney, and Warner Bros. wanted her to play opposite Errol Flynn in a future *Don Juan* project.[14] Aside from radio appearances, Sylvia waited until the end of 1945 before her next screen assignment. *The Searching Wind*, produced by Hal Wallis, was a romantic love-triangle and political-charged indictment based on a play by Lillian Hellman. Hellman's premise was that the U. S. policy of isolationism had roots in high places, and contributed to the extermination of four million Jews. Breckenridge Long, who President Roosevelt appointed Ambassador to Italy in 1933, and head of the State Department in 1939, praised Mussolini as "a most remarkable man." Long thought Hitler's *Mein Kampf* "an eloquent opposition to Jewry."[15] Under Long's leadership the Nazi plan for genocide was suppressed from the American public. He was dedicated to keeping refugees off American soil.

On the set of *The Searching Wind* (1946) with Robert Young. (Paramount)

Although Hellman never mentioned Long specifically, *The Searching Wind* focused on a married American ambassador, Alex Hazen (Robert Young), who is indifferent to the plight of Jews, and absorbed with diplomatic decorum. During his on-going affair with female news correspondent Cassie Bowman (Sidney), he turns a deaf ear to her condemnation of politics that allowed Hitler's rise to power. It's understandable why Sidney would want to be included in this film project. In a *Saturday Evening Post* interview, Sylvia said that her dark, intense portrayal of a disillusioned woman "mirrored [her] own feelings about Europe's prewar problems." Although WWII had ended, she was intent on "doing something to bolster the general argument against appeasement."[16] Politically, Sidney was on the list for Roosevelt during his 1944 reelection campaign.[17]

The Searching Wind begins in 1945. Ambassador Hazen retires from a diplomatic career fraught with error and self-indulgence. Hazen confesses to his wife (Ann Richards), a socialite who has encouraged his diplomatic silence, that he will leave her for their mutual friend and journalist, Cassie. Mrs. Hazen extends an ultimatum to

Cassie to dine with them. During dinner a radio flash announces the death of Mussolini. Hazen cheers the good news, but Cassie reminds him that when it *really* mattered, he did not view the dictator as an enemy to Democracy. In flashbacks, we see Hazen as Ambassador to Italy witnessing Mussolini's *Fascisti* March on Rome. Later in Berlin, where Cassie is investigating the inhumane treatment of Jews, Hazen tells her that the Nazis will never amass any real power. During the Spanish Civil War, the duo's romantic feelings and political discord are resumed. Cassie cautions Hazen that American policy of nonintervention will have dire consequences for Europe. After he refuses to report that German planes are bombing Madrid, Cassie rails at him: "You have nothing to do with death because you have nothing to do with people. You're a diplomat." When Germany annexes portions of Czechoslovakia in 1938, Hazen recommends appeasement and the Munich Pact is signed.

The irony was that Cassie made her living writing for the conservative *Washington Bulletin* (a jab at the Hearst news syndicate) which championed isolationism. She sagely includes herself to be among the frivolous generation she deplored. Hazen's newsman father-in-law (Dudley Digges repeating his Broadway role) also sees through the sham of diplomacy. He is quite articulate about it, but allows his paper to fall into new hands rampant with right-wing rhetoric.

Due to Production Code restrictions, any indication of Alex and Cassie's consummated affair was forbidden (and deleted from the original script). The elaborately posh film was graced with superb performances. Despite intermittent haggling between Cassie and Hazen's wife, the flashback montage builds momentum. Fluid camerawork is the only "action" required as Hellman drives her message home. Bernard F. Dick's 1982 study, *Hellman in Hollywood*, affirms that in

The Searching Wind, "Hellman gave moviegoers a clear and vivid dramatization of the major events and movements that led to World War II. In most World War II movies made in the 1940's, history was the backdrop for the plot; in The Searching Wind, it was embedded in the action like the tiles in a mosaic."[18]

Producer Hal B. Wallis made a number of politically-themed films, including Hellman's *Watch on the Rhine* (1943), which also dealt with isolationism and registered strongly with filmgoers. But, were postwar Americans interested in how appeasement had helped trigger WWII? Reviews were mixed. The sharp-tongued dialogue and perpetual debate proved exasperating to some. "Windy with words," complained the *Kansas City Star*. *The New York Times* felt that weaklings like Alex Hazen received "more sympathy than hate." "No pompous, short-visioned statesmen," griped the review, "are likely to be blown over by this gentle blast." Robert Young later reflected, "I hated my character, a wishy-washy diplomat." Young, who received top-billing, undiplomatically theorized that producer Wallis needed Bette Davis to sell the picture. "Sylvia Sidney is a fine actress," said Young, "but she lacked box office clout."[19]

A Philadelphia critic came to the film's defense. "*The Searching Wind* is neither light or easy entertainment ... relying almost wholly upon brilliantly turned dialogue, characterization and a dissection of world events." The review commended Hellman's effort to end the "periodic slaughter" of genocide and war. "Under William Dieterle's intelligent direction and by means of excellent performances ... the power and purpose of *The Searching Wind* are made impressively apparent. Miss Sidney is warmly sympathetic and intellectually convincing."[20] In 2014, film historian/author James Robert Parish said that he especially liked the film. "It had a lot to say," Parish emphasized, "and got me agitated, which is what the film wanted to do."²¹ *The Searching Wind* qualifies as absorbing, disturbing film drama.

Off camera, Sylvia had warned young Douglas Dick, who played Sam, Hazen's son, to be wary of their director. Dieterle had the habit of singling out one cast member for derision. Sidney told Dick to agree with whatever Dieterle had to say and then follow his own instincts. Before cameras rolled for the film's concluding speech in which Sam denounces his father's isolationism, Dieterle left the set. Perhaps Hellman's leftwing rhetoric made the director uncomfortable.²² (The first Hollywood blacklist would appear the following year). Byron Haskin took to the director's seat. For this, Douglas Dick earned the final close-up and critical applause for conveying Hellman's testament of disillusionment and guarded hope for the future. Years later, Sylvia shared an amusing anecdote about the film,

> I was crazy about that part and I threw myself into it. I remember one day … it was the first day of filming, as a matter of fact … and I was all dressed, my hair fixed just so, everything ready, when we had to wait over four hours because Hal Wallis wasn't satisfied with the way another star, Ann Richards, looked. He was being very protective because … oh, what the hell, because he was sleeping with her … so the rest of us had to sit and cool our heels.²³

The day they shot the bombing scene in a Madrid café, Jody accompanied his mother to the studio. Reporter Gene Handsaker showed up to interview Sylvia, but Jody kept butting in. "Mommy, I want a little sister." Sylvia blushed. Jody climbed upon Handsaker's lap. "Mommy when are they going to change the film in the camera?" Sylvia lifted Jody up and

The Searching Wind love-triangle: Robert Young, Sylvia Sidney, and Ann Richards

sat him firmly upon the box beside her. "Pretty soon, dear." "Mommy, are you going to live 'til the last day on earth?" "No dear, that's a long, long time." "I'm going to live that long ... millions and trillions and billions of years." Sylvia looked over at Handsaker. "This goes on all day!"[24] Jody offered his opinion on Sylvia's acting after watching her long dialogue scene with Robert Young. She asked Jody what he thought, and, as if foretelling the criticism that followed the film's release, he blurted, "All right, but mother, you talk too much."

Jody was more interested in the cameras and lighting equipment than his mother's acting skill, which he estimated was worth about seventy-five cents a week. "He scares me," Sylvia confessed. "Must be something of a genius. He's just learning to read and he's starting out on the dictionary."[25]

On January 11, 1946, Sidney filed for divorce from Luther Adler. "Grievous mental suffering" was the charge. She stated that the official date of their separation was July 1, 1944. They had reached a property settlement and Sylvia had asked for custody of Jody, age 6. The divorce was granted on February 27, on grounds that Luther was "a bachelor at heart." "My husband said that marriage was not for him," Sylvia testified, "that he was too temperamental to be tied down, and just refused to live with me."[26] Sylvia was also awarded two traffic violations that same day: one for parking in a red zone and another for speeding on the way home.²⁷ Luther and Sylvia would remain on good terms, however, and a few years later teamed professionally. In 1972, she was asked about her marriage to Adler. Sylvia offered a "heaven help us" look. Well into her second Bloody Mary, she challenged the reporter, "You can't quote a look dear. I defy you to do it."²⁸ Nonetheless, when asked who the best kisser was among her husbands and lovers, Sidney admitted, "Oh, honey. The best kisser was Luther Adler."²⁹

"I can't act," said George Raft, "I'm a personality."³⁰ It was the last day and the last scene for shooting *Mr. Ace*, a film that teamed Raft and Sidney for the third and last time. Sidney agreed with Raft's assessment that his "craft" was simply self expression. "Of all the actors I worked with," she reflected later, "he was the greatest gentleman. And he never made a pass at me." Sylvia landed her role in *Mr. Ace* (originally *The Congresswoman*) in January 1946, after Raft and Constance Bennett (his original co-star) had a verbal scrap. *The Searching Wind* wrapped a few days later, and Sylvia reported directly to General Service Studios (leased by United Artists). In February, when Raft was hospitalized with pleurisy, director Ed Marin shot around him, trying to keep within the film's small budget. Even so, producer Ben Bongeaus was paying $500 a week to rent a $27,000 mink stole that Sylvia considered a "tacky-looking" fur. When Raft got wind of it he put up a fight to get her a sable. She was completely taken with him.

> I was crazy about George Raft. He was a dear, sweet man who was generosity itself. He never stopped giving, and never ex-

Mr. Ace - with gentleman George Raft (United Artists)

pected anything in return. There were always flowers in my dressing room, and ... just after the war when you couldn't get a pair of silk stockings for love or money, George would come in with cartons of them for me. Cartons of cigarettes...everything. I kept telling him to stop, but you couldn't stop George.[31]

Mr. Ace was a behind-the-scenes exposé of American politics. Congresswoman Margaret Chase (Sidney), a cold-blooded blueblood, is ruthless in her campaign for Governor. She refuses her estranged husband a divorce, because it may cost her votes. She recognizes that connecting to the tough political machine run by suave Eddie Ace (Raft) is her link to being elected ... by a landslide. Having more aspiration than ethics, Sidney's character was on the exact same page as the men who dominated the political scene.

The unsavory pall that hangs over elections and *Mr. Ace* was nothing new. By 1946, two women had been elected Governor, both had husbands who had preceded them in the gubernatorial office, and both were as subject to controversy as their male opponents. Sidney's fictitious character in *Mr. Ace* was not to be confused with Congresswoman Margaret Chase Smith, who would be elected to the U.S. Senate in 1948.

Early portions of *Mr. Ace* intrigue. Sidney and Raft are smooth operators and connect easily. Their celluloid simpatico had mellowed like fine wine. Chase can handle Ace's cliché remarks about women in politics. She isn't fazed in the least. Both are pleasantly aroused by the threats they dish out to each other. The resulting reverie is sealed with kisses at a nightclub while a jazz ensemble neatly performs a wistful tune, "Now and Then." But, the bliss ends there. Despite their mutual attraction, the Congresswoman divides and conquers Ace's political machine. Her double-cross is foiled when Ace strikes a "business deal" with her husband, to file for divorce. Chase drops out of the race. The script subtly leans toward the question: "Will the ambitious combo of Chase and Ace be purified by love?"

Mr. Ace was off-beat territory for tough-guy Raft. The film was thoughtful, adult fare. An intelligently crafted script by Fred Finklehoffe dealt realistically with emotional struggle and transition. The carefully paced direction of Edwin Marin and exquisite camerawork of Oscar-winning Karl Struss (*Sunrise*) capture the pulse of two people who finally take a look in the mirror at themselves. There was no other message, or intention of dealing with pertinent post-war issues.

Reviews were lukewarm. *The New York Times* stated that *Mr. Ace* offered "much believable acting, but little else. Miss Sidney does make her share of the slowly-paced story believable ... her portrayal is warm

Publicity shot, 1946 (United Artists)

and sincere." Critic Eileen Creelman for the *New York Sun* found *Mr. Ace* to be "a powerful treatise against women in politics." She snipped that the glamorous Sylvia "does one stupid thing after another as the ruthless Margaret Chase." "It is an unpleasant part," harped Creelman, failing to mention the manipulating *males* dominating American politics. Racketeering and corporate influence in Washington D.C. wasn't anything new. Many Americans preferred to ignore it … and *Mr. Ace*. Raft biographer Everett Aaker noted, "*Mr. Ace* was an outright box office flop, Raft's first such in many years."[32]

On a positive note, critic/artist Clif Bradt praised, "*Mr. Ace* … one of the sharpest jobs to date, combines analysis of corrupt political practice with emotional dramatic action that is little short of a crusade. Sylvia Sidney stages an excellent screen comeback. The final punch is on the romantic side where everyone suspects it to be."[33] Bradt grasped what the film had to offer. For those who missed seeing the film, Raft and Sidney repeated their roles for a 30 minute adaptation on radio's *This is Hollywood*.

In the spring of 1946, columnists noted that Sylvia and radio producer Carleton Alsop had become a steady twosome. Alsop had separated from actress Martha Scott. That summer, Sylvia and Jody headed to New Jersey to spend a few weeks at the farm until Alsop's divorce was final. Jody's Grandmother Beatrice "Bee" showed up to spoil her little grandson. In August, Sylvia and Jody returned to Hollywood where she signed with Eagle-Lion to co-star with Franchot Tone in *Repeat Performance*. Filming was delayed several months. Sidney opted out. The studio then offered her the lead opposite John Hodiak in a remake of *Love from a Stranger*. Twenty-four hours before cameras rolled for the suspense-thriller, Sylvia and Alsop tied the marital knot on March 5, 1947.

Completing her moderately successful comeback, Sidney had accomplished her main goal: providing Jody an environment that allowed his health to improve. As Jody approached his eighth birthday Sylvia sold her farm in Flemington, concentrated on her new marriage and home in Beverly Hills, and … resumed her stage career.

(Endnotes)

1. Jeff Laffel, "Sylvia Sidney," *Films in Review*, September/October 1994
2. Constance Palmer, "Sylvia Sidney's Best Beau," *Screenland*, July 1946
3. Leonard Lyons, "Heard in New York," *New York Evening Post*, August 2, 1944
4. Harold Clurman to Stella Adler, June 3, 1944. Stella Adler Papers, Harry Ransom Center, Univ. of Austin
5. Jeff Laffel, "Sylvia Sidney," *Films in Review*, September/October 1994
6. Robbin Coons, "Sylvia Sidney Returns to Hollywood With Revised Outlook on Her Career," *State Times Advocate*, October 30, 1944
7. Thomas Patrick Doherty, *Projections of War: Hollywood, American Culture, and World War II*, Columbia University Press, c. 1999, pg. 143
8. *Variety* column, October 25, 1944
9. Louella Parsons column, *St. Petersburg Times*, July 1, 1945
10. James Cagney, *Cagney by Cagney*, Doubleday and Co., c. 1976
11. Jeff Laffel, "Sylvia Sidney," *Films in Review*, September/October 1994
12. Louella Parsons, column, "Sylvia Sidney Develops Unexpected Glamour," July 1, 1945
13. Constance Palmer, "Sylvia Sidney's Best Beau," *Screenland*, July 1946
14. Jimmy Fidler column, *State Times Advocate*, February 21, 1945 (Originally slated for production in 1945, *The Adventures of Don Juan* began filming in October 1947)
15. Kati Martin, *Wallenberg: Missing Hero*, Arcade Pub., c. 1995, pg. 30
16. Sylvia Sidney, "The Role I Liked Best," *Saturday Evening Post*, August 28, 1947
17. David M. Jordan, *FDR, Dewey, and the Election of 1944*, Indiana University Pr., c. 2011, pg. 353 (Telegram, September 20, 1944, Truman Papers - Also on the list for FDR were Luther Adler, Charles Boyer, Joan Bennett, Gregory Peck, Linda Darnell, John Garfield, Walter Huston, Gene Kelly, Agnes Moorehead, Chester Morris, Dick Powell, Teresa Wright, et. al)
18. Bernard F. Dick, *Hellman in Hollywood*, Associated University Presses, c. 1982, pg. 118
19. James Bawden, "Family Man," *Films of the Golden Age*, Fall 2015
20. Mildred Martin, review of *The Searching Wind*, *Philadelphia Inquirer*, September 9, 1946
21. James Robert Parish, email dated November 15, 2014
22. Bernard F. Dick, *Hal Wallis: Producer to the Stars*, University Press of Kentucky, c. 2004, pg. 114
23. Jeff Laffel, "Sylvia Sidney," *Films in Review*, September/October 1994

24 Gene Handsaker, "6-Year-Old Wrecks Interview," *Union Sun & Journal*, January 15, 1946
25 Virginia MacPherson, "Sylvia Sidney's Son Decides She's Worth 75 Cents a Week," *Advocate*, January 4, 1946
26 "Actress Sylvia Sidney Divorces …," *Augusta Chronicle*, February 28, 1946
27 Jimmy Fidler column, *Oregonian*, March 17, 1946
28 Arthur Bell, "Sylvia's Souvenirs," *New York Times*, December 17, 1972
29 quote from Sylvia Sidney, guest artist at the National Arts Club in New York, June 2, 1998
30 Sheilah Graham, "George Raft Says He Can't Act," *Evening Star*, April 3, 1946
31 Jeff Laffel, "Sylvia Sidney," *Films in Review*, September/October 1994
32 Everett Aaker, *George Raft: The Films*, McFarland, c. 2013, pg. 121
33 Clif Bradt review of *Mr. Ace*, *Knickerbocker News*, December 6, 1946

Chapter 10
Jeanne d'Arc & Judy Garland

Sylvia didn't often voice her opinions on films, but if she found a good one she'd watch it dozens of times. *Odd Man Out* (1947) and *Great Expectations* (1946) fit into this category. She was candid about the final film in her quartet of 40's comebacks, *Love from a Stranger*, based on the Agatha Christie short story, *Philomel Cottage*.

> That was the one where John [Hodiak] is a homicidal maniac who marries me because I won the lottery … then plans to murder me, as he has all his wives, at exactly nine p.m. Richard Whorf directed. Whorf was a good director. He was also an actor and he knew how to work with actors. I liked him very much. It wasn't much of a picture, but with all those period costumes I did look gorgeous in it if I do say so myself.

Director Whorf was leery of working with Sidney, and expecting trouble. "I knew that when she lets go she can punch hard and with both hands," he said. But, after the film's release Whorf had to admit, "She never got out of hand."[1] In 1937, *Love from a Stranger* had been a screen success for Ann Harding and Basil Rathbone. Reviews called it a "gripping study" and praised Harding's "compelling authority" in a meaty assignment. The climax in this version, written by veteran Frances Marion, came as a complete surprise and left audiences reeling. The revamped 1947 scenario prompted a *New York Times* critic to remark that the finale exploded with "all the thunder of a cap pistol."

Rathbone had prepared to play the homicidal husband by visiting a London insane asylum. John Hodiak acted as if he went no further than the local barber shop. After all, his character is obsessed with the appearance of his hair. Hodiak offers little beyond a peculiar stare and monotone voice. From the start, the film firmly established the evil nature of Hodiak, clad in a Dracula-like cape. This diminished the build-up of suspense. As the victim, Sidney appears agitated and confused, but little else. *Variety* cited her for a "direct and spirited performance," but most critics were unimpressed, and especially harsh on the inadequacies of her leading man. "Mr. Hodiak, a bad actor in more ways than one," said critic Cecilia Ager, "is in the habit of killing his wives. Miss Sidney changes from one dear silly little frock to another, until it becomes almost a prayer."[2] Sylvia had only high praise for designer Michael Woulfe, who worked on all four of her comeback films beginning with *Blood on the Sun*. In 1946, Sidney was quite vocal about Costume Design being recognized in the annual Oscar race. The Academy listened. The Oscar in that category was first introduced for films released in 1948.

After *Love From a Stranger* wrapped in mid-March, the studio knew they had a turkey on their hands. At the end of May, Sidney and Hodiak were recalled for additional scenes. Eagle-Lion waited another six months before releasing the film. For her efforts Sylvia was

With John Hodiak in *Love From a Stranger* (1947) (Eagle-Lion)

paid $75,000, while top-billed Hodiak was rewarded with $100,000.[3] Producer Bryan Foy took revenge on his lead stars. He told a national news syndicate, "Sylvia Sidney and John Hodiak don't mean a nickel at the box office."[4] It would be five years before Sidney made another film.

After a belated honeymoon to Carmel in June 1947, the new Mrs. Alsop prepared for her stage comeback. She referred to Carleton as

"Pa" and he obligingly accompanied her on tour in *Joan of Lorraine*, by Maxwell Anderson. The play was a phenomenal Broadway hit in the hands of Ingrid Bergman. When Bergman went to Hollywood to do a film version, several actresses took the play on the summer circuit—Luise Rainer, Diana Barrymore and Sylvia Sidney among them. Sidney was quoted as saying, "To me the theater is like violin exercises for a violinist. It gives you a chance to experiment—which movies don't. A motion picture producer isn't going to risk a million dollars in seeing whether or not I can play a certain part. That's why they keep shoving stars in the same kind of roles. And that's how actors get typed. So the logical move is to slip off to some little theater and try yourself out. If you fail it costs little, and nobody's hurt."[5]

Sidney's first performance in *Joan of Lorraine* was at Brooklyn's Flatbush Theatre. The house was packed during her week's stay—standees at every performance, and for good reason. Her interpretation of the role (wisely) made no attempt to follow the Bergman lead. "Miss Sidney is a fragile Joan," observed one critic, "as unlike Miss Bergman as possible." From Brooklyn to Atlantic City to Detroit, Sidney continued mastering her role. Carleton was always on hand. "I stand in the wings and give her criticism after every performance," he said. "I'm the darnedest back stage driver you ever saw."[6] A Philadelphia review praised, "Miss Sidney's performance is entirely individual, and is commendable for its consistency and the clarity with which she unkinks the complexities of the character."

Surprisingly, Sidney avoided the obvious spiritual connection associated with *Jeanne d'Arc*. She played the part as written, choosing not to project the supreme exaltation that Bergman and Rainer put on display. After two months on the road, the Alsops returned to their home on Beverly Drive. Sylvia's next stage appearance came as a surprise. She was an emergency replacement for Laraine Day in the Actors' Company revival of *Angel Street*. With only three hours notice, Sylvia took to the stage with co-star Gregory Peck. She hadn't played the role for five years. She later recalled, "The difficulties of the undertaking were unbelievable and the strain involved made me actually ill a few days later, but somehow I did make the grade and only required one prompt all evening. Without the help of Gregory Peck, Ernest Cossart and Elizabeth Patterson, who backed me every inch of the way ... I shouldn't have been able to complete a single scene."[7]

Sylvia's belief that teamwork alone made a great play endeared her to the troupe, especially Peck, who, along with Mel Ferrer and Dorothy McGuire, had founded Actors' Company. Peck persuaded Sylvia to open their summer season at La Jolla Playhouse.

In the fall of 1947, Sylvia and Carleton began socializing with Judy Garland and her husband Vincente Minnelli. Sylvia first met Garland at an informal party—everyone wearing casual attire, slacks, sweatshirts. When playwright Harry Krunitz arrived with a young woman wearing a spectacular evening gown, Sylvia stared at the girl and asked, "What are ya gonna wear New Year's Eve?" "Well," Sidney related afterward, "Judy heard that and fell off her chair. We became very friendly." When asked about Garland years later, Sylvia just shook her head.

> That poor kid went through some terrible times. She was trying to hide from Louis B. Mayer because he was making her crazy, so she stayed at my house. I wouldn't let Mayer get near her. He told my husband Carleton that if he could, he

1947 - Dining at Ciro's with Judy Garland and Vincente Minnelli

would have me banned from the industry. He even went so far as to say that he would pay one million dollars to be sure that he would never have to see me on the screen again. The son of a bitch. He was a terrible, terrible person.[8]

Garland, who was on a downward spiral emotionally, took to Sylvia's idea of referring to Carleton as "Pa." In 1948, "Pa" became Garland's new agent. Just how much of Carleton's back story was known to these two women is uncertain.

Carleton William Alsop

Carleton William Alsop was the grandson of Samuel Alsop, a pioneer in the Puget Sound salmon fishing industry near Bellingham, Washington. The Alsop trap, off Lummi's shores, was one of the most profitable. Samuel's five sons, however, had to pave their own way. Arthur Alsop (Carleton's father) was a day laborer in Stockton, California, when Carleton (sometimes spelled Carlton), the youngest of four sons, was born October 18, 1900. The following year, Arthur and his wife Jennie moved back to Bellingham, where Arthur began a laundry business. At the age of ten, Carleton was a newsboy for the *Bellingham Herald* and, by 1920, a reporter. The adventuresome lad found himself in Hollywood in 1924, doing free lance reporting while filling in as chauffeur for Fox film star Janet Gaynor. In 1926, Carleton accompanied a Fox film crew to Hawaii. He assisted cinematographers in capturing spectacular eruptions from the Mauna Loa volcano. The footage was used for the feature release *Black Paradise* (1926). Carleton opted to stay in Hawaii for a year, still free-lancing and supporting himself as a salesman for the American Hawaiian Motor Co. In Honolulu, he interviewed multimillionaire William Leeds Jr. (husband of Princess Xenia of Greece). His write up appeared in the *Honolulu Star Bulletin*.[9]

In February 1927, Carleton (and his first wife Lucille) returned to the United States. Nothing is known about Lucille. In 1926, she had sailed to Honolulu signing the ships manifest as "Lucille Alsop." After they separated, Carleton returned to Los Angeles, residing in Burbank, and selling stocks and bonds. Ambition relocated Carleton to New York where he became owner for Alsop Radio Recording, Inc. He ventured into a second marriage in 1935 to Rosalie Hooker Wellington Dixon Melikov (Carleton was her fourth husband). Columnist Cholly Knickerbocker noted that while the couple lived in Miami with their two Great Danes, they were known as "The Battling Alsops." "When Carleton and Rosalie started to bark at each other," said Cholly, "the dogs would join in." The two divorced in 1937, remarried in 1938, and divorced again in 1940. (By 1945, Rosalie was on her eighth marriage, which prompted the moniker "Mrs. Etc.")[10]

In 1938, Carleton hired actress Martha Scott to play the lead in the radio serial *The Career of Alice Blair*—about a struggling young actress in New York. The hero of the series was a man-about-town patterned after Alsop's own reputation. It came as no surprise when Carleton tied his fourth marital knot with Miss Scott, fourteen years his junior, in September 1940. "Older men understand better," purred Martha. "They are more tolerant than young men. They haven't irritating habits."[11] Indeed, a few months later, Martha's "understanding" bridegroom came to her defense on the set of the film *They Dare Not Love*. Director James Whale (*The Bride of Frankenstein*) began to berate his two female leads. One of them, actress Kay Linaker, recalled Whale's desperate emotional state as he ranted, "Not only do I have the two ugliest broads in town, I've got the two lousiest fucking actresses!"[12] Carleton put an immediate stop to it, telling Whale to shut his mouth and "keep it shut … until I come back from talking to Harry Cohn." Cast, crew, and leading man George Brent, sat in a daze until producer Cohn arrived on the scene and quietly informed the director, "You're through."

During WWII Carleton directed the Los Angeles chapter of the Red Cross Blood Bank, setting up mass blood donations at various studios. His radio successes included *The Don Ameche Show* (on which Sylvia would make guest appearances). In 1942, the Alsops greeted a son, Carleton Scott. When she wasn't filming, Martha was touring army camps. She also completed a seven-month Broadway run in *Voice of the Turtle*. Carleton told Louella Parsons that with his wife gone most of the time he was "beginning to feel like a bachelor." Whispers by busybodies were finally confirmed in July 1946, when Martha, age 32, filed for a Las Vegas divorce. After a fifteen-minute wait, she wed Benny Goodman's

1948 - With husband Carleton Alsop

jazz pianist, Mel Powell, age 23. To use a musical metaphor, Martha had "changed her tune" about older men. Gossips were already pairing Carleton and Sylvia. In September 1946, Sidney announced their plans to marry. A quiet wedding took place the following March, on the day after Sylvia was granted her final decree from Adler. The ceremony was held at the First Congregational Church in Hollywood.

Sylvia had been receiving letters from an anonymous man offering marriage proposals and advising her not to marry Alsop. After the wedding he showed up at their home. Carleton answered the door, but the man insisted on speaking to Sylvia. "He says it's personal," Carleton informed her. So, she stepped outside the front door to hear him out. "You know all about me," he said indignantly, "Didn't you think I was serious?" Sylvia realized he really was … and not in a good way. The man departed, unwillingly. It turned out that he was also in trouble with the Pentagon and kept sending back his dishonorable discharge.[13] In hindsight, perhaps Sylvia should have heeded the man's advice, and put her third marriage on hold. As early as September 1948, rumors were rumbling about a marital rift between Sylvia and Carleton. She was preoccupied with reviving her stage career and both were trying to help Judy Garland get back on her feet.

Prior to her return to the stage, Sylvia served as a guest panelist, along with Constance Bennett and Binnie Barnes, for Mutual Radio's *Leave It To The Girls*—touted as an "aggressively feminine" program tackling tough issues. One twenty-nine-year-old bachelor girl complained about her mother waiting by the front door, until she arrived home with her suitors. Constance proposed that she stay out later. Sylvia darkly suggested that she follow the example of the notorious Lizzie Borden. Radio critic John Crosby agreed with Sidney's "sensible, if brutal, solution."

Sylvia opened the summer season (1948) at La Jolla Playhouse in a revival of the Edward Chodorov play *Kind Lady*. The plot involved a kindly, well-to-do woman who befriends a young, homeless man. Before long, she is surrounded by his gang, who literally live off of her—selling her works of art and other valuables until she is on the brink of mental collapse. In the end, she turns the tables on them. When Sidney's tour in the psychological thriller reached Boston, critic Cameron Dewar commented, "Miss Sidney's display of quiet gallantry in the face of unspeakable infamy was something close to perfection."

As for playing a middle-aged spinster, Sidney rationally explained, "My husband's mother is 76; she walks as straight as I do, and her interests are as broad as mine. The way old ladies used to be played on the stage just doesn't hold anymore."[14] After a two-month respite in Hollywood, Sidney and her co-star from Hitchcock's *Sabatoge*, John Loder, were offered the leads in an East coast tour of the Lunt-Fontanne adult comedy *O Mistress Mine*. Loder, recently divorced from the beauteous Hedy Lamarr, had previously tackled the Alfred Lunt role. Carleton informed the usual gaggle of gossips that Sylvia's tour did *not* mean that their own marriage was on the rocks. They were "happy as larks." As the

Christmas holiday approached, Carleton and Jody headed east to join Sylvia. At the Los Angeles train depot, the ticket agent told Alsop that Judy Garland had already paid their fare, as a Christmas gift. In a few months Sylvia had opportunity to repay Garland's kindness.

> Judy Garland called me up, and she was in a state. It seems she was in the midst of shooting some picture, and it was Vincente's birthday—and there was no way that she could organize a party for him. Could I help? For Judy, anything, anytime. 'Leave it to me,' I told her. So I arranged this lovely dinner party for Vincente's birthday and, at the end of the party, when we are doing presents, the doorbell rang. Judy had once told me that Vincente adored Ronald Colman and would love to meet him. So that was my present.[15]

Vincente answered the door. Standing there, adorned in gift wrap, was Ronald Colman next to his wife. Vincente was taken aback ... for a moment. Without missing a beat he moaned, "Oh, this is too much!" and closed the door on them. "We were all convulsed in laughter," Sidney added.

O Mistress Mine took place during WWII. A widow (Sidney) is confronted with difficult decisions when romanced by a titled (and married) British cabinet member (Loder). Loder's character, separated from his wife, finds it inexpedient to divorce her during wartime. He invites the woman of his heart (Sidney) to share his home and tolerant social circle. Their unblessed Eden is interrupted by Sidney's disapproving seventeen-year-old son (Dick Van Patten). Sidney is left to choose between son and lover. The play explored an extra-marital affair with wit and civilized humor.

Sidney succeeded admirably in the footsteps of Lynn Fontanne.

A Cleveland review mirrored the consensus. "I was surprised by the skill and finesse of Sylvia Sidney. She has ... poise, charm, good looks, aptness for comedy, ease in transition to emotional scenes, and, above all, the capacity to make the unlikely believable and to create understanding for conduct which is commonly counted as sinful."[16] A Dallas critic concurred, "There have been more spectacular careers in the theater but no greater talent."

"Playing with Sylvia Sidney is great fun," said Loder. "She has acted in such a succession of drab, wispy parts in films ... lots of people are going to be astonished and delighted to discover how excellently she plays an attractive poised woman of the world with an enchanting sense of fun."[17] The two co-stars weathered a strenuous tour—fifty-three cities in six months. The only mishap occurred in San Antonio, when a bat flew on stage. Sylvia fled, and left Loder, who adlibbed, "Hey you! Come back!" From the wings, Sylvia hollered, "I'll come back as soon as that thing's gone!"

Sidney and Loder willingly allowed twenty-year-old Dick Van Patten to steal a few scenes as the self-pitying son. In 1977, Sidney and Van Patten were reunited on an episode of the popular TV series *Eight is Enough*. For this, Sylvia played a crotchety, sherry-sipping old aunt.

During the *O Mistress Mine* tour, Sylvia squeezed in two other acting assignments. D.C. critic Jay Carmody had high praise for her revival of Eliza Doolittle in *Pygmalion*, but blasted co-star Gavin Gordon. "What Miss Sidney cannot do is also play Prof. Henry Higgins," said Carmody. "That chore is left to Gavin Gordon and he is about as much at home in it as, say, Mickey Rooney might be in *Hamlet*." Poor Gavin

O Mistress Mine - Sylvia and John Loder toured
fifty-six cities in six months (1948-49)

was quickly replaced. For the second play, *The Two Mrs. Carrolls*, Sidney received applause as the second Mrs. Carroll, a wife marked for murder. A Boston review called it "an evening of subdued terror," and gave compliments to the star. "Sylvia Sidney does the honors ... grips it with both hands and gives us a believable portrayal."

Between engagements, Sylvia and Carleton spent time on Cape Cod in the summer of 1949. Judy Garland paid a visit looking, as Dorothy Kilgallen put it, "plump, tan and healthy." Earlier that year, Garland's erratic behavior and failure to report to the MGM set had cost her the lead in *Annie Get Your Gun*. Husband Minnelli, admittedly ineffectual as a helpmate, would phone Alsop at three in the morning to come over at once. A trembling, tear-stained Garland would greet him with, "Pa, I can't face the camera this morning."[18] Louis B. Mayer put her on suspension. Immediately afterward, Carleton accompanied Garland to the home of columnist Hedda Hopper. Garland opened up to Hopper, praising how Sylvia had helped her gain twenty pounds when studio bosses complained she was too thin. "She'd cook food that I liked," said Judy, "and make me stuff myself with it. I felt just like a goose being fattened for the market."[19] On one occasion, Garland admired a pair of silk Chinese lounging pajamas Sylvia was wearing. In a matter of seconds, Sylvia whipped out a tape measure and took Garland's measurements. "I bought some lovely black shantung with gold threading," recalled Sylvia, "and, on her next visit, I presented Judy with her own copy of the pajamas." Garland was less enthusiastic when Sylvia instructed her in needlepoint to "calm her nerves." Nonetheless, Sylvia's nurturing enabled Garland to bounce back and complete *In the Good Old Summertime* (1949).

Garland's recurring downward spirals: fluctuating weight, prescription drugs and nervous exhaustion—exasperated husband Minnelli. The couple separated several times. After losing *Annie Get Your Gun*, Garland was taken by Alsop to a Boston hospital for rest and rehabilitation. While there, she learned to sleep without sleeping pills. Garland had assumed her old vitality by the time she joined Carleton and Sylvia on Cape Cod. They all drove to Tanglewood Summer Theater where Judy sang for over two hours at an after-theater party filled with appreciative young people from the cast of *Best Foot Forward*.

For her birthday on June 10, Judy had a surprise visit from her three-year-old daughter Liza Minnelli. The two dined with Alsop at Boston's Ritz Carlton hotel. Liza, with her long brown hair and huge dark eyes, was quite taken with Sylvia's son, nine-year-old Jody. Although Jody's latest passion was to become a truck driver, he enjoyed little Liza. Liza's nurse, Ms. Duffy, commented, "Liza considers Jody a very special playmate, because he's an older boy who will play with her. Usually older boys don't like to play with little girls."[20] On Independence Day, Carleton, Sylvia, Jody, Judy and Liza were all in Gloucester riding the merry-go-round, and wandering around town followed by admiring crowds.

After her Cape Cod visit, Garland returned to Hollywood—suntanned and enthusiastic. "I don't blame [MGM] for suspending me," she enthused, "I've been a bad girl." Carleton informed the press that Garland was in fine health and had quiet nerves. In many ways, Carleton and Sylvia paved the way for Garland's return to the screen in *Summer Stock* (1950).

Sidney hadn't given up on her film career. Robert Wise had suggested her to play Robert Ryan's wife in *The Set Up* for RKO.[21] Studio boss Howard Hughes preferred more of a starlet-type and settled on Audrey Totter. In December 1948, Sylvia did a screen test at MGM for one of the leads in *Any Number Can Play* starring Clark Gable.[22] A possible run-in with Mayer, or commitment to *O Mistress Mine* precluded filming the picture. Sidney was also considered to play Margo Channing in *All About Eve*. "Mankiewicz nixed me because I looked too Jewish!" she later recalled. "Can you believe that! What was Mankiewicz himself? I would have liked to have done that part. But Davis was great. Davis was almost always great."[23]

In December 1949, Sidney was at Metro once again, filming a test for *Crisis* starring Cary Grant. Richard Brooks, who had written the screenplay for *Any Number Can Play*, directed and penned this political drama in which Sidney would play the wife of a prominent South American dictator—similar to the ill-fated Eva Peron of Argentina.[24] This challenging and fascinating fourth-billed assignment ended up in the hands of Signe Hasso. Of course, Mayer had informed Sidney that he would pay a million dollars never to see her face on the screen again. She had been protective of Judy Garland and would pay the consequences.

Two names from Sidney's past made the news in 1949. Paramount's "It Girl" Clara Bow was residing in a Connecticut sanitarium undergoing shock treatment. B.P. Schulberg was down on his luck and spending his last dime placing a "Situation Wanted" ad in the film trade publication *Variety*. Sidney commented that it was "a shame" that her former boss had to go begging, adding, "I certainly hope Hollywood welcomes him back."[25] They didn't. Following a stroke in 1950, Schulberg retired. His son Budd ended up supporting his father. Budd was now in the limelight and had been ever since the release of his novel *What Makes Sammy Run?* (1941)—a scathing look at Hollywood. His recent novel, *The Harder They Fall*, an exposé on the American prize-fighting racket, would provide Humphrey Bogart his screen swansong in 1956.

In the New Year 1950, Sidney confronted her own problems. Approaching forty, she found herself bedridden, her career on hold, while combating months of crippling arthritis. For three years she had suffered physical pain and panic, hoping that some physician could pinpoint what was wrong. "Some said it was bursitis, others said it was rheumatism," said Sylvia. She would load up on aspirin, and on one occasion walked on stage with her arm in a sling. By May of 1950, she had made vast improvement—no real specifics other than her comment, "I was fortunate in being able to afford good medical attention."[26] In the future, Sidney would intermittently resort to needle treatments (shots) in order for "the show to go on."

Marital stress also aggravated Sidney's emotional and physical health. Her relationship with Alsop was off-again-on-again. In March 1950, Sidney announced that she was "irrevocably determined" to file for divorce. The couple reconciled, which prompted Sylvia to remark, "Sometimes I think I have arthritis of the brain, too, if you know what I mean."[27] By summer, Dorothy Kilgallen hinted, "What's with Sylvia Sidney and Carleton Alsop? He's around the bistros very bachelorish again." To compound matters, Jody fell out of a swing and fractured a vertebra, which delayed his coming east with Carleton to see Sylvia. At that time, she was touring the subway circuit in Maxwell Anderson's historical drama, *Anne of a Thousand Days*.

Playing Anne Boleyn to John Loder's Henry VIII proved a credible, if not completely successful, venture for Sylvia. Critic Louis Sheaffer for the *Brooklyn Eagle* praised her "touching portrayal" of the ill-fated Queen of England: "Most of the credit goes to Sylvia Sidney. Whether she is facing up to the royal bull and bully or battling like a spunky little terrier … Miss Sidney makes a warm, vivid figure of the historic lady. The play is almost invariably at its best when she has the center of the stage." As far as the lusty, ruthless master of royal politics Henry VIII, Sheaffer determined, "John Loder, frankly, isn't up to it." The supporting cast included a young Walter Matthau in the role of Cardinal Wolsey. The play, peppered with frank, racy dialogue, lasted a little over a month on tour. Sylvia opted out for more promising (and contemporary) dramatic turf.

There was also drama closer to home. Judy Garland's addiction to barbiturates had escalated, along with a third suspension from her studio. One evening, Garland got hysterical while conferring with Alsop and Minnelli regarding the future of her career. She had been dropped from her co-starring role with Fred Astaire in *Royal Wedding*. At one point, she ran from the living room, locked herself in the bathroom and reportedly slashed her throat with a broken drinking glass.[28] The suicide attempt, which made front page headlines, was not her first. Garland's career at MGM had come to an end. In 1994, Sidney reflected,

> Judy was great, a wonderful person when she wasn't on drugs. When she was, it was … forget it. One time when she was staying with me, the drug store would send a motorcycle over with what I thought were prescriptions for stuff she needed. What she would do was get the same thing from many different drug stores. I didn't realize until later. But I tell you, when she wasn't on drugs there was no one warmer, kinder, funnier or more talented than Judy. I loved her.[29]

Following the lead of former film queens Madeleine Carroll, Ann Harding and Kay Francis, Sylvia signed on for the popular role of Agatha Reed in the comedy-drama, *Goodbye, My Fancy*. Congresswoman Reed finds herself in a romantic triangle upon returning to her *alma mater* (from which she had been expelled) to receive an honorary degree. Her former professor (and lover) is now the college president. They no longer share the same democratic ideals. Taking on Reed, an outspoken liberal, was a brave move for any actress. Academic freedom was in jeopardy. The loyalty oath had been instituted by President Truman in 1947—the same year that the House Un-American Activities Committee zeroed in on Hollywood. With the recent detonation of the first atomic bomb, author Fay Kanin felt young people had inherited a precarious future. The time was ripe for some healthy debate. She also wanted women to think. Not a popular idea at the time.

Following the opening at Berkshire Playhouse in Massachusetts, a critic for the *Springfield Union* thought the play "first-rate." "From the moment Sylvia Sidney appeared," said the review, "the cast came together in a truly professional manner. She presented a definite growth of character in response to the dramatic issues of the play. When the final curtain went down, the audience had been given the gentlest of lessons that we all have to scrap the comfortable illusions of yesterday and marry the realities of tomorrow." Sidney enjoyed the part and offered successful repeat tours in 1951-52.

Following *Goodbye, My Fancy*, Sylvia decided it was farewell, Carleton Alsop. As finishing touches on their new home on Kings Road in Hollywood Hills were being completed, Sidney moved forward with her intention to divorce husband number three.

(Endnotes)

1   Earl Wilson column, *Omaha World Herald*, January 11, 1948
2   Cecilia Ager, "A Good Costumer Helps Sidney Act Scared," *PM Daily*, November 28, 1947
3   *Variety*, "Film Biz Slump Slight," February 12, 1947
4   Sheilah Graham, "Foy Claims Few Actors Worth Money," *Dallas Morning News*, December 28, 1948
5   Hedda Hopper, "Sylvia Sidney – She's Perfectly Happy," *Chicago Tribune*, July 20, 1947
6   "Rash of Joans Brings Sylvia Sidney (and 'Pa') Back Again," *Brooklyn Eagle*,

August 24, 1947
7. Elinor Hughes, "Sylvia Sidney Discusses Matter of Teamwork on Stage," *Boston Herald*, January 3, 1951
8. Jeff Laffel, "Sylvia Sidney," *Films in Review*, September/October 1994
9. "Bellingham Boy, Now In Honolulu, Writes of Multi-Millionaire," *Bellingham Herald*, June 16, 1926
10. "The Eighth Try," *Buffalo Courier-Express*, August 5, 1945
11. Sheilah Graham column, *Omaha World-Herald*, July 2, 1941
12. Leonard J. Kohl, "Formerly Kate Linaker: Part 3," (Interview), *Scarlet Street*, 2004
13. Harry MacArthur, "Actress Lives a Farce; Another's an Optimist," *Evening Star*, July 2, 1949
14. Howard Hutchison, "Sylvia Sidney Not Daunted By Role Of Kind Old Lady," *San Diego Union*, June 27, 1948
15. Jeff Laffel, "Sylvia Sidney," *Films in Review*, September/October 1994 (In the fall of 1949 columnists misconstrued the story, reporting that Colman showed up to surprise Judy Garland on her birthday. Garland was on Cape Cod at the time)
16. William F. McDermott, review of *O Mistress Mine*, *Plain Dealer*, February 8, 1949
17. Elinor Hughes, "Loder Here, in Rattigan Play, Wonders About Good Scripts," *Boston Herald*, January 12, 1949
18. Gerold Frank, *Judy*, HarperCollins, c. 1975, pg. 240
19. Hedda Hopper column, *Boston Herald*, June 19, 1949
20. Virginia Bohlin, "Judy Garland's Daughter Talented, Friendly Child," *Boston Traveler*, July 14, 1949
21. Doug McClelland, *Forties Film Talk: Oral Histories of Hollywood*, McFarland, c. 1992, pg. 191
22. Edith Gwynn, Hollywood in Review," *Philadelphia Inquirer*, December 26, 1948
23. Jeff Laffel, "Sylvia Sidney," *Films in Review*, September/October 1994
24. Louella Parsons column, *San Diego Union*, December 10, 1949
25. "Schulberg Still Looking For Job In Hollywood," *Daily Illinois State Journal*, October 27, 1949
26. J.A. Wadovick, "Sylvia Sidney Tells How She Fought Arthritis and Won," *Plain Dealer*, December 15, 1950
27. Erskine Johnson column, *Trenton Evening Times*, March 23, 1950
28. "Judy Garland Slashes Throat In Anguish Fit," *Trenton Evening Times*, June 20, 1950
29. Jeff Laffel, "Sylvia Sidney," *Films in Review*, September/October 1994

Chapter 11
Stage, Screen and Television

The *Innocents*, a dramatization of the Henry James psychological thriller *The Turn of the Screw*, occupied Sidney for nine months on tour. Prior to closing, she filed for divorce from Alsop. "We've been married four years," Sylvia explained, "and most of that time we have been separated more than we have been together."[1] More pertinent, unpleasant issues regarding their marriage would be revealed in months to come. Alsop liked to joke about Sylvia's arrangement with the purser of the *Queen Mary* on his return from England in 1949. A cocktail would arrive each evening at six p.m. with the attached note, "I love you." "It was most touching," he mused, "and, by golly, each night at 6 the martini would arrive and ruin each of those shipboard romances."[2] When Judy Garland asked Alsop how it felt to be divorced five times, he sighed, "I feel somewhat like a maple tree that gets tapped every year for its sap." His smug remark was simply a cover-up.

The Innocents was a horror story for adults. Set in 1880's England, a governess of two precocious children has romantic flutters for her employer, their uncle. It appears that she also has an overactive imag-

1950 - *The Innocents* - with Patsy Bruder

ination—a propensity for premonition and hysterics. Audiences were left wondering if the ghosts that terrify her, and the nameless evil possessing the motherless children in her charge, were fact or fiction. Cleveland critic W. Ward Marsh was baffled by what he saw on stage, but had to admit, "*The Innocents* has a kind of harrowing power, and tells just enough to keep one terrified without revealing very much. Sylvia Sidney makes her fears and heartbreaks seem genuine. In her are reflected all the terrors of the play." The eerie set designs by Jo Meilziner added immensely to the sinister atmosphere during the cross-country tour.

For Thanksgiving 1950, Jody, now eleven, left his school in Nyack, New York and traveled alone to Chicago to visit his mother. He enjoyed playing with the two youngsters cast in *The Innocents*, but was more in his element running around the Museum of Science and Industry. "I'm just another mother working as far as he's concerned," said Sylvia. "We get together when we can and we have fun … more so, of course, when I'm out of a job."[3] She elaborated on plans for Christmas in New York, with Grandma Bee in charge of everything but the cooking. Jody had high praise for his mother's poultry. "You get everything nice and brown on the outside," he would tell her, "and juicy in the middle." "He claims I'm a good cook," smiled Sylvia. Jody told his mother that while the food at school was very good, he preferred expensive cooking. "I can tell yours is expensive," he insisted.

Come spring, Sylvia attended a Board of Education screening of *Palmour Street*. The sensitively drawn documentary of an African-American community in rural Georgia illustrated the impact of parental choices in rearing children. Also screened was *Angry Boy*, which promoted clinical counseling for pre-adolescents caught stealing. Sylvia joined William Jansen, Superintendent of Schools, in a panel discussion following the program. Parenting, for Sylvia Sidney, along with acting, involved commitment.

One of the contentions in Sidney's divorce case was that Carleton had refused to let Jody live with them. After conferring with attorney Melvin Belli, she filed suit (March 22, 1951), saying that Alsop had told her he was "fed up with marriage." Following their nuptials in 1947, Alsop refused to support her. "He stopped working and never worked again," she revealed.[4] Alsop's career had definitely been sidetracked by representing Judy Garland. MGM often paid for Carleton's traveling expenses as he monitored Garland's emotional ups and downs. *Variety* reported that Alsop received weekly commission checks from Garland, but she was often, to use her own words, "stony broke."[5] As her agent, Alsop learned that MGM accountants planned retroactive penalties from Garland's salary based on production costs accrued by her failure to show up on the set. As a representative for A&S Lyons theatrical agency, Alsop knew how to investigate such matters. At one point Garland's "debt" at MGM accumulated to a sum of $100,000.⁶ As for the failure of the Garland-Minnelli marriage, Sylvia offered her own opinions after the couple divorced,

> Vincente is a sensitive, intense person who also exhausts himself in his work. His friends are artists and intellectuals. Judy likes romantic novels, soap operas and popular music. She built up a whole new set of inferior feelings in the marriage.⁷

Garland was granted a divorce on the same day that Sidney filed suit against Alsop. In essence, Judy concurrently divorced "Pa." The two had a parting of the ways that some inferred was less than amicable. A few months later it was reported that Carleton had abandoned his stylish *bon vivant* round of night spots and cocktail haunts to live in Washington D.C., and work for the State Department. Several sources indicate that he helped negotiate the film rights to George Orwell's *Animal Farm*.⁸ In 1952, he voyaged to England while working as a consultant for Central Intelligence.⁹ *Variety* indicated that his new position was "hush-hush."

Sidney's summer tours in *Goodbye, My Fancy* and *O Mistress Mine* came as no surprise. The latter re-teamed her with an old flame from Broadway, Romney Brent. The usual round of tongue-wagging proposed that the two had rekindled their romance—some suggested they were engaged. "Where there's life, there's love," replied Sylvia when asked about another marriage. Her divorce from Alsop would not become final until September 1952.

Over the next few years, gossips Dorothy Kilgallen and Ed Sullivan would link Sylvia romantically with top fashion designer Don Loper (who was gay—always sporting patent leather shoes, and devoted to his longtime business partner, Charles Northrup).[10] Loper was all about glamour and style. His motto: "A woman should dress for the man in her life." His clients included Lana Turner, Marlene Dietrich and Lucille Ball. When Loper designed a wardrobe for Frank Sinatra's nightclub act, James Bacon's column headlined: "Gay Wardrobe Costs Sinatra Heavy Ribbing," or "Frank Goes Gay." Comedian Joe E. Lewis wired Sinatra, "Heard about your new Loper wardrobe. Save the first dance for me." When "Old Blue Eyes" was a no-show at an event, Milton Berle quipped that Frank's "zipper got caught in the sequins." Sylvia's friendship with Loper began the first time he designed clothes for her. She told him, "Don, I have a problem. I have a bosom." Loper replied crisply, "You'd have a worse problem if you didn't." "For the first time," Sidney explained, "a designer was structuring clothes for me, instead of restructuring me for them." She added, "Is it any wonder he became very dear to me?"[11] In subsequent years, Sylvia would design needlepoint gifts for Loper and his partner Northrup. Her diligence in making Loper a medieval-design needlepoint of the St. Francis of Assisi prayer, was a testament to their friendship. She was determined to recreate a page from a 12th-century Bible on exhibit at the J. Pierpont Morgan Library. She took her idea to a needlepoint shop for translation. Their suggestions threw the design completely off. Jody ended up coming to his mother's rescue. He showed her how to work the design onto graph paper. His solution worked perfectly and it liberated Sylvia from depending upon store designed canvases.

When Mady Christians took ill before a tour of the English play *Black Chiffon*, Sylvia was paged to take the lead. An émigré from Nazi Germany, Christians had been blacklisted—her name mentioned in the notorious *Red Channels* (1950). Other so-called Communist sympathizers listed in the publication included Edward G. Robinson, John Garfield, Lillian Hellman and Sylvia's ex-husband Luther Adler. While Sylvia toured in *Black Chiffon*, FBI investigations and false accusations against Christians amplified her high blood pressure, contributing to her early death (cerebral hemorrhage). Sylvia herself was listed in Myron C. Fagan's *Red Treason in Hollywood* (1949) and *Red Treason on Broadway* (1954), which included among "Stalin's Stars," Bette Davis and Katharine Hepburn.[12] "Many of the stars named in this book," wrote Fagan, "are craftily piping Red Treason into our homes." Lucille Ball, Gregory Peck, Fredric March, and Frank Sinatra were among 120 stars Fagan listed as rabid pro-Reds "poisoning the minds of children." Right-wing fanaticism zeroed in on the film/theatrical community with inevitable repercussions on careers and lives.

David Clive (son of character actor E. E. Clive) was assistant stage manager for *Black Chiffon*. Clive felt that the play was "spectacularly unsuited to the American heartland." He was right. Sidney played an upper-class woman with an unnatural attachment to her beloved son. After she is arrested for petty theft, her psychiatrist reveals that she subconsciously stole a negligee to create a scandal big enough to halt her son's marriage. After five weeks on the road, *Black Chiffon* closed in Philadelphia. Box office was less than brisk. Matinees attracted only elderly women who had come to see Sylvia Sidney the movie star. They clamored after the play to retrieve Miss Sidney's autograph which, according to Clive, "pleased her no little."

Sidney's career adapted nicely to television. Shortly after essaying Sadie Thompson in *Rain* for radio's *Somerset Maugham Theatre*, Sylvia made her debut in the televised panel discussion *Leave it to the Girls* (1951). She also offered a dramatic sketch, *It Takes a Thief*, by Arthur Miller on NBC's *Kate Smith Evening Hour*. NBC's *Cameo Theatre* cast Sidney opposite her co-star from 1927's *Crime*, Douglass Montgomery, in Abby Mann's first televised script, *The Gathering Twilight*. Sylvia played the frustrated wife of a celebrated artist. To compete, she takes on the hopeless ambition of becoming a professional ballerina.

In early 1952, 20th Century-Fox paged Sidney back to the big screen for a cameo role in an adaptation of Victor Hugo's *Les Miserables*. British actor Michael Rennie, fresh from his success in the science-fiction hit *The Day the Earth Stood Still* (1951), was cast in the iconic role of Jean Valjean. With the reputable Lewis Milestone in the director's seat, *Les Miserables* was projected to be a huge hit. When Rennie and Sidney first met on the set he wagered that she probably didn't remember him from Hitchcock's *Sabotage*. He had been John Loder's stand-in. Sidney admitted she did not. Being back in Hollywood was simply a job to Sylvia, and she made it clear that she preferred New York and its accessibility to good play parts. This was not to be misconstrued as a comeback. "I come out and haunt Hollywood every few years," she remarked.

In *Les Miserables* we follow the journey of Jean Valjean (Rennie), an ex-con who endured years of imprisonment for stealing a loaf of bread. Though he is a victim of injustice, Valjean pursues a new life focused on redemption and good deeds. In a supporting role, Sidney played the ill-fated Fantine, a working class woman who turns to prostitution in order to support her illegitimate daughter Cosette (Debra Paget). We first see Fantine sauntering toward a pub where she is accosted by a drunk. She is accused of assault. The town mayor

Les Miserables (1952) with Michael Rennie and Robert Newton (20th Century-Fox)

(Valjean) comes to her defense. Fantine had lost her job at Valjean's factory. She blames him for her situation. "I'm on the streets because of you!" she cries, spitting on him. Sidney was also allotted a hospital deathbed scene, following Fantine's tender reunion with daughter Cosette. Despite the tampering with Victor Hugo's story, critics were impressed with Sidney. "*Les Miserables* is crammed full of stars," said a Philadelphia critic, "but only Sylvia Sidney, as Fantine … seems to take her part seriously."[13] A Dallas review thought the film left "little impact," but praised Sidney's ability to make her brief "moments valuable with tempered artistry."[14]

Most film historians prefer the handsomely filmed 1935 version of *Les Miserables* starring Fredric March, Charles Laughton and Florence Eldridge as Fantine. Here the players easily connect in a sensitively drawn screenplay. This version was nominated for Best Picture. Rennie's gauntly handsome Jean Valjean in the 1952 film, wasn't the sensation the studio expected. In retrospect, reputable British film critic Leslie Halliwell found the film "lacking the spark of inspiration." Twenty years later, journalist Arthur Bell asked Sidney what it was like to work with Debra Paget. Sylvia mused, "I must have met her. Didn't she play my daughter? Was she Cosette, or was I Cosette? I remember that name, but I don't know who to tag it on to." Bell asked if she was putting him on. "What you see is what you've *got*," snapped Sylvia. "You're asking me things that I don't think about."[15] After *Les Miserables* wrapped, Sylvia and Jody took a vacation in the Bahamas.

One of the more compelling dramatic roles Sylvia essayed on television was for *Tales of Tomorrow*, a precursor to *The Twilight Zone*. The episode *Time to Go* begins with Sidney (Mrs. Davis) frantically trying to reach her husband. In flashback, we see her as a nagging, time-obsessed wife, who lines up chores for her husband—like fixing the leg on a grandfather clock. Mrs. Davis has an account at a new bank, where "time saved" extends the lives of investors. "We in this bank, we're not of your world," the bank manager explains. Suspense builds when Mrs. Davis learns that her account has closed. The bank is going to "borrow" her life at the stroke of midnight. We return to the opening scene to find her barricading the front door, then clinging to the grandfather clock. "It's time, Mrs. Davis," calls a voice from outside. "Time to go." The clock strikes twelve, before collapsing upon its intended victim. It was an eerie, effective piece, and Sidney's skill made the fantastic plausible.

The Gypsies Wore High Hats was scheduled for a Broadway open-

1952 - Sylvia in her dressing room   *The Fourposter* (1952-53) with Romney Brent

ing in October 1952. Sidney gave the new play her best shot for a five-week summer tour. It never reached the Great White Way. Written by Pulitzer Prize Winner Joseph Kramm (*The Shrike*), the play told the story of a Hungarian wife (Sidney) whose husband, a diamond salesman, supplies his family with useless luxuries. She keeps the family from starvation by her endless rounds of eye-straining handiwork. When her daughter confronts the situation, Sylvia helps the girl appreciate the essential generous quality behind the father's eccentricities. *Variety* noted, "Sylvia Sidney's flair for weepy, emotional acting is given a field day. She brings warmth and dignity to the role." Critics felt the play lacked the essentials for Broadway.

The Fourposter was already a proven success when Sylvia joined the Broadway cast. The Tony-Award-winning play, starring Jessica Tandy and Hume Cronyn, had opened in October 1951, at the Ethel Barrymore. The story detailed their marital journey from 1890-1925. A simple set, dominated by a large fourposter bed, accommodated the consummation of their marriage, birth of their first child, an extramarital affair, and preparation for their daughter's wedding. When the play transferred to the John Golden Theatre in December 1952, Sylvia and Romney Brent starred. Sidney admitted that the real challenge in *The Fourposter* was changing from evening clothes into a nightgown in 45-seconds. "I only have time for two puffs from a cigarette the entire evening," she complained. Critic Louis Sheaffer cheered that the Sidney-Brent combo kept audiences happy and provided "an enjoyable, ingratiating evening." The duo kept the play going for five more months. During the run, Sylvia was guest of honor at a luncheon to kick off the 1953 Israel Bond Project.

Broadway Television Theatre offered Sidney the opportunity to enact roles she played on stage: *Angel Street* and *Kind Lady*. During the final rehearsal for a broadcast of Somerset Maugham's *Theatre,* Kay Francis took ill and was hospitalized. Sylvia was paged at the last minute. TV critic Bob Lanigan cheered, "A better substitute than Sylvia Sidney couldn't have been found. Merely great!"

Sidney also tackled two roles associated with Bette Davis: *Dark Victory,* and Maugham's *The Letter*. Christopher Plummer co-starred with Sylvia in *Dark Victory.* "It was like doing summer stock with cameras," he recalled in his autobiography (2009). "I was Sylvia's leading man. Sylvia, who was a superb actress, had large, deep pools of eyes, which right on cue would overflow with tears gushing from their ducts like waterfalls."[16] Cast members were required to enact commercials at the end of each show. "It was humiliating and awful," said Plummer, "particularly for important stars like Sylvia, but we gritted our teeth and did it." Veteran Ian Keith, who costarred in the first act of *Dark Victory*, went out and got drunk before returning to do his bit for Nash Motors. Standing next to a shiny new Nash, he gave it a whack and bellowed, "I want to tell you about my new little MG. Goddamn! ... If she was just a tad smaller, why, hell, I'd take her to bed with me. She sure beats this old piece of tin."[17] Keith was suspended for three months by the American Federation of Television & Radio Artists (AFTRA) for insulting the sponsor product.[18] Keith's reply to his accusers was simply, "How Now Brown Cow!"[19] Plummer admired Keith's ability to separate art from advertising.

On a happier note, in the summer of 1953, Sylvia and ex-husband Luther Adler took Jody to Atlantic City where they co-starred in a successful revival of *Angel Street* at the Quarterdeck Theater. It was the first time since their divorce that Jody had holidayed with his parents. Adler had recently invested in a popular Malibu seafood eatery he named Jody's Lobster Quadrille—a tribute to Jody's passion for lobster.

The only new play that Sylvia tackled in 1953 was the bewitching comedy *Bell, Book and Candle* by John Van Druten. A New York critic nodded, "The lovely Sylvia Sidney weaves some pretty fancy magicwork. Worth seeing too ... is the wardrobe of Miss Sidney."[20] Surprisingly, little news coverage was given to Sidney's narrow escape from death while driving from a summer stock engagement to Hollywood. She was scheduled to report on September 23, to film an episode of *Ford Television Theatre* titled (ironically) *As the Flame Dies*. No one in Stratford, Texas, recognized her after her car overturned en route. Covered in mud, she was unhurt when dragged from the wreckage.[21] The teleplay got around to rolling on September 30, and was sensitively directed by James Neilson. Sylvia's auto mishap triggered what *Variety* called her "excellent portrayal" of a woman physician with heart disease, who contemplates suicide.

Ford Theater (1953) (NBC) with Barry Sullivan. Filmed after Sylvia's automobile wreck in Texas.

In January 1954, Sidney headed to the Sombrero Theater in Phoenix. She and Gene Raymond co-starred in *Design for Living*, Noel Coward's sophisticated ode to *ménage a trois*. The Arizona Republic thought it "jolly good fun" and that Sylvia "was a fine scarlet woman." The review also felt that Raymond outshone his co-star, and carried the provocative play on his "very substantial shoulders." Two decades had passed since he and Sidney teamed in Paramount's *Ladies of the Big House* and *Behold My Wife*. The following month, Sidney, sans Raymond, repeated her role on the island of Bermuda.

In May, Sidney played opposite Rex O'Malley in a revival of *O Mistress Mine* in Miami. She considered the role her most trying, because she was always on stage and never stopped talking. Prior to the opening, Sylvia and Luther met fourteen-year-old Jody at the luxurious Algiers Hotel. This second family reunion was delayed when a motorcycle cop pulled Sylvia over for speeding. Luther was in the passenger seat. The patrol officer inquired if they were married. "Well, not exactly," replied Sylvia. Asked what they were doing in Florida, Adler casually answered,

"Visiting our son." "Not exactly married? Visiting your child?" repeated the officer. "I think we better have a hearing."²² After that ordeal, afternoons were spent poolside at the Algiers. A relaxed Sidney was unusually cordial when a female reporter asked for a photo op. Chuckling to herself, Sylvia struck a pose on the diving board.

Sidney's standout televised performance in 1954, was for *Philco TV Playhouse*. *Catch My Boy on Sunday* was helmed by the young director Arthur Penn (*Bonnie and Clyde*). *Variety* raved that Sidney, as a neurotic stage mother, "socked over in the overwrought, emotional role, underplaying where it was most needed." She evoked exactly what Paddy Chayefsky intended for his teleplay. Chayefsky, who would go on to win three Academy Awards, remarked that Sidney had given "the most perfect performance of any of my characters."²³ TV critic John Crosby raved that Sidney was "perfectly wonderful [as] a shrill possessed neurotic on the verge of a nervous breakdown." Witnessing Sidney in *Catch My Boy On Sunday*, six decades later, one is impressed with the staying power of her remarkable portrayal. When Sidney wasn't nominated for an Emmy for Best Actress, Boston columnist Anthony La Camera took exception as to why she had been overlooked. In recompense, Sidney would be acknowledged for her stage work by the Stage and Arena Guild (New York) as "best dramatic actress" for the spring of 1955.

Columnists such as Jimmy Fidler were now referring to Sylvia as "a star of yesteryear." As far as Hollywood was concerned, if you weren't in films, you didn't exist. In November 1954, it was announced that Sidney was cast in the Clark Gable film *Soldier of Fortune*. For whatever reason, she opted instead to sign on for *Violent Saturday* at 20th Century Fox.

Fighting off bad guy Lee Marin in *Violent Saturday* (1955) (20th Century-Fox)

Filming for the heist caper, shot in Deluxe Color and Cinemascope, began in early December in the copper mining town of Bisbee, Arizona.

Ads for *Violent Saturday* display Sidney's character with the caption: "The Librarian – her life was an open book ... with a very shady chapter!" On screen, Sidney dares the town's bumbling bank manager (Tommy Noonan) to call the police after he catches her with a stolen purse. She knows Noonan's "little secret"—he's the town's peeping Tom. *Violent Saturday* fits classic noir themes. Subplots involve disturbed characters with no redeeming qualities. Despite a tinge of soap opera, the film has fine ensemble work from Victor Mature, Richard Egan, Stephen McNally, Lee Marvin and Ernest Borgnine. Sidney's librarian is almost lost in the shuffle. Deleted scenes in promotional stills suggest there was more to her character. She was billed ninth, but some theater owners ran ads that gave Sidney second billing to Victor Mature.

Director Richard Fleischer was beside himself when he learned that producer Buddy Adler had cast Sylvia in *Violent Saturday*. "The aura of her stardom overpowered me," said Fleischer, "I couldn't imagine in my wildest dreams ever being permitted to direct *Sylvia*

Sidney for God's sake." In his 1993 autobiography, Fleischer recalled how Sylvia sat knitting in her movie trailer, while he nervously explained her character's psychology and motivation. She looked up at him afterward, and, with a devilish smile said, "When we get to the set, you just tell me where to stand. Whenever you need tears ... just tell me when to cry." It must have struck a chord. Fleischer titled his memoir: *Just Tell Me When to Cry: A Memoir*. He thought *Violent Saturday* a "damn good movie."[24] The *Boston Herald* agreed, saying that Fleischer's direction had pace and imagination. *The New York Times* argued the film had no purpose but "to titillate and thrill on the level of melodrama and guarded pornography."

A few film aficionados hold *Violent Saturday* and its assortment of sordid characters, with great esteem. In 2008, Nick Pinkerton for *The Village Voice* wrote, "The cast is a museum exhibit on the nigh-extinct art of scaled-in American bit acting, with the magnificent Sylvia Sidney as the daughter of a prominent family brought low, her flashing pridefulness in tact." When asked about *Violent Saturday* in 1972, Sylvia replied, "I never saw it. Somebody told me that Victor Mature and Ernest Borgnine were in it. I never met them. They were probably grabbing their money and running."[25]

Following location shooting, Sylvia spent the holidays with Jody. While he proudly followed his mother's career, Jody showed no interest in acting. "I really would have helped him," said Sylvia, "if he'd wanted a theatrical career. But—he wants to be an engineer, and now we're going to see to it that he has a chance."[26] As Jody approached his seventeenth birthday he had his eye set on entering Massachusetts Institute of Technology (MIT)—a goal he had had since he was thirteen. Sylvia vowed, "As far as I'm concerned that's where I'll move heaven and earth to send him." In lieu of any real acting opportunity,

Violent Saturday had at least provided Sylvia cash for Jody's college fund. His dream to attend MIT came true the following year.

Television continued to keep Sidney busy in a variety of roles: a cutthroat corporate executive (*Leaf Out of the Book* for *Climax!*), an aging actress who insists on playing younger women (*Toy Lady* for *Star Stage*), a meddling aunt for *Playwrights '56*, and the mother of a suicidal man for *20th Century-Fox Hour*. Sidney Lumet, Sylvia's co-star from *One Third of a Nation*, directed *Toy Lady*. Many broadcasts were "live." This didn't bother her in the least. George Brent, her co-star in *Leaf Out of the Book*, felt otherwise. "I tried just one 'live' show, a *Climax!*" he grimly told *TV Guide*, "and that was my first and last one." Boston critic, Joseph Purcell, felt the handsomely staged teleplay "notches above usual TV fare." "Mr. Brent's performance was the only weak link," said Purcell, "stiff and unyielding throughout. Sylvia Sidney was convincing."

In June 1955, Sylvia was paged to introduce ex-President Truman's daughter Margaret, a semi-professional singer, at the Philadelphia Music Festival. Soprano Leontyne Price was also on hand to dazzle over 4,000 listeners. While in Philadelphia, Sidney began her tour in W. Somerset Maugham's treatise to sexual equality, *The Constant Wife*—a stage success for Ethel Barrymore in 1927. A local critic praised her take on the old chestnut, saying, "All of the poise and serenity inherent in the role—were realized in Sidney's performance."

Star Stage (NBC) Sylvia and director Sidney Lumet discuss *The Toy Lady* (*below*) 1955 - *Leaf Out of the Book* for *Climax!* (CBS) with George Brent and Diana Lynn

Playing the butler, with no dialogue, was sixteen-year-old, future director, Peter Bogdanovich. When the tour reached Michigan, Sidney found out it was his birthday and presented Bogdanovich with a silent butler. The note attached read, "Oh, you *are* the silent one!" "A reference," wagered Bogdanovich, "to my being talkative." In his 2010 autobiography, he wished he had "talked less and asked more questions." "Sylvia Sidney, for God's sake," he lamented, "had worked with Alfred Hitchcock, Fritz Lang, King Vidor ... did I know? No."[27] Forty-five years later, they met again at a Hitchcock centennial. She graciously pretended to remember him. "She was thin and fragile," said Bogdanovich, "had a hard time stepping up to the podium. Her first words to the mike were: 'Getting old is a bitch!'"

In early 1956, Sidney teamed with Tom Tully for the prison melodrama, *Behind the High Wall* (Universal-International)—a remake of *The Big Guy* (1939). Things looked promising for the "B" programmer. Tully had recently been nominated as Best Supporting Actor in *The Caine Mutiny*. In *Behind the High Wall*, he played a warden who is kidnapped by convicts during a prison break. When his captors are killed in a car wreck, Tully hides the stolen cash, in order to provide security for his invalid, wheelchair-bound wife (Sidney). He allows an innocent mechanic (John Gavin) to be accused of the crime. When Tully reveals the truth to Sidney, she is crestfallen, blaming herself. "You wouldn't have done it," she tells him, "if I wasn't more than half a wife."

Decidedly downbeat, *Behind the High Wall* was depressing screen fare with no surprise twists. *Variety* was unimpressed, but felt that of the two co-stars, Sidney came off best. "Tully's characterization of a prison warden," said the review, "fails to register." Another critic praised, "Acting in a wheelchair throughout, Sidney dominates her scenes ... a fine and sensitive performance." Tully's uneven interpre-

Behind the High Wall (1956) with
Tom Tully (Universal-International)

tation goes through the motions. His death scene is one of cinema's most unconvincing. In his *Prison Pictures in Hollywood,* author James Robert Parish wrote, "Thankfully, veteran actress Sylvia Sidney gave meaning and intensity to her role as the wheelchair-bound wife."[28] John Gavin, in his official screen debut, was predicted to be "a likely candidate for bigger things." Sidney, however, wouldn't make another film for seventeen years.

Dabbling in Hollywood didn't satisfy Sidney. Her preference was the stage, which afforded more *real* opportunities … and, a chance to play comedy. In the summer of '56, audiences howled giddily during Sidney's *Anniversary Waltz* tour. Written by Jerome Chodorov and Joseph Fields, this frothy concoction was held together by bold jokes, sex, child psychology, and television. She portrayed the wife of Barry Thomson (real-life husband of Ruth Chatterton), a harried advertising executive who kicks in the TV set when their "progressive" daughter reveals on a "live" broadcast that her parents had engaged in premarital sex. The resulting marital spats and reconciliations between Sidney and Thomson were praised as "believable, warm and humorous." A Boston critic thought Sylvia offered a "nicely timed, crisp job" as a woman desperate to save her marriage. Last billed in a Hyde Park Playhouse production was a twenty-year-old newcomer named Buddy Reynolds (later known as Burt).

William Inge's Pulitzer Prize drama *Picnic* gave Sidney the opportunity to shine in the role of Rosemary, a spinster schoolteacher living with a combustible family of frustrated women. During its week-long engagement at Legion Star Playhouse in Pennsylvania, director Walt Witcover found *Picnic* his most rewarding of the summer season. He held Sidney in high esteem and in 2004 gave an insider's impression of what it was like to work with her.

> Sylvia Sidney was a joy, and a lesson to work with. With no star airs, she plunged into our rehearsals with full seriousness and professional commitment. She gave it her all. And in my experience, her all was unique. During our week of rehearsals, she wandered slowly through her role, slowly following my staging, glasses alternately up and down her nose, as she peered in turn at her script and then at her fellow actors, never raising her voice, and never trying to "act."

I had no idea whatsoever of what kind of performance might emerge. I managed to keep my anxieties to myself, though the rest of the cast were somewhat unnerved by her unusual approach. And then—then, at our first dress rehearsal, when she had mastered the part and had put down the script, she astonished us all. A brilliant performance emerged—fully developed, funny, painful, and almost unbearably touching as the spinster schoolmistress.[29]

The ensemble spirit of *Picnic*, with several major characters, had no real lead role. The catalyst for change was Hal, a sexy, out-of-work vagabond who comes to town to reconnect with a wealthy former college buddy. Hal unwittingly lights a sexual fire that enthralls the local women. Following the climactic "picnic" of the title, Rosemary finds herself on her knees begging her steady beau Howard to marry her. Witcover felt that Sidney's performance was the highpoint of the play, and the season. "Though I only worked with Sylvia for one week," he recalled, "I can never forget her Rosemary. I treasure the memory, and I count myself very lucky, and proud, to have been able to work with her."

(Endnotes)

1. Louella Parsons column, *Sacramento Bee*, November 6, 1950
2. Leonard Lyons, "The Lyons Den," *Advocate*, April 1, 1951
3. Dorothy Parnell, "Phone Call to Son Perks Up Actress Sylvia Sidney," *Milwaukee Sentinel*, November 29, 1950
4. "Mate Loafed Since Wedding," *Boston Traveler*, July 25, 1951 (Sidney's interlocutory decree was obtained in July 1951. Her final divorce decree from Alsop was entered in Superior Court on September 19, 1952)
5. *Variety* article, June 29, 1950
6. Gerald Clarke, *Get Happy: The Life of Judy Garland*, Delta, c. 2001, pg. 248
7. Mary X. Sullivan, "Judy Garland: Rainbow at Last!" *Boston Record*, August 15, 1954

8 Tony Shaw, *Hollywood's Cold War*, Univ. of Massachusetts Press, c. 2007, pg. 76 (In 1954, Alsop retired from the agency and remained on friendly terms with J. Edgar Hoover. Many refute the reports that Alsop worked undercover at Paramount, preparing lists of individuals to be blacklisted. There is no direct evidence for such a claim. Alsop is not connected to anti-Communist Joseph Alsop, who also worked for the CIA. Carleton's brothers names were: Arthur Jr., Fred and Robert)
9 UK Outward passenger list, September 24, 1952 (Listed profession on manifest as: government)
10 Mark Griffin, *A Hundred Or More Hidden Things: The Life and Films of Vincente Minnelli*, DeCapo Press, c. 2010, pg. 74 (interview with scenarist Irving Brecher saying, "Loper was out and I mean *out.*")
11 Sylvia Sidney, *Sylvia Sidney Needlepoint Book*, Reinhold, c. 1968, pg. 11
12 Anthony Slide, *Actors on Red Alert: Career Interviews with Five Actors and Actresses*, Scarecrow Press, c. 1999, pg. 5
13 Barbara L. Wilson review of *Les Miserable*, *Philadelphia Inquirer*, September 6, 1952
14 Rual Askew review of *Les Miserables*, *Dallas Morning News*, October 16, 1952
15 Arthur Bell, "Sylvia's Souvenirs," *New York Times*, December 17, 1972
16 Christopher Plummer, *In Spite of Myself: A Memoir*, Knopf, c. 2009, pg. 123
17 Christopher Plummer, *In Spite of Myself: A Memoir*, Knopf, c. 2009, pg. 124 (Plummer mistakenly noted the sponsor was General Motors)
18 "Keith Suspended by AFTRA For TV Commercial Antics," *Billboard*, December 12, 1953
19 Eve Starr, "Inside TV," *Greensboro Record*, December 19, 1953
20 Al Larimore, "Pretty Sylvia Sidney Weaves Magic Work in Astor Show," *Free Press*, November 4, 1953
21 Erskine Johnson column, *Lubbock Avalanche-Journal*, October 11, 1953
22 Leonard Lyons, "The Lyons Den," *Advocate*, May 20, 1954
23 James Robert Parish, *Paramount Pretties*, Castle Books, c. 1972, pg. 278
24 *Dark Page Two*, Oak Knoll Press, c. 2009, pg. 92
25 Arthur Bell, "Sylvia's Souvenirs," *New York Times*, December 17, 1972
26 Ron Burton, "Sylvia Sidney's Son Eyes Career As Engineer," *Star News*, February 20, 1956
27 Peter Bogdanovich, *Who the Hell's in It: Conversations with Hollywood's Legendary Actors*, Random House, c. 2010, pg. 9
28 James Robert Parish, *Prison Pictures from Hollywood*, McFarland, c. 1991, pg. 25
29 Walt Witcover, *My Road, Less Traveled: Becoming an Actor, a Director, a Teacher*, Watson-Guptill, c. 2004, pg. 235

As *Auntie Mame*. On tour 1958-59

Chapter 12
Auntie Sylvia

Brainwashing behind the Iron Curtain was big news during the 1950's. Sidney signed on for the melodrama *Protective Custody* scheduled to open on Broadway in April 1956. The plot involved an American newswoman who is kidnapped, then indoctrinated by Russians. Greer Garson turned the role down. Fortunately, Sidney also backed out of this project, which was delayed until December. Critics found the end result tedious, saying audiences were "brainwashed" along with the leading lady (Faye Emerson). It lasted three performances. Instead of a brainwashing, Sidney took the opportunity to work with Italian opera singer Ezio Pinza in a play produced by David Susskind.

A Very Special Baby by Robert Alan Aurthur (ex-husband of actress Bea Arthur) was to begin rehearsals in September. Advance sales were brisk and Pinza's name had guaranteed a spot on Broadway. The director was the reputable Martin Ritt. On August 24, Pinza suffered a brain hemorrhage. A slew of group cancellations meant losing the Belasco Theater—a prime location. As a compromise, producer Susskind booked The Playhouse. As for a new leading man, associate producer Michael Abbott recalled, "We got Luther Adler, who was a wonderful actor, but he wasn't Ezio Pinza."

After getting Jody ready for fall semester at Oakwood Friends School (New York's co-educational college prep facility, near Poughkeepsie), Sylvia headed for tryouts in Philadelphia and Boston. Abbott recalled that Adler and his ex-wife didn't exactly get along. "You can imagine the rehearsals," said Abbott. "And scenes with them together, he would push her, she would push him. She always called him noodle head."[1]

A Very Special Baby opened in November—and wasn't so special after all. Critics found it overwrought. Adler played a wealthy immigrant who holds his spinster daughter (Sidney) under his thumb, as well as his pampered thirty-something son Joey (the special baby in question). When Joey asks for money to start a business, the old man's true feelings surface. "It's your fault I'm alone," he wails. "You son-of-a-bitch, you killed my wife." Joey's mother had died during childbirth. Columnist Walter Winchell didn't wait to see what happened next. He walked out of the theater. "It put me to sleep after the first 10 minutes," he griped. "Unattractive people and their bickering ... this is not entertainment." Was friction backstage the problem? When asked about Adler, Sylvia remarked, "He's a wonderful man, but work with him! I'd rather die."[2] A month prior to this statement she told another reporter that she and Adler were "very good friends, now that we are not emotionally involved."[3] Adler was present on this occasion. He may have been wearing the gray cashmere sweater she had knitted for him.

New York critic John M'Clain admitted that the latter half of *A Very Special Baby* was superior theater. "The second act comes almost immediately alive," he observed. "The performances are uniformly brilliant. Sylvia Sidney, most handsome and beguiling, gives a magnificent account of herself."[4] Ward Morehouse concurred, "Sylvia Sidney is extraordinarily effective as the withering, but unwilling spinster." He found the second act achieved "considerable power" and that Adler was effective as the "pathetic monster of a father."

Sidney and Adler never worked together again. The following year, columnist Mike Connolly revealed that an episode of *Playhouse 90* was a takeoff on the battling ex-mates. The 1957 teleplay (also written by Robert Alan Aurthur) *The Thundering Wave* cast Joan Bennett as an aging actress reunited on stage with her ex-husband (Franchot Tone). Martin Ritt, who directed *A Very Special Baby*, was also in the cast. Perhaps to avoid libel, the script included not a teenage son, but a daughter. *The Thundering Wave* was greeted with rave reviews.

The real bond between Sylvia and Luther was Jody, who continued to excel in science and was set on moving to Boston to attend MIT. "Jody may be here next year," enthused Sylvia to a Boston reporter. "The dean at the school he attends said he is such a genius in mathematics that he will be accepted by any college he chooses." In May, both parents were beaming. Jody was accepted into MIT—the only one in his class to be selected. Since the fall of 1953, he had thrived at Oakwood Friends School—guided by Quaker principals of conscience, compassion and accomplishment. A number of parents in the performing arts enrolled children there: James Cagney, Zachary Scott, and Lena Horne.

Jody's fellow students christened him "Patron Saint of Senior Math." He was always eager to share his knowledge. Classmates were used to hearing him say, "Now look, it's very simple." Friend and classmate Jonathan Talbot recalled in 2014 that he and Jody enjoyed "deep and serious discussions about philosophy and mathematics during our two years together."[5] Jonathan was inspired by Jody to build a digital computer. However, when he explained to the pacifist faculty that computers could be used to aim weapons, they insisted it be disassembled. In the Class of '57 yearbook Jody cautioned his friend, who was being pulled between science and art, not be become a jack-of-all-trades—to find "the correct balance" in pursuing a discipline. Jody's pen closed his message to Talbot with a sagacious dash of humor:

> The hungry soul seeks a cause to dedicate himself. Neither calculus or music can save the human race. Sex can.

In keeping with its Quaker roots, Oakwood discouraged discrimination on the basis of race or gender. Talbot recalled that when James Cagney arrived to see his adopted daughter Cathleen "Casey" in a play, he found her holding hands with a boy "with substantially darker skin than her own."[6] Cagney panicked. He immediately withdrew Casey from Oakwood and made an uproar with the school's Board of Managers. The headmaster resigned. Talbot, who became a professional artist, felt these tensions and experiences were part of his education. He observed, "Jody seemed more comfortable in his own skin than many of us. I remember him as gentle and noncompetitive." Talbot further emphasized,

> Jody helped many of us with math and his help was not limited to class assignments. Jody guided me in learning the

1957 - Jody's senior portrait from Oakwood Friends School (courtesy of Jonathan Talbot)

basics of both the binary number system (something our teacher knew nothing about) and factorials. While binary numbers are relatively familiar to many since the advent of personal digital computers, in those days they were relatively unknown. I needed Jody's guidance … and he gave me the benefit of his expertise freely and generously. Jody was a genius. There is no doubt about that.[7]

Classmate Hugo Sonnenschein and Jody shared many classes together. Hugo contacted me in 2015, pointing to Jody as being "kind and friendly," and that Oakwood was a "good place" for his substantial intellectual gifts to be acknowledged. When the top math students were having difficulty with their teacher (Mr. Gardner), they met outside of class, where Jody became their self-appointed instructor. "I recall feeling … that I was learning more from Jody than I was Mr. Gardner," said Hugo.[8] Upon enrolling at MIT Jody decided to tackle the controversial study of nuclear physics.

1957. For years, Sidney maintained the same Manhattan residence at 11 East 73rd Street—a palatial Venetian Renaissance mansion built for publisher Joseph Pulitzer in 1904. It was later converted into apartments. Among the tenants were Moss Hart and Kitty Carlisle. "It's home and I'm rooted there," Sylvia explained. However, by the time Jody graduated from Oakwood, she relocated to 161 West 54th Street—the Congress Apartments, built in 1923 and home to such celebrities as composer Oscar Levant.

Taking a spring break from acting, Sylvia was seen about with fashion photographer Serge Balkin (famous for his portraits of Marlon Brando). She began the habit of wearing all three of her wedding rings to remind herself and warn others, as she put it, "not to make a fourth mistake." Sidney also signed on with Elizabeth Arden's salon in Manhattan to design bejeweled Easter Eggs—exclusively advertised as being created by the "dramatic hand of actress Sylvia Sidney." The eggs were painstakingly covered with tiny beads—special initials could be preordered for a pricey sum.

For all the attention Sylvia and Ben Schulberg had received during their three-year relationship in the early 1930's, her name was ignored in news reports of his death (February 25, 1957). Many headlines read, "Budd Schulberg's Father Dies." The forgotten movie tycoon passed away in his sleep at the age of sixty-five in Key Biscayne, Florida, where he had lived since 1952. He was survived by his second wife, Helen. Budd carried the Schulberg legacy forward—at any cost. After it was revealed that he was a former member of the Communist Party, Budd testified before the House Un-American Activities Committee (HUAC) as a "friendly witness" (May 1951). He was then free to return to Hollywood and continue his career as a writer/producer. Budd teamed with director Elia Kazan, another "friendly witness," for the Academy Award-winning film, *On the Waterfront* (1954). Budd won an Oscar for Best Story and Screenplay, and Kazan won for Best Director.

Budd was indeed a gifted writer, but the act of "naming names" before the HUAC was seen by many as cowardly. To many, his rationalization for doing so seemed hollow. Budd named a dozen acquaintances, who he had once shared a vision of social justice. Most of them became blacklisted and four spent time in prison.[9]

The Helen Morgan Story (1957) (CBS) - with Polly Bergen and Hoagy Carmichael

The *Playhouse 90* presentation *The Helen Morgan Story* provided Sidney with a major opportunity. The ninety-minute drama about the torch singer who pulled the heartstrings of F. Scott Fitzgerald's "lost generation" was well-received. Smooth direction by George Roy Hill (*The Sting*) was above par. Jack Gould for *The New York Times* nodded that Polly Bergen "acquitted herself very nicely" singing Morgan's trademark songs like "Why Was I Born?" Gould commented that as Helen's mother, "Sylvia Sidney portrayed with quiet hopelessness." Lulu Morgan was, admittedly, unable to refuse her daughter's demand for drink as her popularity waned. Helen died penniless at the age of forty-one.

Sidney, who also acted as narrator, helped prepare the dramatization. Bergen admitted, "I couldn't have done it without her."[10] When Bergen looked at the script, she almost fainted. She was in practically every scene. As filming began, Sylvia tucked a note into Polly's costume which read, "I can only wish you what I would have wished for myself, had it been my first." Bergen walked away with an Emmy for

Best Single Performance—competing with the likes of veteran Helen Hayes. *Playhouse 90* received its highest ratings. A film version, *The Helen Morgan Story* (1957) was postponed for release until September.

In a surprise turn, Sylvia signed for a tour in the Pulitzer Prize winner *The Old Maid*, starring Miriam Hopkins. Hopkins took the title role, and Sidney played the older sister (Hopkins' character in the 1939 film that had starred Bette Davis). Hopkins' young niece, Margot Welch, played her illegitimate daughter. The John Drew Theatre on Long Island played to capacity audiences for six evenings beginning July 22. The tour lasted all of one week. Hopkins, much to the consternation of Sidney and the cast, stood in the wings mouthing the young novice her lines. The poor girl was overwhelmed. New York columnist Burt Boyar offered a hint as to the reason for tour's demise when he asked, "What's this about Sylvia Sidney and Miriam Hopkins battling it out at an East Hampton theater last week?" Whatever transpired between the two women had staying power.

In January 1964, Hopkins created chaos during a tryout of the play *Riverside Drive*—showing up late; drinking too much; not knowing her lines. As things went downhill, co-star Donald Woods broke out in a nervous rash. When Miriam was a no-show for a crucial rehearsal, producer Stanley Raiff called her agent, who also represented Sidney. Raiff asked for Sidney to replace Hopkins. Hopkins found out and arrived at the theater within the hour—gracious and charming as ever. Raiff told her she was sacked. "You can't fire me from some tacky little off-Broadway theater," she railed. "I'm Miriam Hopkins!" Playwright John Donovan recalled, "It was a sad thing. Curiously enough, while

Riverside Drive was not a successful evening of theater, it was very good for Sylvia, and Miriam could have had the same kind of tremendous personal notices."[11] With less than two weeks rehearsal, Sidney impressed critics.

Turning to Color TV, Sylvia, wearing glittering makeup and gown to match, played Farley Granger's mother in *Circle of Fear* for *Kraft Theater*. Granger played an insanely jealous actor who nearly destroys the life of his protégé (Lee Remick). When Sidney shows up in the third act, viewers discover the source of Granger's neurotic behavior. "As the bad boy's bad mama," said TV critic Harry Harris, "Sylvia Sidney was exasperating." Another reviewer agreed, "Veteran actress Sylvia Sidney provided the only substantial drama in an electric third act."

In 2009, director Walter Grauman recalled a mishap from "live" TV's *Matinee Theater*. Sylvia, despite Grauman's pleas, refused to rehearse the closing line (considered bad luck) in *The Gift and the Giver*. The shot involved a close-up of her bending over to kiss her husband's grave. "We get on the air," said Grauman, "the show goes beautifully, and there is Sylvia at the gravesite. She leans down to kiss it, backs up and ... silence. Absolute silence. She bows her head. So, I say, 'Fade to black.' She had forgotten the line that she refused to rehearse."[12]

With nothing better to do, Sylvia agreed to guest star on Polly Bergen's short-lived musical variety series. Sylvia, singer Julius LaRosa, and Jack Carson played themselves advising Bergen on how to do her show. The trio ended up in a shouting match. "A more unfunny exercise would be harder to imagine," said one review. "So bad it was embarrassing," said another. Afterward, Sidney was brutally frank with syndicated columnist Hal Humphrey about the dearth of acting assignments for women her age.

> I'm not doing movies because no one has asked me. As for television, how many dramatic shows are there? I manage to do four or five in a year. If you do a *Climax!* it means CBS won't use you on *Playhouse 90* for six months. TV has replaced everything else the actor used to do. Even tougher is the fact that we're on our own. Movie studios and legit theater producers used to sign us to contracts and see that our talents were built properly over the years.[13]

Sidney went on to say that in TV or movies a middle-aged woman must never fall in love with a younger man. Her considerably older male contemporaries were allowed to romance women half their age. Humphrey asked if she ever watched her old movies on TV. "Heaven's no!" she answered. "I can learn nothing from a girl of 20." Sylvia didn't have to wait much longer to tackle one of her most popular stage vehicles.

Auntie Mame

Auntie Mame, based on the novel by Patrick Dennis, opened on Broadway in October 1956. Rosalind Russell's triumphant turn as a free-spirited socialite, who nurtures her orphaned nephew on the art of how to *really* live, became her trademark role. Other actresses eagerly lined up to play Mame. Greer Garson succeeded Russell on Broadway. Constance Bennett began a touring production. In April 1958, Sylvia opened *Auntie Mame* in New England. For ten months she played to enthusiastic audiences cross-country. By the time she had concluded her run, she was considered by many to have given the performance closest to the author's conception of the role.

Opening night in Utica, reportedly attracted 3,000 patrons. *Daily Press* enthused that Sidney "supplied the bounce that was necessary and demonstrated considerable depth in the role." "For the most part," said the critic, "she played strictly for laughs ... and got them." Several weeks later in Hartford, a critic raved, "Miss Sidney, hitherto associated with dramatic roles, has the comedienne's instinct and facility. She can turn a phrase with irreverent humor, flash a deadening glance, prattle nonsense with an air of wisdom and be casually pleasant to the most eccentric. Also, she wears stunning gowns—with flair."[14]

Sylvia relished Mame's parade of Travis Banton fashions—a Chinese lounging robe, a befeathered negligee, velvet and gold lame pajamas, to mention a few. She admitted that she patterned her interpretation of Mame after Rosalind Russell. "You'd be nuts if you didn't," she said. "It's a dream part for an actress—millions of laugh lines and the most beautiful clothes you've ever seen." Laced with laughter and gin, Sidney's Mame, as one critic put it, "[tore] away at the banquet of life like a two-fisted gourmand."[15]

Sylvia and Constance Bennett both recognized that they literally carried the show on their backs. The two stars were considered the most temperamental by *Mame* cast and crew members. Bennett biographer Brian Kellow noted that with Constance, "Anyone caught performing at less than maximum potential was likely to feel her wrath."[16] Ditto for Sidney. Cast member Philip Bosco, who played the hack Irish poet, was asked about Sidney in 2004. "She was so mean and vicious, an absolute horror," he recalled. Bosco quit after three-weeks. At one performance, a cheeky twelve-year-old took an inopportune moment, during curtain call, to ask Sylvia for her autograph. Diva

Sidney took one look at him, slapped his face, and said "Get lost!"[17] Following Sylvia's record-breaking run at Lambertville Music Circus, the company began an annual "Sylvia Sidney Award" for the person most difficult to work with. By the fall of 1958, Dorothy Kilgallen disclosed that supporting players who worked in both the Sidney and Bennett companies enjoyed debating which star was the worst to work with. As to who was more "Auntie Mean" than "Auntie Mame," Dorothy Kilgallen summed up, "It's a draw."

Apparently, Sidney's wrath was not cast upon the boy playing her nephew. In 2012, Edward Spence, who played the nephew role in Portland and during the tour's final months, fondly recalled, "I played young Pat to Sidney's magnificent *Auntie Mame*. Her interpretation was anything but mean!"[18] Spence indicated that Patrick Dennis was most pleased with Sidney's performance. Jerome Lawrence, who had adapted the play, acknowledged Sidney's performance as one of the finest based on "sheer acting ability."

Playing "Auntie Mame" was no easy task. She is rarely off center stage. Sylvia used a pedometer and measured 2 ½ miles per performance. Vocal demands proved difficult. Veteran Broadway critic John Chapman caught Greer Garson sounding like "a pondful of frogs." "Bea Lillie," said Chapman, "couldn't be heard beyond the third row." When Chapman saw Sidney she had been four months on the road and sounded like "a newsboy trying to get rid of the last few copies of the extra edition." After curtain call, Sylvia sat in her dressing room brushing her hair. "I'm so miserably tired," she sighed to news writer Eleanor Kennedy. "Nineteen costume changes, four wigs, and I don't know how many hats." Kennedy's questions drew little warmth from the star until the subject of Sylvia's ten-month-old pug Madame Too, came up. Kennedy asked about the trouble of taking a dog along.

Sylvia set her straight on the subject. "Any amount of trouble would be worthwhile," she smiled. "She's a *wonderful* companion."

Sidney's romance with pug dogs began when Lena Horne returned from England (c. 1957) with an adorable, fawn pug. "The vision of him haunted me for a long time," said Sylvia. While shooting a television play in Hollywood, Sidney and co-star Patricia Neal would pass by a pet shop during lunch break. "One of them must have bought me the moment she saw me," said Sylvia. "She seemed to be waiting every time I passed, and she stared with such an appealing look in her eyes that I felt myself losing my heart to her. Finally, I had to give in and buy her. I named her Madam Oi-Vingh. She died when she was only fourteen months old. I was shattered. I began to experience the most acute loneliness."[19] Sidney then opted to buy two pugs (Madame-Too and Mister Oi-Vingh), who eventually made their stage debut in a production of *Kind Sir*.

Auntie Mame headed west with solid reviews. The *Omaha World* cheered, "It is doubtful that Sylvia Sidney in the title role could be surpassed, on this, or any other stage." Upon reaching Seattle, Jody, now a sophomore at MIT, joined his mother for the Christmas holiday. The *Daily Times* applauded that Sylvia "slayed 'em" at the city's Moore Theater—playing to packed houses. A Portland critic pointed to the basic *difference* that Sylvia offered to *Mame*. "Sylvia Sidney gives the role the merry abandon it demands and sprinkles it with a deep and emotional love for a young boy." In 1989, Sidney revealed to director Richard Kramer the difference between her Mame and the others. As she put it, "I found the heart." Sidney's relationship with Jody provided the key to her performance. Sylvia may have lavished affection on her pugs, but a staff writer for the *Oregonian* keenly observed that Jody was the most important person in his mother's life.

The critical acclaim and turnout for *Auntie Mame* road companies somehow failed to generate enough cash to cover production costs. Touring professional theater was becoming a thing of the past. Even big name stars could not avoid the terrific operating losses. *Variety* reported, for example, that Sidney's tour had lost its entire $100,000 capitalization. Producer Richard Barr felt everything was overproduced—weighed down with royalties to authors and stars. The disgruntled Barr also implied that Sidney acted unprofessionally.[20] No specifics. During the last lap of Sidney's tour, still playing to packed houses, the film version of *Auntie Mame* starring Rosalind Russell hit theaters.

Touring in *Auntie Mame* put Sidney's TV work on hold. In early 1960, Sylvia co-starred with Lee J. Cobb in the well received *General Electric Theater* politically-charged drama, *The Committeeman*, directed by African-American Lloyd Richards. TV columnist W. Rhoades Weaver offered Sidney "a bouquet for her performance." Crime series like *Naked City* (1961), in which Sylvia teamed successfully with newcomer Robert Duvall, proved rewarding. Duvall played a psychotic murderer, who holds his long-suffering aunt (Sidney) hostage. When the aunt reveals the unhappy truth about the uncle Duvall had idolized, the story, *A Hole in the City*, takes an unexpected turn. The 2010 publication *Cornucopia of Crime* describes the episode as a "superb telefilm noir—worth whatever trouble you have tracking it down."

In the popular series *Route 66*, Sidney showcased her talent in seedy surroundings. Looking slim and attractive in Capri pants, she drowns her sorrows in drink, chaperoning showgirls who con cowboys into gambling their paychecks. The pivotal scenes involved

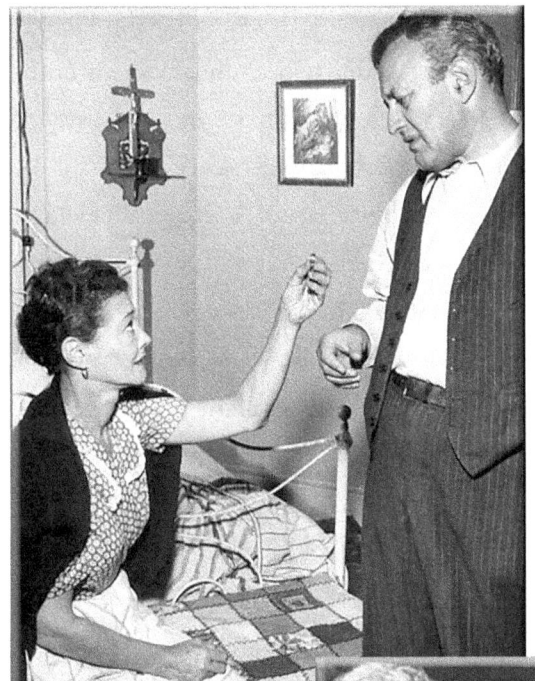

General Electric Theater (CBS) *The Committeeman* (1960) with former Group Theater member, Lee J. Cobb

Route 66 (CBS) *Like a Motherless Child* with Martin Milner and George Maharis

Sidney (who had once abandoned her baby boy) and co-star George Maharis (who grew up an orphan). The two connect over a bottle of liquor, in a poignant display of sorrow and tenderness, to provide *Route 66* one of its strongest entries: *Like a Motherless Child.*

NBC advertising for singer Bobby Darin's TV special (1961), made the mistake of saying Sidney would appear with her "all-mother harmonica band." She sued for $350,000 in damages. Sylvia and attorney Paul Caruso petitioned in Superior Court, charging defamation, invasion of privacy and misappropriation of her name for commercial purposes. The ad implied that Sidney had become "something less than an actress."[21] The case was settled out of court for an undisclosed sum.

Sidney was the sole figure on camera in the NBC special, *Change of Life*, playing a middle-aged, menopausal woman overwhelmed with loneliness and insecurity. Sidney's poignant, virtuoso performance tackled an unflinchingly adult subject. Boston critic Eleanor Barnes was outraged. "Is nothing sacred any longer?" she railed. "This was once a subject discussed only in the privacy of a doctor's office." Times *were* changing. The taboos and forbidden subject-matter of a Production Code that had compromised the film/TV industry for decades was finally being challenged.

Sidney moved on to an Emmy nomination for her standout role as the estranged mother of a criminally insane man in *The Defenders* (1962), a series which tackled tough subjects. When the role was offered, Sylvia wasn't feeling well (back problems). Her cousin, Dr. Albert Sabin, with whom she was staying in Cincinnati, encouraged that she could and should take on the assignment. The two-part drama *Madman*, directed by Stuart Rosenberg (*Cool Hand Luke*), challenged the legal definition of insanity. Sidney's character mirrors the erratic behavior of her son. It is implied that brutal childhood beatings had emasculated him—he was unable to perform sexually. "I don't think of myself as being his mother at all," she protests when served a subpoena. Critics concurred that Sidney was "magnificent" and "superb." *Madman* received five Emmy nominations. Director Rosenberg took home an Emmy, but Sidney lost out to Kim Stanley, who had received a career jump-start in 1947 as part of Sidney's *Joan of Lorraine* tour. Instead of an Emmy, Sidney took home a nomination plaque. "I have [it] in my john," she told a reporter for *The New York Times*.[22]

Big screen opportunities for Sylvia never materialized. In November 1959, she signed to play the wife of James Mason in scenarist Ben Hecht's *Brotherhood of Evil*. Mason, set to play an Italian-American Mafia boss in the heroin trade, came down with pneumonia and bowed out of the film, which was abandoned. Shortly afterward, producer Jerry Wald planned to cast Sylvia as the mother in *High Heels*. This project was aborted by studio strikes, and eventually, Wald's death. In the fall of 1960, Sylvia tested for a role in *Birdman of Alcatraz*, starring Burt Lancaster. According to Sidney's publicist, John Springer, producer Ross Hunter and Rock Hudson also expressed interest in featuring Sidney in one of their films. Hudson admitted to a long-distance crush on Sylvia when he was a youngster. He had what he hoped was a perfect role for her (a socialite) in *The Spiral Road* (1962)—which turned out to be a contrived tangle of religious conversion, leprosy, and "goona-goona" (voodoo) in the East Indies. Sidney escaped being in this uninspired mess.

1960 - Stylish at fifty - Sidney wearing capris

Norman Krasna's battle-of-the-sexes play *Kind Sir* (filmed as *Indiscreet* in 1958) provided Sylvia another comedy—as a famous actress who is outraged upon learning that her current lover isn't really married. Sidney arrived for rehearsals in Milwaukee in February 1960, accompanied by her pugs. She explained to a reporter that, when it came to acting, she had no causes or ideologies. "When people buy tickets for a play," she said, "you can't expect them to join you on a hike through the mud of human suffering. I don't mean that a play must be built of pure fluff ... the minute you cut the heart from it, it dies." By the time *Kind Sir* closed outside Cleveland, six months later, critics were still referring to it as "a rather fluffy little piece." Sylvia, on the other hand, thought *Kind Sir* "a hell of a clever, funny show."

Sylvia's wardrobe for *Kind Sir*, designed by her friend Don Loper, was a display of deep reds, mustard tones, black fox, and a sheath with flying tunic—all shown to advantage by extremely pointed high heels. The real topper was the moment Sidney rushed on stage with her pugs, adorned in reddish-gold ponchos. Critic Joe Boyd countered Sidney's high opinion of the play, but conceded, "The Sidney-Loper combination triumphs over the ... inanities." Sylvia wore Loper's designs off stage as well—"When I can afford him," she cautioned.

Juxtaposed between Sidney's play dates in *Kind Sir* was William Inge's *The Dark at the Top of the Stairs*. For this, she replaced an ailing Janet Gaynor for producer Harold J. Kennedy. Inge's humor and tenderness highlighted the story of a Midwestern family in the 1920's. Sylvia played the central role of Cora Flood, who fears the loss of her husband's love, while over-pampering her young adult children. Playing to full houses at Spa Summer Theater in New York, *Dark at the Top of the Stairs* was considered "best of the season."

Tennessee Williams was new turf for Sylvia. She stepped easily into lead roles in *Sweet Bird of Youth* and *The Glass Menagerie*. She balanced these heavier plays with comedies: *The Pleasure of His Company*, and a five week tour in Thornton Wilder's *The Matchmaker*. The latter, directed by Harold Prince, also featured Sada Thompson. Critic John M. Gordon felt that Sidney was "awash" in this period piece about a middle-aged woman who ties matrimonial knots for friends and anyone else ... for a price. "Miss Sidney does not provide the dander this needs," snipped Gordon. The *Springfield Union* was inundated with complaints about his review—patrons did not agree. Sylvia had her own complaints during a tour of one-night stands. Doctors demanded that she take two-hour breaks, daily, for disc therapy. She was in constant pain, except when on stage ... "and then the part takes over," she explained. "I'm not myself anymore and I don't hurt!"

Sidney passed on the opportunity to play Barbra Streisand's mother in the musical *I Can Get It for You Wholesale*. This was nineteen-year-old Steisand's Broadway debut. Sylvia was tentatively cast when the production was titled *What's in it For Me?* (Fall of 1961). Her role eventually went to Lillian Roth.

In November 1962, Sylvia took a few months off to recoup. Come spring, she welcomed the opportunity to return to Broadway. *Enter Laughing*—a lampoon of the acting craft, was based a Carl Reiner novel. After serious revisions in Philadelphia, the play opened at the Henry Miller Theater. Sidney was top-billed. The play was an unheralded "sleeper" that convulsed Broadway for a whole season and made a star of young Alan Arkin. Sidney played the mother to Arkin's gawky, stage-struck youth. She and her husband, a conventional Jewish couple, want Arkin to be

1963 - Enter Laughing with Alan Arkin

a druggist. Arkin joins a flea-bitten troupe of players instead, headed by an old ham named Marlowe (Alan Mowbray). This all takes place in the 1930's. A plethora of funny lines, obvious as matzo balls, was served with Jewish humor. When Sylvia's husband makes amorous advances in one scene, she moans, "Aw, go to sleep. It's bad for your hernia."

Several months later, Sidney announced that she was leaving the play. Dorothy Kilgallen, after gabbing with cast members, implied that Sylvia's sudden exit spelled backwards meant that she was fed up with someone. In October, Sidney was replaced by Mae Questel, best known for dubbing voices for Betty Boop and Olive Oyl. Alan Arkin's son Adam related a story to director Richard Kramer which solved the riddle of Sylvia's sudden exit from *Enter Laughing*. The original billing placed Sidney above Arkin. Following his rave reviews, ads featured Arkin's name alone, above the title. "Sylvia was not happy," said Kramer.[23] She "had words" with Arkin over this turn of events.

It was announced that Lillian Hellman had written a play with Sidney in mind. Titled *Emma*, it focused on the 19th-Century Jewish-American poet Emma Lazarus, who championed the idea of a Jewish homeland. Lazarus is best-remembered for her 1886 sonnet to The Statue of Liberty, "Give me your tired, your poor, your huddled masses." Plans for the play fell through, but Sidney did sink her teeth into a 1966 revival of Hellman's *The Little Foxes*. "Miss Sidney is very good in this play," praised one critic. "She employs her husky, deeply vibrant voice to good effect, as well as her large blue eyes. She is not above showing a generous helping of décolletage."[24]

For Yom Kipper 1963, Sidney appeared in Stephen Chordorov's *In The Last Days*. The CBS special detailed turmoil in a Jewish family when the son decides to visit a concentration camp where relatives had been slain by Nazis. Also that fall, Sylvia was honorary chairman for the National Cancer Foundation campaign to raise $90,000. The funds went toward free counseling and patient care for low and middle income families in the greater New York area.

Jody, after two lonely years at MIT, enrolled at New York University where he graduated. He enrolled at Amherst for post-graduate work, and found himself fascinated with scientific photography. Columnist Louis Sobol described Jody as "a rather esthetic looking young chap with an expensive camera strapped to a shoulder."[25] Sobol spotted the 23-year-old in January 1963 mingling with actors at a theater district coffee shop in New York. Jody admitted to Sobol that he wanted no part of acting. Apparently, Jody was coming out of his shell. Classmate Jonathan Talbot recalled that while at Oakwood Jody "appeared to choose solitude rather than social engagement—content to be ignored as he was often deep in thought ... exploring subjects which were far beyond what many others were able to understand."[26]

Jody was now going by "Jacob." His lifelong pal, novelist Raymond van Over, explained that upon reaching adulthood, Jacob disliked the diminutive tone of "Jody." "Our relationship covered a long time," said van Over, "from when he was eighteen and I in my early twenties. We first met while both were working in the original Sam Goody's record store in NYC."[27] Van Over added that Jacob enjoyed taking photographs of him and his wife Camilla. Jacob was also pursuing an interest in long distance bike riding.

Despite a hectic schedule of touring, television roles, and fundraising, Sylvia Sidney, the consummate actress, recognized her main focus was to continue supporting her son's post-graduate work and aspirations.

(Endnotes)

1. Stephen Battaglio, *David Susskind: A Televised Life*, MacMillan, c. 2010, pgs. 159-160
2. Earl Wilson column, *Aberdeen Daily News*, November 21, 1956
3. Mary X. Sullivan, "Sylvia Sidney and Luther Adler Work as a Team for 'Baby,'" *Boston Record American*, November 4, 1956
4. John M'Clain, review of *A Very Special Baby*, *Springfield Union*, November 18, 1956

5   Email from Jonathan Talbot to author, December 30, 2014
6   Jonathan Talbot, "1955-57 – Oakwood Friends School," http://www.talbot1.com/chronology/subpages/1955-57/oakwoodfriends.htm, c. 2010-2012
7   Jonathan Talbot, correspondence dated January 19, 2015
8   Hugo F. Sonnenschein, correspondence dated January 28, 2015
9   C.P. Trussell, "Schulberg Tells of Red Dictation," *New York Times*, May 24, 1951 (Schulberg named: Richard Collins (also a friendly witness), John Howard Lawson (Hollywood 10), V.J. Jerome (3 years in prison), Waldo Salt (blacklisted), Ring Lardner Jr. (Hollywood 10), Lester Cole (blacklisted), John Bright (blacklisted), Paul Jarrico (blacklisted), Gordon Kahn (blacklisted), Herbert Biberman (Hollywood 10), Meta Reis Rosenberg (friendly witness), Stanley Lawrence (deceased at the time))
10 Hedda Hopper, "Looking at Hollywood," *Times-Picayune*, May 23, 1957
11 George Eells, *Ginger, Loretta and Irene Who?* Kangaroo Book, c. 1976, pgs. 120-121 (*Riverside Drive* closed after 15 performances at off-Broadway's Theater de Lys)
12 Walter E. Grauman, interview, Archive of American Television, April 17, 2009
13 Hal Humphrey, "Sylvia Sidney Brutally Frank About Lack Of Role Assignments," *St. Petersburg Independent*, January 26, 1958
14 Louise Mace, review of *Auntie Mame*, *Springfield Union*, June 4, 1958
15 William C. Glacken, ""Sylvia Sidney Scores Success as Auntie Mame," *Sacramento Bee*, January 23, 1959
16 Brian Kellow, *The Bennetts: An Acting Family*, University of Kentucky Press, c. 2004, pg. 379
17 Ed Mottershead, (Ed recalled his youthful encounter with Sidney on Broadwayworld.com.) March 16, 2008
18 Edward (Spence) Sandler, comment in author David Noh's blog, *Noh Way*, October 31, 2012
19 Sylvia Sidney, *Sylvia Sidney Needlepoint Book*, Reinhold, c. 1968, pg. 69
20 David A. Crespy, *Richard Barr: The Playwright's Producer*, SIU Press, c. 2013, pg. 76
21 "Actress Sues N.B.C.," *New York Times*, November 29, 1961
22 Arthur Bell, "Sylvia's Souvenirs," *New York Times*, December 17, 1972
23 Conversation with Richard Kramer, May 12, 2015
24 Dana Stevenson, review *The Little Foxes*, *Trenton Evening Times*, July 27, 1966
25 Louis Sobol, "New York Cavalcade," *Greensboro Record*, January 31, 1963
26 Jonathan Talbot, correspondence dated January 19, 2015
27 Raymond van Over, email to author, November 22, 2015

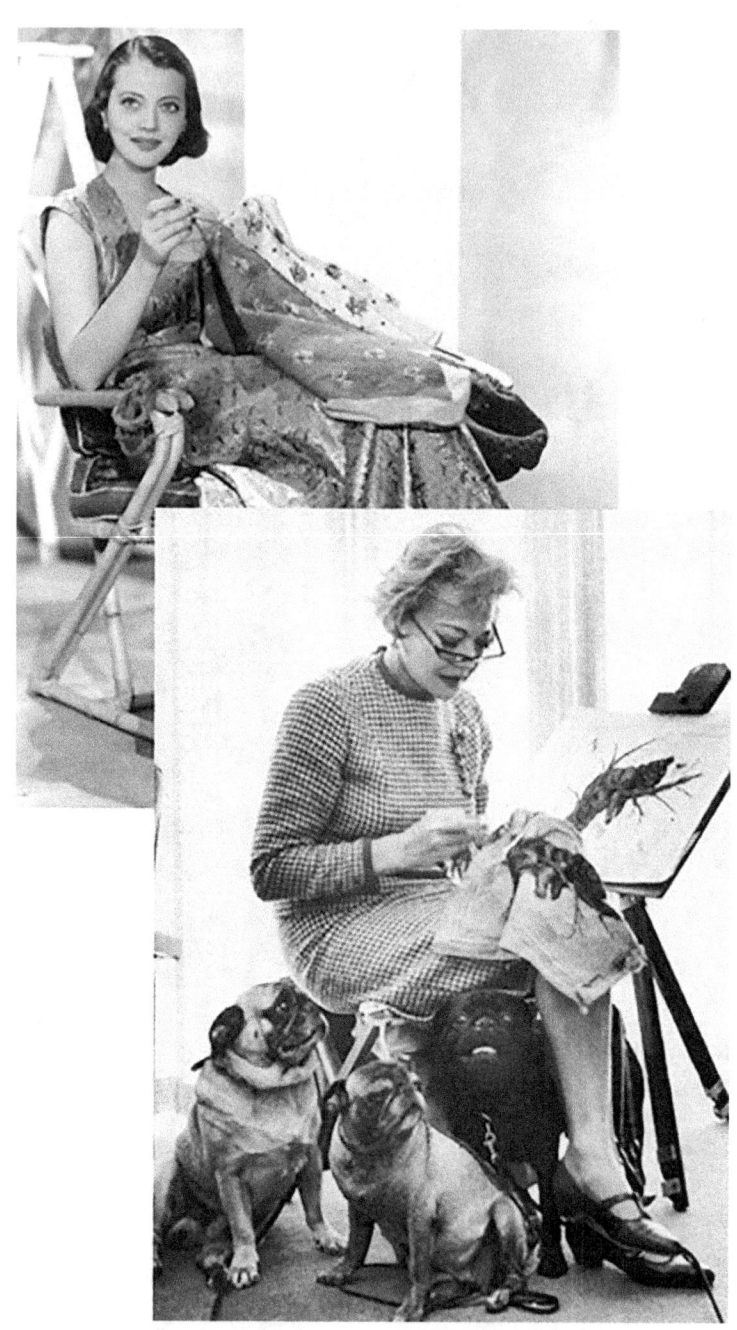

1938/1968 Needlepoint and pugs: Madame Too,
Small Wonder, Captain Midnight

Chapter 13
Exit Laughing …
All the Way to the Bank

In his 1961 farewell address, President Dwight Eisenhower warned the nation about the military-industrial complex. His message fell on deaf ears. Munitions makers began lobbying for lucrative government contracts as the Vietnam War got underway. The corporate model of capitalism pushed for war and profit. The corporate trend had also integrated itself into the arts, and not without controversy.

Sylvia watched the gradual demise of theatrical touring companies. As early as 1956, she had commented to prominent theatrical critic Ward Morehouse about what a "rat race" theater had become since making her debut in 1925. Sipping iced coffee in the Cub Room at the Stork Club, she opened up.

> Kids come to me these days and ask, 'How do you get started in theater?' I think that if I were now 16 and just beginning that I couldn't last six months. There used to be a wonderful atmosphere about it all; the managers had charm. And there was a great deal of courtesy. There's very little of it today. I

feel that the theater is kind of tragic for kids today. At 16 or 17 a success might mean a career, but it can be a very short career. They've always said I made a hit in *Crime*. Well, after that I had five flops in a row, but it didn't matter. New plays were always starting, always opening. In those days we had more than 200 plays on Broadway in a season. What do we get now—around 70?[1]

Sidney also complained to columnist Hal Humphrey, "For every Broadway success there used to be four road companies sent out. That's over." Television, amplified with commercials, was now devouring people's attention. If Americans weren't watching TV, they were shopping. Who had time for theater? Sidney admitted to her own personal penchant for the almighty dollar. "I fell into some nasty habits which could only be gratified by making good money," she said. "What nasty habits? Well, things like eating well and wearing good clothes."[2] To supplement her "nasty" habits, Sidney found guest spots on numerous talk shows throughout the 1960's: *Jack Paar*, *Here's Hollywood* (accompanied by her fashion-designer Don Loper), *The Today Show*, *Mike Douglas*, *Gypsy Rose Lee*, and *The Joan Rivers Show*. When asked about her film career, Sidney was usually dismissive, saying, "I was always ironing somebody's shirt." This remark referred to her role in *Dead End* where she stood at the ironing board pressing a shirt for kid brother Billy Halop. On Educational Television's *Living in the 1960's* Sidney discussed her favorite subjects: raising pug dogs, and creating needlepoint. Her prize pug Madame's recent litter sold for, what Sidney called, "fancy prices." "I know how to arrange for perfect pug puppies," she boasted.

It was rare for Sidney to talk about personal finances. In 1978, she was unusually frank with reporter Marian Christy. Nervously puffing away on a cigarette, Sylvia revealed a crisis that occurred prior to 1960. The day after her accountant died, her bank called to report that Sidney had $90 left to her name—period. "None of the taxes had been paid and the money that was to be put in a trust for my son wasn't. I owed the government a lot of money. The manager, you see, had spent the money *himself*." Sylvia resisted going off the deep end. She nodded, "I had my son, thank God. The fact that he existed prevented me from doing something dumb, like going on drugs. I was always fighting the feeling that I wanted to hide."[3] In the aftermath, Sidney's pursuit of money seemed relentless. Syndicated columnist Alex Freeman reported that on occasion, Sylvia could be seen standing quietly in line at the New York unemployment office on Second Avenue and 89th. "She isn't broke," noted Freeman, "but feels she's entitled to her unemployment check when she isn't working—which isn't often."[4]

Sylvia's need for cash did not preclude her generosity. She supported her mother, Beatrice, who had lived in Miami Beach since 1956. There was also Jody's education to think of. Although he preferred to go by "Jacob" at this point, Sylvia still used his nickname. Jody was about to enter a Master's program at the University of Massachusetts, where he would also serve as an instructor in advanced calculus. "But, he lets me talk to him about mundane things," Sylvia reassured one interviewer. Unfortunately, Jody would eventually face an irreparable and costly health crisis.

Sylvia continued with stage revivals of *Angel Street*, *The Glass Menagerie*, and Sidney Howard's 1926 play, *The Silver Cord*, playing a possessive mother. For the National Repertory Theatre (NRT), she toured with Eva LeGallienne in well-received productions of *The Madwoman of Chaillot* (as Constance) and Sheridan's 1775 comedy of manners *The Rivals*, as Mrs. Malaprop—the woman with a talent for using "the wrong word in the right place." Sylvia arrived for NRT rehearsals directly from the dentist's chair, telling reporters that she lacked "a full set of uppers" and was functioning with "sort of a temporary arrangement." They found her candor and lack of false vanity appealing.

In his review of *The Rivals*, critic Marty Jacobs cheered, "Mr. Sheridan's slaughter of the English language was never in more capable hands than those of Sylvia Sidney. Couple with this brittle dialogue her ability for facial gymnastics and an innate sense of comedy timing and you come up with an unforgettable Mrs. Malaprop." The director also allowed Sylvia's "alarmingly active" pugs, Madame Too and Captain Midnight to saunter on stage. "Those two dogs go with me everywhere," declared Sylvia. "I'd never see the light of day if I didn't have the dogs. They're great discipline for me because I have to get up and walk them in the morning." The pugs, both prize-winning show dogs, also took Sylvia's mind off of herself.

In the fall of 1966, Sidney kept audiences rolling in the aisles with a successful tour in Neil Simon's *Barefoot in the Park*. She was then invited by Oakland Repertory Theatre for a successful turn as Lady Bracknell in Oscar Wilde's *The Importance of Being Earnest*. After a months' run, Sidney was asked to return to Broadway (April 1967) and repeat her role in *Barefoot in the Park*, Simon's longest-running hit. Sidney replaced Ilka Chase as the meddling mother-in-law, and received bouquets from the critics: "Sylvia Sidney proves that she is still

1966-67 - with Don Fenwick on tour in *Barefoot in the Park*

one of the first ladies of the American Theater"; "Miss Sidney wins her audience from the beginning"; "Sylvia Sidney knows her part like the inside of her palm. Her comic timing is unerring ... perfectly priceless."

Backstage at the Biltmore, Sylvia placed sign on her dressing room door: NO VULGAR LANGUAGE ALLOWED HERE. As she put on her makeup, Sylvia clarified to reporters that the vulgarities she had in mind were four-letter words like "cute" and "love." When asked about the precarious situation of Broadway economics, she replied, "I don't think about it. Nothing bothers me except if the puppy has worms. I just want to keep on working and keep out of debt."[5] Sidney stayed with *Barefoot in the Park*, until it closed its three-and-a-half year run. She referred to the play as "one of the best comedies written in the last 25 years." She loved her role and would sign on to do it as late as 1973.

"Simon's really my bread and butter playwright," she said at the time. "I've been doing *Barefoot* ... for eight years. He's a great craftsman. He develops scenes marvelously and they work every time—for both actor and audience."[6]

NRT paged Sidney to play Mrs. Hardcastle in Goldsmith's 1773 comedy *She Stoops to Conquer*. During its brief run, Sylvia was interviewed by D.C. reporter Emerson Beauchamp, son of a former Kentucky senator. He caught Sylvia in a typical mood, asking her how she got to Hollywood. "How did I get there?" she repeated. "On a *train!*" When he asked why she married Luther Adler in England, she replied, "Why! Because he was *there*! What else is on your mind? I've got to go to the Safeway and buy cottage cheese for the dogs." Not long after this exchange, Sylvia was robbed at the supermarket. Her losses totaled around $1,500. Her purse, containing a pearl necklace, cash, checkbook and credit cards, was snatched from her grocery cart. She may have been preoccupied with the upcoming D.C. event, "Ladies and Their Dogs," in which Sylvia and her black pug, Captain Midnight, would show up in matching Chinese garb.

In 1969, Sylvia opted for a coast-to-coast tour in another Neil Simon hit. *Come Blow Your Horn* was strictly for laughs, and a tad risqué. Samuel Hirsch, for the *Boston Herald*, was pleased with Sylvia's self-pitying, scatterbrained mother of two playboy sons. "She milks her individual scenes for every ounce of laughter," applauded Hirsch. "Her way with a shrug and a frown and a helpless gesture is frosting on the wedding cake of the consummate Jewish mother." Sylvia's main competition on stage was the statuesque Hugh Hefner discovery June

1965-66 - (l-r) Margaret Webster, Sylvia, Leora Dana, Eva Le Gallienne rehearse for the NRT revival of *The Madwoman of Chaillot*; (*below*) Scene from *Madwoman*... with Sylvia, Eva Le Gallienne and Leora Dana

Wilkinson, who measured: 46-21-37 (according to her press agent). The former *Playboy* centerfold, who was billed above Sidney (!) as "the new dimension in entertainment," sold tickets. Hirsch noted that Wilkinson capably displayed her figure, along with "a natural dumb Dora quality ... necessary for the role."

When the play reached New Orleans, one review headlined "*Come Blow Your Horn* Has Two Major Assets." It was not referring to Wilkinson, who had left the cast. The praise was reserved for the dialogue and Sidney's acting. "Acting honors go definitely to Miss Sidney, looking chic and never overindulging the colloquialisms of her Jewish mother role." With Wilkinson out of the cast, Sylvia was now billed above the title next to Keefe Brasselle, who had replaced Sammy Jackson as the eldest son. Sidney's major concern wasn't the billing. When asked why she toured in *Come Blow Your Horn*, she quipped, "I did it for my sins. I'd do anything for money. I have to make the loot so I can afford my needlepoint." The fact was, Sidney was simultaneously on an extensive book tour for her publisher. She was becoming a best-selling author.

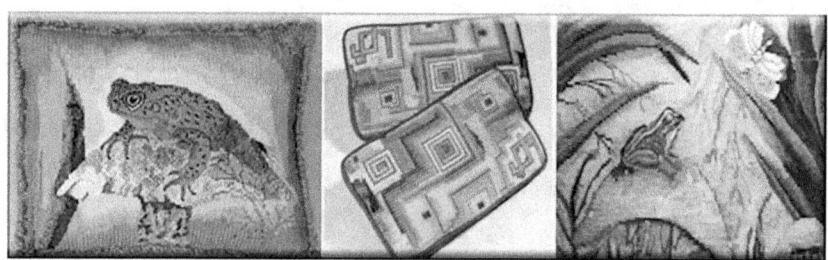

Sidney needlepoint designs

"Needlepoint ... keeps my hands off people's throats ..."

Sylvia learned about her cataracts the hard way. She was pulled over and arrested for driving down the middle of the highway. She admitted to the officer that she couldn't see the white line.[7] She went directly to a hospital for the first of several cataract operations. Despite cataracts, Sylvia perfected the craft of needlepoint, for which she had a genuine instinct. Her interest in needlecraft began at the age of seven. "My grandmother taught me how to knit a washcloth," she explained. "When I became an actress I was at it all the time between scenes." She jested that she was "hooked on the needle."

In the early 60's Sidney won first prize in a needlepoint competition sponsored by the New Hope Historical Society in Pennsylvania. She was also among celebrities contributing their artwork for the United Nations Annual Art Club Exhibition—a benefit for UNICEF. By 1968, Sylvia left behind what she called "the gray chiffon world of cataracts" to become a prominent expert and author on the subject of needlepoint. Besides 20-20 vision, it meant more money in the Sidney coffers. She had also relocated to Roxbury, Connecticut. "My New York apartment got too small for my dogs," she explained.

The well-received *Sylvia Sidney Needlepoint Book*, garnered outstanding reviews. Sylvia had worked tirelessly on needlepoint projects for the book. Her friend Joan Perry, along with Jody, assisted with the book's photos. Jody, now working in New York with computer electronics for the phone company, made use of his mathematical mind to translate his mother's designs onto graph paper. Sidney mentioned to one columnist that the girls Jody dated "look a little like I used to."[8]

Sylvia's one-of-a-kind creations using wool, silk and metallic gold threads, detailed her skill and originality. The finer details required a sharp needle, along with a large magnifying glass. As one critic put it, "The desire to have a life-like gleam in the eye of a frog or a pet pug led her to try a shiny bead for a highlight, with exciting results." Some pieces took as long as seven months to finish. Sylvia's own whimsical designs of pugs, turtles and tigers sold at specialty shops for as much as $1,250. "They will last for hundreds of years," she said proudly. "And so will the work of hundreds of people—men included—who have learned from my book. I consider it a contribution to the world far more constructive than any acting I have done."[9] Sidney frequently contracted to do special requests for clients. She didn't always enjoy doing them. "They're a headache, but a challenge," she admitted. "When they get too sentimental I dislike them."[10] Though her needlepoint was often illuminated in the Medieval lettering of monks—phrases she selected were not necessarily fit for public consumption. Her unwed mothers prayer, for example: "O Lord, Give me a Bastard with Talent."

Among Sylvia's more famous clients were Joan Fontaine, playwright Clifford Odets, and the Duke and Duchess of Windsor—avid pug-lovers. Sidney created a needlepoint of their royal pooch. Initially, the Duchess invited Sylvia and her pug Captain Midnight for luncheon. On the appointed day, Sylvia was reluctant to take three-month old "Cappy" out in the rain. A mutual friend told Sylvia not to bother going without her pug, advising, "It's not *you* she wants to meet."

Critics of needlepoint craft agreed that Sidney had written an informative and highly readable contribution to the art. In her book, Sylvia emphasized, "Anyone who has ever sewn a button or knitted a simple scarf can learn to do what looks like the most complicated piece of petit or gros point. So my book is written for all those people who are ready to take the next small step."[11]

At book signings, Sidney was praised for her sharp needle, sharp mind ... and acid tongue. Retailers invited customers to let Miss Sidney show them basic stitching in person, and have "great fun." "Look, this is rough work," Sylvia explained. "I'm not a stand-up comic. The ladies crowd around. Sometimes you get creeps who ask questions, won't go away and buy nothing. I try not to be rude." Sidney didn't try very hard. One lady asked Sylvia what to do with her chairs. Sylvia told her to "sit on them." Typically, she never held back during guest appearances, or in the numerous interviews she gave over lunch, for which she always arrived precisely on time.

In Pittsburgh, columnist Ruth Heimbuecher watched Sylvia peer at the menu through granny glasses. "I *am* eating for three," warned Sylvia before the reporter could open her mouth. Indeed, there was enough steak, shrimp, French fires and salad for three hungry stomachs. Heimbuecher braved asking Sidney about her reputation for being temperamental. "Not anymore than anyone else is," Sylvia snapped. "Temperament is an interesting, exciting quality. A person without temperament is dull." Interview over, Sylvia bundled up the lunch remains for her pug dogs, Madame Too and Small Wonder, whom she referred to as her "two-year-old bitch."

Sidney proved her point about being "anything but dull" over lunch again during an interview with David Cuthbert at the New Orleans' Downtowner. Sylvia instructed the waitress that she wanted no butter in her Chicken St. Pierre. "Butter makes me violently ill," she said. The waitress gushed, "Aren't you a character actress?" After a silent pause, Sylvia answered, "No dear. I'm an actress *without* character." When the order arrived, Sylvia poured ketchup over her Chicken St. Pierre. Cuthbert, watching in horror, asked if she liked the play. "Like it?" she repeated. "Of course I *like* it. Otherwise I wouldn't be doing the thing." He quickly changed the subject, inquiring about why she took up needlepoint. Sylvia looked up and said, "It keeps my hands off people's throats."[12]

When *Come Blow Your Horn* headed west, an audience of 2,000 gave Sidney their approval in Omaha. One critic observed, "It got so every time Sylvia Sidney opened her mouth, applause rippled across the theater." Seattle critic John Voorhees cheered, "The stage came to life when Sylvia Sidney took charge of things. Miss Sidney made one more aware of the fact that there's nothing like a pro. Miss Sidney knows just how far to carry invention, overstatement and all the necessary shtick to make the play work. Unfortunately ... when Miss Sidney isn't on stage, *Come Blow Your Horn* is a bummer." Voorhees had a point. A 1961 comedy of playboy mentality felt dated. The play closed in October, shortly after its engagement in San Francisco—which had become a haven for hippies and the "love generation." Sylvia told a reporter for the *Arizona Republic* that she approved of the youthful rebellion, that without it there would be no progress.

Without skipping a beat, Sidney continued guest author appearances along with her "in your face" attitude—much to the delight of her fans. First stop, the Windy City. Upon facing a welcoming committee from the Needlework and Textile Guild of Chicago, Sylvia shook her head. "Don't *welcome* me to Chicago. I've been coming here since I was six!" Sipping vodka on the rocks, she told them, "My book is in its fourth printing in a year! Can you imagine what I could have done if I'd written a dirty book?"[13]

Columnist Liz Smith, who would become a close friend, called Sylvia's tome to needlepoint "gutsy." "I had a ball," wrote Smith, after reading it. "The introduction and first four chapters alone are worth the price. In her absorbing, chatty first half, Miss Sidney reveals herself as that incredible rarity—an instant writer. I can hardly wait for *The Son of the Sylvia Sidney Needlepoint Book*, which will, let's hope, be a full autobiography to the point and sans the needle."[14] When asked if she was working on one, Sylvia was matter-of-fact. "God no! I've spent years forgetting things." On another occasion she wailed, "Do you really think I'm going to spend the next few years of my life trying to recall what I'm glad to forget?"[15] Sidney had indeed demolished her nostalgic career ties and tossed all her albums and press clippings in the trash. "It's like carrying a load on your back," she insisted. "Keeping things like that is sick, sick."[16]

August 1970. Dressed in beige, and wearing a ton of gold rings, bracelets, pins, while holding a gold cigarette lighter, Sidney settled into a luncheon table to be cross-examined by a reporter for the *Boston Herald*. The waiter informed her that lunch would be a stuffed shrimp. "How do you stuff a shrimp?" Sidney asked, waving her cigarette into a question mark. She was on tour in *Cabaret* playing Fraulein Schneider, an aging landlady in 1931 Berlin. Lotte Lenya originated the role on Broadway. "This is the first time I've been near a musical," said Sidney. "I'll be 60 years old this month."[17] The five-week tour starred Anna Maria Alberghetti as Sally Bowles—entertainer at the decadent Kit Kat Club. *Cabaret*'s disturbing glimpse of Nazi Germany's moral rot and disintegration into fascism was at the play's core. Sidney cautioned, "If anyone takes offense, it's because of what they have brought to the theater with them. The show filters through the person's attitudes, hang-ups, feelings. Hopefully with *Cabaret* you have a personal hostility toward the master of ceremonies. Charles Abbott is just brilliant as the M.C." Critics agreed that it was Abbott, in *Cabaret's* first national tour, who kept things going at a sparkling pace.

Sylvia and company broke a twenty-year attendance record at the Cohasset South Shore Music Circus. The managing director thought Sidney "fabulous" in her first singing role. She actually "talked" her songs, in what critic Irv Vogel described as a "Tallulah Bankhead voice." Vogel praised, "She is convincing in her role of a spinster who has a bitter-sweet romance with one of her roomers, a Jewish grocer sympathetically portrayed by Woody Romoff." Upon closing the tour in Cleveland, critic Glenn Pullen agreed, "Although Miss Sidney's singing voice may not be very strong, she and Woody Romoff are excellent in their dueting. Their acting has more tender honesty than anybody would expect to find in such a sophisticated show."[18]

In spite of her tours in *Come Blow Your Horn* and *Cabaret*, by the summer of 1971 the media referred to Sidney as "coming out of retirement." She had signed on for a TV "Movie of the Week," titled *Do Not Fold, Spindle Or Mutilate*. For some, visibility on the big or small screen was all that mattered. It had been two years since she appeared with her co-star from *Trail of the Lonesome Pine*, Fred MacMurray, in his long-running sit-com *My Three Sons*. As a tyrannical English teacher of MacMurray's son Ernie (Barry Livingston), Sylvia exuded the stubborn air of academia until faced with her own error in judgment. It was a nicely essayed guest-star stint.

The ABC suspense-comedy *Do Not Fold, Spindle Or Mutilate* was

Do Not Fold, Spindle, or Mutilate (ABC) (l-r) Mildred Natwick, Helen Hayes, Vince Edwards, Sylvia, Myrna Loy

an early foray into virtual reality. Sylvia was in good company, starring with Helen Hayes, Myrna Loy, and Mildred Natwick. The quartet of ladies play a practical joke on "today's society" by creating an imaginary young woman for a computer dating service. They are having a great time reading responses and letters from potential suitors, until things backfire. One man turns out to be psychotic. Ultimately, they find themselves face-to-face with a killer.

Prior to filming, director Ted Post received phone calls from Myrna Loy, then Sylvia, both requesting to be in the cast.[19] Post couldn't believe his luck. Sidney admitted to having a "great time" during the twelve day shoot. Loy agreed, "We all got along so well and laughed so much." The vintage co-stars were royally feted at a press conference—where Sylvia's champion pug, Captain Midnight, a scene stealer, attracted the most attention.

Do Not Fold, Spindle Or Mutilate had a top-twenty rating, but reviews were tepid. Vince Edwards, who played the psychotic, offered tedious off-screen narrations that hampered the proceedings. The real delight was the camaraderie of Hayes, Loy, Sidney and Natwick. They worked beautifully together. John Mitchum (brother of Robert), playing a minor role, found them to be "consummate pros," and recalled, "I found myself beaming inwardly to have been asked to work in such exalted company."[20] Hayes received an Emmy nomination. It came as no surprise. She was given the choice lines. English film critic David Quinlan noted that director Post allowed "Helen Hayes and Mildred Natwick to hog too much of the limelight at the expense of Myrna Loy and Sylvia Sidney."[21] "I probably had the dullest part," Loy admitted, "but Sylvia was marvelous."[22] Sidney returned the compliment when the Academy of Motion Picture Arts and Sciences paid *A Tribute to Myrna Loy* (1985). As friend and admirer, Sidney stepped on stage to detail Loy's early life on a Montana Ranch, her move to Los Angeles at age 15, and the ironic twist of a girl with Irish/Welsh roots being typecast as an Asian in silent movies and early talkies.

Except for a Bayer aspirin commercial, it would be another year before Sidney faced the camera. Veteran columnist Dorothy Manners asked why she had abandoned acting. "I don't intend to abandon anything," Sylvia replied. "I get abandoned. But I'll never retire. When I'm not working I needlepoint. My book has been a best seller in sewing circles for three years." In the Bayer commercial she was seen doing needlepoint, confiding to viewers that she always reached for Bayer during an arthritis attack. When a reporter asked if she really had arthritis she jumped all over him. "Are you out of your box?" she asked, thrusting out her hands with enlarged joints. The *Sylvia Sidney Needlepoint Book* reached its seventh edition, capitalizing on the world-wide revival of the craft. Sylvia signed on for an eight-week tour promoting her new kit designs for Paragon Needlecraft. They sold at Gimbels and numerous other department stores. New designs included simple floral and fruit patterns, and geometric abstractions.

An eyewitness at a Washington D.C. promotion watched Sidney giving "orders like a jaded master sergeant and criticizing workmanship put before her like a school marm." Sidney's blunt assessments failed to discourage anyone. To one worshipful needlepointer Sylvia demanded, "What are you still doing here? I thought I finished with you." To another, she huffed, "*Darling*, I would *never* work on someone else's canvas." To a news reporter, "You've taken up enough space, why don't you move out of the way?" When someone asked if Jody was married, Sylvia answered pertly, "He wasn't when I left [home]." When they persisted the subject, she argued, "All I can say is if he wants to he will." "She gets away with it," wrote one baffled reporter. "People come happily back for more and more." Sylvia didn't even hold back when the manager of D.C.'s Sheraton-Park Hotel asked her to christen their annual Christmas tree. After fifteen unsuccessful smacks at the tree's base with a champagne bottle, she tossed it (along with a few choice words) into the hotel swimming pool.

Designer Don Loper had admonished Sylvia regarding her reputation of being less than "Miss Charm." "He told me to stop my nonsense and practice being more affable," she admitted. Loper died in 1972 from a lung puncture. As a memento, on one of her long necklaces, Sylvia attached a pair of tiny gold monkeys that belonged to him. "When he left I was given these," she explained. "No, he wasn't a lover. He saw me through three marriages." Loper had three unsuccessful marriages of his own (the first at age 17) before pairing with his business partner/lover Charles Northrup. Loper, a former dancer, launched his career into fashion design in the early 1940's.[23]

Instead of being more affable, Sylvia persisted that honesty was the best policy and wouldn't budge. She blamed her own insecurities, and gauged that her attitude toward life made an about turn while working with the Group Theatre. "I lost my faith in people in the bargain," she admitted. "Still, looking back, I cannot, will not blame anybody. I asked for it. Who said I had to be so dumb and innocent? I was no virgin child. I had lovers and two husbands by then. If people stepped on me, who said I had to let them? Eleanor Roosevelt once said, 'Nobody can give you an inferiority complex without your consent.'"[24]

The needlepoint kit promotion paved way for Sidney's second best-seller, *The Sylvia Sidney Question And Answer Book On Needlepoint* (1974). By then, Sylvia Sidney had received a long overdue Academy Award nomination.

It had been seventeen years since Sidney's last film. In the fall of 1972, she faced cameras as the demanding mother of Joanne Woodward in *Summer Wishes, Winter Dreams*. Woodward's character faces a midlife crisis after her estranged son leaves for Amsterdam to cohabit with his new boyfriend. She regrets how she dealt with the situation. Sidney and Woodward are seen lunching together, then attending the Ingmar Bergman film *Wild Strawberries*, during which Sidney dies unexpectedly. Woodward's emotional conflicts find resolve when she and husband Martin Balsam visit Europe. While there, his steady demeanor shatters while facing his own ghosts and trauma from WWII. Woodward is finally able to take her mind off herself and move forward.

Stewart Stern, who had written *Rebel Without a Cause* (1955), the iconic tale of troubled youth, demonstrated his skill in translating similar themes of anxiety in middle-aged Americans. As Sidney read the script she saw characterizations that were deep and real. She was hell-bent on getting the part. According to Sylvia, she told director Gilbert Cates, "It would be a bomb without me."[25] "I also told him I'd practice voodoo on him if he didn't let me have the role and he thought I was enough of a witch to do it." Sylvia had heard through the grapevine that producer Jack Broosky wasn't all that enthused about casting her. "All she can do is cry," he lamented.[26] The shoot went smoothly, and Cates earned Sidney's admiration. "He will only direct what he has feeling for," she said. "He puts his mark on scenes and on an actor—and its always for the best."

During filming, Sylvia scheduled an interview with Arthur Bell for *The New York Times*. As usual, it was over a leisurely lunch. Bell watched as she shooed away the maitre d', who attempted to light her cigarette. "I can do it," she shrugged, ordering a Bloody Mary. She briefly reminisced about "being paid by the teardrop" and "always ironing somebody's shirt" during her Hollywood heyday, then settled into talking about the present. The present was more to her liking. She talked about her home in Roxbury, "a real town with real people," and her pugs. "They really don't do anything but love people—and themselves," she laughed. "God knows how they love themselves." Then the subject of money came up. "I couldn't ever afford not to work, " she admitted. "I make a lot, but spend too much. I spread it around. On who? Friends, mostly." When Bell delved into the past once more, Sidney admonished, "None of this stuff you're asking me has anything to do with me now." She didn't stop there.

Going through that schmaltz-ridden past just doesn't interest me anymore. I don't live in the Variety-Hollywood Reporter world, so I don't know what the hell is going on. What was, was. If a part's there, I do it. If it isn't, I do something else. I'm a better person now, a better actress. Look, we've been here a long time. I've got to go figure out how to make a death scene funny.[27]

The next day, Bell showed up on the set to see Sylvia Sidney at work. At Studio Cinema on Broadway and 66th Street, Sylvia fiddled with her needlepoint waiting to do her death scene. Joanne Woodward was chewing gum and reading about Orson Welles. Seventy extras gathered onto the movie-house set, then Joanne and Sylvia sat in the designated seats next to each other. "Roll the projector," announced Cates. *Wild Strawberries* was cast upon the screen. The crews' eyes were on Sylvia. Bell observed, "Suddenly, Sylvia slumps forward in her seat, sighing, sobbing, moaning, coughing, wheezing, gagging, emulating death. Her cries send shivers. At the sound of 'cut,' the crew, as one, applauds. It's a wrap." Out came the champagne bottles, and a toast from director Cates. "This is for you, Sylvia. Let me drink to you. You are really a delightful lesson to us all." Sylvia was dumbfounded. She took a look around. "Who's paying for this?" she asked. "You are," replied one of the grips. Sidney doubled up with laughter and offered a toast to the crew. Audiences would wait ten months before they got to hear Sylvia utter her character's poignant last words: "Cancel my appointments."

Sidney's confidence in Gilbert Cates was justified. *Summer Wishes, Winter Dreams* received Academy Award nominations for Best Actress (Woodward) and Supporting Actress (Sidney). Critics lined up to applaud. Judith Crist rated the film "deeply affecting." Crist commented on Sidney's "still stunning-eyes and dramatic intensity." The *Daily News* praised Sidney's "chilling desperation as the mother." Columnists Jill Jackson, Charles Champlin, and Bob Thomas predicted a Sidney Oscar win.

Sylvia played a great-grandmother in *Summer Wishes, Winter Dreams*, and remarked, "I could be too, if my son Jody weren't such a slow starter." Obviously, Jody was more interested in his career than matrimony. Sylvia brushed off her own attempts at marriage. "I lived to see each of my ex-husbands marry someone else—and make it," she said. "Obviously I was not marriage material." "Don't think," she added, waving her forefinger, "that I haven't had a man since then."[28]

Prior to the release of *Summer Wishes, Winter Dreams*, a nod to Sylvia's contribution to cinema was offered by publicist John Springer in March 1973. *Legendary Ladies of the Movies*, held at New York City's Town Hall, was detailed by author Ronald Bowers.

> Miss Sidney, silver-maned, wearing a royal blue satin dress, walked out leading one of her prize-winning pugs, who lay at her feet unimpressed with the evening's proceedings. Her fourteen film clips were divided into five segments – The Tragic Sidney, The Joyous Sidney, Sidney in Trouble, Sylvia in Love and Sylvia Sidney, Character Actress.
>
> In her question and answer period, Miss Sidney read each question herself, wearing half-glasses. She was abrasively curt and humorous with her responses. This lady does not

reminisce. Her avocation of needlepoint (which was on exhibition in the lobby) came about by her suppression of desires to "wring the necks" of directors Fritz Lang, William Wyler, and Josef von Sternberg.[29]

The most amusing question involved the prophylactics inspired by her performance in *Madame Butterfly*. Sylvia said that she regretted not collecting royalties. As the evening came to an end, Sylvia offered a nod to the host, "As long as there are men like John Springer, old actors and actresses will never be forgotten. He won't even let them fade away." Other "Legendary Ladies" in the series included Bette Davis, Myrna Loy, Joan Crawford, Rosalind Russell and Lana Turner.

The National Board of Review awarded Sylvia Sidney as Best Supporting Actress of 1973. The Golden Globes, National Society of Film Critics, and British Academy of Film and Television Arts nominated Sidney in the same category. On February 20, 1974, Academy Award nominations were announced. After forty-four years in the industry, Sidney was finally listed among the contenders. Among those championing Sidney for the win was co-nominee Madeline Kahn (*Paper Moon*), who fondly recalled working alongside Sylvia during a brief run of Peter Shaffer's *Black Comedy*. Kahn reasoned, "I don't see how you can compare what a child does, however remarkable, to what an experienced actress like Sylvia Sidney does."[30] The child actresses that Kahn referred to were nominees Linda Blair (*The Exorcist*) and eight-year-old Tatum O'Neal (*Paper Moon*). Critic Vincent Canby was baffled by the inclusion of Blair and O'Neal. He pointed to the

Summer Wishes, Winter Dreams (1973) playing mother to Joanne Woodward (Columbia)

"souped-up electronics and editing" that enhanced Blair's performance (her devil-voice dubbed by Mercedes McCambridge), and questioned the "preconditioned responses" elicited from O'Neal.

Scott MacDonough, a unit publicist for *Summer Wishes, Winter Dreams*, related how neither Woodward or Sidney thought they would win the coveted Oscar. Woodward rationalized, "They hate Paul and me in L.A. and I'll never get another Oscar." Sidney was even more blunt. "They'll never give me the damned Oscar," she snapped. "They'll give it to one of those rotten kids!"[31] Sidney agreed to attend the ceremony on April 2, if she could be one of the presenters.

The 46th Academy Awards Ceremony had among its hosts singer Diana Ross, who welcomed "a very talented lady who was finally discovered by Hollywood this year, Miss Sylvia Sidney." Dressed in an elegant, floor-length, deep-purple gown, Sidney joined Paul Winfield to present the award for Best Art Direction (*The Sting*). When the time arrived, host David Niven welcomed Charles Bronson and Jill Ireland to the stage to present the category of Best Supporting Actress. When Tatum O'Neal was announced the winner, cameras caught Sidney offering an "I thought so" smile. News coverage for the Awards focused mainly on a naked man who dashed across the stage to show off, as Niven put it, "his shortcomings." The phenomenon of "streaking" was all the rage. The next presenter, Elizabeth Taylor, nervously quipped, "That's a pretty tough act to follow."

Sidney loved repeating a story about Bette Davis that took place the day of the Awards. Davis was on tour with John Springer for *Legendary Ladies of the Movies*. During the question and answer segment someone yelled out, "Who do you want to win the Oscars?" When telling the story, Sylvia did a dead-on impersonation of Davis. "I don't know, and I don't care," said Davis, "as long as Miss Sylvia Sidney wins. She has paid her dues." When Davis and Springer retreated to their hotel to watch the awards on television, it became obvious that Davis was dead serious. Her eyes were glued to the TV set when Bronson and Ireland appeared to do the honors for Best Supporting Actress. Bronson announced, "And the winner is .....," handed the card to Ireland who said, "Tatum O'Neal." Bette Davis got up from the couch, slammed off the TV and said, "All right. That's that. Let's get drunk." In 1990, Sidney reflected back.

> You know, a lot of people thought I was going to win that year. Maybe I did, too. But … . Why did the kid win? Who knows? More screen time? More studio backing? But what has she done since … nothing! They rush to give these awards to these young kids. Maybe they're right … who knows? Ancient history.[32]

O'Neal later revealed in a televised *Hollywood Reporter* episode (2014) that it wasn't so much acting as it was doing "take, after take, after take." She would simply mimic director Peter Bogdanovich. She had no desire to be an actress. Bogdanovich admitted doing up to 53 takes, calling it a "manipulated performance."[33]

Along with her Oscar nomination, *Summer Wishes, Winter Dreams* opened a new chapter for Sylvia Sidney. She had more visibility, and acquired a life-long friendship with Joanne Woodward and husband Paul Newman, who also lived in Connecticut.

(Endnotes)

1. Ward Morehouse, "Sylvia Sidney Stars With Ex-Mate in New Play," *Star Journal*, October 9, 1956
2. "Sylvia Must Face Facts; Her Face Is For Crying," *Trenton Evening Times*, June 30, 1963
3. Marian Christy, "Lifestyle: Sylvia Sidney, Older, Wiser," *Oregonian*, November 28, 1978
4. Alex Freeman column, *Morning Advocate*, June 15, 1964
5. Rebecca Moorehouse, "Sylvia is Back on Broadway," *Springfield Sunday Republican*, April 30, 1967
6. Cy Rice, "A Toehold on 'Barefoot'," *Milwaukee Sentinel*, June 29, 1973
7. David Dempsey, "How Much Do You Know About Your Eyesight?" *Boston Herald*, July 20, 1975
8. Harold V. Cohen, "*Dream Girl*," *Pittsburgh Post-Gazette*, July 18, 1969
9. Harold Heffernan, "Rosy's Now in Stitches," *San Diego Union*, August 29, 1971
10. Doris Dale Reynolds, "She Soothes One Art With Another," *Greensboro Daily News*, October 6, 1965
11. Mildred Rauschkolb, "Blows Needlepoint's Horn," *Plain Dealer*, January 8, 1969
12. David Cuthbert, "Miss Sidney in New Orleans; Recalls Good, Bad Films," *Times-Picayne*, July 2, 1969
13. Stephanie Fuller, "Needlepoint's Why She's Here," *Chicago Tribune*, October 30, 1969
14. Liz Smith, "An Actress Gives Us The Needle," *Chicago Tribune*, December 8, 1968
15. Arlene Abrahams, "Movie Heroine Enjoys Knitting," *Wichita Eagle*, March 23, 1969
16. William Glover, "Sylvia Sidney Acts Again," *Evening Star*, October 17, 1965

17 Donald Cragin, "'Cabaret' Comediennes," *Boston Herald*, August 2, 1970
18 Glenn Pullen, "Showmanship Makes 'Cabaret' Successful," *Plain Dealer*, August 25, 1970
19 John Mitchum, *Them Ornery Mitchum Boys*, Creatures at Large, c. 1988, pg. 266
20 John Mitchum, *Them Ornery Mitchum Boys*, Creatures at Large, c. 1988, pg. 265
21 David Quinlan, *Quinlan's Film Directors*, B.T. Batsford, c. 1999, pg. 263
22 Myrna Loy, *Being and Becoming*, Knopf, c. 1987, pgs. 337-338
23 Passport from May 1941, lists Loper's full name as: Lincoln George Hard Loper, born August 28, 1907 in Toledo, Ohio. Loper's first marriage was to Violet Hughes, April 25, 1925 (Michigan Marriage Records)
24 Bernard Drew, "Sylvia Sidney-Return of a Star," *Herald Statesman*, September 21, 1973
25 John Hartl, "Sylvia Sidney: an Oscar in April?" *Seattle Daily Times*, January 25, 1974
26 Bernard Drew, "Sylvia Sidney-The Return of a Star," *Herald Statesman*, September 21, 1973
27 Arthur Bell, "Sylvia's Souvenirs," *New York Times*, December 17, 1972 ("a real town with real people" taken from "Tenement Girl in the Country," *The Hour*, December 31, 1977)
28 Marian Christy, "Lifestyle: Sylvia Sidney Older, Wiser," *Oregonian*, November 28, 1978
29 Ronald Bowers, "Legendary Ladies of the Movies," *Film in Review*, June-July 1973
30 Robert Berkvist, "Woses Are Wed, Madeline's a Wow!" *New York Times* March 24, 1974
31 Scott MacDonough, comment on *Summer Wishes, Winter Dreams*, IMDB, January 26, 2013
32 Jeff Laffel, "Sylvia Sidney," *Films in Review*, September/October 1994
33 Mason Wiley, Damien Bona, *Inside Oscar - 10th Anniversary Edition*," Ballantine, c. 1996, pg. 482

Chapter 14
"I've Been Playing Those Rotten-Mother Type Roles"

Sylvia Sidney (1978)

In 1973, Sidney withdrew from a Broadway revival of *The Women* by Clare Boothe Luce. The project was shelved several times and Sylvia got tired of waiting around. (Her close friend, Jan Miner, would eventually play the Countess role assigned to Sidney.) In the interim, Sidney had portrayed the formidable Violet Venable in Tennessee William's *Suddenly, Last Summer*—a role that Katharine Hepburn had essayed on screen. In Chicago, Hepburn's niece, Katharine Houghton, joined Sidney on stage as the young woman who Venable institutionalizes for telling "vile" stories surrounding the death of her homosexual son, Sebastian. Critic Ron Offen complained that Houghton failed to pace her performance and slipped "in and out" of her Southern accent. "Sylvia Sidney, on the other hand," said Offen, "showed her stuff throughout." Sidney was nominated for Chicago's Joseph Jefferson Award for Best Guest Artist of 1973.

When *The Women* finally began its two-month run, Sylvia opted for a tour in *Barefoot in the Park*. "Miss Sidney consumes the role with vigor," observed one critic, who then added, "With all due respect, she often looks a bit like a pug." During a press interview, New Orleans critic Frank Gagnard studied Sidney's little pug earrings and her doghead print blouse adorned with a large doggie lapel pin. "She looked like a walking kennel commercial," he cattily commented, noting that her humor was a "little more feline." Gagnard loved her spunk. When he retired in 2006, he declared Sidney "one of the funniest actresses I've ever interviewed." Sylvia gave reporter Cy Rice a good chuckle as he got up to leave her hotel apartment. Rice headed for the wrong door. Sylvia grabbed his arm, steering him to the exit. A bit abashed, he said, "Really, I'm not trying to get into your bedroom." Sylvia laughed, "Neither is anyone else."

Sidney was set to join William Shatner, and old-timers Margaret Hamilton and Lon Chaney Jr., in a revival of *Arsenic and Old Lace* for Ohio's Kenley Players. By the time the play opened (July 31), Chaney Jr.'s body had been donated to the USC School of Medicine—his liver and lungs on display to show the dangers of alcoholism and cigarettes.[1] Hamilton bowed out. Sidney and Shatner remained the star attractions. The play told of two zany old ladies who comfort lonely, elderly gentlemen by poisoning them, then offering a proper Christian burial in their basement. Critics found the production, "rollicking." Sidney was praised for her "polish and class." Shatner, as the mentally balanced nephew who discovers his aunts' grisly hobby, was praised for his "gusto and great timing."

In his 2009 autobiography, Shatner mentioned that producer John Kenley was "an ... interesting man. Or woman. Or both." Kenley spent his winters in Florida as a woman named Joan Kenley. At the

Fall 1977 - Window shopping with her pugs in New York City

cast party, Kenley, the man, insisted on the first dance—with Shatner.[2] Apparently, Sidney's part in *Arsenic and Old Lace* appealed to her. She appeared in subsequent productions.

In January 1974, Seattle Repertory teamed Sidney with Gale Sondergaard for the American premier of Julian Mitchell's *A Family and a Fortune*. The turn-of-the-century English comedy was promptly panned. Exposing the bitchiness lying beneath the niceties of well-bred people was intended to be "delicious and disturbing." "The play itself is a tiresome bore," complained *The Seattle Daily Times*. Critics praised Sidney and Sondergaard, but not the three-hour "unplayable play." "I love doing period pieces," said Sidney. "The play needed cutting and I've sensed the audience tiring of the repetition. I can't say the reviewers were wrong." Co-player Sondergaard was the first Academy Award recipient in the Best Supporting Actress category in 1936 (*Anthony Adverse*). Her career came to a standstill in 1951 when she was blacklisted. She returned to acting fifteen years later. Sondergaard recalled of Sidney, "We had been civil to each other ... not what you might call fast friends." Three years later, they arranged to meet again. The two spent the day talking, not as actresses, but woman to woman. "It was so pleasant to get to know her that way," said Sondergaard.[3]

Prior to a second *Arsenic and Old Lace* tour, Sylvia joined a panel of judges at the 1974 Miss U.S.A. Pageant in Niagara Falls. Dr. Joyce Brothers, actor George Peppard, and former football player Paul Hornung were also onboard watching beauty contestants in evening gowns and bathing suits. When contestant Karen Jean Morrison mentioned she wanted to meet Israeli Premier Golda Meir because of the "marvelous things" Meir had done for her people—she was a shoo-in to win, especially with Jewish celebrities like Dr. Brothers and Sylvia making the call.

A revival of *Sabrina Fair* reteamed Sidney with Katharine Houghton in the fall of 1975. At the helm was Sylvia's champion from Group Theater, producer/director Harold J. Kennedy. Also in the cast was Maureen O'Sullivan. The romantic tale of Sabrina Fairchild had proved a popular film in 1954, starring Audrey Hepburn. Houghton was assigned the Hepburn role, O'Sullivan and Sidney were delegated, respectively, to future mother-in-law and the doddering "Aunt" Julia. Wit and skillful playing induced much laughter from Toronto to Detroit to Buffalo to Ottawa, before wrapping in Pittsburgh. *The Pittsburgh Press* singled out Sylvia's performance. "Miss Sidney is a joy every time she opens her mouth with a wry, raspy delivery."

When not on stage, Sidney was very much "in charge," especially when told that her prize pugs got on the wrong plane. "If you want to see a commando in action," recalled Kennedy, "you should have seen Sylvia." Sidney somehow managed to get on the Detroit airport communications system. "Ground that Minneapolis plane!" she barked into the microphone. Traffic froze on the runways. In the aftermath, it was discovered that her pugs were safe and on the *correct* plane.

The cast of *Sabrina Fair* fared better when traveling by bus. Producer Kennedy, who brought along his dog Poogie, offered details.

> One of the most joyous trips we ever had during the tour [was] when we had to charter a bus from Buffalo to Ottawa. The whole cast was aboard ... four dogs, all of them jubilant

to be out of their kennels and most of whom behaved better than the actors. We all brought bottles of vodka, tons of tomato juice, cold chickens, stuffed eggs, all the makings for martinis, and lots of scotch. The Bloody Marys flowed until one in the afternoon; then came the wine with the cold lunches; and at about four-thirty the martinis ... at about eight-thirty in the evening we arrived in Ottawa and floated off the bus and into our beds.[4]

Aside from the steady cash flow, it is easy to understand the appeal that touring had for Sidney. Kennedy also cast Sylvia in *Me Jack, You Jill*—a play that never saw opening night. When Kennedy urged Peggy Cass to join the production, she hemmed and hawed. "Are you afraid of the play?" he asked. "No," said Cass. "I'm afraid of Sylvia Sidney." Lisa Kirk signed on instead. She thought Sylvia was fun, and told reporters, "I'm a tremendous fan of hers. She gets better all the time." After sixteen previews, the fun stopped. Kirk decided to drop out. Kennedy referred to it as the "most unpleasant experience of my theatrical life." "But Sylvia," he emphasized, "was a dream and a professional throughout." Hardly anyone cared about the play's demise. Lisa and Sylvia sat toasting each other in Kirk's dressing room. "It was a good thing to close it," shrugged Sylvia, "to get rid of it. Wash it off. Forget it."[5] Co-player Russ Thacker had his own opinion regarding his "chummy" co-stars. Months afterward he commented, "The mystery is how we all got through it alive. Sylvia Sidney, Lisa Kirk and Barbara Baxley ... absolutely hated each other. I've never seen three women behave so childishly. They would even poke each other in the ribs when they passed each other on stage. Sylvia Sidney didn't like me, either. During one performance she threw a bottle of champagne at me. It missed my head by inches. If the show hadn't closed when it did I'm sure one of us would have been killed."⁶

Kennedy was impressed by how Sidney had evolved since her days with Group Theater. She was "no longer in awe ... or under anybody's thumb," he observed. "She will sweep into a rehearsal with her champion pugs, all three of them yapping, and in ten minutes she can intimidate an entire company. I don't know quite how she does it but I've seen her do it and I rather enjoy it. Don't we always enjoy seeing the underdog strike back!" A few months later, Kennedy persuaded Sylvia and Maureen O'Sullivan to repeat their roles in *Sabrina Fair*, with interesting results.

Kennedy trusted Sidney's basic acting instincts, which he felt were "excellent." A *Chicago Tribune* critic praised Sidney and O'Sullivan as "the two best performances in a uniformly splendid cast." Critic Joan E. Vadeboncoeur, who had a reputation for being tough, nodded to Sylvia, saying, "It would be worth the ticket price just to see Miss Sidney inch herself down the stairs, coffee cup in shaky hand, and say, 'I have just a teensy, weensy, hangover this morning.'" By the time the tour reached Syracuse, former teen icon Sandra Dee inherited the role of Sabrina from Heather MacRae. Unfortunately, Dee, looking spunky and appealing, came across as shrill—killing her lines with meaningless gestures. While facing audiences, she was also facing alcohol/drug problems and panic attacks, and carrying the burden of childhood sexual abuse. Dee would never fully recover. Her attempt to do stage work can only be seen as courageous.

Everyone got along fine on tour, until Kennedy had to leave. Twenty-four hours later, he was inundated with frantic phone calls. Sylvia was trying to redirect the play. "Maureen O'Sullivan fought with her," said Kennedy. "Sandra Dee hid from her; and the leading man threatened to strangle her." By the time *Sabrina Fair* opened at Elitch Gardens in Denver, no one was speaking to Sylvia. When she pleaded with the company to do a benefit for Colorado flood victims, they flatly refused. Kennedy, again, came to Sylvia's defense, saying she was being "unfairly maligned." "Her bark," argued Kennedy, "like the yapping of her pugs, doesn't mean anything. And like them, she also is a champion."

Following her "comeback" in *Summer Wishes, Winter Dreams*, Sidney was content to do a mix of TV films and guest appearances. For $10,000 she did a pilot titled *Maureen* starring Joyce Van Patten. The nagging mother (Sidney)-frustrated daughter (Van Patten) combination failed to find a sponsor. Sidney also guest-starred as a Catholic nun with Jewish roots in a few episodes of the long-running daytime soap opera *Ryan's Hope*. She then showed up as a tough crime boss on the popular cop-thriller series *Starsky and Hutch*.

NBC's *The Secret Night Caller* (1975) starred Robert Reed as a repressed IRS executive, stuck in a loveless marriage, who resolves to fantasy and obscene phone calls. The *Los Angeles Times* thought it a convincing, compassionate look at "a phenomenon that most of us would rather not think about." Sidney, as Reed's dominating mother, "scintillated in an unsympathetic role." NBC's *Winner Take All*, delved into the world of a compulsive gambler (Shirley Jones) whose marriage is falling apart. Her nagging mother (Sidney), on the verge of tears, begs her daughter to "quit cold." "God would forgive you," she pleads. "Would she?" Jones replies sarcastically. Director Paul Bogart does a smart, realistic job of capturing the relentless nightmare of out-of-control gambling—to the point of making the viewer uneasy, un-

1975-76: Nun habits, and wigs, *Ryan's Hope* and *Starsky and Hutch* (ABC)

comfortable. There was little, if any, comic relief, but casino manager Joan Blondell pulls off the best line when she advises Jones, "Why don't you throw yourself in front of a train?"

Sidney summed up her career at this juncture, saying, "I've been playing those rotten mother type roles."[7] When asked to join the cast of *WKRP in Cincinnati* (as Mama Carlson, the tough, ornery owner of the station)—her answer was, "What the hell, why not?" She lasted the pilot episode. The 2006 DVD commentary featured director Hugh Wilson and *WKRP* costar Loni Anderson. After mentioning the mink coat Sylvia allowed her two little pugs to sit on between takes, Anderson remarked, "She thought we were just all ridiculous." "Sylvia Sidney was not all that pleasant," confirmed Wilson. "That's why we changed mom. Carol Bruce replaced her. She was lovely." "What a sweetheart," agreed Anderson.

When asked to join WKRP (CBS), Sidney answered, "What the hell, why not?"

Sidney, Joan Blondell and Dorothy Lamour signed on for ABC's *Death at Love House* (1976). It was shelved for over a year. This absurdity involved Robert Wagner and Kate Jackson investigating the life of Lorna Love, a deceased 20's movie queen who died tragically in a fire. Filmed on location at the old Harold Lloyd estate in Beverly Hills, the film, at least, *looked* authentic. In a surprise twist, we learn that Lorna is very much alive, acting as the housekeeper (Sidney) at her old mansion. Her disfigured "face" has been hidden behind a rubber mask. TV critic John Voohees thought the old-time stars gave this "90-minute time-waster" a "welcome lift." Others called it "high camp." Sidney's career choices were peppered with clunkers like *Death at Love House*, but her next film almost defies description.

The big screen beckoned Sidney back for *God Told Me To* (1976).

Sixty minutes into this radical horror flick, Sidney shows up to explain how she was impregnated by aliens inside a spaceship back in 1941. She gave the baby up for adoption. We believe her. Tony Lo Bianco plays a New York homicide detective—the alien son in question. Lo Bianco discovers the truth of his own "past" while investigating a series of serial killings in which the perpetrators insist, "God told me to"—a concept rooted in the Old Testament story of God telling Abraham to kill his son Isaac—the same God who cast plagues upon Egyptians. "Kill a multitude and you can convince a nation," remarks one savvy investigator. The surreal plot thickens when Lo Bianco discovers that he has an alien androgynous sibling "bathed in a halo of light," who is behind the recent killings. Writer-director Larry Cohen creates a cinematic first wherein this androgynous "God" shows his pulsating vagina to Lo Bianco, in an attempt to seduce him into creating a new species. "The movie is ill-natured," warned Copley News critic James Meade. "Cohen's story is farfetched and unpleasant despite the professional manner in which he has handled it." Sidney's career choices would continue to be … unpredictable.

It was during the filming of *Death at Love House* (May 1975) that Sylvia first made mention of Jody's long-term illness to Hollywood columnist Bob Thomas. She didn't elaborate about the nature of his condition, but in a private letter that Jody wrote to his Aunt Stella Adler, the previous year, we get some details. It was dated June 16, 1974.

> Dear Aunt Stella,
> You have watched my condition deteriorate as have others. I imagine it must be rather sad. But all I can do is cope the best

I can, and not worry about how others may feel. I have no place in my life for those who are weak, and no use for those who cannot speak to me openly and directly. This evening I shall leave for the National Institute of Health in Bethesda, Md. Also, Aunt Stella, I want you to know that I know too much to expect miracles. I rather expect that my fight against this disease will take years. So I am preparing myself for a protracted battle.[8]

A month later, he wrote Stella with a confirmation:

Last week I got out of the National Institute of Health. They confirmed that I have Amyotrophic Lateral Sclerosis [ALS], for which there is no treatment. One day I may not be able to feed myself. No matter, it's not important. What is important is that I am able to communicate with others, share ideas, thoughts, feelings. It may seem strange Stella, that in spite of the distance I seem close to you, as though our spirits reached out for each other.[9]

Stella was dealing with her own sorrow after the death of her third husband, writer/physicist Mitchell Wilson. When she escaped on a world tour, she invited Jody to stay in her apartment on Fifth Avenue. Upon her return, Jody took pen in hand. His letter, dated September 3, indicated the deep affection they had for each other.

Dear Aunt Stella,
I received your letters, yet clearly don't know how to answer them. Both of us are trapped. I by my disease. In some ways I am more fortunate than you, yet I envy anyone who can

get on a bus . . . I think of you often. The trip around the world was very good for you. And you said that in Israel you learned that you were just a plain Jewish girl. This I got to see! An uncomplicated Adler![10]

As he approached the age of thirty-five, Jody embraced a wisdom beyond his years. Stella Adler biographer Sheana Ochoa indicated, "Jody's letters ... undoubtedly reminded Stella of the strength of her family and its spirited fight for life."[11] Although Stella's teaching had revolutionized modern-day acting, she still had periods of self-described "falling down into somewhere." Ochoa points out that it was "a classic case of clinical depression."[12]

In reality, both Sylvia and ex-husband Luther Adler had learned the truth of their son's illness long before he did. They kept it from Jody. After observing him tripping, and dropping things, Sylvia got Jody to Mt. Sinai Hospital in New York. Sylvia received the results of Jody's tests in early 1973. On the advice of her cousin, Dr. Albert Sabin, the diagnosis was kept secret from Jody, who was functioning well enough at the time. Years later, Sidney offered specifics. "We spent a year of his life playing games," she said. "That couldn't last. Jody was too bright." As he indicated in letters to Stella Adler, Jody did his own investigating. Then, he called his mother. "I know what I have," he told her. "Don't lie to me anymore. I know that the prognosis is death. I can't handle it anymore."[13] It was at that point (early 1975) that Jody came home to live with Sylvia.

In September 1976, Sidney was reported in "fair condition" at Danbury Hospital for an undisclosed illness, but bounced back in time to join Peter Finch, Martin Balsam and Charles Bronson for NBC's *Raid on Entebbe* (1977). The film dramatized a true incident. Recent news headlines had detailed how a hijacked plane, filled with mostly Jewish passengers, was held in Uganda by a radical Palestinian group. They were backed by the corrupt regime of Idi Amin. Their demand: the release of imprisoned terrorists. The latter half of the film focused on the successful Israeli commando rescue mission. Peter Finch (in his final performance) won an Emmy as Israeli Prime Minister Yitzhak Rabin.

Raid on Entebbe proved more engrossing than its televised predecessor *Victory at Entebbe* (1976), which had starred Burt Lancaster, Kirk Douglas, Elizabeth Taylor, and Helen Hayes. Hayes had essayed the same role as Sidney, a seventy-four-year-old widow named Dora Bloch who was transferred to a Kampala hospital, prior to rescue. The *Jewish Observer* deemed *Raid on Entebbe* "more factually accurate and authentic," but thought Hayes "had the edge" over Sidney. *The Spectator*, on the other hand, thought Sidney performed "unforgettably." The film's epilogue claimed that the whereabouts of Dora Bloch were unknown. It was later verified that Bloch had been dragged from her hospital bed and shot—her disfigured body dumped near a sugar plantation.

Less memorable was *Snowbeast* (1977). For this, Sidney was a last minute replacement for Gloria Swanson, who wised up before filming began (doctor's orders). Swanson was busy with talk shows, cooing about her healthy sex-life, and promoting her new husband's book, *Sugar Blues*. While Sylvia was on location in Colorado, Swanson, in reality, was being crowned Queen of a Mardi Gras feast in Hollywood. Sidney was compensated with a pay check, this time for playing the matriarch of a popular ski lodge. Her character doesn't want authorities to

I Never Promised You a Rose Garden (1977) with
Kathleen Quinlan (New World Pictures)

divulge that Big Foot is randomly killing skiers on the slopes. She argues it's bad for business. Besides, she is eager to crown the Carnival Snow Queen—a crown she wore fifty years ago. Instead, Sidney is almost crushed to death by Winter Carnival celebrants as they flee from the beast. She drops the crown, falls to the floor, and watches a man's "big foot" demolish it. She wails in agony, "The crown! The crown!" Sylvia is carried away in an ambulance, but the viewer must endure another hour until Big Foot is finally killed with a ski pole, no less. *Snowbeast* captured the top spot in Nielsen ratings the week it premiered.

On the big screen, *I Never Promised You a Rose Garden* presented Sidney inside a mental institution, unable to cope with the outside world. Her character is an educated woman, a former math instructor with a salty tongue. Jody must have been pleased with his mother's professional debut as a mathematician, spouting lines like: "Pussycat, did I ever tell you what happens when a straight line bisects an 80 degree angle?"

The film was based on the best-selling novel by Joanne Greenberg.

Kathleen Quinlan played the teenager who resides in a self-created world—a certified schizophrenic. Quinlan's character comes to terms with her demons in a contained performance. The young actress made an observation about her co-star Sidney. "With Sylvia Sidney, all I can say is don't ever try to mess around in a scene with her. She knows everything there is to know about ... camera angles, where to stand, and lighting. Once she was sitting on the sidelines with her needlepoint. I asked her who were the best actors she'd ever worked with. She kept right on with her needlepoint, looked up at me for an instant, and said, 'Tracy and Cagney.' Then she went right back to her work. I thought to myself, 'To be able to drop the names Tracy and Cagney, just like that!' That seemed awesome."[14]

A Dallas critic thought Sidney's portrayal "expertly crafted." *The New York Times*, praised her "achingly pathetic" characterization. There was talk of Sidney being a candidate for Best Supporting Actress. Though reviewers found a few critical thorns in *I Never Promised You a Rose Garden*, they deemed it intensely disturbing and worth seeing.

Adhering to the Hollywood commandment for sequels to box-office hits, came *Damien - Omen II*. This successor to *The Omen* (1976), received mixed reviews, but an almighty $20 million dollar profit. In *Omen II*, Damien reaches puberty and comes to terms with his true identity: the Anti-Christ. The Anti-Christ, or Beast, is derived from Biblical "visions" of a seven-headed monster who brings doom and gloom upon the world. On film, Damien (Jonathan Scott-Taylor) is being raised by his father's brother (William Holden), CEO of an multinational conglomerate. Sidney does a credible job as Holden's wealthy Aunt Marion, who controls a sizeable chunk of the firm. She shakes her finger at everyone while trying to convince Holden that his nephew spells trouble. Although Damien lacks the horns and seven heads as prophesized, Aunt Marion instinctively senses something unsavory. Moments later, a raven—the devil's motif, pays Marion a visit in her bedroom where she succumbs to the inevitable. Critic Bernard Drew described Sidney's demise as "a realistic choking death that brings shivers."

British film director Mike Hodges was enthused about the assignment. "The sequel," said Hodges, "was far more interesting because the subject was highly political." He elaborated: "The corporation owned by Damien's uncle [Holden] was cornering the world's food markets and introducing genetically modified food. It was unwittingly anti-capitalist and here I was being offered it by an American conglomerate, 20th Century-Fox. Very amusing. So I said yes!"[15]

After three weeks of shooting, Fox studio sacked Hodges. "I was making a political film," explained Hodges, "whereas they were making a horror film. What they wanted was the antithesis of everything I stood for in filmmaking." Although "unseen forces" got in the way, *Omen II* retains its anti-conglomerate edge, as Damien moves closer toward a corporate world in which everyone is at his mercy. The film entertains. The remainder of the shoot was completed by actor/director Don Taylor, who received sole credit for complying with the powers that be.

Initially, Sylvia turned down the role of Aunt Marion. "I didn't particularly like it," she stated. "I was feeling fat and rich, so they shot a lot of footage without me. I don't know what happened, but they had a crisis ... then called me frantically. It was December, and I figured I could use the loot for Christmas presents." Sidney was blunt about her performance and director Taylor, who told her, "Now chew up the scenery, Sylvia, otherwise we'll have no movie." After each take, Taylor kept screaming, "More,

more, more!" "I don't know how the other actors felt about it," Sidney said afterward. "I got the feeling they didn't like it much, but I came on strong and carried on without much motivation and now you know why."[16]

Lovers in 3-B, a film for CBS, was shot prior to *Damien - Omen II*. It reteamed Sidney with Martin Balsam. During a press conference at the Manhattan 21 Club, Sylvia quipped, "You know, this is the third time Marty and I have done a picture together. I played his mother-in-law in *Summer Wishes, Winter Dreams*, I was his friend in *Raid on Entebbe*, and now finally Marty and I are lovers." When asked why he took the role, Balsam gave Sylvia a wink and said, "Sylvia Sidney." Retitled *Siege*, the film was a knockout. UPI critic Joan Hanauer found it "beautifully acted and savagely engrossing." Inner city neighborhoods were changing, and *Siege* tackled serious issues.

During the shoot, Sylvia stayed at a midtown hotel. "Mayor Beame may not like to hear this," she told one reporter, "but I've gotten a little disillusioned with the Big Apple." One of the reasons Sidney, an avid walker, had moved to Connecticut, was to distance herself from what she determined "an alarming place to live." When she walked her dogs at night, the hotel doorman cautioned her, "If you're not back in a half-hour, I'm calling the police."

Struggles that faced a youthful Sylvia Sidney in *Street Scene*, had transmuted, over time, into the tragic struggle of elderly people, victimized by urban street gangs. The topic made news headlines, but had been ignored by the film industry. Shot in New York City, *Siege* details the reality of self-proclaimed kingpins who control neighborhood thugs. Dorian Harewood offered an uncompromising portrait

Siege (1978) (CBS) Doomed lovers. A stellar opportunity for Sidney and Martin Balsam

as a young, charismatic black leader who destroys lives in a decaying, minority neighborhood. Sidney's character, the widow Lillian, after repeatedly being victimized, finally removes herself from the battleground. Critic David Cuthbert determined: "Lillian Gordon is probably the best part Sylvia Sidney has had in years. No compromise is made with her appearance; Miss Sidney is playing a frail, old woman and she looks it. Still, there is no disguising the lady's innate style. She projects what might be called 'elderly chic.' She also turns in a shatteringly effective portrayal that builds almost unbearably to the character's efficient, horribly convincing suicide."[17]

Sidney and Balsam carry the film—the first *real* "Sylvia Sidney Movie" since *Love From a Stranger* in 1947. From the scene where her battered face is on display at the police station, until her carefully orchestrated suicide, Sidney captivates. Her intensity, her truthfulness, make her both beautiful and authentic. Sidney and Balsam make a persuasive love match from the moment she waltzes into his arms at a senior social. The scene where Balsam presents Sidney with her stolen wedding ring, carries something that only seasoned players can accomplish. Sylvia found the scenario realistic. "I was so crazy about this script," she said. "The subject material is extremely important, about what unprotected, defenseless elderly people face."[18]

Sidney's performance, coupled with the exquisitely tender, twilight romance she shared with Balsam, was overlooked when the Emmys were announced. In lieu of an Emmy, Sylvia received a Gold Venus Medal (Life Achievement Award), at the 10th Annual Virgin Island Film Festival (1977) held on the island of St. Thomas.

In the Spring of 1977, Sidney took her final bow on Broadway. Tennessee Williams began writing *Vieux Carre* in the 1930's while living in a New Orleans boarding house. He created a montage of characters residing in the pungent decay of the city's French Quarter. Sidney played Mrs. Wire, the landlady, based on the many abrasive, strong women in Williams' life. Theater critic Glenn Currie surmised that Williams was trying to get something "off his chest." He felt the play was "neither theatrical nor revealing." However, Currie did single out Sidney. "Vieux Carre has little to recommend it but a couple of excellent performances: by Tom Aldredge as the painter, and by

Sylvia Sidney as the sluttish, suspicious landlady who gets her jollies by pouring boiling water through the cracks in the floor onto a gay photographer and his fellow orgiasts in the apartment below."[19]

"Having another one of his orgies!" wails Mrs. Wire. "That's the last one he's going to have, by God, and by Jesus! The society people in this city, *they* tolerate vice, but not me!" Broadway's William A. Raidy praised that Sidney captured "the madness, lost gentleness and cruelty of the character." Sylvia's analysis was typically brusque. "I play an old bitch," she said. "My dogs don't think so, but some people think that's what I am. They're welcome to their opinion." When Sylvia shared the stage with a naked man, audiences raised quite a hubbub. "I ceased to be Mrs. Wire in that scene," remarked Sylvia. "I became white-haired Sylvia Sidney up there on the stage, and wasn't she always such a nice girl and what's she doing up there with a naked boy. It stopped the show in a very noticeable and unintentional way."[20]

Vieux Carre opened at the St. James on May 11. It closed after six performances. Williams' biographer, Donald Spoto, wrote that Sidney had foreseen difficulty for *Vieux Carre*. The cast dealt with numerous rewrites. Williams himself was nowhere around. "There were terrific problems," admitted Sylvia. "None of us saw Tennessee for a long time, until we had major problems with several scenes. By the time he arrived ... it was almost too late." Sidney kept calm during the eight weeks of rehearsal. "Nobody has seen me throw a fit about anything," she said. While Williams was commuting from his home in Key West, Spoto pointed to the "coterie of young men, of dubious value to him, who clung to him constantly." Sidney later disclosed,

> I don't think he was helped much by the group of hangers-on and sycophants that surrounded him then, either. We were

nervous, and he was sad. He was frightened of getting old, terrified that he was no longer attractive ... that he couldn't attract young men except with his money. Meanwhile, we were in trouble. The set was impossible, clumsily built, and the production was misconceived.[21]

After *Vieux Carre* closed, Sidney shared her personal feelings about the playwright. "I love him. I don't denigrate Williams. You learn from failure. You don't learn from success. I want to do more Williams plays. He's been bruised. He hurts easily."[22] In turn, Williams acknowledged his admiration for the actress, saying,

My mother and I adored her and her films. She was always so fragile and plaintive. She appeared to need protection. Let me tell you: Sylvia needs no protection. She may look fragile, but look in that exquisite purse she carries with her: it contains the balls of thousands of men who annoyed her; the hearts of those who crossed her; and the locations of those who betrayed her.[23]

Sylvia returned to the stage the following year in a revival of Emyln Williams' 1934 psychological thriller, *Night Must Fall*, which paired her with David McCallum. When I asked McCallum what it was like to work with Sidney, he responded, "She was cool and very professional. Liked to have a drink after the show. Loved her dog - or was it dogs?"[24] (The pugs, at this point in time, were: Star Sapphire and Ladybug). On stage, Sidney was an elderly woman who took fancy to her pregnant housekeeper's beau, Dan (McCallum). Sidney's niece suspects that Dan is not what he seems, but a murderer. The action proceeds to validate her suspicion with unexpected results. A review for the *Palm Beach Daily News* noted the "unique and sensitive mingling of McCallum and stage great Sylvia Sidney. Their ease in working together makes the pair seem like bookends."

Early in 1979, The Chicago Art Institute paid tribute to Sidney's career. "I don't know why they're doing this," was her response. "Maybe if I get enough tributes, they'll say, 'Maybe she's employable.' They don't write much for gray-hairs." As a self-declared "spendaholic" she ballyhooed her availability. When Greer Garson phoned Sidney about doing *The Matchmaker* in Santa Fe as a last minute replacement for Vivian Vance, Sylvia told her, "I haven't done the role in twenty years—so I'll be there tomorrow."

Sylvia next flew to Florida to film the ill-fated Jerry Lewis project *That's Life*—a parody about sex in an adult retirement community. After a week on location, the shoot came to an abrupt halt. Lewis read a letter to the cast, saying that the production's financial balloon had burst. The assembled stars included: Sylvia, Red Buttons, Molly Picon, Danny Thomas, James Darren, among others. Liz Smith reported that Lewis had gotten Sidney out of a previous commitment to do the film. It was payback for Sylvia's kind gesture in 1946, when she caught Lewis' act with Dean Martin at the 500 Club in Atlantic City. Sidney called a reputable agent "and the rest," reported Smith, "is history."[25] *That's Life* was put on hold, permanently.

With nothing better to do, Sidney signed on to lead a scholarly

16-day tour of French needlework and tapestry art: Paris, Aubusson, Angers, and Beauvais. Museums such as the Louvre, a tapestry factory, the Loire Valley and Normandy were included on the itinerary. Prior to departure on October 13, she enthused, "I haven't been to France since one of my honeymoons [1938]."

Upon her return from the Continent, Sidney signed with Universal for the primetime feature, *The Gossip Columnist*. For this slam on tinseltown Sylvia played a washed-up Hedda Hopper-type. She loses her column to a much younger Kim Cattrall. Before long, Cattrall's gossip hits a highly political nerve in the film community. She runs into Sylvia at a posh bar. Sylvia greets her with, "Welcome to the North Pole, dear. I read your column. Naughty, naughty. Even I can't afford to be seen with you." *The New York Times* called *The Gossip Columnist* "the electronic equivalent of junk food." D.C. critic, Judy Flander, sang praises for Sidney and co-star Martha Raye. "The two old pros run away with the movie, knocking over the leads without missing a step." Numerous young actors and pop stars in the cast tested their acting chops. When asked about this new crop of thespians, Sidney readily admitted that she couldn't wait to finish working with them. "Some make it seem they're doing you a great favor to be talking with you. One young actor approached me after a day's shooting and said, 'Hey, you did OK.'" Sylvia chuckled, "I'm glad he told me." [26]

Cattrall had high praise for Sylvia, finding her "ballsy and gutsy." When she asked Sidney for a cigarette, Sylvia peered at her intensely and snapped, "Go bum it off someone else!" On another occasion, Cattrall accidentally nudged Sidney, who then turned around and belted her! "But we became friends," assured Cattrall, "and we went to lunch together. With Sylvia its tears through the laughter."[27]

If anything, *The Gossip Columnist* afforded Sylvia the opportu-

The Gossip Columnist (1980) (OPT) as a Hedda Hopper clone

nity to vent her personal feelings about vultures like Hedda Hopper and Louella Parsons (both safely dead).

Louella Parsons, Hedda Hopper, Sheilah Graham, Jimmy Fidler and Walter Winchell, were all feared and sometimes despised by the stars. I was scared to death of all of them myself because of the enormous power they had. I learned Louella's technique for worming out all the personal stuff that could make headlines. She'd begin by crying and telling me about her own personal problems. To make her feel better ... I'd confess the truth about my entire life. The next day I'd read it in headlines. I'd get furious with myself and promise not to talk to her again. Thank God, I had a few secrets I managed to keep to myself.[28]

Sylvia had her own theory about the demise of the Heddas and Louellas of yesteryear. "The way we all live today," she said, "it's difficult to shock anyone. There's an openness about two unmarried people sleeping together. How can newspaper readers be shocked by what the stars are doing when they are involved in the very same things? The scandal that brought about the end of the era of gossip columnists was Ingrid Bergman's affair with Roberto Rossellini and the child they had out of wedlock. After that, everything seemed to be anticlimactic."

For *F.D.R.: The Last Year* (1980), Sidney was paged to play Franklin Delano Roosevelt's talkative spinster cousin Polly Delano. The TV drama featured Jason Robards in the title role, and detailed Roosevelt's negotiations with Churchill and Stalin; his battle with congestive heart failure; and, relationships with wife Eleanor (Eileen Heckert) and mistress Lucy Mercer (Kim Hunter). Both Robards and Heckert received Emmy nominations. Robards avoided impersonation, yet caught the Roosevelt style. A UPI critic found Sidney "delightfully scatty." *The New York Times* commented, "Sylvia Sidney and Jan Miner, as the President's cousins, narrate the story most authentically."

Sylvia enjoyed a long friendship with actress Jan Miner, who, coincidentally, had made her stage debut in a 1945 revival of *Street Scene*. The two worked together in *The Dark at the Stop of the Stairs* (1960) and *Light Up the Sky* (1964). Miner's most lucrative claim to fame was as "Madge the Manicurist" for Palmolive commercials. When Sylvia gifted Miner with two exquisite needlepoint pillows (c. 1961), Miner said, "You're crazy!"—insisting that the needlepoint should sell for fancy prices. She took out a checkbook and gave Sylvia her first order. Two years later, Miner showed up at Sylvia's to announce that she had fallen in love. Sylvia, once again, spun her magic with needle and thread. In May 1963, Jan and set designer Richard Merrill stood at the altar—a double-ring ceremony graced with a needlepoint ring pillow designed by Sylvia herself. Sidney, along with Myrna Loy, were the appointed bridesmaids.

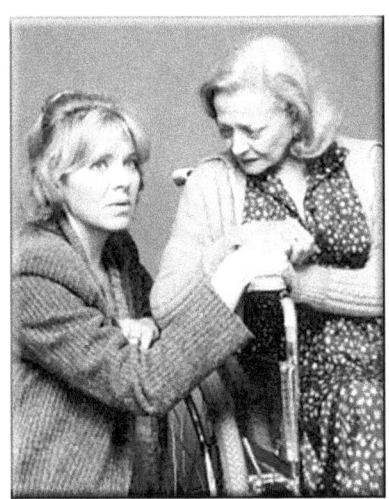
The Shadow Box (1980) (ABC) with Melinda Dillon

After Sidney opted out as a last minute replacement in a production of Michael Cristofer's *The Shadow Box* (directed by Richard Chamberlain), Paul Newman and Joanne Woodward visited her at home in Connecticut. Newman made mention of directing his first television movie, which happened to be, *The Shadow Box*. Woodward suggested that Sylvia be cast as the elderly woman, but Newman had rewritten the part for Laurence Olivier. Sylvia butted in, "I could compete with any other dame, but not with Olivier."[29] Olivier turned Newman down. Newman went directly to Sylvia and offered her the role.

The Shadow Box was based on a Pulitzer Prize play. ABC agreed to televise the production after some of the dicey language was omitted. The emotional, upbeat drama, explored the lives of three terminally ill patients who reside at a seaside hospice. Director Newman's powerhouse cast included: Joanne Woodward, Christopher Plummer and Valerie Harper. Sylvia played Felicity, an elderly woman who puffs away on cigarettes while riding along in her wheelchair. Her abrasive character is offended when doctors refer to her as "the patient." "Patient?" she rails. "Hell, I'm the corpse! I have one lung, and two springs and a battery where my heart used to be." Her devoted daughter Agnes (Melinda Dillon) acts as caregiver. Felicity's "hope" is bolstered by letters from Claire—a favored, younger daughter who has died. The letters are inventions that Agnes writes to make her mother happy. Felicity is determined to bargain with death until Claire shows up. *The Shadow Box* shows how *hope* gets in the way of letting go.

Newman relished the irreverence of a script that allowed viewers to get in touch with *feelings* and, as he envisioned, "make every day count." *The New York Times* praised the "outstanding production" and the "superb performances." Sylvia had deep respect for Newman's talents. "He's very calm, he's very specific," she said. "The thing I love about him ... he made me do things that never occurred to me to do. He's very inventive as a director. He sees things from an actor's point of view."[30] Sidney also waxed poetic about Woodward: "My beautiful Joanne. She is one of the dearest human beings ever born."[31]

By the time *The Shadow Box* wrapped, Sidney had signed for Francis Ford Coppola's *Hammett*, directed by German filmmaker Wim Wenders. It was a fictionalized detective yarn paying homage to author Dashiell Hammett, who once referred to Sylvia as his favorite actress—his "ugly little baby" from *City Streets*, a story he had written for the screen. *Hammett* turned out to be a three year project for Coppola's ill-fated Zoetrope Studios. After months of rewrites and disagreements, Coppola shut down production. Filming resumed in November 1981 with a new cinematographer, and premiered at the Cannes Film Festival (to mixed reviews) in June 1982.

Set in San Francisco 1928, Hammett (Frederic Forrest) investigates the case of a missing Chinese call girl. As manager of the Occidental Mission House, where the girl had once taken refuge, Sidney offers Hammett some clues ... but, has she been duped? Sidney's screen time was allotted one minute, fifteen seconds. The brevity of her role didn't bother her. "I need the money," she said. "There are bills to be paid. So, I work for a living like everybody else." Sylvia seldom refused offers. "After all," she explained, "how many parts are there for little old gray-haired ladies?" Critics were drawn to Sidney's performances, no matter how small. Vincent Canby, for *The New York Times,* said the film "isn't quite the mess one might expect. ... It's not ever boring. Sylvia Sidney, beautiful, gallant woman, plays a tiny role as one of the people who aid Sam's investigation."

One distinct plus for Sidney at this juncture, was pointed out by veteran Hollywood reporter Vernon Scott: "Unlike many stars of her heyday, Sylvia willingly allows camera close-ups disclosing the alterations that time has etched in the hauntingly beautiful face of the girl she once was." Sylvia's attitude? "I think it's dumb to be something you're not. Everything ages. Trees age. Beauty is in the eye of the beholder. You can't fight aging. It happens."[32] A few years later, she bluntly determined,

> I've changed as a woman. Three marriages, a child, a couple of offbeat lovers, the loss of friends, the loss of parents, the loss of teeth, the loss of eyes, all change you. After 74 years, you have to change. You're going to look awful ugly, still acting 17 or 18 with that face.[33]

(Endnotes)

1 Greg Mank, Tom Weaver, "Evolution of a Horror Star," *Films of the Golden Age,* Summer 2015
2 William Shatner, *Up Till Now: The Autobiography,* MacMillan, c. 2009, pgs. 159-160
3 John Voorhees, "Gale Sondergaard: Trying to Turn Authoress," *Seattle Daily Times,* November 18, 1977
4 Harold J. Kennedy, *No Pickle, No Performance,* Doubleday, c. 1978, pg. 192
5 Earl Wilson. "Even the Actors Didn't Like the Show," *Aberdeen Daily News,* March 19, 1976
6 Harry Bowman, "'Breaks' Not Always Welcome for Thacker," *Dallas Morning News,* August 26, 1976
7 Dan Lewis, "Sylvia Sidney, 67, Eyes New TV Series," *Boston Herald,* April 25, 1978
8 Jody Adler to Stella Adler, June 16, 1974, Stella Adler Papers, Harry Ransom Center, University of Austin

9   Jody Adler to Stella Adler, July 11, 1974, Stella Adler Papers, Harry Ransom Center, University of Austin
10 Jody Adler to Stella Adler, September 3, 1974, Stella Adler Papers, Harry Ransom Center, University of Austin
11 Sheana Ochoa, *Stella! Mother of Modern Acting*, Applause, c. 2014, pgs. 253-254
12 Sheana Ochoa, *Stella! Mother of Modern Acting*, Applause, c. 2014, pg. 180
13 Kathy Larkin, "Actress Helps Son Cope with *Lou Gehrig's Disease*," *Centre Times*, September 21, 1983
14 Philip Wuntch, "Texpo Honors Quinlan," *Dallas Morning News*, February 4, 1978
15 Mark Adams, *Mike Hodges: The Pocket Essential Guide*, Oldcastle, c. 2001, pg. 42
16 Bernard Drew, "At 68, Sylvia as Rebellious as Ever," *Herald Statesman*, July 14, 1978
17 David Cuthbert, review of *Siege*, *Times-Picayune*, April 23, 1978
18 Dan Lewis, "Sylvia Sidney, 67, Eyes New TV Series," *Boston Herald*, April 25, 1978
19 Glenn Currie, "Now Tennessee Can Return to Playwriting," *Evening Star*, May 22, 1978
20 Anna Quindlen, "The Indomitable Sylvia Sidney," *New York Times*, June 9, 1977
21 Donald Spoto, *The Kindness of Strangers: The Life of Tennessee Williams*, Da Capo, c. 1997, pgs. 324-325
22 Earl Wilson, "Modest Star Who Shuns Fame," *Dallas Morning News*, June 6, 1977
23 Dan Callahan, "Sylvia Sidney: Jailhouse Blues," *The Chiseler*, blog, c. 2014
24 David McCallum, message sent to author, August 28, 2015
25 Liz Smith, column, *Plain Dealer*, July 15, 1979 (Smith erroneously named Abe Lastfogel (William Morris Agency), when, in fact, it was indie agent Abby Greshler who signed the duo of Martin & Lewis after catching their act the Atlantic City's 500 Club)
26 Marilyn Beck, "Actress Plays Old Bag," *Star-News*, March 6, 1980
27 David Cuthbert, "*Gossip Columnist* 'Fun Trash,'" *Times-Picayune*, March 23, 1980
28 Vernon Scott, "Actress Who Feared Gossip Columnists Gets to Play One," *Omaha World*, January 6, 1980
29 "People in the News," *Greensboro Daily News*, October 28, 1979
30 Camilla Snyder, "Sylvia Remembers the Old Days," *Marietta Journal*, March 16, 1980
31 Susan King, "Sylvia Sidney - Not the Retiring Type," *Los Angeles Times*, December 31, 1992
32 Millie Wolff, "The Magic Still Works for Actress Sylvia Sidney," *Palm Beach Daily*, February 8, 1978
33 Marylynn Uricchio, "Sylvia Sidney: A Real 'Pro for the Public Theater," *Pittsburgh Post-Gazette*, September 28, 1984

Chapter 15
A Mother's Shrine to Her Son

In the summer of 1980, Budd Schulberg made mention that he was writing his memoirs, tentatively titled, *Home Sweet Hollywood*. As Sylvia approached seventy, any anxiety that she anticipated from what Budd might reveal was assuaged (temporarily) by her friends Joanne Woodward and Paul Newman. Woodward offered Sylvia a role in *Come Along With Me*, which began filming in Chicago that fall. It marked the directorial debut of Woodward, and aired on *American Playhouse*.

Sylvia told a journalist for the *Chicago Tribune*, "Working with Joanne as a director is a true joy." The feeling was mutual. "I always believe in casting my friends," remarked Woodward.[1] For *Come Along With Me* she cast Estelle Parsons as a widow with paranormal abilities. Sylvia was among the quirky characters who attend a séance Parsons holds at a rooming house. *Variety* wasn't exactly enthusiastic, but conceded, "*Come Along With Me* at least provides marvelous acting ground for the incomparable Estelle Parsons, for Barbara Baxley and for Sylvia Sidney. Nuf said." When filming wrapped, Sylvia made a guest appearance on *Over Easy* (PBS)—aimed at older viewers. The episode focused on vision and allowed Sylvia to talk about her cataract operations. Her comments were juxtaposed with an historical sketch of the vision-impaired Impressionist Claude Monet and how cataracts influenced his art before he had them surgically removed in 1923.

Sidney kept busy as usual, queuing up with other vintage stars for the popular *Love Boat* TV series. She played a Jewish mother who makes frequent asides to her dead husband regarding their son's shipboard flirtation. Who was the dead husband? The photo she placed next to her bed was of none other than Bennett Cerf (Cerf had died in 1971). Sylvia also transformed herself into a bag lady who acts as a "mule" for drug dealers, in the CBS movie *A Small Killing*. Filmed in a Los Angeles slum area, Sylvia's character gets bumped off for doing a little dealing on the side.

For the stage, Sylvia toured in *Mornings at Seven*, a comedy revival that was concurrently having a successful Broadway run starring Maureen O'Sullivan. While playing in Fort Lauderdale, critic Skip Sheffield thought it an "exemplary production," and praised the top-billed Sidney as "warm, dignified and sensitive." As for her priggish husband (Dana Andrews), Sheffield thought him appropriately "handsome, cold and stiff." In a close-knit family of four sisters, Sylvia played the eldest. The cast was also close-knit. In a 2015 conversation with co-player Patricia O'Connell, who played Sylvia's youngest sister, she related, "Sylvia was a fun, and a funny lady. I went to see Maureen O'Sullivan in *Mornings at Seven* and told her that I was going on tour with it. After a pause, she said, 'I hear you are doing this with Sylvia Sidney.' I said, 'Yes, I am.' 'You have to stand up to her,' O'Sullivan warned me. And, it was true. She got along with people who stood up to her."[2]

O'Connell recalled that Sylvia would always leave her dressing room door open, so when cast members walked by, they had to greet her. At the end of each week she would throw a cast party, with fancy *hors d' oeuvres* and drinks. "It was really a wonderful company," enthused O'Connell, who had obvious affection and admiration for Sylvia.

Closer to home, Sidney put heart and soul into an ALS benefit concert to be held at Carnegie Hall. Eight years had passed since Jody was stricken with the progressively damaging disease. Sylvia had been a tireless volunteer for the National ALS Foundation. In charge of the honorary committee for the Carnegie event, she put together a star-studded list, and began making phone calls. Sylvia didn't hesitate to ask people like Woody Allen, Robert Preston and Joanne Woodward, but when it came to telephoning violinist Isaac Stern, one of her heroes, she admitted, "I contracted butterflies and hesitantly dialed the Stern home." The phone rang and Sylvia asked to speak to Stern. During the silence she almost hung up in terror. Before long she heard an enthusiastic, "Sylvia Sidney! My God, I've been in love with you for years."[3] Stern gladly joined Miss Sidney's committee.

Patricia O'Connell made mention of how often Sylvia was asked why she was working so hard at her age. "She had to," said O'Connell. "Sylvia paid for all of Jody's health expenses at the facility where he was residing." I asked her about Luther Adler. "He didn't pay a penny," said O'Connell. Aside from Aunt Stella, few of the Adlers were participating in Jody's life.

As the neuromuscular system of his body slowly deteriorated, Jody's mind remained active. Sylvia's home in Connecticut was 55 miles from Brandywine Nursing Home, in Briarcliff Manor, New York, where Jody lived. Together, the two of them had decided on the location. Jody's life narrowed down to visits from his mother and a decreasing number of visits from his old friends. His closest friend, Raymond van Over, recalled "One of Jacob's joys as the disease was catching up with him was photography, along with his long distance bike riding"— both of which came to an inevitable standstill.

Just off the living room in Sylvia's home was the bedroom Jody had stayed in before it became imperative that he have constant medical care. The room was now redecorated, but photos of Jody were displayed throughout the house—from the small, laughing boy hugging his dog, to the good-looking young man. Home had become a shrine of memories. Sidney's collection of thimbles, her collection of pugs in art and china, her needlepoint and her own paintings, made the atmosphere highly personal. Jody would be turning forty-two in October. Sylvia watched the devastation of a disease that attacked the productive years—destroying talented human beings with much to give. "Like my son," she said softly, "a constructive intelligent, bright human being. It's rough, but Jody is extraordinary. Something going on inside keeps him interested in the world, and in life."[4] Weighing only 115 pounds, Jody spent time listening to his favorite music, and reading with the aid of an electronic device that turned the pages. "There seems to be nothing of him now," Sylvia quietly observed.

When Budd Schulberg's book, *Moving Pictures: Memories of a Hollywood Prince*, was finally released in July 1981, Sylvia wasn't quite prepared for what was inside. *Variety* made a point of saying that Sylvia was "far from happy" with Schulberg. She was upset and rightly so. "What he thinks of me is his own business," she told reporters, "but I object strongly to the inaccuracies—even to things as easy to check as roles I never played and the misspelling of my name."⁵ A British review commented, "Sylvia Sidney also receives special—though less kindly—mention." Some called Schulberg's memoir a "masterpiece." Others weren't as impressed. In his review for the Associated Press, Phil Thomas referred to Budd's book as an oversized "haphazard collection" of memories. Reviewers rarely took time to check facts. Budd's revisionist slant on actual events was inclined to accommodate his narrative. While he did an admirable job of detailing the mixed messages he received while growing up—a mother who preached socialism, but practiced capitalism; an industry that promoted "morality" on screen but did just the opposite off—"Prince" Schulberg managed to reinvent and twist information to suit himself.

Budd wraps up his commentary on Clara Bow by mentioning that immediately after the infamous Daisy De Voe trial, Bow's next film role was taken over by Peggy Shannon. While Shannon would replace Bow in a subsequent film (*The Secret Call*), it was Sylvia who initially filled in for Bow (*City Streets*). Budd wasn't quite ready to introduce Sylvia. She makes her grand entrance 170 pages later during a screaming match between Budd's parents in which Ad refers to Sylvia as "nothing but a little *hoor*. Cheap little *kike!*" Budd erroneously informs the reader, "Ben and Ad had seen the 20-year-old Sylvia in the risqué hit, *Strictly Dishonorable*." *Bad Girl* was the play in question. Budd carelessly referred to Sylvia's mother as "Sophie Kosow"—never Beatrice Sidney.

Budd goes into some detail about film director Marcel De Sano. The two attended the Rose Bowl together in 1929. "Fade in—ten years later," writes Budd. "The scene: my mother's townhouse in London." He then describes De Sano's proposal of marriage to Ad Schulberg, who wanted to help Marcel resurrect his career. De Sano told her that if she did not accept his offer, he would jump out of a window. According to Budd, that's exactly what he did.[6] The problem with Budd's ten-page treatise on De Sano, is that De Sano committed suicide three years earlier, on March 17, 1936, near Paris, not London. He had fixed a rubber tube to a car's exhaust and inserted it in his mouth. After De Sano's demise, Bebe Daniels revealed that shortly before he took his life he told her that he had made two previous attempts, and was determined to succeed.[7]

Numerous other fabrications and errors fill Schulberg's memoir. His ramblings, however misconstrued, have now become part of Hollywood lore. He readily admitted, "I am my own team of archeologists digging down in time and the memories are scattered shards."[8] Among these "shards" is Budd's dutiful analysis of Conrad Nagel's penis, while visiting the actor in his dressing room on the set of *Divorce in the Family* (1932).

Budd was pleased with himself and his book. "I can smell a new season of success," he crowed at one book promo. "People are suddenly calling me from all over the country. All sorts of invitations are arriving ... . I just take it in stride."[9] His modesty no doubt resulted from escaping Hollywood at the tender age of eighteen. "I felt very threatened by the sexuality of the town," he explained. "I despised all girls. I thought they were all predators who wanted favors. My home was threatened by Clara Bow and other women ... ." Budd joked that he was an "impossible Puritan" at the time. By 1981, he had succeeded in chalking up four marriages to Sylvia's three. Even so, Budd's juvenile approach in relating the story of his father and Sylvia Sidney lacked the hindsight and wisdom that comes with maturity.

Prior to the release of Schulberg's book, Sylvia referred to her relationship with Budd's father. "My antics—which caused such waves a half a century ago," she stated, "wouldn't even cause a ripple of excitement today."[10]

Next up, Sidney returned to the stage for a revival of Moss Hart's *Light Up The Sky*, all about a bunch of conniving Broadway characters. *The New York Times* pointed to Sylvia and co-player Phyllis Newman for the play's success. "Our allegiance goes to the evening's voice of reason ... the star's mother played with regal disdain by Sylvia Sidney. Miss Sidney's droll, deadpan performance is matched by that of Phyllis Newman as the producer's wife. An early-morning, two-handed colloquy between Miss Sidney and Miss Newman is at the heart of the evening's humor. Others in the cast do not all function on the level of these two estimable ladies."[11]

In 2013, Phyllis Newman reflected back. "Sylvia and I shared a teeny dressing room, and the first time we actually used it ... Sylvia stared at me, and in her whiskey soaked voice said, 'For a little girl, you sure have a big ass!' (It still tickles me). We gave a cast party at our house and we rented *Sabotage* as a surprise. We watched a much older Sylvia look at herself as a young, fragile beauty whose huge eyes were staggeringly compelling. It was not sad, because those eyes were exactly the same in this still delicate looking, but tough old broad whose talent deepened all the time."[12]

More offbeat casting greeted Sylvia when she signed to play the wealthy grandmother of punk rock star John Lydon (Johnny Rotten of the Sex Pistols) in *Corrupt*, starring Harvey Keitel. Keitel, a shady police investigator, shows up at Sidney's mansion to learn more about Lydon, with whom he has entered a bizarre sadomasochistic relationship. She's obliging, believing her grandson is missing, when, in fact, he is bound and gagged, lying naked in Keitel's bathtub. Keitel feeds Lydon out of a dog bowl and keeps an eye on him through a peephole. *Corrupt* (released in 1983), shot in New York and Rome, was directed by Italian director Roberto Faenza. Keitel, who studied under Stella Adler, played his trademark brooding, thug. British author, Hugh Fleetwood, on whose book the film was based, recalled in 2013, "I was on the set for the whole shooting, enjoying it enormously. The person I got on with best was Sylvia Sidney. She had lots of great stories about Hollywood."[13] *Variety* thought Lydon's quirky persona the film's "big asset." *Corrupt* was an acquired taste. *The Film Journal* noted, "Sylvia Sidney is quietly eccentric as Leo's wealthy grandmother, in a small but surprisingly pleasing role. She is ... an oasis of harmless oddness in a milieu overrun by the dangerously bizarre." New York critic Janet Maslin thought *Corrupt* "irredeemably wild," and concluded, "The whole thing might just as well be taking place on the moon."

In November 1982, Sylvia was a recipient of the George Eastman Award for Distinguished Contribution to the Art of Film. Joining her in this category were: Myrna Loy, Joan Bennett, Louise Brooks, Maureen O'Sullivan, Luise Rainer, and Dolores Del Rio. Sylvia closed 1982 in the TV-Movie *Having It All*, playing the puzzled mother of Dyan Cannon, a bicoastal bigamist juggling two husbands. This frantic comedy, according to *The New York Times*, came off as "basically inert." Sidney brought in the New Year as a champagne-guzzling KGB agent in TV's seriocomic *Magnum P.I.* starring Tom Selleck. She arrives in Hawaii with a killer parrot perched on her shoulder, and plans to shoot a former Hungarian freedom fighter. She's foiled before getting her man, but manages to pull off the best lines. "I have trouble sleeping," she tells Selleck. "Old people often do. They're afraid

KGB agent Sidney and her killer parrot visit *Magnum P.I.* (CBS)

they won't get up." Sidney said of Selleck, "He is the closest thing we have today to the great movie heroes of the past."[14]

By midsummer 1983, Sylvia was on location in Danbury, Connecticut. She joined the cast of *The Brass Ring*, co-produced by and starring Dina Merrill. Based on a young adult novel by Jocelyn Riley, the story centered on a teenager (April Lerman) trying to cope with the mental issues plaguing her mother (Merrill). Sidney played the disgruntled grandmother, who reminds Merrill, "I'm not the crazy one in this family." *The Brass Ring* was tossed off kilter by relentless scenes of Merrill chain-smoking, in lieu of focusing on a teenager trying to deal with Mom's "issues"—the center of the novel. Merrill may have been hauled off to a mental institution, but it was fourteen-year-old Lerman who carried the story.

One of Sidney's more convoluted roles was that of Robert Preston's delusionary wife in HBO's *Finnegan Begin Again* (1985). It was a sensitively drawn portrait of a woman who lost touch with reality following the death of her young son. A former dancer, she waltzes around her disheveled home in elegant gowns, emotionally unavailable to anyone. Preston's glib vitality takes it all in stride, until Sidney has a stroke. We see him feeding her in the hospital, lovingly combing her hair, while she struggles to mouth words. "We did not rehearse that scene," recalled Sidney. "Joan Silver, the director, was surprised how fast we did it. Preston was such a wonderful actor to work with! After the film, he became ill himself, and later died of cancer [1987]."[15] The film also starred Mary Tyler Moore, a single woman who bends Preston's ear with her own love problems. New York critic Kevin Thomas found the bittersweet tale to be "a real winner ... heartwarming and funny. Sidney is extraordinary as a vague, drifting woman jolted back into focus by severe illness."

While filming in Virginia, Sylvia was interviewed inside Richmond Memorial Hospital. "I die a lot in movies these days. Pleasure in my work? It is not enjoyment. It is a satisfaction that goes with doing a good job." When asked about contemporary films, Sidney felt they didn't measure up. "We had real escapist films. Now you want to escape from some of them." She preferred the controlled studio atmosphere to location filming—no barking dogs, honking cars, or planes flying over. "As a result," she concluded, "we don't have scenes like Lubitsch and Hitchcock used to shoot." As for being forthright with her opinions, she admitted, "When you reach a certain age you let it all hang out."[16]

'night Mother brought Sidney back to the stage after a three year absence. The play, by Marsha Norman, had won a Pulitzer Prize. Sylvia was the featured star in a 1984 Pittsburgh revival. Playing a simple country woman, Sidney is faced with her epileptic, unemployable daughter's calm, nonchalant revelation that she plans to commit suicide by morning. Margaret Reich, founder and manager of the theater, recalled in 1999, "During rehearsals [Sylvia] got scared and tried to back out of the show. So Bill [Gardner, producer] contracted with an actress from the Guthrie Theater to stand by for her. Then Sylvia began to relax—she needed that security."[17] Fortunately, 'night Mother, despite its downbeat theme, was a record-setting hit. Critic Marilyn Posner was impressed with Sidney's emotional range: "... frustration, brutal honesty, desperation, and even humor. Her tears are real, the anguish harsh." A critic for *The Pittsburgh Post* called *'night Mother* "the most moving experience I've ever been involved with ... theater at its most shattering and devastating." The play was Sidney's stage swansong.

On December 8, 1984, ex-husband Luther Adler, after a long illness, passed away at the age of eighty-one. Obituaries touted his starring roles from *Golden Boy* to the Broadway musical, *Fiddler on the Roof*. He and his wife, Julia, whom he married in 1959, had resided on a 40-acre farm in Kutztown, Pennsylvania. In 2015, Jody's friend Raymond van Over shared vivid memories of Luther's last visits with his son. Van Over recalled Luther banging on his apartment door at 11 p.m., tears running down his cheeks. He needed to talk with van Over after he and Jacob had quarreled. Van Over also elaborated on the final father-son visit.

> I wheeled Jacob into Luther's bedroom after his last stroke, a few months before his death. It was an overwhelming, poignant scene: both paralyzed, unable to move or speak—except for Luther's fingers on his left hand that grasped Jacob's gnarled fingers and hung on for the whole time we were there. Since they couldn't talk, they sat there staring at each other, both desperate for some sort of rapprochement. It brought tears to my eyes and I had to leave and let them commune in their silence with whatever means they could.[18]

Sylvia continued getting numerous TV offers, which she gladly accepted. When columnist Harry Haun asked Sidney what kind of role she played on the teen-themed *Whiz Kids*, she shrugged, "Oh, one of those old bags they always think of me for." For this, she donned a rubber mask to rob a convenient store, after her Social Security check was waylaid. In another TV guest spot, Sylvia locked horns with Pernell Roberts on *Trapper John, M.D.* She played a tyrannical productivity consultant who spies on the hospital staff and champions a surgeon who performs unnecessarily risky, but financially lucrative, operations. "A hospital is a business," she tells Roberts, who replies, "And, the patients are customers, and we're just a bunch of salesmen." The storyline is still relevant. In 2010, the Institute of Medicine reported that thirty percent of health care spending ($750 billion per annum) was spent on "unnecessary health care services."[19] After shooting wrapped in Los Angeles, Sylvia returned home to Connecticut to find that her water pipes had frozen to the tune of a $20,000 repair bill.

In the early 1980's, Sylvia lost three close friends to the AIDS virus. For her, the logical step was to lend her name and money to help fight what was considered a deadly disease. In 1985, she jumped at the opportunity to be in the first televised production tackling the AIDS epidemic. Sidney wasn't concerned about any flak to which she might be subjected—she was already used to it. "I donated a considerable amount of money to a recent AIDS benefit," she said, "and when certain people found out about it, they yelled and screamed at me. People were offended that I wanted to help fight the killer."[20]

In NBC's *An Early Frost*, Sidney played the understanding grandmother whose grandson is stricken with AIDS. Aidan Quinn played

New York, April 15, 1985 - with Mayor Ed Koch at a benefit for the Museum of the Moving Image

the grandson, a Chicago attorney. He and his lover of two years, Peter (D.W. Moffet), separate, and Quinn travels home to his parents who live in New England. The time had arrived to inform them that he was gay ... and had contracted AIDS. His search for love and support finds answers in unexpected places.

The time had arrived for Hollywood to challenge die-hard prejudices that targeted those living with AIDS. When Sidney received the offer from director John Erman, he told her, "Get on the plane tomorrow. We need you!" Filming had already started and the actress assigned to play the grandmother was off key. Erman read some of the script to Sylvia over the phone. She agreed to do the role, but only under the condition that she receive Jody's approval. It would be a solid three week shoot. Jody was in the last stages of ALS. Sylvia later reflected, "We knew that it was only a matter of time. I was with him just as often as I could be, and that was a good deal of the time. Just then, I was offered a role in the first television film to deal with the subject of AIDS, a subject that meant a great deal to me, for so many wonderful people, many of my friends, were dying of it." Flying to California meant leaving Jody behind. She went to the hospital. "At that point," said Sidney, "my son couldn't speak. He could only move his eyes. He was hooked up to an interpretive instrument." "Should I go and do this TV movie?" she asked. Through the machine Jody said, "Take the money and run, Mom!"[21]

During rehearsals Sidney celebrated her seventy-fifth birthday. When she returned to the hotel a small bunch of carnations were waiting for her. "Who the hell in California knows I love white carnations," she asked herself. She read the card,

Dear Mom,
I remember so well the day you told me the story of *Candide*.
Happy Birthday.
Love, Jacob

Sidney recalled the story's poignant ending, when the doctor tells Candide, "Get on with your life and cultivate your garden!" Jody died two days later at the age of forty-five. In all likelihood he had encouraged his mother to leave, in order to release himself from the ties that bound him to physical reality. Upon hearing of Jody's death, producer Perry Lafferty offered to shut down the production of *An Early Frost*, or release Sylvia so that she could return East. She insisted that they remain on schedule and keep her busy. Jody had been cremated. It was over. "He was already gone physically when he died," she told them,

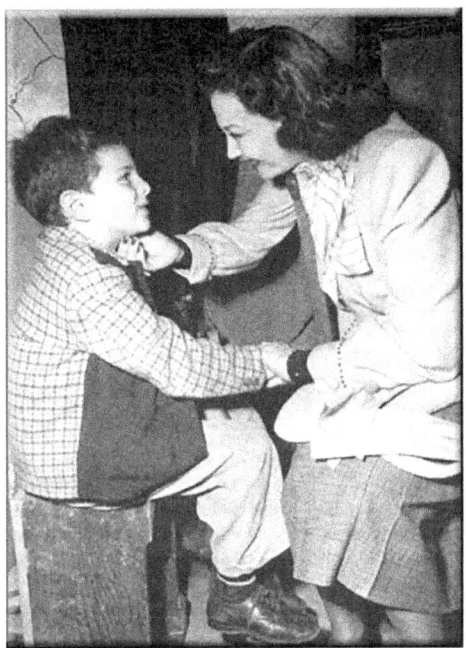

Sylvia and Jody, 1944

"but he will never be truly gone from me for as long as I live. What a marvelous, loving human being he was."[22] Jody's childhood dream had been cut way too short.

"Mommy, are you going to live 'til the last day on earth?"
"No dear, that's a long, long time."
"I'm going to live that long … millions and trillions and billions of years."

Prior to the broadcast of *An Early Frost* there were concerns about audience reaction to what was considered a highly controversial subject.

Sidney told reporters, "Whatever backlash there might be is not important. For those of us who have some experience with these things, it is … about people in trouble—that is what's important." "The film to me," she added, "is not so much about homosexuality and AIDS. Its point is how you handle a difficult situation. I didn't have to do research as to how I felt about a grandson having a terminally ill disease. My son died of ALS. The film is about relationships and supporting people. Forty-five years ago this film could have been about cancer. Or, when I was a little girl, it could have been about tuberculosis. People at those times knew just as little and were just as afraid of those diseases."[23]

Sidney's skill as an actress easily fuels two tear-inducing scenes in *An Early Frost* that provide emotional release for the viewer, and drive the message home. They take place after Michael (Aidan Quinn) has been subjected to his father's (Ben Gazzara) outrage, as well as his sister's refusal to touch him. While Michael is hospitalized following a seizure, we see his mother (Gena Rowlands) and grandmother Beatrice (Sidney) outside trimming roses. Sidney shares her fear that an early frost could "come along and nip them in the bud"—then Rowlands reveals the truth about Michael, "We're going to lose him, mom." Sidney underscores their anguish. "When your father died," she says, "I told myself I'd never have to cry again, because I'd be the next to go. I've lived my life. Michael's so young … life is just beginning … he … ." At a loss for words the two embrace—sharing their heartache.

Sidney is not at all pleased with son-in-law Gazzara's attitude. She offers him stony stares at the dinner table when he refuses to pass the butter to Peter (Michael's lover who unexpectedly shows up). When Michael walks his grandmother out to her car that same evening, she reaches for an embrace. He backs away. "Come on," she encourages him. "Give your Grandma a kiss." It is at this juncture that she tells him, "It's a disease,

Cast for the critically acclaimed *An Early Frost* (NBC): Aiden Quinn, Gena Rowlands, Ben Gazzara, Sylvia Sidney; (*below*) Sidney and Aiden Quinn

not a disgrace." She explains how people treated Michael's grandfather before he succumbed to cancer. "That's how people are," she says.

The acting is uniformly excellent. Quinn goes through the emotional gamut with grace and believability. A dash of unexpected comic relief is provided by John Glover as an outré gay man dying of AIDS who befriends Michael at the hospital. The performances are bolstered by an Emmy-winning script by Ron Cowen (*Queer As Folk*) and Daniel Lipman. In true ensemble spirit, the characters reach the power point of unconditional love.

On the night it aired (November 11, 1985) *An Early Frost* was number one in the Nielsen ratings—watched by 34 million people. Even so, NBC had difficulty finding sponsors and took a loss of $500,000 in revenue.[24] Typically, corporate America was leery of any potential controversy, refusing to have their products advertised during such a broadcast. They were concerned about profit, not human beings. Deservedly, the film was honored with broadcasting's Peabody Award for meritorious public service, and fourteen Emmy nominations, including a nod for Sidney's performance as Best Supporting Actress. Sidney gave *her* praises to Ben Gazzarra as the father who comes to grips with his own homophobia. "*That's* the best performance in the whole movie," she insisted. "It knocked you out! Especially the close-ups of his eyes. He couldn't stand the fact that his son had AIDS, but still loved the boy. He couldn't resist him!"[25] Sidney lost the Emmy, but did receive a Golden Globe Award in the same category. In her acceptance speech, Sylvia referred to the loss of her own son. "I think I'm probably about the oldest person in this room," she began, giving the audience a good chuckle. "I only have to thank Perry Lafferty and John Erman for their support and their help during a bad time ... they permitted me to continue with the film. And, thank you all, very much."

An Early Frost managed to transcend clichés. It was instructive on the ramifications of the AIDS virus, and dispelled the numerous rumors surrounding it. *An Early Frost* made people think about the senseless vitriol that was being aimed at the gay community. In this respect, the broadcast fueled an enduring operative for that community and the world at large: love and compassion are stronger than fear. Sidney, director Erman (whom she adored working with), Quinn and several other cast members would (understandably) donate a part of their salary to AIDS research and counseling.

Sidney observed that her role in *An Early Frost* echoed her relationship with Jody. "The loss of someone you love isn't the hardest part," she said. "The worst is watching the suffering they have to go through."[26] Naturally, thoughts of Jody didn't fade easily. Several years later during an interview at Gallagher's Steakhouse in Manhattan's Theater District, Sylvia looked around the dining room and remarked, "I've been coming here forever. Luther and I used to take Jody here when he was just a baby. He loved the food. He had his first soft shell crab here. 'Mommy, good,' he said, 'More, Mommy, more.'" With a wistful smile she looked into her drink, remembering. "Ach," she sighed, looking up, shaking her head. "Memories."[27]

In 1990, Sidney once again played a grandmother in the AIDS-themed adaptation of Terrence McNally's *Andre's Mother*, for PBS. Richard Thomas played Cal, the lover of a young man named Andre who had recently died from AIDS. At the memorial service, Cal is confronted with Andre's conservative mother, Katherine (Sada Thompson), who has never accepted her son's homosexuality. Their edgy relationship is explored in a series of flashbacks in, what one critic called, "an achingly honest story."[28] *The*

New York Times thought Sidney "played feistily" as Andre's supportive grandmother. She is perpetually at odds with her daughter Katherine. In one flashback, Cal invites Andre's mother and grandmother to lunch. The conversation is strained. Katherine asks her mother to stop rattling. Sidney complains to Cal, "I only rattle when my daughter's around. It's like speaking to an enormous void." On this sour note Cal excuses himself from what he refers to as a "miserable meal." After he's gone, Sidney talks matter-of-factly about men who are smitten with each other. She asks the waiter if he is gay. "Yes," he smiles. She gives a nod toward her daughter and says, "Then would you please tell *her* it's not the end of the world?"

Critic John Voorhees praised, "The scenes between Katherine and her outspoken mother, played with great panache by Sidney, are rich with subtext."[29] Their frosty, uneasy relationship was sensitively depicted. The dialogue had dashes of the theatrical, but was always emotionally on cue. Sidney's earthy character and acerbic wit is perhaps the easiest to like.

An article from *New York Magazine* emphasized that television had acted more responsibly than the federal government in handling the AIDS crisis. TV movies and documentaries had "acquainted us with the victims and reminded us of community."[30] *Andre's Mother* received an Emmy for Outstanding Writing. The National Board of Review named it Outstanding Television Movie of the Year. The broadcast of *Andre's Mother* did meet some snags. A Milwaukee PBS station refused to air it during their pledge drive due to the subject matter. Some stations dropped it entirely.[31]

For Sylvia, life without Jody did not mean abandoning work on behalf of ALS. Hers, was a lifetime commitment. She urged friends and family to contribute to ALS chapters in memory of Jacob Luther Adler. Contributions were put into a Patient Services fund that provided counseling to deal with depression that often accompanies chronic disease. The funds also procured ventilators, which allowed patients to continue breathing as their diaphragm muscles began to fail—respiratory failure being the most common cause of death.

From what his friends shared about Jody, he was comfortable in his own skin. He eagerly pursued his passion/fascination for the world of mathematics and science. Sylvia understood her son; nurtured his dreams; and, in so doing, quashed any possibility for self-doubt. From Jody's obituary, which ran on August 18, 1985 in *The New York Times*:

> **Jacob Luther Adler** - Died August 11, 1985
> Son of actress Sylvia Sidney and the late Luther Adler. Brilliant scientist, accomplished musician, talented Bridge player, devoted son. Even though ALS cut his young life too short, he enjoyed life to the fullest, sharing his wonderful and charming personality. ... The ALS Association extends their heart-felt sympathy to his mother, Sylvia Sidney, who works tirelessly to raise money ... to conquer this disease.

In 2015, Jody's former classmate at Oakwood, Henry Greenberg, an M.D. and Epidemiologist, contacted this author, and offered these observations about the young man he knew.

> Looked at thru today's mirror, Jody was disabled and I realize he was the first of my peers to be so. He was at best ungainly and most surely afflicted with a neurological disorder. He could not compete in athletics nor was he ever a rival in

the adolescent fixation on sex or conquest. He was smart, collegial, friendly, and open. What I now realize is that he was never a victim. He was who he was and what he was. He was comfortable being that person. He sought no pity nor did ever act in a way that would evoke it. For an adolescent child, and one who is on his own in a boarding school, that is actually quite remarkable. Considering that both his parents were "stars," his casual and comfortable sense of himself is even more remarkable. I would have to conclude that the subject of your biography and her husband must have had something to do with that.[32]

Sylvia had observed Jody's generous nature, commenting that he was the kind of thoughtful young man "who was more concerned with giving to the time he lives in than with getting." "These are the important things in life," she emphasized, "not what it's like to have kissed Spencer Tracy or Gary Cooper."[33] Following her son's death, it would be several months before Sylvia had any desire to return to acting.

(Endnotes)

1. Vernon Scott, "Joanne Skillfully Directing Life," *Dallas Morning News*, January 28, 1981
2. Conversation with Patricia O'Connell, May 27, 2015
3. Albin Krebs, "Notes on People," *New York Times*, January 22, 1981
4. Kathy Larkin, "Actress Helps Son Cope with Incurable 'Lou Gehrig's Disease,'" *Centre Daily Times*, September 21, 1983
5. *Variety* article, July 30, 1981 (Sidney was misspelled "Sydney" on page 356)
6. Budd Schulberg, *Moving Pictures: Memories of a Hollywood Prince*, Stein and Day, c. 1981, pg. 145
7. Lloyd Pantages, "He Did It - Marcel Bumps Himself Off," *San Antonio Light*, May 4, 1936

8   Phil Thomas, "Haphazard Collection," *Mobile Register*, October 4, 1981
9   Sandra McElwaine, "Schulberg: The Sweet Smell of Success Again," *Evening Star*, July 17, 1981
10 "Ask Them Yourself," *Trenton Evening Times*, March 16, 1980
11 Mel Gussow, review of *Light Up the Sky*, *New York Times*, August 18, 1981
12 Phyllis Newman, "The Last Time I Looked," personal blog, July 21, 2013
13 Hugh Fleetwood interview with Richard T. Kelly, April 2013 (from the Introduction of *The Order of Death*, Faber & Faber, c. 2013)
14 Roderick Mann, "Movie Motto: Selleck Sells," *Plain Dealer*, March 17, 1983
15 Gregory J.M. Catsos, "Sylvia Sidney," *Filmfax*, November 1990
16 Carole Kass, "Actress Maintains Edge On, Off Screen," *Richmond Times Dispatch*, July 14, 1984
17 Christopher Rawson, "O'Reilly Theater: Triumphant Triumvirate," *Pittsburgh Post-Gazette*, December 5, 1999
18 Raymond van Over, email to author, November 22, 2015
19 Atul Gawande, "Overkill," *New Yorker*, May 11, 2015
20 Alan W. Petrucelli, "Aiding the Situation," *Mobile Register*, November 8, 1985
21 Gregory J.M. Catsos, "Sylvia Sidney," *Filmfax*, November 1990
22 Jeff Laffel, "Sylvia Sidney," *Films in Review*, September/October 1994
23 Bill Hayden, "Film Examines Relationships, AIDS," *Register Star*, November 10, 1985, and Mark Lorando, "Sylvia Sets Us Straight," *Times-Picayune*, November 10, 1985
24 Anabel Dean, "Topic That Frightened Advertisers But Not the Viewers," *Sydney Morning Herald*, March 17, 1986
25 Gregory J.M. Catsos, "Sylvia Sidney," *Filmfax*, November 1990
26 Robin Adams Sloan column, *Marietta Journal*, October 2, 1985
27 Jeff Laffel, "Sylvia Sidney," *Films in Review*, September/October 1994
28 John Burlingame, "*Andre's Mother* tackles AIDS topic," *Augusta Chronicle*, March 14, 1990
29 John Voorhees, "A Dynamic *Andre's Mother* Will Reach Out And Touch You," *Seattle Times*, March 11, 1990
30 John Leonard, "Sons and Lovers," *New York Magazine*, March 12, 1990
31 Mike Drew, "Andre's Mother," *Milwaukee Journal*, May 16, 1990
32 Henry Greenberg, M.D., email to author, February 2, 2015
33 James Watters, *Return Engagement*, Crown Pub., c. 1984, pg. 15

Sidney acquired a new generation of fans in *Beetlejuice* (1988) (Warner Bros.)

Chapter 16
Beetlejuice & Beyond

Sidney returned to acting in the series *Morningstar/Eveningstar* (1986), about orphans who live in a community of senior citizens. "Man," says one of the youngsters, "we've ended up in the waxworks!" *People* magazine agreed, wisecracking, "May they melt quickly." The cliché-ridden plot lasted seven episodes. Sylvia waited another ten months before making the TV-Movie *Pals* (1987), playing the trailer trash "Mama" of George C. Scott. He and his old WWII buddy (Don Ameche) accidentally discover a suitcase stuffed with three million dollars. They assume new identities, and take "Mama" along for a taste of the "high life." Highlight: Sylvia sitting in the backseat of a luxury convertible, her blonde wig blowing in the breeze, yelling, "Eat your heart out Cyndi Lauper!" Funnier still, "Mama" spending her "hot" cash. As a salesman launches his pitch on the latest television set, she barks, "Shut up! I'll take four." At the finish, Sidney gets rid of the "bad guy" by scrambling his pacemaker with her remote.

Michael Norell, who wrote the screenplay for *Pals*, recalled Sidney being "a very salty old lady." Before "Mama" leaves her motor home, she grabs a special photograph, and declares, "I ain't leavin' without my picture of Captain Hank Stanley! He's my idol." During rehearsal

Sylvia demanded, "Who the hell is Captain Hank Stanley?" Norell explained that it was a character he played on the TV series *Emergency!* He thought all two of his fans would get a kick out of it. "Aw, that's cute," she said.[1] Most critics got a "kick" out of *Pals*. *Variety* found it to be "an amusing, never dull affair." As for Sylvia, *The New York Times* surmised, "Miss Sidney [is] too practiced a trouper to play third fiddle." Following this, Sylvia took on an assignment that endeared her to a whole new generation of filmgoers.

Beetlejuice

When Sidney signed with director Tim Burton for *Beetlejuice* (1988), she had no idea that she was helping to create a new film genre. She had turned down the offer several times. "I had never heard of Tim Burton," said Sylvia. "I couldn't understand the script." She tossed it in the garbage. It took a long phone conversation with Burton, before Sidney agreed to read the script again. He sent her a new one. She finally relented, and flew to California. Burton met her upon arrival. "We had breakfast together," recalled Sidney. "We had lunch together, and I was in love ... his sensitivity, how he thought about scenes."[2] Sidney began to understand the young director, who had spent his youth watching classic horror films, and drawing cartoons. On the set, Sidney's chain-smoking character was required to emit smoke from a slit in her neck. "They hired me because I'm the only one left who smokes," she jested to a reporter from *Variety*. Burton refuted the idea. "We want her for 'gravity,'" he insisted.

As Juno, the dour case-worker in the after-life, Sidney exudes "gravity" and, as columnist Faye Zuckerman put it, gives the "movie enough spirit to keep you pleasantly entertained." "Never trust the living," Juno advises a ghostly couple (Alec Baldwin and Geena Davis) hell-bent on ridding their earthly home of its new owners, a greedy salesman, his wife, and their young daughter (Winona Ryder). The degenerate, disembodied Betelgeuse (Michael Keaton), Juno's former assistant, arrives on the scene to resolve the problem. Can he be trusted?

The film's deft exposé on privatization, has the new owners marketing the property as a ghost-ridden amusement park. Betelgeuse himself is a huckster, who fancies marketing souls. Keaton, as the oversexed poltergeist, was hilariously offensive. The National Society of Film Critics awarded him Best Actor of the year. Ironically, Keaton had also turned Burton down for the role ... three times. "I didn't know how to do it," he admitted, "so, I just said, 'No thank you.'" Once Keaton got into the Betelgeuse makeup, however, it liberated him. "What it did for Michael," said Burton, "was it allowed him to play someone who wasn't a human being." "*Beetlejuice* was a romp," enthused Keaton in 2012. "I've never had so much fun in my life!"[3]

Burton agreed with Sidney's initial reaction to the script. "It had no real story. It didn't make any sense," he wrote in his 1994 memoir *Burton on Burton*. Burton succeeded in shaping the scenario's incongruities into something unique. Audiences were enthusiastic. The film grossed over $72 million. The hopeless tangle of afterlife bureaucracy was original, funny, and irreverent. As Geena Davis advises the young, disillusioned, death-obsessed Ryder, "Being dead doesn't make it any easier."

Sidney herself was impressed with *Beetlejuice*. "Look what happened with that film," she said. "Alec Baldwin, Geena Davis, Winona Ryder. She was just a baby then. She used to hang around me a lot. I think because her mother said, [whispering] 'She's an old actress.'" Sidney was amazed by her new fan base: youngsters. "Kids look at me now and say, 'Look! That's the witch in *Beetlejuice*!' That goes to show you how smart kids are today, because I didn't even know what the character was!"[4] Sidney's performance was honored at the 16th Annual Saturn Awards for Best Supporting Actress.

Following the release of *Beetlejuice*, Sidney was the honorary chairperson at an auction for homeless AIDS victims living in Danbury, Connecticut. Valuable antiques from historic homes, works of art, and designer fashions were donated for the cause. Sylvia continued to engage the small screen with interesting results. One memorable guest-star role teamed her with Judd Hirsch in his well-received, *Dear John*. Hirsch, as the easy-going, divorced high school teacher, discovers the true spirit of Christmas from Mrs. Lumenski (Sidney), an elderly Polish woman in a neighboring apartment. She has sass, and he takes a shine to her. Lumenski talks about her husband Branislav, who was lost in the war, and how poor they were. "Yeh" nods Hirsch, "but I bet you were happy." "Don't be stupid," she snaps. "We were miserable."

The humor in the script, and Sidney's feisty character, with a slight accent, come across as authentic. She mentions a Franz Lehar song, *Gern hab' ich die Frau'n gekusst*, that she and Branislav used to dance to on Christmas Eve. Hirsch locates the original recording. On Christmas Eve, as he prepares for a sexual rendezvous, Mrs. Lumenski knocks on the door. He gives her the recording. She is overcome. "Mrs. Lumenski, are you okay?" he asks. She looks up at him and smiles. He plays the record for her. They dance. "I don't want you to have Christmas dinner alone," she insists. "I know what it's like. Who wants to have dinner with a cranky old lady like me?" Her radiance and joy give Hirsch pause. He tosses aside his plans for the evening.

They dance again to the music. Mrs. Lumenski nods, "You know what? You remind me of Branislav, my husband. He was also a lousy dancer." Hirsch's holiday enters the realm of the unexpected ... with charming results.

After appearing as a judge on the Emmy-winning crime series *The Equalizer*, Sidney went directly onto the set of the baby boomer-themed *thirtysomething*. The popular series wasn't without controversy. Writer/director Richard Kramer's script for the episode *Strangers*, caused as much uproar as the fall of the Berlin Wall, which occurred two days after *Strangers* aired. The problem: two gay males having a post-coital conversation in bed. Writer Graceann Macleod, who grew up in Milwaukee, found it to be "a completely innocent scene." "After *Strangers* aired," observed Macleod, "the ridiculous number of complaints would make you think that the station had shown Hitler stomping on kittens."[5] ABC reported a $1.5 million loss in advertising revenue. The episode never aired again; further proof of how a profit-driven economy managed to derail gay visibility in the media.

In the *thirtysomething* episode, *Be a Good Girl*, Sidney played Rose, the chain-smoking, imperious grandmother of Melissa (Melanie Mayron). *Entertainment Weekly* called it "the finest episode" of the series. Sidney was dazzling to watch, as Rose loses her grip on life, following a series of mini-strokes. When the elegantly attired matriarch offers Melissa, a professional photographer, the opportunity to take over her dress shop, Melissa boldly refuses. Rose is not happy. "What's your life?" she demands. "You snap a few pictures. You live like a bum. You dress like a freak!" Sidney's face registers all that separates one generation from another. The courageous Melissa finally tells Rose, "You don't know what's best for me. I love you Nana, but you can't have me." Mayron received an Emmy Award for Outstanding Actress

Sylvia and Melanie Mayron feel the generation gap in *thirtysomething* (1989) (ABC)

in a Drama Series that season. She was impressed with Sidney and told this author in 2014, "Oh wow! Sylie was fantastic. We had a ball together."[6] "Sylie" had become Sylvia's pet name for herself. She personalized her Connecticut license plate: *SYLIE*.

In my conversation with Richard Kramer, he enthused, "I wrote *Be a Good Girl* specifically for Sidney. I always had adored her. I first saw her in *Summer Wishes, Winter Dreams*. Shortly afterward, I saw *Fury* on campus [Yale]—I had become a *cineaste* [film enthusiast]. I also enjoyed her in *Beetlejuice*. We sent her the script and she called back to say that she would do it. I asked her to bring along her needlepoint, wardrobe and photos from when she was young. She brought her suits—all Chanel. She looked gorgeous. She also brought her pugs. Sylvia was fun to work with. It was a huge privilege for me."[7]

Sylvia was instantly liked by cast and crew. Shooting an outdoor flashback provided another memorable moment for director Kramer.

As they set up the scene, he felt a tug on his sleeve. "What is *this*?" Sylvia asked. Kramer explained that the flashback would reveal the trauma Rose underwent the day her mother died. Sylvia was incredulous. "That was the *best* day of my life!" she told Kramer. Beatrice had passed away at the age of ninety-two, May 17, 1979, at Hebrew Home for the Aged in Miami Beach. Most likely, Sylvia saw it as one less worry and financial responsibility.

Kramer reflected, "Sylvia was easy to direct. Before her character drops the bomb at the party [regarding her granddaughter's inheritance], she rehearses her speech in the mirror. We lit it beautifully. Sylvia acted so internally. She had wonderful subtlety ... so malleable and so present. .... and so funny! She liked me. She liked that I knew her history." After a thoughtful pause, Kramer concluded, "Sylvia carried enormous light with her without ever being foolish, pompous or pretentious. She was committed."

On the evening of April 23, 1989, Sidney, along with thirty other distinguished women, was formally inducted into New York's Players Club, the century-old male bastion started by Edwin Booth, the noted Shakespearean actor (and brother of John Wilkes). Other inductees that evening included: Helen Hayes, Lauren Bacall, Carol Burnett, Lillian Gish, Kitty Carlisle, Leontyne Price, Angela Lansbury, Dina Merrill, columnist Liz Smith et al. In 2013, Smith wrote an article about the event, titling it "Remembering the Divine Sylvia Sidney."

> None of us were bursting with youth save for Dina Merrill and Lauren Bacall. Many of the honorees could barely climb

the three steps to the theater stage. When one of them stumbled, Sylvia whispered, 'Liz, when they call our names, let's RUN down the aisle like we're crazy and jump up on stage. Let's show them we've still got something.' Sylvia was wearing a neck brace covered with chiffon, recovering from an accident. But when they did call her name, she did indeed run down the aisle like a breeze. She leapt up onto the stage and accepted her bouquet of crappy gladiolas from the famous *Odd Couple* actor Jack Klugman. Sylvia promptly seized her flowers and slapped Jack across the face with them, to what was—in her mind—a playful gesture. Klugman was taken aback and she had to smother him in a warm embrace before he got it that she was kidding. Needless to say, after that, nobody could 'follow' such a star. Here's to her sense of fun. We should all practice more of that.[8]

Sylvia then signed on for *The Witching of Ben Wagner*—a Disney film with a hint of the supernatural. It was shot in the vicinity of Utah's Mirror Lake. Sidney's decision to do the film wasn't without controversy. She was on a hiatus from filming the psychological thriller *The Exorcist III* playing the mother-in-law of George C. Scott. Sidney was still involved with the Disney project when *The Exorcist III* producer Carter De Haven asked her to return to the big-screen cameras in Washington D.C. According to De Haven, her scenes ultimately had to be reshot with Barbara Baxley "at considerable expense and trouble."

The Witching of Ben Wagner was adapted from juvenile fiction.

The contemporary setting had Sidney playing Grammy to a mysterious young girl named Regina (Bettina Rae). Townsfolk suspect the two of practicing witchcraft. When Regina's high school chum Ben (Justin Gocke) suddenly earns better grades and makes the basketball team, he begins to wonder if he's under some kind of spell. We first see Sidney in her rustic kitchen, asking Ben to try some of her soup. "It's been brewing for about a week," she smiles. "What's in it?" he marvels. "Don't ask," she laughs. She's a happy old bird. Was it the *soup* that helped him make the team? We next see Sidney with Ben's dad (Sam Bottoms), a realtor who has his eye on her property. "I'll put a curse on anyone who tries to interfere with me!" she cackles. By the finish, Grammy takes Ben's face into her hands and confesses, "There's no such thing as curses. Believe in *yourself*." *The Witching of Ben Wagner* offers other life lessons: the danger of corporate greed, the worship of money and the people who have it, and the environmental issues that compromise our natural world. Bottoms, who puts a wrench into his realtor boss's scheme to grab Grammy's land, comes to the realization that life is about "people first-things later"—a lightweight precursor to George Clooney's *The Descendants* (2011).

Upon completing the Disney film, Sylvia left Utah and returned home to Connecticut, her pug dogs, and needlepoint. She read a great deal, and watched TV—"anything except old Sylvia Sidney movies," she emphasized. That fall, there was talk about producer De Haven contesting the money he owed the veteran actress for *The Exorcist III* after she reneged. Sylvia let it be known that the fault was with her agent (whom she dismissed). He had told her that she was in the clear to juggle both projects. The Screen Actors Guild backed Sidney's position in the case.[9]

In early 1990, Sidney again tackled age-related issues, on and off-screen. In the *Equal Justice* (ABC) episode *The Art of the Possible*, she coaxes her son Eugene (Cotter Smith) to help reinstate her revoked driver's license. When he learns the truth about her moving violations he explains, "Mother, you really can't drive anymore." It's not what she wants to hear. "I want to be able to do for myself!" she pleads. "Next thing you'll want to put me in a home – watching game shows in some hell hole." She finally admits that since her stroke things weren't the same. She relents with the remark, "Eugene, I'm scared." Sidney, true to form, easily pulls a reluctant tear from the viewer.

When *Equal Justice* aired, Sylvia was in the intensive care unit at Danbury Hospital recovering from a serious bout with double pneumonia. She had fallen ill while returning home from a Caribbean cruise, and fell into a coma. For several weeks doctors believed Sidney would not survive.[10] On Thursday, March 29, Sylvia regained consciousness. Facing her was Albert Sabin, now retired, who had been at her bedside. "Oh my God," she said, "I haven't seen you in years. Let's have some champagne."[11] Dr. Sabin got the champagne, allowing some of the bubbly to touch his cousin's lips before she fell back to sleep. His presence lifted her spirits when she most needed it. Upon release, she was required to make use of a cane. She hoped to be well enough to appear as an honoree for the telecast, *Night of 100 Stars* (NBC). Publicist John Springer arranged to show a selection of clips ranging from *City Streets* and *Fury*, to *Beetlejuice*. The gala occasion was held in Manhattan. While Katharine Hepburn appeared on crutches, Sidney simply wasn't up to it.[12] She was too weak to even get in a wheelchair.

On November 30, 1990, Sidney's film career was (finally) honored by the Film Society of Lincoln Center. The Society's President, Roy L. Furman (who would co-produce *The Color Purple*, and *The Book of*

Mormon), acted as host. Tony Randall was Master of Ceremonies. The evening began with a showing of Sylvia's personal film favorite, *Mary Burns, Fugitive*. True to form, Sylvia had indicated to John Springer that she did not wish to sit through the picture. She arrived in time to see the film highlights of her career. Special guest tributes followed: Joanne Woodward, Teresa Wright, John Springer, and columnist Liz Smith. Then Sylvia took stage center, bounding onto the stage to take charge in her own inimitable manner. The high spot was the appearance of Sylvia's beloved cousin, Dr. Albert B. Sabin, who shared the following:

> John Springer suggested that I say a few words about 'what Sylvia means to me'—Sylvia whose beautiful mother was my father's sister. Sylvia, I have loved since I first saw her about seventy years ago. She has been a source of pride to me ever since. I began to admire her efforts to master the art of acting at the Theatre Guild School about sixty-five years ago—so that, already, at the age of 16 she could achieve a starring role in a play on Broadway.
>
> And, why did I so greatly admire my cousin Sylvia's efforts to master the art of acting? It is because I have always looked upon good theatre and good films as enriching our lives in ways that all art forms do—to make us see and understand what ordinarily escapes our consciousness—by making it possible for us to add fantasy to reality and thus add another dimension of pleasure to our sometimes dreary lives. And this, Sylvia, my beloved cousin, has achieved. And so, I thank all of you for the tribute you are paying her tonight. It is good medicine for her old heart and young soul.[13]

Sabin would die two years later. Sylvia commented shortly afterward, "There isn't a day goes by that I don't miss him; that I don't want to pick up the phone and call him. What a wonderful man. What a story there is in *that* man's life."[14]

After the tribute, AP reporter Hillel Italie called upon Sylvia in her Gramercy Park Hotel suite. Typically, the relentless barking of two black pugs greeted her. "Petey! Malcolm!" Sylvia called out. "You be quiet in there!" Italie aptly described Sylvia as "a tiny woman built to last."[15] Sidney no longer needed a cane. She stated that luck and excellent medical care were her only health secrets. As far as her tribute at Lincoln Center, Sylvia shrugged it off. "If they don't get to it now," she said, "God knows what is going to happen." Dressed in black leather pants and vest, along with her trademark gold rings and bracelets, she calmly revealed, "I plan to die without a nickel. I will be penniless, but not a pauper. It will all be gone. At least what's in cash. The rest will be disseminated among my friends." According to plan, Sidney continued to charm audiences for another eight years before she arrived at her envisioned demise, and tease of pennilessness.

Susan King, for the *Los Angeles Times*, asked Sidney if she had any intentions to retire. "As long as I have a good brain and can remember the lines," quipped Sylvia, "and they pay me well, I will do it." King praised Sidney's appearance in the big-screen comedy-drama *Used People* (1992). "Though the film boasts the talents of three Oscar-winning actresses," wrote King, "Sidney effortlessly steals every scene she is in." The three actresses in question were: Shirley MacLaine, Jessica Tandy and Kathy Bates. Asked if she enjoyed filming it, Sidney

On the set with Shirley MacLaine in
Used People (1992) (20th Century-Fox)

snapped, "What's fun about it? That's my job. I act. I work. I haven't seen the picture." Family pictures weren't her cup of tea, she insisted.

Although slim on plausibility, *Used People* entertains with humor and heart. The Italian-Jewish courtship of the dreamy-eyed Marcello Mastroianni and a joyless widow (MacLaine) keeps getting sidetracked by family problems: MacLaine's daughters, and her bickering mother (Tandy). This all takes place in Queens, New York. *Newsweek* applauded the film as "the season's most pleasant surprise. A comedy that can make you cry. Jessica Tandy and Sylvia Sidney are masterfully directed." *The New York Times* concurred, "Jessica Tandy and Sylvia Sidney fare best as two wisecrack-trading old friends." Whether haggling over bets, or arguing what qualifies as officially being "mugged," the old cronies are scene stealers. Situations often border on the surreal, as when Sidney and Tandy visit a retirement community right out of Fritz Lang's *Metropolis*. These eccentricities are part of the charm, and *Used People* was worth the effort. The script, by Todd Graff, allowed each character moments of truth. Perhaps the best line wasn't in Graff's script, but said off-camera. This occurred when Sylvia leaned toward Marcello at one point to tell him, "I like you. If I were two or three years younger ... ."[16]

Sidney found the film's British director, Beeban Kidron, "very, very easy to work with." Writer Eve Golden, for *Movieline* magazine, asked Sidney for her opinion on Kidron. "I've worked with woman directors before, honey," said Sylvia. "I worked with Dorothy Arzner back in the 30's." When Golden mentioned Arzner's being openly gay at that time, Sidney shrugged, "In those days, honey, we didn't know what gay *was*. We knew some people were different, but no one ever talked about it." Golden also brought up the subject of Sidney being the only actress to have a condom named after her. Sylvia laughed, "God, I think I still have some of those 'Sylvia Sidneys' around. For years, honey, men would stop me on the street, wink and say, 'Remember Shanghai?'"[17] Golden recently recalled of Sidney, "Everyone warned me, 'be careful! She is *such* a bitch!' Well, she was delightful: funny and charming and gave me great stories."[18]

When Golden attended a memorial for Lillian Gish, she ran into Sidney once again. Golden mentioned their interview from the previous year. "Oh," replied Sidney, "was I a bitch?" Golden reassured Sylvia that she was "very pleasant." "That's funny," she replied. "I'm usually a real *bitch*."[19] On that score, Sylvia had competition: a Jewish drag queen who called himself "Sylvia Sidney - The Bitch of Boston." The bawdy, 6 ' 4," 62-year-old entertainer, known for his insults, crashed Boston's St. Patrick Day's Parade in 1992, in defiance of the parade organizers' Supreme Court-sanctioned ban on gay marchers. The ban was not lifted until 2015.

Writer for New York's *Gay City News*, David Noh, describes Sidney as "a complex woman, one of Hollywood's greatest, yet strangely-underappreciated actresses." He jokingly refers to her as "Auntie Mean" and "Salty Sylvia." Noh was chums with Sidney's publicist and champion John Springer, who routinely cautioned the actress, "Oh, Sylvia!" whenever she pounced on people with four letter words. Noh recalled a man at Bloomingdale's, raving at her, "Oh Miss Sidney, I'm such a fan! I have over 200 photos of you." Noh looked on, as Sylvia gave the man her owl look, and snapped, "You're fuckin' crazy! Your house must be a mess!"[20] Noh qualified his remarks, saying,

> In her defense, she was civil—even nice and welcoming to me. Although, one time, Springer had to remind her who I was, just as (I think) I was about to feel the lash of her tongue. I think she really preferred pugs and needlepoint to people. A New York Public Library appearance was memorable for her very moving mention of the early death of her son. You wonder if that's what might have caused her behavior.[21]

After founding the National Actors Theater (NAT), Tony Randall was delighted when Sylvia agreed to co-star as the devoutly religious Rebecca Nurse in a revival of Arthur Miller's *The Crucible*. By the time rehearsals began at the Belasco Theatre (October 1991), she was busy filming *Used People*. Randall got Martha Scott as a replacement. Sidney was also in the news for attending a campaign event for Bill Clinton at the National Arts Club (July 1992). It would be another year before she took an acting assignment—Dick Van Dyke's series, *Diagnosis Murder* (1993). When filming wrapped in Denver, Sylvia fell and shattered her hip. She ended up in a New York hospital intensive care unit. She bounced back, but placed her career on hold. She was picky about with whom she would work, and unimpressed with the new crop of directors. "I think I'm too tough for Spielberg," she announced. She made an exception for Tim Burton, who had written a role for her in *Mars Attacks!*—a spoof of 50's alien invasion movies and 70's all-star disaster epics.

In the fall of 1995, Sidney met with Burton. She agreed to play the doddering, ill-tempered Grandma Norris who foils alien invaders from Mars. Filming would begin in February with a $70 million dollar budget. Jack Nicholson, Rod Steiger, Glenn Close, Michael J. Fox and other top-liners also signed on. Unfortunately, Sylvia was hit by a car in New York City—a near fatal, hit-and-run incident that put her in the hospital. Burton was soon at her bedside, reassuring her that they would postpone filming her scenes. Sidney was overwhelmed by his generosity. She said it went beyond anything she had ever experienced during her entire career. "He *really* made me feel like a movie star!" she enthused.[22] Burton was exceptionally persuasive. *Mars Attacks!* Co-star, Sarah Jessica Parker, cheered, "If Tim asked me to stand on my head, and shoot flames out of my ass, that's what I would do."[23]

Sidney solves the alien problem in *Mars Attacks!* (1996) (Warner Bros.)

Mars Attacks!

In *Mars Attacks!* aliens circle the earth, while government officials and hawkish military brass strut their stuff to no avail. When they deploy a nuclear missile, the Martians capture and suck out the contents as if it were laughing gas. Meanwhile, Grandma Norris (Sidney) resides in an old-folks home listening to recordings of country star Slim Whitman. Grandma actually enjoys all the mayhem created by the big-brained aliens. "They blew up Congress!" she cackles. At the climactic finish, Grandma inadvertently destroys the pesky intruders by blasting their brains out with Whitman's version of *Indian Love Call*—his piercing falsetto is more than they can tolerate. Sidney looked as if she was having jolly good fun doing this role. In his 2014 tome devoted to science fiction, *Outer Limits*, author Howard Hughes nodded, "Sylvia Sidney stole the film as dotty Grandma Florence Norris, who inadvertently ... possesses the solution to the alien problem." For her relaxed, engaging, sweet tempered (!) performance, Sidney walked away with the Congressional Medal of Honor (on screen, that is).

The New York Times thought Burton's film was "spinning its wheels." The review argued that most of the actors ended up as "wasted opportunities," while aliens "gleefully" killed them off. AP journalist Ted Anthony found *Mars Attacks!* a "pointless hodgepodge," but praised Rod Steiger and Sylvia Sidney, finding her "delightful as the demented grandmother." Chicago film critic, Jonathan Rosenbaum, gave the film a thumbs-up, praising *Mars Attacks!* for being "in love with silliness," and achieving a level of non-seriousness that kept him "enthralled."[24]

Mars Attacks! has gained a cult status in the years since its release. In the 2006 publication *Disaster Movies*, authors Glenn Kay and Michael Rose concur that the film was "unfairly rejected by audiences," but went on to achieve a following of fans who "see it in the spirit in which it was intended." The authors rave about the "visual inventiveness and absurd energy that fuels the film ... boosted by excellent performances and direction." *Mars Attacks!* was the perfect follow-up to Burton's *Ed Wood* (1994)—a parody of the eccentric director's *Plan 9 From Outer Space* (1959). "I think most people thought I'd actually become Ed Wood," said Burton. "[*Mars Attacks!*] wasn't really received very well here. It was received well in Europe. If I ever have trouble in this country, I'll maybe just move to France."[25]

It could be that *Mars Attacks!* held the mirror too close to home—from the posturing President (Nicholson) and his pretentious wife (Close)—to the country's spiritual Mecca, Las Vegas, and the heartland, where gun-toting trailer trash solve nothing while utilizing their beloved "right to bear arms." Corporate racketeers and their media shills feed the fear. Arrogant educators and airy New Agers were not left unspared. At the finish, Sidney's grandson (Lukas Haas) suggests that, in the future, they should all live in teepees—an obvious slam at the white alien invasion of Native America. While Europe laughed their heads off at *Mars Attacks!*, Americans stayed away. The film barely broke even at the box-office. One person who came out ahead from the film's release was Slim Whitman. It was a bit of a career booster for the 73-year-old singer. "I'm proud of it," said Slim. "The President, the Army, they couldn't do it. So, here comes Whitman."[26] He was hoping for a world tour, and waiting for the phone to ring.

In 1998, Sidney rang the curtain on her career for the revamped *Fantasy Island* series. For this, she signed a seven-year contract, then took a ten-hour flight to Hawaii.[27] Upon her arrival at the Hotel Hana-Maui, she found an "Aloha!" note from producer Barry Johnson. In typical style, she promptly returned the gesture, telling him, "'Aloha,' yourself! Thank you for turning my sunset years into a living nightmare." (She was referring to the 52-mile, four-hour-long journey on a winding road to the isolated hotel.) Scenes were also shot inside a refurbished Halawa warehouse on Oahu.

Sidney's character, Clia, spent her time knitting, wisecracking, and chain-smoking inside a gloomy travel agency, where she and veteran actor Fyvush Finkel recruit unsuspecting candidates for fantasy vacations. The island host, played by Malcolm McDowell, offered a more sinister version of "Mr. Roarke" (Ricardo Montalban's role in the original series.) McDowell's supernatural powers, coupled with dark humor, go so far as to change the gender of one gentleman guest in the episode, *Estrogen*. The new series was mature, adult fare.

Variety rated the premier episode: "Clever and creepy ... noth-

Sidney signed a seven-year contract for
Fantasy Island **(1998) (ABC)**

ing short of spellbinding. Fyvush Finkel and Oscar nominee Sylvia Sidney supply a deft comic touch." Critic Kevin McDonough, raved, "Don't dare miss this show. This new version of *Fantasy Island* comes close to Tim Burton's *Beetlejuice*. Sylvia Sidney reprises her role as the cranky receptionist to another realm." *The New York Times*, however, found the series "bleak." Audiences expecting the more pleasant excursions of the 1978 series, may have been disappointed. The final, and thirteenth episode of *Fantasy Island*, an idea ahead of its time, aired in January 1999.

To promote the new series, Sidney agreed to do a phone interview with Shawna Malcolm for *Entertainment Weekly*. Malcolm caught Sidney in one of her moods. She asked how she was, and if she liked her role. In-between "cigarette-induced coughing fits" Sylvia rasped, "Do you really fuckin' care? For Christ's sake don't call it a role. It's a part. A part is a part. It's a job." The only bright spot in this conversation was when the subject of Tim Burton came up. "I adore him," she swooned. "He's one of the most talented men who ever lived. I think we were lovers in another life." When asked about her youthful success in the movies, Sylvia moaned, "Oh God. You want me to remember 50 years ago?"[28] This PR for *Fantasy Island* was, understandably, Sidney's only one. Due to health issues, Sylvia appeared in only seven episodes.

Upon her return to New York, Sidney was invited by film historian Foster Hirsch, to appear as guest star at the National Arts Club. She accepted, and arrived on the scene in rare form. Hirsch introduced her as having one of the longest careers in American film. Her only competition on that score were Lillian Gish and Helen Hayes. "Yeh, but they're both dead!" interrupted Sylvia. "I'm still employable." When Hirsch introduced a clip from *Sabotage*, he made the mistake of saying it contained "a great performance by Sylvia Sidney." She admonished, "It was *not* a great performance. No, no, no. No, no, no." The film soundtrack cut her off. You could hear her in the background, facing the audience, shouting, "I can't tell *what* the hell you're watching." Following the clip, Hirsch asked her about the key to good acting. Sidney calmed down long enough to reply, "Honesty, and belief in what you say." When Hirsch mentioned the importance of "the eyes," Sylvia bounced back, "Honey, if the camera isn't on you, you can fuck around with your eyes for the rest of your life." Hirsch maintained his cool. "What are you so nervous about?" she asked him. Sidney was a far cry from the timid 21-year-old, who wailed for her mama at the New York premier of *An American Tragedy*.

During a Question & Answer session, Sylvia cracked her whip, giving orders to those brave enough to raise their hand: "You're not making any sense!" "Stand up and be heard!" "Take your hand away from your mouth!" "None of your business!" "My best picture? I'm still *alive!*" When the hands stopped raising, she barked, "What happened? Did everybody dry up?" Finally, one lone soul braved asking if Sylvia still auditioned. "Audition? At my age? Are you *nuts*?"[29]

One of the last Sidney interviews (1999) was filmed in her Upper West Side apartment, on Broadway. She sat in her easy chair, surrounded by her collection of ceramic pugs, while being questioned about her career by designer/illustrator Mel Odom. Odom describes what led up to this memorable meeting.

> My friend Ira Gallen asked me to come with him to pay a visit to Sylvia, and I reluctantly went with him. I say reluctantly, because I felt I didn't know enough about her career to intelligently converse with her. Anyway, the night before, I watched *Street Scene* and was knocked out by the film and especially her performance.
>
> She had chemo that morning and originally kicked us out, which I totally understood. I was angry with Ira for his including me in this intrusion into her privacy. She called us back and we sat down and the interview happened. I suspect she was lonely. She died a few weeks later.[30]

Archivist Ira Gallen had known Sidney for a long time. He brought along his camera. At one point, Sylvia remarked, "What are you doing with that piece of shit? Put it on the floor!" What Gallen managed to film was priceless. We see Sylvia admiring illustrations from Odom's lushly erotic book, *Dreamer*. "Your drawings of the guys proves you're gay," she chuckled, turning the pages. "Boy, are you a giveaway. Jesus Christ!" Odom's reply? "Well, there you go!" Odom offered his compliments about her performances in *Street Scene, An Early Frost,* and *Beetlejuice*. Ira then made the mistake of referring to producer Schulberg as Budd. "It was *B.P.* Schulberg who was the producer," corrected Sidney. "Get your facts straight!" The conversation was amusingly interrupted with barks and yaps from Sidney's teenage pug, Malcolm. (Gallen would post the interview, interspersed with scenes from *Street Scene,* on Youtube.)

When I talked to Odom, he mentioned that upon leaving, Sylvia presented him with a 1930's portrait taken of her by George Platt Lynes. Lynes is especially known for his sensuous portraits of male nudes. Odom was sorry that he had met Sidney so late in her life, and wished he had had another opportunity for a private one-on-one conversation. Odom, put it best when he described Sidney's acting as "emotionally naked." There was no second guessing how she felt in any given performance.

Sylvia Sidney died at Lenox Hill Hospital in Manhattan, on July 1, 1999. She was eighty-eight. Her battle with throat cancer was over. Chemotherapy treatments had merely allowed her to enjoy smoking awhile longer. Her body was cremated. Obituaries designated Sidney as the ideal Depression heroine. While she joked about being "paid by the teardrop," her moist-eyes and suffering had epitomized the working class girl.

The New York Times followed up its obit with an addition, saying that they failed to mention Sylvia's two half-brothers: Albert and Edgar Kosow. Sidney had never uttered a word about either half-sibling, who were now retired and living in Florida. In a 2016 conversation, Albert (age 90) told me that he first met Sylvia in 1943. An acquaintance encouraged him to go backstage following a Manhattan performance of *Jane Eyre*. At 18, Albert had just passed his physical for the Army Reserve Corps. It was his only opportunity to meet his half-sister before leaving for overseas. Sylvia and Luther were cordial, and there was some contact between the two siblings over the next few years. Albert made news himself when he was captured by the Germans during the Battle of the Bulge (December 21, 1944). He was liberated by the Russians in June 1945, making the *Long Island Daily Press* "Honor Roll of Heroes." "Coming home from Europe," said Albert, "I was given time to go home to New York. I told people about my horrendous experiences as a P.O.W., but no one wanted to listen. I told them anyway. That's why I'm still alive."[31] My conversation with Albert occurred at an uncanny moment. He happened to be looking at a photograph of Sylvia when he picked up the phone. It was quite evident that Albert and Edgar had a great deal of affection for their famous sister. Before Edgar passed away in 2014, he paid homage to Sylvia on the database *Find a Grave*: "As one of the two surviving members of the original Kosow family ... Rest in Peace big sister."

A memorial service honoring Sidney was held August 9, at the National Arts Club on Gramercy Park South. There was a presentation of film clips, followed by guest speakers: Joanne Woodward, Paul Newman, Tony Randall, Betty Comden and Adolph Green. Sylvia's pug, Malcolm, was bequeathed (along with a sizeable amount of money) to the club. It was familiar territory for the pooch. Club President Aldon James mentioned that he and Sylvia were dining out one evening when the subject of Malcolm came up. "She said it was a horse race, who was going to go first, she or Malcolm," recalled James. "I said, 'If you need anyone to take care of Malcolm, the club and I will take care of him.' And she said, 'You're on, kid.'"[32]

Upon his arrival at the club, Malcolm was put on a diet. He was overweight and sullen. When it was time for his walk he didn't want to go. Malcolm's grief eventually subsided. Perhaps it was Sylvia's Ferragamo slipper that did the trick. Malcolm kept it next to him in his little bed. If they removed it, he wouldn't sleep. The evening that Aldon James and board members were reviewing film clips for Sidney's upcoming memorial, Malcolm was in his room. "We were watching *Trail of the Lonesome Pine*," said James. "Malcolm heard Sylvia's voice, and he came running in with her red Ferragamo slipper in his mouth."[33] The pug became fond of Club members Yoko Ono, Patricia Neal and sex-therapist Dr. Ruth Westheimer. Malcolm (posthumously) became a celebrity his own right, starring in the 10-minute short, *Puttin' on the Dog* (2002)—all about his life at the National Arts Club, where he passed away, age 16, in 2001.

The Legacy ....

In an article for *Films in Review*, John Springer designated Sylvia Sidney "*the* finest" of the screen's "emotional actresses." Springer's clients included Bette Davis, Joan Crawford, and Marlene Dietrich, who were all very much alive at the time (1966). While these women held out for starring roles, Springer was impressed that Sidney never regretted the loss of stardom. Being an actress is what mattered. "She says it in a way that makes you believe her," he stressed. While Sidney didn't enjoy watching her own films, she once commented, "I do like to watch Bette Davis films, especially *Jezebel* or *Mr. Skeffington*. She had a different look in her eyes for each character. In pictures you mostly look the same, but not her—not she. I can't say as much for myself."[34] Sidney's self-effacement was a reflection of her own honesty and understatement as an actress.

One of the highest compliments that Sylvia Sidney received was from African-American author James Baldwin, whose writing depicted the obstacles hindering the assimilation of the poor, blacks and gays into the American mainstream. In his 1976 essay, *The Devil Finds Work*, Baldwin focuses on cinema—and, his experience watching movies as a youngster. He stressed,

> Sylvia Sidney was the only film actress who reminded me of a colored girl, or woman—which is to say that she was the only American film actress who reminded me of reality. All of the others, without exception, were white, and, even when they moved me ... some instinct caused me profoundly to distrust the sense of life they projected. My reaction to Sylvia Sidney was certainly due, in part, to the kind of film she appeared in during that era. ... It was almost as though she and I had a secret: she seemed to know something that I knew. ... I always believed her.[35]

In 1995, Sidney was a guest at Cinecon 31, a classic movie marathon held in Hollywood. The *Los Angeles Times* nodded that the high point of the weekend was a question-and-answer session with the "feisty, wisecracking Sylvia Sidney." Jere Guldin, vice-president of Cinecon, engaged in numerous phone conversations with Sidney prior to her arrival. She was enthused, and looking forward to the event. "From the time she arrived," said Guldin, "she was all bad-mood Sidney, and her temperament only worsened as the weekend wore on."[36] She took to the stage following a screening (per her request) of *Trail of the Lonesome Pine*. "What the hell are you talking about?" was her frequent response to questions. Sidney threw a tantrum during the banquet, making for, what Guldin referred to, as "an unforgettable guest." In attendance was author Max Pierce. "Sylvia seemed to be a woman who lived in the present," Pierce told me, "and Cinecon members are anything but. Her assessing the crowd with, 'You people need to stop living in the past,' still makes me smile."[37] Before walking off stage, Sylvia told the audience: "I have a very important message. Old age sucks!" She managed to disappear before eager autograph hunters could descend upon her.

One thing that seemed to underscore Sidney's interviews during the 70's, 80's and 90's was her intent on *living* in the present. While she candidly opened up about her film work, the actors and directors that she had worked with, she always brought it back to the moment at hand—like some evolved, albeit cranky, Zen master. A perfect example was her 1994 meeting with author Jeff Laffel. They met in front of Gallagher's restaurant on West 52nd Street for lunch. Sylvia stepped out of a cab and before entering Gallagher's, she paused. "What a minute," she told Laffel. "You see that theater down there?" Laffel looked in the wrong direction. Losing her patience, Sylvia physically maneuvered him to look in the right direction. "Not there. *There*," she instructed. "That's where the Theatre Guild used to be ... and their school. I went to that school." She laughed. "But that was a million years ago." She gestured to the restaurant entrance. "This is today. Let's eat."[38]

(Endnotes)

1. Richard Yokley, Rozane Sutherland, *Emergency!: Behind the Scene*, Jones & Barlett, c. 2007, pg. 351
2. Hillel Italie, "Sidney Wastes No Time on Nostalgia," Daily Gazette, December 7, 1990
3. Daniel Kellison, "Dinner With Daniel: Michael Keaton," *Grantland*, July 13, 2012
4. Gregory J. M. Catsos, "Sylvia Sidney," *Filmfax*, November 1990
5. Graceann Macleod, email to author, February 23, 2016
6. Melanie Mayron, message to author, September 27, 2014
7. Conversation with Richard Kramer, May 12, 2015
8. Liz Smith, "Remembering the Divine Sylvia Sidney," *New York Social Diary*, July 1, 2013
9. Marilyn Beck column, *Washington Times*, October 24, 1989
10. "Sylvia Sidney To Be Honored By The Film Society Of Lincoln Center," drc.libraries.uc.edu/, November 1990
11. Tom Poster and Phil Roura, "Sylvia Sidney, Though Ailing, Bubbly Adherent," *Los Angeles Times*, April 2, 1990
12. James Brady, "In Step – With Michael Caine," *Herald Journal*, September 23, 1990
13. Albert B. Sabin, handwritten letter, DRC, University of Cincinnati https://drc.libraries.uc.edu/bitstream/handle/2374.UC/683268/sidney_1978-90_011.pdf?sequence=1
14. Jeff Laffell, "Sylvia Sidney," *Films In Review*, September/October 1994
15. Hillel Italie, "Sidney Wastes No Time on Nostalgia," *Daily Gazette*, December 7, 1990
16. Kevin Thomas, "The Sweet Life With Marcello," *Los Angeles Times*, July 4, 1999
17. Eve Golden, "Grand Dame," *Movieline*, December 1992
18. Eve Golden, ladymirror.com, December 23, 2013
19. Eve Golden, email to author, April 14, 2015
20. David Noh, "Sylvia Sidney: Human Conundrum," *Noh Way* (blog), August 9, 2012
21. David Noh, comment to author, Facebook, November 2015
22. Liz Smith column, *Daily Advocate*, June 24, 1996
23. Robert J. Emery, *The Directors-Take Three*, Allworth Press, c. 2003, pg. 190
24. Jonathan Rosenbaum, review of *Mars Attacks!*, *Chicago Reader*, December 13, 1996
25. Robert J. Emery, *The Directors-Take Three*, Allworth Press, c. 2003, pg. 191
26. "Names in the News," *St. Albans Daily Messenger*, December 16, 1996
27. "Sylvia Sidney, 30's Film Heroine, Dies at 88," *New York Times*, July 2, 1999 (Sidney's agent, John Springer, mentioned her seven year contract in this

obituary, which mistakenly stated that Jody died in 1987)

28 Shawna Malcolm, "Sylvia Sidney Refuses to Retire," *Entertainment Weekly*, October 30, 1998
29 Sylvia Sidney, interview, filmed at the National Arts Club, June 2, 1998. https://www.youtube.com/watch?v=d0GCZotng2c
30 Mel Odum, e-mail, December 2, 2015
31 Conversation with Albert C. Kosow, February 28, 2016
32 Sharon Krengel, "Put Pet in Will So It's Not Homeless," *Register Star*, February 4, 2001 (Carol Wilder's 10-minute film *Puttin' on the Dog*: https://www.youtube.com/watch?v=oYU0CT16F_M)
33 *New York Daily News* item, August 6, 1999
34 Joseph G. Boyd, "Sylvia Sidney Is Still a Presence to Reckon With," *Milwaukee Sentinel*, October 11, 1978
35 James Baldwin, *The Devil Finds Work: An Essay*, Dial Press, c. 1976, pgs. 21-22
36 Jere Guldin, Cinecon Forum, November 26, 2003
37 Max Pierce, email to author, July 1, 2015
38 Jeff Laffell, "Sylvia Sidney," *Films in Review*, September/October 1994

1908 ed. *Lonesome Pine* women:
Sidney as June Tolliver, and Rose Morgan

Acknowledgements

"That's Not Your Story, Baby"

The above quote was Sidney's retort after author/journalist Anna Quindlen approached the subject of Sylvia's relationship with B.P. Schulberg. It was 1977. Sidney said that she was contemplating a book about her life. "I don't think I should let too much dribble out," she cautioned, lighting a cigarette. "I should save it in case I decide to do the book."[1] Her motto, for years, was variations of: "I'm not going to dig up all that junk." In 1987, Sidney told Army Archerd (*Variety*) that she had been approached to write her memoirs. "The publisher sent someone over and she asked me, 'Did you sleep with Bogart?' I said, 'No.' She asked, 'Did you sleep with Tracy?' I said, 'No ...' She stopped me with, 'You've got no book!'"[2] Two years later, Sylvia put a lid on the subject. "Since I was 16, they've been hanging my drawers on the line for everyone to look at. I've said all I want to say about myself in two books. What I've wanted to reveal, I've already revealed."[3]

The subtitle "Paid by the Tear," was from Sidney herself, uttered many times during the last twenty-five years of her life. My Uncle Moroni Parker, who saw almost every film that came to Salt Lake in the 30's and 40's, nodded when he saw the subtitle, "Oh, yeah. She was always crying."

When author James Robert Parish mentioned to me that Sylvia Sidney was long overdue for a biography, I had to agree. As soon as I took on the task, I had a flashback ... to 1957. A childhood friend and I attended a Saturday matinee revival of *Trail of the Lonesome Pine* at the Stockton Theater (California). It was the first time I had seen an "old" movie, and I was mesmerized, particularly by Sylvia as the mountain girl torn between two worlds—the one in which she grew up, and the one that threatened everything she had known. When my mother picked us up after the movie, I was anxious to tell her that what had occurred on screen *really happened*. "Oh, Scott, it did not," she cautioned me. Credit Sylvia Sidney—I still wasn't convinced. Mother then reminded me that my Grandma Rose (Morgan) had a copy of the book—her favorite since girlhood. Aside from the Bible, it was the only book she owned. Grandma Rose, like June Tolliver, was from pioneer stock—they understood each other. A sobering thought for my ten-year-old mind.

Writing a biography is a team effort. James Robert Parish pitched in with resources and contacts, and provided access to hard-to-find films. His 1972 publication *Paramount Pretties* (Castle Books) offers an excellent overview of Sidney's career. Once again, my proofreader/editor, Graceann Macleod, came to the fore with inspired suggestions, accompanied with her astute grammatical expertise. This London-based writer is an aficionado of silent and early-sound film, and the recipient (twice) of the Apex Award of Excellence for Magazine & Journal writing. Author Joseph Egan was also on board with excellent suggestions. I can easily recommend his well-researched, long overdue, *The Purple Diaries-Mary Astor and the Most Sensational Hollywood Scandal of the 1930s* (DiversionBooks).

I was especially pleased when director Richard Kramer agreed to write the Foreword. He had a personal connection to Sylvia, and captures something special in what he has to say. Kramer's debut novel *These Things Happen* (2012) was nominated for a Lambda Literary Award. In this, he tells a coming-of-age story with humor, heart, and a fascinating mix of characters.

I appreciate the responses I received from Sylvia's co-stars from stage and TV: Patricia O'Connell, David McCallum, and Melanie Mayron. Brian Kellow (author of *The Bennetts - An Acting Family*) put me in touch with O'Connell, who was generous with her observations on Sidney and Luther Adler. When I talked with Ed Asner at a showing of the documentary *My Friend Ed* (2014), which details his work on behalf of human rights, Asner smiled and nodded, "Sylvia Sidney was a wonderful actress." The two had co-starred on TV's *Naked City* (1961) and the TV movie *A Small Killing* (1981). Asner couldn't recall any specifics about working with Sylvia, but his admiration for her was obvious.[4]

Author Eve Golden (*John Gilbert: The Last of the Silent Film Stars*) shared her memories of interviewing Sylvia, as did artist/illustrator Mel Odom (*Dreamer*), who, along with film archivist Ira H. Gallen (*D.W. Griffith: Master of Cinema*) offered Sidney her final interview. David Noh, reporter for New York's *Gay City News*, shared his interactions with Sylvia. Noh's affinity for classic film offers insightful commentary in his blog: *Noh Way*. Writer Max Pierce (*At the Crossroads*) offered his amusing take on Sylvia at Cinecon 31. Film historian/author Ron Bowers, a friend of Sylvia's publicist John Springer, penned an excellent article (*Films in Review*) about her 1973 appearance at Town Halls' Legendary Ladies. Bowers (co-author with James Robert Parish for *The MGM Stock Company*) also offered suggestions and contacts to help Sylvia's story unfold.

G.D. Hamann (*Sylvia Sidney in the 30's*) provided a treasure-trove of vintage articles from Los Angeles newspapers. Hamann's countless hours viewing microfilm made my task much easier. Two of the most important interviews that Sidney offered toward the end of her life, were detailed by writers Gregory J.M. Catsos for *Filmfax* (1990) and Jeff Laffel in *Films in Review* (1994). I must express my thanks for their getting candid, informative answers from the actress.

Always on board for my writing projects, providing me resources and stills, are good friends Jenny Paxson and Larry Smith, archivists at the Library of Congress facility in Culpeper, Virginia. John Drennon, who has met and corresponded with many vintage film stars, sent me a packet filled with Sidney articles and photos. Writer Moira Finney, moderator for the classic film websites *Silver Screen Oasis* (SSO) and TCM's *Movie Morlocks*, offered her encouragement and insight. Finney's excellent SSO interview with author Sheana Ochoa (*Stella! Mother of Modern Acting*) enabled me to connect with Ochoa, who provided access to personal letters between Stella Adler and Sylvia's son Jody.

Essential to the telling of Sidney's story, were comments from the friends of her son Jacob "Jody" Adler. I am very grateful to Jonathan Talbot for sharing memories of his classmate at Oakwood Friends School. Talbot connected me with other students: Harry Greenberg, Hugo F. Sonnenschein, and Steven Vogel. Jody's lifelong friend Raymond Van Over also offered a personal glimpse into Jody's life toward the end, as he struggled with ALS. My conversation with Albert Kosow, opened another door to Sylvia's story that few know about. Her interactions with an admiring half-brother, may have eased the painful memories she had regarding their father, Victor Kosow.

Lastly, I must thank Sylvia Sidney herself. It is ironic that a woman who enjoyed a comfortable lifestyle, from girlhood to old-age, would become known as the iconic face of the less privileged during the Depression. As author James Baldwin noted, Sidney was able to project "reality." I appreciate the fact that during the last twenty-five years of her life, Sylvia provided candid, in-your-face answers regarding her career. As far as her cranky personality, I think Sylvia knew that a majority were chuckling inside at her audacity. I know I was.

(Endnotes)

1. Anna Quindlen, "The Indomitable Sylvia Sidney," *New York Times*, June 9, 1977 (Quindlen wrote: "mention her past relationship with the movie mogul B.P. Schulberg ... and she will stop you with a smiling 'That's not your story, baby.'")
2. Army Archerd, "Just for Variety," *Variety*, April 13, 1987
3. Sharon Cromwell, "Sylvia Sidney: Yesterday's Star Talks of Today," *Boston Herald*, March 4, 1979
4. Conversation with Ed Asner, Sebastopol Center for the Arts, March 5, 2016

August 1975 - *Sabrina Fair* cast: (*front row*) Sandra Dee, Russell Nype, Maureen O'Sullivan, Sylvia Sidney (historiclitchtheatre.org)

Credits

STAGE CREDITS

(Note: cast members varied on tour)

1924
March 14, 1924 - Little Theatre; Sylvia Sidney (impersonations/recitations)

1926
Prunella (by Laurence Houseman and Granville Barker) Garrick Theatre; D: Winthrop Ames; Cast: Sylvia Sidney (Prunella), Ben Lackland, Earl McDonald, Marguerite Churchill, Charles Allais, Linda Watkins

The Challenge of Youth (by Ashley Miller) on tour; D: Priestly Morrison; Cast: Charles Waldron, Sylvia Sidney (Desire Adams), Sue Van Duzer, Phyllis Tyler

1927
The Squall (by Jean Bart) 48th Street Theatre; D: Lionel Atwill; Cast: Blanche Yurka, Lee Baker, Sylvia Sidney (Anita), Romney Brent, Horace Braham, Henry O'Neill

Crime (by Samuel Shipman and John. B. Hymer) Eltinge Theatre; D: A.H. Van Buren; Cast: Douglass Montgomery, Sylvia Sidney (Annabelle Porter), Chester Morris, James Rennie, Kay Johnson, Kay Francis (billed as Katherine Francis), Jack LaRue

1928

Mirrors (by Milton Herbert Gropper) Forrest Theatre; D: Albert Lewis; Cast: Sylvia Sidney (Mary), Hale Hamilton, Marie Nordstrom, Raymond Guion (later known as Gene Raymond), Albert Hackett

Don't Count Your Chickens (by Robert Riskin and Edith Fitzgerald) on tour; D: Hassard Short; Cast: Mary Boland, Sylvia Sidney, Maude Eburne, Raymond Hackett

The Breaks (by J.C. Nugent and Elliot Nugent) Klaw Theatre; D: Augustin Duncan (brother of Isadora); Cast: Sylvia Sidney (Amy), Elliot Nugent, Claude Cooper

Elitch Gardens, Colorado; Plays included: *The Command to Love, The Second Mrs. Tanqueray, Baby Cyclone, Nightstick, The K-Guy, Behold the Groom*; Cast: Fredric March, Isabel Elsom, Sylvia Sidney, Florence Eldridge, C. Henry Gordon

Gods of the Lightning (by Maxwell Anderson and Harold Hickerson) Little Theatre; D: Hamilton McFadden; Cast: Charles Bickford, Horace Braham, Sylvia Sidney (Rosalie), Leo Bulgakov, Eva Condon, Robert Brister, Barton MacLane, Ian Wolfe

1929

The Royal Family (by George S. Kaufman and Edna Ferber) Temple Theatre, Rochester; D: Elmer Brown; Cast: Sylvia Sidney (Gwen), Alexander Kirkland, Aline MacMahon, Julia Stewart, Alden Chase

The Silent House (by John G. Brandon and George Pickett) Temple Theatre, Rochester; D: Elmer Brown; Cast: Sylvia Sidney (T'mala), Alexander Kirkland, Alden Chase

The Trial of Mary Dugan (by Bayard Veiller) Temple Theatre, Rochester; D: Elmer Brown; Cast: Sylvia Sidney (Mary Dugan), Alexander Kirkland, George Graham

Nice Women (by William A. Grew) Longacre Theatre; D: W.B. Friedlander; Cast: Sylvia Sidney (Elizabeth Girard), Robert Warwick, Verree Teasdale, George Barbier

An Old Fashioned Girl (by Maurine Watkins) Flatbush Theatre; D: Joseph Graham; Cast: Sylvia Sidney (Kerry Lane), Edward Arnold, Helen MacKellar

Cross Roads (by Martin Flavin) Morosco Theatre; D: Guthrie McClintic; Cast: Sylvia Sidney (Patricia), Franchot Tone, Irene Purcell, Peggy Shannon, Dennie Moore

1930
Many a Slip (by Robert Riskin and Edith Fitzgerald; formerly titled *Don't Count Your Chickens*) Little Theatre; D: Robert Riskin; Cast: Sylvia Sidney (Patsy), Douglass Montgomery, Maude Eburne, Tom Brown, Dorothy Sands, Elisha Cook Jr.

Bad Girl (by Vina Delmar and Brian Marlow) Hudson Theatre; D: Marion Gering; Cast: Sylvia Sidney (Dot), Paul Kelly, Sacha Beaumont, Charlotte Wynters

1933
Liliom (by Franz Molnar) Pasadena Playhouse; D: Frank Reicher; Cast: Sylvia Sidney (Julie), Arthur Lubin, Lloyd Corrigan, Nydia Westman, Montague Shaw

1937
To Quito and Back (by Ben Hecht) Guild Theatre; D: Philip Moeller; Cast: Sylvia Sidney (Lola), Leslie Banks, Joseph Buloff, Evelyn Varden

1938
Accent on Youth (by Samson Raphaelson) on tour; D: Oliver Barber; Cast: Sylvia Sidney (Linda), Richard Hale, Joseph Cotten, Dorothy Matthews, Boyd Davis

Pygmalion (by George Bernard Shaw) on tour; D: Arthur Sircom; Cast: Sylvia Sidney (Eliza), Philip Huston, Mary Brian

1939
The Gentle People (by Irwin Shaw) Belasco Theatre; D: Harold Clurman; Cast: Sylvia Sidney (Stella), Franchot Tone, Sam Jaffe, Elia Kazan, Karl Malden, Roman Bohnen, Lee J. Cobb, Martin Ritt

1940
No Time for Comedy (by S.N. Behrman) Amherst Drama Festival; Cast: Sylvia Sidney (Linda), Luther Adler

1941
Accent on Youth - on tour; D: Samson Raphaelson; Cast: Sylvia Sidney (Linda), Luther Adler, James Gregory, Dorothy LiBaire, Kevin McCarthy

Two on an Island (by Elmer Rice) Music Hall, Kansas City; D: Ilya Motyleff; Cast: Sylvia Sidney (Mary), Luther Adler

Golden Boy (by Clifford Odets) Maplewood Theatre, N.J.; Cast: Luther Adler, Sylvia Sidney (Lorna), Joseph Buloff

1942
Angel Street (by Patrick Hamilton) on tour; D: Shepard Traube; Cast: Sylvia Sidney (Mrs. Manningham), Victor Jory, Ernest Cossart, Judy Parrish

Little Women (by Marian DeForest, based on the novel by Louisa May Alcott) Amherst Drama Festival; D: Robert M. Perry; Cast: Sylvia Sidney (Jo), Nancy Duncan

Jane Eyre (by Helen Jerome, based on the novel by Charlotte Bronte) Cape Playhouse; D: Arthur Sircom; Cast: Sylvia Sidney (Jane), Luther Adler, Harry Ellerbe, Cora Witherspoon

Pygmalion - on tour 1942-43; Cast: Sylvia Sidney (Eliza), and in various productions: Philip Huston, Horace Sinclair, Audrey Lindley, Staats Cotsworth, Richard Temple

1943

We Will Never Die (by Ben Hecht) Madison Square Garden, and Constitution Hall; D: Moss Hart; Cast: Sylvia Sidney, Luther Adler, Jacob Ben-Ami, Paul Muni, Edward G. Robinson, Herbert Rudley, Kurt Baum

Jane Eyre - on tour 1943-44; D: Luther Adler; Cast: Sylvia Sidney (Jane), Luther Adler, Ellen Hall, Katherine Allen, Cora Witherspoon, Ruth Gregory, John Ireland

1947

Joan of Lorraine (by Maxwell Anderson) on tour; D: Arthur L. Sachs; Cast: Sylvia Sidney (Joan of Arc), Harry Irvine, Ann Coray, Charles Ellis, Henry Jones, Kim Stanley, James Kirkwood Jr.

Angel Street - Biltmore Theatre, Los Angeles; D: Shepard Traube; Cast: Sylvia Sidney (Mrs. Manningham), Gregory Peck, Elizabeth Fraser, Elizabeth Patterson

1948

Kind Lady (by Edward Chodorov) on tour; Cast: (La Jolla Playhouse) Sylvia Sidney (Mary), Tom Helmore, Sig Rumann, Dennis Hoey, Doris Lloyd

O Mistress Mine (by Terence Rattigan) on tour 1948-49; D: Harald Bromley; Cast: Sylvia Sidney (Olivia Brown), John Loder, Dick Van Patten, Edna Preston

1949

The Two Mrs. Carrolls (by Martin Vale - pen name for Mrs. Bayard Veiller) on tour; D: George Somnes; Cast: Sylvia Sidney (Sally Carroll), Edward Andrews, Nancy Marchand

Pygmalion - on tour; D: Harry Ellerbee/Eldon Winkler; Cast: Sylvia Sidney (Eliza), Gavin Gordon, Donald Foster, Morton L. Stevens

1950

Anne of a Thousand Days (by Maxwell Anderson) on tour; D: Maury Tuckerman; Cast: Sylvia Sidney (Anne Boleyn), John Loder, Walter Matthau, Erik Rhodes

Goodbye, My Fancy (by Fay Kanin) on tour; Cast: Sylvia Sidney (Agatha Reed), Janet Fox, William Roerick

The Innocents (by William Archibald, based on the story *Turn of the Screw* by Henry James) on tour 1950-1951; D: Stanley Gould; Cast: Sylvia Sidney (Miss Giddens), David Cole, Patsy Bruder, Regina Wallace

1951

Arms and the Man (by George Bernard Shaw) Bermudiana Theatre, Bermuda; Cast: Sylvia Sidney (Raina), Romney Brent

Goodbye, My Fancy - on tour; Cast: Sylvia Sidney (Agatha Reed)

O Mistress Mine (two weeks in Chicago) Cast: Sylvia Sidney (Olivia Brown), Romney Brent

Black Chiffon (by Lesley Storm) on tour; D: William Miles; Cast: Sylvia Sidney (Alicia Christie), Henry Daniell, Alan Marshall

1952

Goodbye, My Fancy - on tour; Cast: Sylvia Sidney (Agatha Reed), Conrad Nagel

Kind Lady - Bucks Co. Playhouse, Pa.; Cast: Sylvia Sidney (Mary), Edward Ashley

The Gypsies Wore High Hats (by Joseph Kramm) on tour; Cast: Sylvia Sidney (Fanny), Stephen Bekassy, Helen Auerbach, Judy Edwards

The Fourposter (by Jan de Hartog) Golden Theatre on Broadway 1952-53; D: Jose Ferrer; Cast: Sylvia Sidney (Agnes), Romney Brent

1953
Angel Street - Miami; Cast: Sylvia Sidney (Mrs. Manningham), Luther Adler

Bell, Book and Candle (by John Van Druten) Cast: Sylvia Sidney (Gillian), Herbert Patterson

1954
Design for Living (by Noel Coward) Sombrero Playhouse, Arizona (and Bermuda with different co-stars); D: John O'Shaughnessy; Cast: Sylvia Sidney (Gilda), Gene Raymond, Thayer Roberts

The Man (by Mel Dinelli) (filmed as *Beware, My Lovely*) Palm Beach Playhouse; D: Cast: Sylvia Sidney, John Barrymore Jr., Wakefield Poole

O Mistress Mine - Biltmore Playhouse, Miami; Cast: Sylvia Sidney (Olivia Brown), Rex O'Malley

The Fourposter - on tour; Cast: Sylvia Sidney (Agnes), Frank Albertson

Angel Street - Avondale Playhouse, Indianapolis; Cast: Sylvia Sidney (Mrs. Manningham)

1955
The Constant Wife (by Somerset Maugham) on tour; Cast: Sylvia Sidney (Constance), Tom Helmore, Margery Maude, Margot Stevenson, Peter Bogdanovich

Angel Street - on tour; Cast: Sylvia Sidney (Mrs. Manningham), John Straub

1956
Angel Street - Ephrata, Pa. Cast: Sylvia Sidney (Mrs. Manningham)

Anniversary Waltz (by Jerome Chodorov) on tour; D; Richard Barr; Cast: Sylvia Sidney (Alice), Barry Thompson, Burt Reynolds

Picnic (by William Inge) Legion Star Playhouse, Pa.; D: Walt Witcover; Cast: Sylvia Sidney (Rosemary)

A Very Special Baby (by Robert Alan Aurthur) Playhouse Theatre; D: Martin Ritt; Cast: Sylvia Sidney (Anna), Luther Adler, Jack Warden, Jack Klugman, Carl Low

1957
Anniversary Waltz - Sombrero Theatre, Phoenix; Cast: Sylvia Sidney (Alice)

A Room Full of Roses (by Edith Sommer) Cast: Sylvia Sidney (Nancy)

September Tide (by Daphne du Maurier) Carousal Star Theatre, S.C.; D: Ray Boyle; Cast: Sylvia Sidney (Stella)

The Old Maid (by Zoe Akins, from the novel by Edith Wharton) John Drew Theatre, Long Island; D: Robert Hartung; Cast: Miriam Hopkins, Sylvia Sidney (Delia), Alan Shayne

1958-1959
Auntie Mame (by Patrick Dennis) on tour; D: Charles Bowden (patterned after Morton Da Costa) Cast: Sylvia Sidney (Mame), Guy Russell, Mark O'Daniels, Sudie Bond, Betty Sinclair, Edward Spence

1960
Kind Sir (by Norman Krasna) D: Ray Boyle; Cast: Sylvia Sidney (Jane Kimball), Mark O'Daniels, James Coco, Marion Paone, Mary Gordon, Annie Miller

Dark at the Top of the Stairs (by William Inge) on tour; D: Harold J. Kennedy/George Mallonee; Cast: Sylvia Sidney (Cora Flood), William Adler, Rayetta Gale, Amy Taubin, Jan Miner, Mark O'Daniels

1961
Sweet Bird of Youth (by Tennessee Williams) Cast: Sylvia Sidney (Alexandra Del Lago), Richard Kneeland, J. Thomas Adkins

1962

Pleasure of His Company (by Samuel Taylor) Berkshire Playhouse, MA.; D: Edward Payson Call; Cast: Sylvia Sidney (Katherine), John Straub, Constance Wolf, Jessica Poole

The Matchmaker (by Thornton Wilder) on tour; D: Harold Prince; Cast: Sylvia Sidney (Dolly Levi), Ralph Williams, Sada Thompson, Ralph Dunn, Casey Walters, Woody Romoff

1963

Enter Laughing (by Joseph Stein, based on Carl Reiner novel) Henry Miller's Theatre, N.Y.; D: Gene Saks: Cast: Sylvia Sidney (Mrs. Kalowitz), Alan Arkin, Vivian Blaine, Alan Mowbray, Irving Jacobson, Michael J. Pollard, Monroe Arnold

1964

Riverside Drive (by John Donovan - two one-act plays: *Damn You, Scarlet O'Hara & All My Pretty Little Ones*) Theatre de Lys; D: Douglas Seale; Cast: Sylvia Sidney (Beatrice/Leslie), Donald Woods

Angel Street - Dobbs Theatre, N.Y. D: Peter Waldron; Cast: Sylvia Sidney (Mrs. Manningham), Kent Smith, Wood Romoff

Kind Lady - Corning Theatre, N.Y. Cast: Sylvia Sidney (Mary), James Lockhart

The Silver Cord (by Sidney Howard) Berkshire Playhouse, MA. D: Joan White; Cast: Sylvia Sidney (Mrs. Phelps), William Swan, Angela Wood, William Shepard

Light Up the Sky (by Moss Hart) Playhouse on-the-mall, N.J. D: Ken Costigan; Cast: Sylvia Sidney (Frances Black), Jeffrey Lynn, Jan Miner, Vincent Gardenia, Jeanne Bolan

1965

The Glass Menagerie (by Tennessee Williams) Moorestown Theatre, N.J. Cast: Sylvia Sidney (Amanda), Jill Haworth, Robert Salvio, Peter Coffeen

Candida (by George Bernard Shaw) Comedia Repertory Co., Palo Alto, CA. Director: Dean Goodman; Cast: Sylvia Sidney (Candida)

The Rivals (by Richard Brinsley Sheridan) NRT tour 1965-66; D: Jack Sydow; Cast: Sylvia Sidney (Mrs. Malaprop), Leora Dana, G. Wood, Diana Frothingham

The Madwoman of Chaillot (by Jean Giraudoux) NRT tour 1965-66; D: Margaret Webster: Cast: Eva Le Gallienne, Sylvia Sidney (Constance), John Straub, Alan Oppenheimer, John Garfield Jr., Leora Dana, Sloane Shelton

1966
The Little Foxes (by Lillian Hellman) Moorestown Theatre, N.J. Cast: Sylvia Sidney (Regina), John Beal, Iris Pitney

Barefoot in the Park (by Neil Simon) on tour 1966-67; D: Woody Romoff/ Philip Lawrence; Cast: Sylvia Sidney (Mrs. Banks), Woody Romoff, Pamela Grey, Don Fenwick, Joan Van Ark

1967
The Importance of Being Earnest (by Oscar Wilde) Oakland Repertory Theatre, CA. Cast: Sylvia Sidney (Lady Bracknell)

1968
She Stoops to Conquer (by Oliver Goldsmith) NRT, Ford's Theater, D.C.; D: James D. Waring; Cast: Sylvia Sidney(Mrs. Hardcastle), Susan Sullivan, Patricia Guinan

Black Comedy (by Peter Shaffer) Philadelphia; Cast: Sylvia Sidney, Madeleine Kahn, John Horn

Come Blow Your Horn (by Neil Simon) on tour 1968-69; D: Richard Vath; Cast: Sylvia Sidney (Mrs. Baker), June Wilkinson, Sammy Jackson, Keefe Brasselle, Jay Lewis

1970
Cabaret (musical based on John Van Druten's play *I Am A Camera*, based on *Berlin Stories* by Christopher Isherwood) on tour; Director: Bert Convy; Cast: Anna Maria Alberghetti, Sylvia Sidney (Frau Schneider), Woody Romoff, Charles Abbott

1972
Butterflies Are Free (by Leonard Gershe) St. Louis, MO. Cast: Sylvia Sidney (Mrs. Baker), Gary Tomlin

1973
Suddenly, Last Summer (by Tennessee Williams) on tour; D: George Keathley; Cast: Sylvia Sidney (Violet Venable), Katharine Houghton, Joel Stedman, Allen Carlson

Barefoot in the Park - on tour; D: Patrick Baldauff; Cast: Sylvia Sidney (Mrs. Banks), Ginger Flick, Roger Miller, Woody Romoff

Arsenic and Old Lace (by Joseph Kesselring) on tour; D: Leslie B. Cutler; Cast: William Shatner, Sylvia Sidney (Abby Brewster), Peter Lupus, Joy Garrett, Nan Wilson

1974
Life in a Love (based on letters/poems of Elizabeth Barrett and Robert Browning) Kiva Auditorium, Kent State University, OH. Cast: Sylvia Sidney (Elizabeth), Richard Hudson

A Family and a Fortune (by Julian Mitchell, from the novel by Ivy Compton-Burnett) Seattle Repertory Theater; D: W. Duncan Ross; Cast: Sylvia Sidney (Matty Seaton), Gale Sondergaard, Jeannie Carson, Biff McGuire, Douglas Seale

Arsenic and Old Lace - Cast: Sylvia Sidney (Abby Brewster), John Carradine, Tony Roberts

1975

Arsenic and Old Lace - Cabrillo College, Aptos, Ca. Cast: Sylvia Sidney (Abby Brewster)

Sabrina Fair (by Samuel Taylor) on tour 1975-76; D: Harold J. Kennedy; Cast: Robert Horton, Katharine Houghton, Russell Nype, Maureen O'Sullivan, Sylvia Sidney (Julia), Art Fleming, Sandra Dee, Martin Milner, Roland Winters, Heather MacRae, Robert Ulrich

1976

Me Jack, You Jill (by Robes Kossez) John Golden Theatre (16 previews before closing); D: Harold J. Kennedy; Cast: Sylvia Sidney (Tessie), Lisa Kirk, Barbara Baxley, Russ Thacker

1977

Vieux Carre (by Tennessee Williams) St. James Theater; D: Arthur Allan Seidelman; Cast: Sylvia Sidney (Mrs. Wire), Richard Alfieri, Tom Aldredge, Diane Kagan

1978

Night Must Fall (by Emlyn Williams) on tour Cast: Sylvia Sidney (Mrs. Bramson), David McCallum, Barbara Caruso, Linda Cook

Come Blow Your Horn - on tour; Cast: Sylvia Sidney (Mrs. Baker), Kevin Tighe, Lou Jacobi

1981

Mornings at Seven (by Paul Osborn) on tour; Cast: Sylvia Sidney (Esther), Dana Andrews, King Donovan, Patricia O'Connell, Nancy Coleman, Mimi Cozzens, Lizbeth Pritchett

Light Up the Sky - John Drew Theatre, Long Island; D: Harold J. Kennedy; Cast: Sylvia Sidney (Stella), Gloria Graham, Phyllis Newman, Russell Nype, David O'Brien, Danny Aiello, Patrick Desmond

1984

'night Mother (by Marsha Norman) Pittsburgh Public Theatre; D: Peter Bennett; Cast: Sylvia Sidney (Thelma Cates), Sonja Lanzener

FILM CREDITS

Sorrows of Satan (1926) Paramount; P/D: D.W. Griffith; Cast: Adolphe Menjou, Ricardo Cortez, Carol Dempster, Lya de Putti, Ivan Lebedeff, Sylvia Sidney (bridesmaid)

Prince of Tempters (1926) First National; P: Robert Kane; D: Lothar Mendes; Cast: Lois Moran, Ben Lyon, Lya de Putti, Ian Keith, Mary Brian, Sylvia Sidney (extra)

Broadway Nights (1927) First National; P: Robert Kane; D: Joseph C. Boyle; Cast: Lois Wilson, Sam Hardy, Philip Strange; Guest stars: Sylvia Sidney, Barbara Stanwyck, June Collyer, Texas Guinan

Dance Magic (1927) First National; P: Robert Kane; D: Victor Halperin; Cast: Pauline Starke, Ben Lyon, Louis John Bartels, Isobel Elsom, Helen Chandler, Sylvia Sidney (bit)

Thru Different Eyes (1929) Fox; P: D: John G. Blystone; Cast: Mary Duncan, Warner Baxter, Edmund Lowe, Sylvia Sidney (Valerie), Stepin Fetchit, Natalie Moorhead, Florence Lake, Stuart Erwin

Five Minutes From the Station (1930) Warner Bros. (Vitaphone short) D: Arthur Hurley; Cast: Lynne Overman, Sylvia Sidney (Dot), Berton Churchill

City Streets (1931) Paramount; D: Rouben Mamoulian; Cast: Gary Cooper, Sylvia Sidney (Nan), Paul Lukas, William Boyd, Guy Kibbee, Wynne Gibson

Confessions of a Co-Ed (1931) Paramount; D: Dudley Murphy and David Burton; Cast: Sylvia Sidney (Patricia), Phillips Holmes, Norman Foster, Claudia Dell, Dorothy Libaire, Bing Crosby and the Rhythm Boys, Dickie Moore

The House That Shadows Built (1931) Paramount; Documentary celebrating Paramount's 20th anniversary; Scenes from *An American Tragedy* are included.

An American Tragedy (1931) Paramount; D: Josef von Sternberg; Cast: Phillips Holmes, Sylvia Sidney (Roberta), Frances Dee, Irving Pichel, Charles B. Middleton, Emmett Corrigan, Claire McDowell, Lucille LaVerne

Street Scene (1931) United Artists; P: Samuel Goldwyn; D: King Vidor; Cast: Sylvia Sidney (Rose), William Collier Jr., Estelle Taylor, Beulah Bondi, David Landau, Matt McHugh, Russell Hopton, John Qualen, Marcia Mae Jones

Ladies of the Big House (1931) Paramount; D: Marion Gering; Cast: Sylvia Sidney (Kathleen), Gene Raymond, Wynne Gibson, Rockliffe Fellowes, Earle Foxe, Purnell Pratt, Louise Beavers, Jane Darwell, Noel Francis, Robert Emmett O'Connor

The Miracle Man (1932) Paramount; D: Norman McLeod; Cast: Sylvia Sidney (Helen), Chester Morris, Irving Pichel, John Wray, Robert Coogan, Boris Karloff, Ned Sparks, Hobart Bosworth, Lloyd Hughes, Virginia Bruce, Florine McKinney, Jackie Serle

Merrily We Go To Hell (1932) Paramount; D: Dorothy Arzner; Cast: Sylvia Sidney (Joan), Fredric March, Cary Grant, Skeets Gallagher, Kent Taylor, George Irving, Esther Howard, Adrianne Allen

Make Me a Star (1932) Paramount; P: B. P. Schulberg; D: William Beaudine; Cast: Joan Blondell, Stuart Erwin, ZaSu Pitts, Ben Turpin, Ruth Donnelly; Guest stars (as themselves): Sylvia Sidney, Claudette Colbert, Gary Cooper, Maurice Chevalier, Tallulah Bankhead, Jack Oakie, Fredric March, Charlie Ruggles, Clive Brook, Phillips Holmes

Madame Butterfly (1932) Paramount; P: B. P. Schulberg; D: Marion Gering; Cast: Sylvia Sidney (Cho Cho San), Cary Grant, Charlie Ruggles, Irving Pichel, Helen Jerome Eddy, Dorothy Libaire, Shiela Terry

Pick-Up (1933) Paramount; P: B. P. Schulberg; D: Marion Gering; Cast: Sylvia Sidney (Mary), George Raft, Lillian Bond, Louise Beavers, William

Harrigan, Purnell Pratt, Charles B. Middleton, Robert McWade, Clarence Wilson, Jane Darwell (voice)

Jennie Gerhardt (1933) Paramount; P: B. P. Schulberg; D: Marion Gering; Cast: Sylvia Sidney (Jennie), Donald Cook, Mary Astor, Edward Arnold, H. B. Warner, Dorothy Libaire, Greta Meyer, Cora Sue Collins, Frank Reicher, Jane Darwell

Good Dame (1934) Paramount; P: B.P. Schulberg; D: Marion Gering; Cast: Sylvia Sidney (Lillie), Fredric March, Jack LaRue, Noel Francis, Russell Hopton, Walter Brennan

Thirty-Day Princess (1934) Paramount; P: B.P. Schulberg; D: Marion Gering; Cast: Sylvia Sidney (Catterina/Nancy), Cary Grant, Edward Arnold, Vince Barnett, Henry Stephenson, Robert McWade, Lucien Littlefield

Behold My Wife (1934) Paramount; P: B.P. Schulberg; D: Mitchell Leisen; Cast: Sylvia Sidney (Tanita Storm Cloud), Gene Raymond, Laura Hope Crews, H.B. Warner, Juliette Compton, Ann Sheridan, Monroe Owsley, Kenneth Thompson, Dean Jagger, Eric Blore, Charles B. Middleton, Virginia Hammond, Eddie "Rochester" Anderson, Matt McHugh

Accent on Youth (1935) Paramount; P: Douglas MacLean; D: Wesley Ruggles; Cast: Sylvia Sidney (Linda), Herbert Marshall, Phillip Reed, Astrid Allwyn, Holmes Herbert, Dick Foran, Catherine Doucet, Ernest Cossart, Lon Chaney Jr., Samuel S. Hinds, Donald Meek

Mary Burns, Fugitive (1935) Paramount; P: Walter Wanger; D: William K. Howard; Cast: Sylvia Sidney (Mary), Melvyn Douglas, Alan Baxter, Brian Donlevy, Pert Kelton, Wallace Ford, Esther Dale, Fuzzy Knight, Cora Sue Collins, Dennis O'Keefe

The Trail of the Lonesome Pine (1936) Paramount; P: Walter Wanger; D: Henry Hathaway; Cast: Sylvia Sidney (June), Fred MacMurray, Henry Fonda, Beulah Bondi, Fred Stone, Nigel Bruce, Robert Barrat, Spanky McFarland, Fuzzy Knight, Samuel Hinds, Alan Baxter, Clara Blandick, Charles B. Middleton

Fury (1936) MGM; P: Joseph L. Mankiewicz; D: Fritz Lang; Cast: Sylvia

Sidney (Katherine), Spencer Tracy, Walter Abel, Bruce Cabot, Edward Ellis, Frank Albertson, Walter Brennan, George Walcott, Esther Dale, Leila Bennett, Ward Bond, Terri (dog)

Sabotage (1936) (*The Woman Alone* in the U.S.) Gaumont-British; P: Michael Balcon; D: Alfred Hitchcock; Cast: Sylvia Sidney (Mrs. Verloc), Oscar Homolka, Desmond Tester, John Loder, Joyce Barbour

You Only Live Once (1937) United Artists; P: Walter Wanger; D: Fritz Lang; Cast: Sylvia Sidney (Joan), Henry Fonda, Barton MacLane, Jean Dixon, William Gargan, Jerome Cowan, Chic Sale, Margaret Hamilton, Warren Hymer, Ward Bond, Jack Carson

Dead End (1937) P: Samuel Goldwyn; D: William Wyler; Cast: Sylvia Sidney (Drina), Joel McCrea, Humphrey Bogart, Wendy Barrie, Claire Trevor, Allen Jenkins, Marjorie Main, Billy Halop, Gabriel Dell, Huntz Hall, Bobby Jordan, Leo Gorcey, Ward Bond

You and Me (1938) Paramount; P: Fritz Lang; D: Fritz Lang; Cast: Sylvia Sidney (Helen), George Raft, Robert Cummings, Barton MacLane, Roscoe Karns, Harry Carey, George E. Stone, Warren Hymer, Guinn Williams, Matt McHugh, Joyce Compton

One Third of a Nation (1939) Paramount; P: Harold Orlob; D: Dudley Murphy; Cast: Sylvia Sidney (Mary), Leif Erickson, Myron McCormick, Sidney Lumet, Hiram Sherman, Muriel Hutchison, Iris Adrian

The Wagons Roll at Night (1941) Warner Bros.; P: Harlan Thompson; D: Ray Enright; Cast: Humphrey Bogart, Sylvia Sidney (Flo), Joan Leslie, Eddie Albert, Sig Ruman, Cliff Clark, John Ridgley, Clara Blandick

Breakdowns of 1941 (1941) Warner Bros. short with outtakes from *The Wagons Roll at Night*; with SS, Humphrey Bogart, Sig Ruman

Blood on the Sun (1945) United Artists; P: William Cagney; D: Frank Lloyd; Cast: James Cagney, Sylvia Sidney, Wallace Ford, Rosemary De Camp, Robert Armstrong, John Emery, Jack Halloran, Frank Puglia, Philip Ahn, Rhys Williams, Marvin Miller, Porter Hall, Leonard Strong, Gregory Gay, Hugh Beaumont

The Searching Wind (1946) Paramount; P: Hal B. Wallis; D: William Dieterle; Cast: Robert Young, Sylvia Sidney, Ann Richards, Douglas Dick, Dudley Digges, Albert Basserman, Dan Seymour, Norma Varden, Ian Wolfe, Bess Flowers

Screen Snapshots: The Skolsky Party (1946) Columbia; D: Ralph Staub; 10 minute short of producer Sidney Skolsky's party for the premier of *The Jolson Story*. Guests include: SS, Alan Ladd, William Powell, John Garfield, Jack Haley

Mr. Ace (1946) United Artists; P: Benedict Bogeaus; D: Edwin Marin; Cast: George Raft, Sylvia Sidney (Margaret Wyndham Chase), Roman Bohnen, Stanley Ridges, Sid Silvers, Sara Haden, Jerome Cowan, Alan Edwards, Bess Flowers

Love From a Stranger (1947) Eagle-Lion; P: James Geller; D: Richard Whorf; Cast: John Hodiak, Sylvia Sidney (Cecily), Ann Richards, John Howard, Ernest Cossart, Isobel Elsom

Screen Snapshots 1860: Howdy Podner (1949) Columbia; D: Ralph Staub; 10 minute short with celebrities arriving in Las Vegas: SS, Clara Bow, Rex Bell, Roy Rogers, Dale Evans, Yvonne DeCarlo

Les Miserables (1952) 20th Century-Fox; P: Fred Kohlmar; D: Lewis Milestone; Cast: Michael Rennie, Debra Paget, Robert Newton, Edmund Gwen, Sylvia Sidney (Fantine), Cameron Mitchell, Elsa Lanchester, Florence Bates, Rhys Williams

Violent Saturday (1955) 20th Century-Fox; P: Buddy Adler; D: Richard Fleischer; Cast: Victor Mature, Richard Egan, Stephen McNally, Virginia Leith, Tommy Noonan, Lee Marvin, Margaret Hayes, J. Carroll Nash, Sylvia Sidney (Elsie), Ernest Borgnine

Behind the High Wall (1956) Universal-International; P: Stanley Rubin; D: Abner Biberman; Cast: Tom Tully, Sylvia Sidney (Hilda), Betty Lynn, John Gavin, Don Beddoe

Summer Wishes, Winter Dreams (1973) Columbia; P: Jack Brodsky; D: Gilbert Cates; Cast: Joanne Woodward, Martin Balsam, Sylvia Sidney (Mrs. Pritchett), Tresa Hughes, Dori Brenner, Ron Richards

> Academy Award Nomination: Sylvia Sidney for Best Supporting Actress
>
> Golden Globe Nomination: Sylvia Sidney for Best Supporting Actress
>
> National Board of Review Award: Sylvia Sidney for Best Supporting Actress

God Told Me To (1976) New World Pictures; P/D:Larry Cohen; Cast: Tony Lo Bianco, Deborah Raffin, Sandy Dennis, Sylvia Sidney (Elizabeth), Sam Levene, Robert Drivas, Richard Lynch, Andy Kaufman

I Never Promised You a Rose Garden (1977) New World Pictures; D: Anthony Page; Cast: Bibi Andersson, Kathleen Quinlan, Ben Piazza, Lorraine Gary, Darlene Craviotto, Reni Santoni, Susan Tyrrell, Signe Hasso, Norman Alden, Sylvia Sidney (Miss Coral), Dennis Quaid, Jeff Conaway, Diane Varsi

Damien: Omen II (1978) 20th Century-Fox; P: Harvey Bernhard; D: Don Taylor and Mike Hodges (uncredited); Cast: William Holden, Lee Grant, Jonathan Scott-Taylor, Robert Foxworth, Nicolas Pryor, Lew Ayers, Sylvia Sidney (Aunt Marion), Lance Henricksen, Elizabeth Shepherd

Hammett (1982) Warner Bros. (produced at Zoetrope Studios); Executive Producer: Francis Ford Coppola; D: Wim Wenders; Cast: Frederic Forrest, Peter Boyle, Marilu Henner, Roy Kinnear, Lydia Lei, Elisha Cook Jr., R.G. Armstrong, Richard Bradford, Michael Chow, David Patrick Kelly, Sylvia Sidney (Donaldina), Jack Nance

Order of Death (1983) (a.k.a. *Corrupt*) New Line Cinema (RAI) D: Roberto Faenza; Cast: Harvey Keitel, John Lydon, Sylvia Sidney (Margaret Smith), Leonard Mann, Nicole Garcia

Beetlejuice (1988) Warner Bros.; D: Tim Burton; Cast: Michael Keaton, Alec Baldwin, Geena Davis, Winona Ryder, Jeffrey Jones, Catherine O'Hara, Sylvia Sidney (Juno), Annie McEnroe, Mark Ettlinger, Robert Goulet, Dick Cavet, Susan Kellermann

> Saturn Award: Sylvia Sidney for Best Supporting Actress

Used People (1992) 20th Century-Fox; D: Beeban Kidron; Cast: Shirley MacLaine, Marcello Mastroiani, Kathy Bates, Marcia Gay Harden, Jessica Tandy, Sylvia Sidney (Becky)

Mars Attacks! (1996) Warner Bros.; P: Tim Burton/Larry Fanco; D: Tim Burton; Cast: Jack Nicholson, Glenn Close, Annette Bening, Pierce Brosnan, Danny DeVito, Martin Short, Sara Jessica Parker, Michael J. Fox, Rod Steiger, Tom Jones, Lukas Haas, Natalie Portman, Jim Brown, Lisa Marie, Sylvia Sidney (Grandma Florence), Pam Grier, Paul Winfield, Jack Black, Christina Applegate

RADIO CREDITS (major appearances)

Campbell Playhouse, The (CBS) Mercury Theater

January 24, 1941 - *Golden Boy* with Luther Adler, Sylvia Sidney

Chesterfield Hour, The (CBS) (Paul Whiteman)

March 11, 1938 - guest: Sylvia Sidney

Columbia Radio Workshop (CBS)

July 17, 1945 - *The Undecided Molecule* with Groucho Marx, Sylvia Sidney, Robert Benchley, Vincent Price, Keenan Wynn

Don Ameche Show, The (The Drene Show Review) (NBC)

July 31, 1946 - scene from *Angel Street* - Sylvia Sidney

September 15, 1946 - guest: Sylvia Sidney

December 8, 1946 - guest: Sylvia Sidney

Gotham Nights (WHN)

January 16, 1939 - *The Gentle People* (scenes); guests: Sylvia Sidney, Franchot Tone

Green Valley U.S.A. (CBS)

March 12, 1944 - Guest Sylvia Sidney plays a waitress

Hedda Hopper Show - This is Hollywood (CBS)

January 25, 1947 - *Mr. Ace* - with George Raft, Sylvia Sidney

Hollywood Hotel (CBS) (Louella Parsons)

April 18, 1934 - Guests: Sylvia Sidney, Cary Grant perform a sketch about "charm"

Hollywood Playhouse (NBC)

April 24, 1940 - *Shadow Light* - with Charles Boyer, Sylvia Sidney

Hollywood Star Time (CB S)

September 7, 1946 - *Mission Perilous* with Sylvia Sidney, Dane Clark

Kate Smith Hour, The (ABC)

October 21, 1937 - scenes from *Dead End*; Guest: Sylvia Sidney

February 9, 1939 - scenes from *The Gentle People*; Guests: Sylvia Sidney, Franchot Tone

March 8, 1940 - scenes from *Voices*; Guests: Sylvia Sidney, Luther Adler, Richard Haydn

Leave It To The Girls (Mutual) (panel show)

March 12-June 11, 1948 (Fridays) - moderator: George Brent; panelists: Sylvia Sidney, Constance Bennett, Binnie Barnes

Lux Radio Theatre (CBS)

January 6, 1936 - *The Third Degree* with Sylvia Sidney, Morgan Farley

December 3, 1945 - *Blood on the Sun* with James Cagney, Sylvia Sidney

Memoirs of the Movies (WNYC)

January 7, 1962 - *Requiem for a Writer* - Sylvia Sidney hosts screenwriters Anita Loos, Henry Myers, Samuel Spewack, Dorothy Parker, Marc Connelly, Joseph L. Mankiewicz, Ben Hecht, Reginald Denham, Leo Rosten, and story editor Kenneth McKenna

Paula and Phil (Mutual)

August 28, 1945 - Paula Stone interviews Sylvia Sidney

Philip Morris Playhouse, The (CBS)

August 15, 1941 - *Dark Victory* with Sylvia Sidney, Agnes Moorhead

September 19, 1941 - *Angels with Dirty Faces* with Sylvia Sidney

October 17, 1941 - *Wuthering Heights* with Sylvia Sidney, Raymond Massey

Pretty Kitty Kelly (CBS)

January 15-March, 1940; daytime serial: Arlene Blackburn, Sylvia Sidney (herself)

Radie Harris Show (CBS)

July 31, 1945 - interview with Sylvia Sidney

Screen Guild Theater (CBS)

October 29, 1945 - *You Only Live Once* - with Sylvia Sidney, Henry Fonda

Silver Theater, The (CBS)

July 8, 1945 - *Broken Destiny* with Sylvia Sidney

Somerset Maugham Theatre (CBS)

June 2, 1951 - *Rain* with Sylvia Sidney

Theater Guild on the Air (ABC)

October 5, 1952 - *Morning Star* with Gertrude Berg, Sylvia Sidney, Joseph Buloff

Twenty Questions (Mutual)

April 19, 1952 - guest: Sylvia Sidney

United Jewish Appeal Campaign (ABC special)

May 6, 1947 - *Barbed Wire Sky* - with Sylvia Sidney, John Garfield, Paul Muni, Edward G. Robinson, Agnes Moorehead

We Take Your Word (CBS)

June 25, 1950 - guests: Sylvia Sidney, Abe Burrows

Miscellaneous:

November 23, 1930: (WMCA) *Bad Girl* (scenes); guests: Sylvia Sidney, Paul Kelly, Charlotte Wynters, Sascha Beaumont

September 16, 1933: (BBC) *Romeo and Juliet* (scenes); guests: Sylvia Sidney, Ion Swinley

April 12, 1943: (WINX) *We Will Never Die!* with Paul Muni, Edward G. Robinson, Sylvia Sidney

TV CREDITS

1951:
Leave it to the Girls (NBC) - Dorothy Kilgallen, Maggi McNellis, SS (guest panelist)

Kate Smith Evening Hour (NBC) - SS and Sidney Blackmer enact a dramatic sketch from Arthur Miller's *It Takes a Thief*

1952:
Cameo Theater (NBC) - *The Gathering Twilight* (by Abby Mann) with SS, Douglass Montgomery

Schlitz Playhouse of Stars (CBS) - *Experiment* (by Joel Hammill) with SS

Tales of Tomorrow (ABC) - *Time to Go* (by Mann Rubin) D: Don Medford; with SS

Lux Video Theater (CBS) - *Night, Be Quiet* (by S. Lee Pogostin) D: Richard Goode; with SS

    Pattern for Glory (by Abby Mann and Bernard Drew) D: Richard Goode; with SS, Robert Cummings

Hollywood Screen Test (ABC) - guest: SS

Broadway TV Theatre (WOR-TV) - *Theatre* (by W. Somerset Maugham) with SS, Jack Whiting, Ted Newton

    The Letter (by W. Somerset Maugham) with SS, Gene Raymond, Joel Ashley

1953:

Strike it Rich (CBS) guest: SS

Broadway TV Theatre (WOR-TV) - *The Climax* (play by Edward Locke) with SS, Russell Hardie

    Dark Victory (by George Brewer, Bertram Block) with SS, Christopher Plummer, Ian Keith

    Kind Lady (by Edward Chodrov) with SS, Christopher Plummer

    Angel Street (by Patrick Hamilton) with SS, Victor Jory, Melville Cooper

Joseph Schildkraut Presents (DuMont) *A Candle in the Sun* (by Tad Mosel) D: Barry Shear; with SS, Peter Fernandez

    Shortcut with SS, George Matthews

Kraft Television Theatre (ABC) *Johnny Came Home* (by Frank Gilroy) D: Stanley Quinn; with SS, Frank McHugh, John Connell

Ford Theater (NBC) *As the Flame Dies* (by Herbert Little, David Victor) D: James Neilson; with SS, Barry Sullivan, Richard Webb, Whit Bissell, Gloria Henry

1954:

Philco Television Playhouse (NBC) *Catch My Boy on Sunday* (by Paddy Chayefsky) D: Arthur Penn; with SS, Martin Rudy

1955:

Pond's Theatre (ABC) *The Hickory Limb* (by John Van Druten) with SS, Mary Astor, Gene Raymond, Mildred Dunnock

Climax! (CBS) *The Leaf Out of the Book* (teleplay by Morton Fine, David Friedkin; book by Margaret Cousins) D: Allen Reisner; with SS, George Brent, Diana Lynn, Hugh Beaumont

Ford Theater (NBC) *Deception* (by Ted Thomas and Jan Leman) D: Peter Godfrey; with SS, John Howard, June Vincent

Star Stage (NBC) *The Toy Lady* (by Max Watson) with SS, Lorne Greene, Jeffrey Lynn (host)

Playwrights '56 (NBC) *The Heart's a Forgotten Hotel* (by Arnold Schulman) Aired October 25, 1955; D: Arthur Penn; Cast: SS (Sophie), Edmond O'Brien, Paul Hartman, Arleen Whelan, Jack Krushchen (note: Sidney was paged for the role on Broadway, retitled *A Hole in the Head* (1957), but it was given to Kay Medford)

Celebrity Playhouse (NBC) *The House Between Flags* (by Montgomery Pittman, Frederick Brady) D: James Neilson; with SS, Stephen McNally

The 20th Century Fox Hour (CBS) *Man on the Ledge* (story by Joel Sayre; teleplay by Steve Fisher) D: Lewis Allen; with SS, Cameron Mitchell, Vera Miles, Alan Hale Jr., William Gargan, Joseph Cotton (host)

1956:

Celebrity Playhouse (NBC) *More Than Kin* (by John McGreevey) D: Gerald Freedman; with SS, Tom Tully, Gigi Perreau

Talk Show: *Home* (NBC) SS, Arlene Francis (host)

1957:
Climax! (CBS) *The Gold Dress* (by Stephen Vincent Benet) D: Buzz Kulik; with SS, Leif Erickson, June Lockhart, William Lundigan (host)

Playhouse 90 (CBS) *The Helen Morgan Story* (teleplay by Leonard Spigelgass and Paul Monash; story by Lulu Morgan) D: George Roy Hill; with Polly Bergen, SS, Hoagy Carmichael, Reginald Denney, Ronnie Burns, Dana Wynter (host)

Kraft Television Theatre (ABC) *Circle of Fear* (by Samuel Elkin) with SS, Farley Granger, Lee Remick, Don Dubbins

Matinee Theatre (NBC) *The Gift and the Giver* (by Harold Gast; novel by Nelia Gardner White) with SS

1958:
Playhouse 90 (CBS) *The Gentleman from Seventh Avenue* (by Elick Mall) D: Allen Reisner; with SS, Robert Alda, Patricia Neal, Walter Slezak, Amanda Randolph, Dana Wynter (host)

Climax! (CBS) *No Time at All* (by Charles Einstein) D: David Swift; with William Lundigan, Betsy Palmer, Jane Greer, Keenan Wynn; Cameos: SS, Chico Marx, Buster Keaton, Sheppard Strudwick, James Gleason, Jack Haley, Reginald Gardiner, Charles Bronson, Cliff Edwards, Regis Toomey

1960:
General Electric Theater (CBS) *The Committeeman* (by Joseph Stefano) with Lee J. Cobb, SS, Timmy Everett, Ronald Reagan (host)

June Allyson Show (CBS) *Escape* (teleplay by Bruce Geller; story by Gene Roddenberry) D: Paul Henreid; with SS, Frank Lovejoy, Margaret O'Brien, Brian Donlevy, June Allyson (host)

Talk/Panel Shows: *Jack Paar, Here's Hollywood*

1961:
Naked City (ABC) *A Hole in the City* (by Howard Rodman) D: David Lowell Rich; with SS, Robert Duval, Ed Asner, Martin Balsam, Robert Blake

Route 66 (CBS) *Like a Motherless Child* (by Howard Rodman, Betty Andrews) D: David Lowell Rich; with SS, George Maharis, Martin Milner, Ben Johnson, Jack Weston

Change of Life (NBC Special) (by George Lefferts) with SS, Pauline Frederick (host)

1962:

The Defenders (CBS) *The Madman* (Emmy Award for writing by Robert Thom, Reginald Rose) D: Stuart Rosenberg (Emmy Award); Cast: SS (Emmy Nomination), Don Gordon (Emmy Nomination), John Beal, E.G. Marshall, Robert Reed

Emmy Nomination: Sylvia Sidney for an Actress in a Leading Role

1963:

The Eleventh Hour (NBC) *Five Moments Out of Time* with SS, Wendell Corey, Patricia Barry, Norman Fell, Patrick O'Neal, Pat Crowley, Jack Ging

In the Last Place (CBS) (Yom Kippur Special) (by Stephan Chodorov) with SS, Henderson Forsythe, Ira Barmak

The Doctors (NBC) *Twinkle, Twinkle Big Star* with SS, Richard Roat

Talk/Panel Shows: *The Today Show, Girl Talk*

1964:

Route 66 (CBS) *Child of a Night* (by Stirling Silliphant, Herbert B. Leonard) D: Allen Miner; with SS, Chester Morris, Herschel Bernardi, Martin Milner, Glenn Corbett

The Nurses (CBS) *To All My Friends on Shore* (by Allan E. Stone) D: Stuart Rosenberg; with SS, Zina Bethune, Shirl Conway, Will Kuluva

Talk/ Panel Shows: *Girl Talk, Get the Message*

1965:

Talk/Panel Shows: *Girl Talk, Mike Douglas, Today with Inga, Gypsy Rose Lee*

1966:
Talk/Panel Shows: *Living for the Sixties* (NET) (SS discusses raising pugs), *Gypsy Rose Lee*

1967:
Talk/Panel Shows: *Living for the Sixties* (NET)

1968:
Talk/Panel Shows: *Panorama* (Fox)

1969:
My Three Sons (CBS) *Teacher's Pet* (by Freddy Rhea) D: Frederick De Cordova; with SS, Fred MacMurray, Barry Livingston, Don Grady, William Demarest

Talk/Panel Shows: *That Show, With Joan Rivers/The Joan Rivers Show* (NBC)

1970:
Talk/Panel Show: *Mike Douglas* with SS, Jane Powell, Rosie Greer, Jackie Vernon

1971:
Do Not Fold, Spindle, or Mutilate (ABC Movie of the Week) (teleplay by John D.F. Black; novel by Doris Miles Disney) D: Ted Post; with SS, Myrna Loy, Helen Hayes, Mildred Natwick, Vince Edwards, John Beradino, John Mitchum

1974:
46th Annual Academy Awards - SS Nominee for Best Supporting Actress (*Summer Wishes, Winter Dreams*); Co-presenter, Best Art Direction-Set Decoration

Talk/Panel Shows: *Good Morning!*, *Sonja Hamlin Show*

1975:
The Secret Night Caller (NBC Movie) (by Robert Presnell Jr.) D: Jerry Jameson; with Robert Reed, Hope Lang, SS, Michael Constantine

Winner Take All (NBC Movie) (by Bill Garner, Caryl Ledner) D: Paul Bogart; with Shirley Jones, Laurence Luckinbill, SS, Joan Blondell, Joyce Van Patten

Bicentennial Minute (CBS) SS narrated one segment on August 9, 1975

Ryan's Hope (ABC) SS played in three episodes

1976:
Maureen (CBS pilot) with Joyce Van Patten, SS

Death at Love House (ABC Movie) (by James Barnett) D: E.W. Swackhamer; with Robert Wagner, Kate Jackson, SS, Joan Blondell, Dorothy Lamour, John Carradine

Starsky and Hutch (ABC) *Gillian* (by William Blinn, Benjamin Masselink, Amanda J. Green) D: George McCowan; with David Soul, Paul Michael Glaser, SS

1977:
Raid on Entebbe (NBC Movie) (by Barry Beckerman) D: Irvin Kershner; with Peter Finch, Charles Bronson, SS, Martin Balsam, Yaphet Kotto, Horst Buchholz, John Saxon, Jack Warden, James Woods

Snowbeast (NBC Movie) (by Joseph Stefano) D: Herb Wallerstein; with Bo Svenson, Yvette Mimieux, Robert Logan, SS, Clint Walker

Westside Medical (ABC) *Tears for a Two Dollar Wine* (by Barry Oringer) with SS

Eight is Enough (ABC) *Children of the Groom* (by William Blinn, Thomas Braden, Hindi Brooks) D: Philip Leacock; with Dick Van Patten, Betty Buckley, SS, Adam Rich

Talk Show: *Elliot Norton Reviews* (WGBH, Boston) SS talks about *Vieux Carre*

1978:
Siege (CBS Movie) (by Conrad Bromberg) D: Richard Pearce; with SS, Martin Balsam, Dorian Harewood, James Sutorius

WKRP in Cincinnati (CBS) Pilot (by Hugh Wilson) D: Jay Sandrich; with Howard Hesseman, Gordon Jump, Gary Sandy, Loni Anderson, SS

Kaz (CBS) *A Fine Romance* (by Carol Roper) with Ron Leibman, Patrick O'Neal, SS

Talk Show: *Good Day* (WCVB, Boston) SS, Al Martino, John Willis (host)

1979:

Supertrain (NBC) *Superstar* (by Larry Alexander) D: David Moessinger; with Dennis Dugan, Renee Heller, SS, Bo Hopkins

California Fever (CBS) *Movin' Out* (by Dan Polier) D: Marc Daniels; with Lorenzo Lamas, Jimmy McNichols, SS, Nancy Malone, Marc McClure

1980:

The Gossip Columnist (OPT Movie) (by Michael Gleason) D: James Sheldon; with Kim Cattrall, SS, Martha Raye, Joan Blondell, Robert Vaughn, Bobby Sherman, Dick Sargent, Bobby Vinton, Lyle Waggoner, Joe Penny

F.D.R. The Last Years (NBC Movie) (teleplay by Stanely R. Greenberg; book by Jim Bishop) D: Anthony Page; with Jason Robards, Eileen Heckart, Kim Hunter, SS, Jan Miner, Olympia Dukakis, Michael Gross, Kathryn Walker

The Shadow Box (ABC Movie) (by Michael Cristofer) D: Paul Newman; with Joanne Woodward, Christopher Plummer, SS, Melinda Dillon, Ben Masters, Valerie Harper, James Broderick, Curtiss Marlowe

Talk Show: *Over Easy* (PBS) "Vision" - SS talks about her cataract operations

1981:

The Love Boat (ABC) *Mama and Me* (by Harvey Bullock) D: Earl Bellamy; with SS, Eddie Mekka, Gavin MacLeod, Fred Grandy, Bernie Kopell

A Small Killing (CBS Movie) (by Burt Prelutsky; based on *The Rag Bag Clan* by Richard Barth) D: Steve Stern; with Edward Asner, Jean Simmons, SS

1982:

Come Along With Me (PBS Movie) (Teleplay by June Finfer, Neal Miller; story by Shirley Jackson) (filmed in the fall of 1980) D: Joanne Woodward; with Estelle Parsons, Barbara Baxley, SS

Night of 100 Stars (ABC) All-Star Variety Special that included SS among the guests

Having it All (ABC Movie) (Teleplay by Ann Beckett, Elizabeth Gill; story by Elizabeth Gill) D: Edward Zwick; with Dyan Cannon, Barry Newman, SS

Talk Show: *Tom Cottle: Up Close* (Syndicated) with SS

1983:

Magnum P.I. (CBS) *Birdman of Budapest* (by Louis F. Vipperman) D: Mike Vejar; with Tom Selleck, John Hillerman, SS, Joseph Wiseman, Fritz Feld

The Brass Ring (Filmed summer of 1983; Released on Cable TV January 1985) (based on *Only My Mouth Is Smiling* by Jocelyn Riley) D: Bob Balaban; with Dina Merrill, SS, April Lerman

1984:

Whiz Kids (CBS) *The Lollipop Gang Strikes Back* (by Lynn Barker) D: Dennis Donnelly; with SS, Elisha Cook Jr., Dan O'Herlihy

Trapper John, M.D. (CBS) *Aunt Mildred is Watching You* (by Jeff Stuart) D: Gregory Harrison; with SS, Pernell Roberts, Gregory Harrison, Ray Wise

Domestic Life (CBS) *Small Cranes Court* (by Howard Gewirtz, Ian Praiser) D: Michael Lessac; with Martin Mull, Megan Follows, SS

1985:

Finnegan Begin Again (HBO) (by Walter Lockwood) D: Joan Micklin Silver; with Mary Tyler Moore, Robert Preston, Sam Waterston, SS, David Huddleston

An Early Frost (NBC Movie) (teleplay by Ron Cowen, Daniel Lipman; story by Sherman Yellen) D: John Erman; with Gena Rowlands, Ben Gazzara, SS,

Aidan Quinn, D.W. Moffet, John Glover

    Emmy Nomination: Sylvia Sidney for Best Supporting Actress

    Golden Globe Award: Sylvia Sidney for Best Supporting Actress

1986:
43rd Annual Golden Globes Awards - SS Winner: Best Actress in a Supporting Role (Motion Picture made for TV: *An Early Frost*)

38th Annual Emmy Awards - SS Nominee: Best Actress in a Supporting Role (*An Early Frost*)

Morningstar/Eveningstar (CBS) Various writers/directors. Seven episodes. Cast: SS, Fred Savage, Joaquin Phoenix, Teresa Wright, Scatman Crothers, Melissa Francis

1987:
Pals (CBS Movie) (by Michael Norell, Michael Siegel) D: Lou Antonio; with George C. Scott, Don Ameche, SS, Susan Rinell

1988:
Going Hollywood: The War Years (Disney) Documentary; D: Julian Schlossberg; with SS, Doug Fairbanks Jr., Joan Leslie, Jackie Cooper, Dane Clark, Van Johnson (host)

Dear John (NBC) *Dancing in the Dark* (by Gina Goldman); D: Arlene Sanford; with Judd Hirsch, SS

1989:
The Equalizer (CBS) *Trial by Ordeal* (by Coleman Luck) D: Marc Laub; with Edward Woodward, Keith Szarabajka, SS, Robert Lansing

thirtysomething (ABC) *Be a Good Girl* (by Richard Kramer) D: Richard Kramer; with Melanie Mayron, SS, Phyllis Newman, Herb Edelman

American Masters (PBS documentary) *Broadway's Dreamers: The Legacy of the Group Theatre*; D: David Heeley; with SS, Stella Adler, Ellen Burstyn, Harold Clurman, John Garfield, Katharine Hepburn, Paul Newman, Joanne Woodward, Shelley Winters

1990:

Andre's Mother (PBS) (by Terrence McNally) D: Deborah Reinisch; with Sada Thompson, Richard Thomas, SS, Haviland Morris

Equal Justice (ABC) *The Art of the Possible* (by Glenn Merzer) D: Kevin Hooks; with George DiCenzo, Cotter Smith, SS, Cotter Smith, Sarah Jessica Parker

The Witching of Ben Wagner (Disney Channel) (book by Mary Jane Auch; teleplay by Michael Marmorstein) D: Paul Annett; with Justin Gocke, Sam Bottoms, SS, Bettina Rae

1991:

The Man in the Family (ABC) *Honor Bound* (by Ed Weinberger, Gina Wendkos) D: John Rich; with Ray Sharkey, Anne De Salvo, SS

1993:

Diagnosis Murder (CBS) *Miracle Cure* (by James Kramer); D: Michael Lange; with Dick Van Dyke, Scott Baio, SS, Robert Guillaume, Barry Van Dyke

1998-99:

Fantasy Island (ABC) 7 episodes; various writers and directors; with Malcolm McDowell, Louis Lombardi, Edward Hibbert, SS, Fyvush Finkel

2001:

American Masters (PBS) *Goldwyn: The Man and His Movies* (based on the biography by A. Scott Berg); includes interviews with SS, Farley Granger, Ann Blyth, Teresa Wright

2002:

Biography (A&E) *Clara Bow: America's Silent Sexpot*; D: John Griffin; with SS, Baby Peggy, Rex Bell Jr., Budd Schulberg, Fay Wray

Sylvia's needlepoint of her champion pug, Captain Midnight

AUTHOR CREDITS

Sylvia Sidney's Needlepoint Book (1968) Reinhold Book Corp, Galahad Books, 120 pages

Sylvia Sidney: Question and Answer Book on Needlepoint (1974) Von Nostrand Reinhold, 128 pages

Photo Credits

Every effort has been made to trace the copyright holders of photographs included in this book; if any have been inadvertently overlooked, the author and publisher will be pleased to make the necessary changes.

Paramount photos c. Paramount Pictures. All Rights Reserved

Warner Bros. photos c. Warner Bros. Entertainment Inc. Co. All Rights Reserved

MGM/Eagle-Lion photos c. Metro-Goldwyn-Mayer Studios Inc. All Rights Reserved

20th Century-Fox photos c. 20th Century-Fox Film Corp. All Rights Reserved

Columbia photos Columbia Pictures-Sony Entertainment. All Rights Reserved

Universal photos c. Universal Studios. All Rights Reserved

Thanks also to: Jonathan Talbot; http://kehilalinks.jewishgen.org/lunna/Kosowski.html; DRC, University of Cincinnati; and, historicelitchtheatre.org

Index

A

A Very Special Baby 283-285
Accent on Youth 122-*124* (film), 203-*204*, 205 (play)
Adler, Jody (Jacob)
  childhood *194*, 195-201, 211, 213, 217-218, 224-225, 229-230, 253
  education 260-261, 274-275, 284-286, 287, 295, 304-305, 311
  and ALS 345-347, 367-368, 375, 423
  death 378-*379*, 383, 385-386
Adler, Luther 167, 172, 177-*179*, 180-*181*, 195-198, 201-202, *204*-205, 207-*210*, 213, 218, 230-231, 270-271, 283-284, 347, 367, 375
Adler, Stella 177-*179*, 189-190, 207, 218-219, 345-347, 367
Alsop, Carleton 202-203, 235, 241-247, 248-249, 251-253, 255, 257, 259, 261-262
An American Tragedy 46-47, 56-57, 59-61, 70, 72, 74, 104, 409
An Early Frost 376, 378-*381*, 382-383, 411
An Old Fashioned Girl 36-37
Andre's Mother 383-384
Angel Street 205-*207*, 243, 269-270, 312
Anne of a Thousand Days 255
Arkin, Alan 302-*303*
Arnold, Edward 37-38, 101, 115
Arsenic and Old Lace 336
Arzner, Dorothy 71, 81-82, 402
Astor, Mary 102, 138-139, 201, 421
Auntie Mame xv-*xv*, xvi, *283*, 292-296

B

Bad Girl 42-45, 100, 133, 369
Baldwin, James 414
Balsam, Martin 326, 348, 352-353, 354
Barefoot in the Park 312-*313*, 314, 336
Baxter, Warner 32-34, 109
Beetlejuice 388, 390-392, 394, 398, 411
Behind the High Wall 277-278
Behold My Wife 120-*121*, 122, 271
Bergen, Polly *289*, 291
Bickford, Charles 30, 54
Blood on the Sun 220-*221*, 222-*223*, 224
Bogart, Humphrey 168-169, 199-*200*, 201-203, 254, 419
Bogdanovich, Peter 147-148, 153, 175, 277
Bondi, Beulah 69, 143
Bow, Clara 47-48, 51, 64, 92, 254, 369-370
Boyer, Charles 173, 196
Brent, George 199, 201, 246, 275-276
Brent, Romney 262, *268*
Broadway Nights 23
Brown, Tom 40
Burton, Tim 390-391, 404-406, 409

C

Cabaret 321-322
Cagney, James 54, 196, 199, 201, 220-*223*, 285-286, 350
Cerf, Bennett 40, 42, 91, *132*, 133-139, 149, 366
Challenge of Youth, The 16-19, 27
Chevalier, Maurice 107, 109

City Streets 47-48, 50-56, 61, 74, 94, 362, 369, 398
Clurman, Harold 185-186, 218-219
Colman, Ronald 71, 249
Come Blow Your Horn 314, 316, 320, 322
Confessions of a Co-Ed, 56, 61-62, 63-64, 185
Cook, Donald 102-*103*
Cooper, Gary 50, 52-53, 54, 69, 79, 86, 93, 99, 107, 386
Cornell, Katharine 22-23
Crawford, Joan 65-66, 99, 330
Crime 20, 265
Crosby, Bing *63*, 100
Cross Roads 38-39, 187
Cukor, George 35, 85

D

Damien - Omen II 350-351
Dark at the Top of the Stairs, The 301
Davis, Bette 36, 38, 42, 147, 167, 199, 201, 228, 253, 264, 269, 290, 330, 332, 413-414
Dead End xii, 160, 165-169, 171, 176, 310
Dee, Sandra 341, *424*
Do Not Fold, Spindle Or Mutilate 322-323
Dreiser, Theodore 47, 56-57, 59-60, 101, 103-104
Duvall, Robert 296

E

Enter Laughing 302-*303*, 304

F

Fairbanks, Doug Jr. 66, 85, 112, 122
Fantasy Island 407-*408*, 409
Finnegan Begin Again 373-374
Fonda, Henry 141-*142*, *143*-144, 146, 155-156, 161-*163*, 164, 172
Fourposter, The 268-269
Francis, Kay 21-22, 54, 256, 269
Fury xii, 144-*147*, 148, 164, 176, 394, 398

G

Garfield, John 165, 187, 201, 213, 264
Garland, Judy 243-244, 247, 249, 251-256, 259, 261-262
Gentle People, The 185-189, 198
Gering, Marion 42-43, 45, 64, 72, 101, 104, 112-114, 118, 138
God Told Me To 344-345
Gods of the Lightning 29-31
Good Dame 112-*113*
Goodbye, My Fancy 256-257, 262
Gossip Columnist, The 358-359
Grant, Cary 82-83, 85-87, 88, 93, 114-*116*, 117-118, 254
Griffith, D.W. 16, 69
Group Theatre 167, 172, 180, 185-189, 195, 197-198, 205, 326, 341

H

Hammett, Dashiell 52, 55, 362
Harding, Ann 35, 64, 71, 240, 256
Hayes, Helen xiii, xix, 88, 290, 323-324, 395, 409
Helen Morgan Story, The 289
Hellman, Lillian 55, 165, 168, 225, 229, 264, 304
Hepburn, Katharine 85, 264, 335, 398
Hitchcock, Alfred 124, 149-*151*, 152-155, 248, 277
Hodiak, John 235, 239-*241*
Holmes, Phillips 56-57, 58-59, 61-62, *63*, 71, 74
Hopkins, Miriam 36, 64, 134, 290-291
Hopper, Hedda 109, 176, 203, 358-359
Howard, William K. 124-128

I

I Never Promised You a Rose Garden 349
Innocents, The 259-260

J

Jane Eyre 208-*210*, 211, 213, 412
Joan of Lorraine 242, 299
Jennie Gerhardt 60, 101-*103*, 104

K

Karloff, Boris *80*
Kazan, Elia 186-187, 288
Kelly, Paul 43-*45*
Kennedy, Harold J. 196-198, 301, 339-342
Kind Lady 248, 269
Kosow, Albert 7, 412, 423
Kosow, Edgar 7, 412
Kosow, Victor *xx*, 1-4, 7-8, 85, 111-112
Kramer, Richard xi-xvii, 98, 295, 393-395, 421

L

Ladies of the Big House 64, 71-72, 73, 93, 121, 271
Lamarr, Hedy 173, 248
Lang, Fritz xvi, 124, 144-146, 148, 161-164, 173-*175*, 277, 330, 402
Les Miserables 265-*266*, 267
Libaire, Dorothy 64, *89*, 102, 118, 136, 138, 204
Liliom 14, 101
Little Foxes, The 304
Loder, John 150-*151*, 152, 248-251, 255
Loper, Don 263, 301, 310, 325-326
Love From a Stranger 235, 239-*241*
Loy, Myrna 107, 323-324, 330, 360, 372
Lumet, Sidney 182, 184-185, 275-276

M

MacLaine, Shirley 400-*401*
MacMurray, Fred 141-*142*, 143-144, 322
Madame Butterfly 85-87, 88-89, 98-99, 330
Madwoman of Chaillot, The 312, *315*
Magnum P.I. 372-373

Mamoulian, Rouben 47-48, 51, 53, 55, 94, 118
Many a Slip 39-*41*
March, Fredric 29, 81-*83*, 84, 93, 96, 112-113, 114, 264, 266
Mars Attacks! 404-*405*, 406-407
Marshall, Herbert 96, 111, 122-*124*
Mary Burns, Fugitive 124-*127*, 135, 399
Mayer, Louis B. 92, 94-96, 147, 243-244, 254
Mayron, Melanie *x*, xii-xiii, xvi, 393-394, 421
McCallum, David 356-357, 421
McCrea, Joel *160*, 165, 168-169
Merrily We Go to Hell vii, 79, 81-*83*, 84
Miner, Jan 360
Minnelli, Vincente 243-244, 252, 256, 262
Miracle Man, The 79-80, 81, 99
Mirrors 27
Montgomery, Douglass 21-22, 39, 265
Moore, Dickie 63
Morris, Chester 21, 23, *80*-81, 109, 219
Mr. Ace 224, 231-232, 233-234
Murphy, Dudley 62, 64, 182-185

N

Newman, Paul, xv, 333, 362-362, 365
Newman, Phyllis *x*, xiv, xvii, 371
Nice Women 36-37
'night Mother 374-375
Night Must Fall 356-357

O

O Mistress Mine 248-251, 253, 262, 271
O'Connell, Patricia 366-367, 421
Odets, Clifford xiii, 189, 198, 318
One Third of a Nation 181-*183*, 184
O'Sullivan, Maureen 339, 341, 366, 372, *424*

P

Pals 389-390
Parsons, Louella 65, 118, 176, 246, 358-359
Peck, Gregory 243, 264

Pick Up 99, 100-101
Picnic 279-280
Plummer, Christopher 269-270, 361
Preston, Robert 367, 373-374
Prunella 14-15
Pygmalion 185, 206-207, 220, 250

Q

Questel Mae xv, xvii, 304

R

Raft, George 86, 99, 100, 118, 174-175, 231-232, 233-234
Raymond, Gene 28, 71-72, 120-121, 271
Rennie, Michael 265-266
Route 66 296-297

S

Sabin, Albert 5, 10-11, 12-13, 16-18, 70, 109-110, 176-177, 298, 398-400
Sabotage 84, 149-152, 153-155, 248, 265, 371, 409
Sabrina Fair 29, 339-342, 424
Schulberg, B.P. xvi, 42, 43, 46-47, 51, 64-65, 74, 85, 89-92, 93-98, 107-109, 117-119, 120, 122, 138, 149, 254, 288, 411, 419
Schulberg, Budd xvi, 45-46, 48, 74-75, 92-97, 118, 254, 288, 365, 368-370, 411
Searching Wind, The 225-230
Shadow Box, The 361-362
Shatner, William 336, 338
Shearer, Norma 66, 97
Sheridan, Ann 120-121
Siege 352-353
Sidney, Beatrice 1-3, 4-5, 6-10, 12, 16, 85, 90, 111, 156, 180, 235, 260, 311, 369, 395
Sidney, Sigmund 2-3, 8-10, 16, 85, 111, 180
Sidney, Sylvia
    Childhood 1-15
    Death 411-413
    Marriages 135-136 (Cerf), 180-181 (Adler), 235 (Alsop)
    Needlepoint 316-321, 324-326
    Pugs 294-295, 327
    Romance with B.P. Schulberg 47, 48, 74-75, 89-91, 93-97, 109, 118-119
Smith, Liz 83, 321, 357, 395-396
Sondergaard, Gale 338
Sorrows of Satan 16
Squall, The 19-20
Street Scene 66-67, 68-70, 74, 94, 166, 170, 410-411
Suddenly, Last Summer 335
Summer Wishes, Winter Dreams xi, 326-328, *331*, 333, 394
Swanson, Gloria 64, 348

T

The Defenders 298-299
The Way to Love 107-*108*, 111
Thirty Day Princess 114-*116*, 117
thirtysomething x-xvii, 393-394,
Thru Different Eyes 31-32, 70
To Quito and Back 170-171
Tone, Franchot 38, *185-188*, 189, 235, 285
Tracy, Spencer 128, 145-*147*, 148, 350, 386, 419
Trail of the Lonesome Pine 136-137, 139-*142*, 143-144, 149, 322, 413, 415, 420

U

Used People 400-*401*, 402, 404

V

Vieux Carre 354-356
Violent Saturday 272-273, 274
von Sternberg, Josef 56-59, 330

W

WKRP in Cincinnati 343-344
Wagons Roll at Night, The 199-200, 201
Wanger, Walter 84, 124, 128, 136-137, 139, 155-156, 161, 167, 173, 176-177
We Shall Never Die 207-208
West, Mae 86, 88
Williams, Tennessee 301, 354-356
Woods, Al 20, 22-23

Woodward, Joanne 326, 328, *331*, 333, 361, 365, 367
Wyler, William 166-169, 201, 330

Y

You and Me 173-176
You Only Live Once 156, 161-*163*, 164
Young, Robert *226*, 228, *230*
Yurka, Blanche 19-20

About the Author

Scott O'Brien has written five film biographies of players from Cinema's Golden Age: Kay Francis, Virginia Bruce, Ann Harding, Ruth Chatterton and George Brent. He has contributed articles for *Films of the Golden Age, Classic Images* and *Filmfax*. O'Brien has done interviews for classic cinema blogs: TCM's *Movie Morlocks, Silver Screen Oasis, Let's Misbehave* and *Close-Ups and Long Shots*. His guest appearances include the San Francisco Silent Film Festival, KRCB's *Outbeat Radio* and *A Novel Idea, Yesterday USA Radio*, as well as Jan Wahl's "Inside Entertainment," for KRON-TV in the Bay Area. He has introduced the film classics *Trouble in Paradise* (1932) and *Double Harness* (1933) at the Library of Congress' Packard Theater in Culpeper, Va. Scott appeared in two film documentaries: *Queer Icon – the Cult of Bette Davis* (2009), and Irish television's *Reabhloidithe Hollywood* (2013) that chronicled the career of George Brent, who had been a dispatcher for the IRA. Scott lives with his partner Joel Bellagio in Sonoma County. (website: www.scottobrienauthor.com)

www.ingramcontent.com/pod-product-compliance
Lightning Source LLC
Chambersburg PA
CBHW050322230426
43663CB00010B/1705